The Reel Story

In his quest for fame & fortune, he found a pearl of great value.

LARRY D. VAUGHN

Saber Publishing

The Reel Story
Larry D. Vaughn

Edited by Greg J. Kuzmic

© 1998 Larry D. Vaughn
Saber Publishing Company
P.O. Box 25473
Greenville, South Carolina 29616

Cover design © 1998 American Business Forms
    Cover and internal design by Matt Donovan
    Some cover images © 1998 PhotoDisc, Inc.

ISBN 0-9662343-0-8

Printed in the United States of America

15   14   13   12   11   10   9   8   7   6   5   4   3   2   1

To my Lord and Savior Jesus Christ.
It is because of His wonderful grace working in my life that there is a
real story to tell. May this book go as far as He would have it to go.

Contents

One   The Luck of the Draw   *1*

Two   The Lie   *7*

Three   Ernest Watson   *11*

Four   Greenville   *17*

Five   Victor   *27*

Six   The Break   *33*

Seven   The Fever   *39*

Eight   Changes   *53*

Nine   The Metal Box   *61*

Ten   Introduction to Hollywood   *71*

Eleven   The Sale   *77*

Twelve   Doneata   *85*

Thirteen   Starting Over   *93*

Fourteen   The Making of a Film Buyer   *103*

Fifteen   Two Years   *119*

Sixteen   Going Overboard   *135*

Seventeen   The Payoff   *151*

Eighteen   Shallow Faith   *173*

Nineteen   A Vapor   *191*

Twenty   The Struggle Within   *209*

Twenty-One   The Compromise   *227*

Twenty-Two   Broad Horizons   *239*

Twenty-Three   The Unexpected Bouquet   *257*

Twenty-Four   Decisions   *279*

Twenty-Five   The Controversy   *295*

Twenty-Six   The Dark Cloud   *311*

Twenty-Seven   The Brief Friendship   *325*

Twenty-Eight   Responsibilities   *347*

Twenty-Nine   The Prelude   *363*

Thirty   Carrots, Carrots, Carrots!   *373*

Forward

Hollywood may be a large part of your world. If so, you're hardly alone. Prime-time television, cable pay-per-view, satellite access, in-flight movies, corner video rentals, and public libraries have given it a nearly ubiquitous presence in American culture. Daycare workers, school teachers, politicians, and even ministers assume that not only adults but also the smallest children know the names and catchy lines of current movie actors and producers. Disney stores cut a brisk business in malls and airport terminals, fast-food restaurants entice diners with colorful toys of the latest animated movie characters, and the ever-present sound of musical themes from current blockbusters pervades not only the radio waves, but creates the ambiance of clothing stores, specialty shops, health spas, doctors' and dentists' offices, and even the corner grocery. Somebody has been incredibly successful at saturating society with movies.

When Larry Vaughn and his wife first visited our church in the spring of 1994, I was unaware of his occupation. Warmly introducing himself and his wife in the lobby after a morning service, he did not (nor would I have expected him to) relate to me that his business was in the movie industry. Instead, he made a point of saying that they would be back the next week to hear the continuation of our then-current series on the Ten Commandments. When he mentioned that they were from Myrtle Beach, I thought that I had misheard what he said about returning the next Lord's Day. It's a four-and-a-half-hour drive from Myrtle Beach to Greenville! But when I asked again about their intentions, both he and Doneata assured me earnestly that they would be back. Their willingness to travel all those miles to return piqued my curiosity. But had I known the spiritual distance they had covered to show up in our church that morning, I'm sure that I would have been something far beyond curious.

Only later did I find out that when the Vaughns visited with us that day, they were taking some of the last steps to exchange worlds. Larry's world had been light-years removed from the one which our church represents. Gambler, film buyer, and movie marketer, Larry had dedicated most of his adult life to promoting movies. And he had been successful. So for him to find anything desirable in a conservative, biblical church was nothing short of a series of miraculous acts of God.

I say a "series" of miraculous acts because the road from the film industry to biblical Christianity has been a long one for the Vaughns. Actually, they have changed worlds twice. The first change occurred when they were "delivered from the power of darkness" and "translated into the kingdom of his dear Son" (Colossians 1:13). Although more dramatically life altering, it was, in many ways, much easier. The second change has taken much longer, has been more materially costly, and is for professing Christians the more instructive of the two.

Some who read this book will be non-Christians. If you are of that number, I know I'm safe in saying that Larry warmly welcomes you to his story and prays that it proves to be God's means of rescuing you for His Son, the Lord Jesus Christ.

But the majority reading this page will be, like me, professing Christians. For us, the most intriguing part of Larry's story is the after conversion years when his new world was Christ *plus the film industry*. What is life like for a man who can sincerely testify that being a Christian is the most important part of his life but who gives six days a week to a world which is, in his own words, "totally controlled by darkness"? What sort of Christian life is it to talk with Sylvester Stallone about movies one day and then try to pay tribute to Christ the next?

Actually, this part of the story is not merely about one professing Christian's attempt to merge movies with Christ; it's about a widely diffused philosophy of Christian living. It's about attempting, as a matter of chosen Christian policy, to marry new life in Christ with certain aspects of the old life before Christ in order to ensure the retention of wealth, power, and worldly prestige. It's about living with a protesting conscience clamoring for radical change but listening to well-meaning Christian friends counseling realistic caution. It's about coming to the brink of scriptural convictions only to be wooed and won again by compromising proposals. In short, it's an exposé of the kind of Christianity that attempts to live between two irreconcilable worlds.

That is the life from which the Vaughns were taking their last steps the morning they introduced themselves in the lobby of our church. Through the months since then that Larry was recuperating from a surgery and writing the chapters of this book, I couldn't help but hunger for an awakening of the many, many professing Christians who have not yet emerged from that confusing maze of a compromised Christianity. I wish that they all could be reached by this account.

The Reel Story is the fascinating, well-written, inspiring story of one family's pilgrimage out of darkness through bewildering haze into the Lord's marvelous light. But now that Larry is sharing it, I and many others are prayerful that God will use it to provide answers for many others who, beleaguered by the world but hopeful in Christ, are attempting to find their way through to the clean living of an uncompromised commitment to Christ.

Dr. Mark Minnick

One

The Luck of the Draw

Doneata and I arrived at the Park Terrace Theatre forty-five minutes before the feature showing was to begin. No, we didn't get to the theatre early for good seats, because our seats were already reserved. Halfway down in the center of the auditorium a row of seats had been set aside for us along with other ABC home-office personnel in the special VIP section of the auditorium. My reason for wanting to get to the theatre early was to get caught up in the excitement—yes, excitement—of watching over seven hundred moviegoers all but stampede into the auditorium to secure a seat for themselves, their dates, mates, or steadies. They, like me, wanted to be the first movie patrons in Charlotte, North Carolina, to see the sneak preview of what was rumored to be one of the biggest motion pictures ever made.

The director of the film was at that time relatively unknown outside the film community. Earlier in his career he had directed a very good, intense, and highly suspenseful made-for-television movie, *Duel,* starring Dennis Weaver. (Dennis Weaver played Chester in *Gun Smoke.*) The sheer terror of that movie, with its unseen villain and sweaty hero, still gives me the creeps!

After his success with *Duel,* the director was later asked to direct a Goldie Hawn film, *Sugarland Express,* which turned out to be a good film, though not a great one. However, this film that we were about to see, *Jaws,* was supposed to be nothing short of sensational. *Jaws* was the film that was supposed to make its director, Steven Speilberg, a household name.

All the advance publicity from Universal Films was true: *Jaws* was two hours of edge-of-the-seat entertainment. About forty-five minutes into the film, the great white shark came roaring up out of the ocean for the first time, and when it did, I almost flipped backwards out of my seat into the lap of the man sitting behind me. I was thankful that, at that surprising moment, I didn't have a drink in my hand.

After the showing of *Jaws* was over, I raced to the back of the auditorium to listen to all the jabber as excited customers came filing out of the theatre, talking excitedly to each other about the movie and how they couldn't wait to see *Jaws* again. I knew I had just seen the biggest motion picture of the year, and quite possibly the biggest motion picture ever made. *Jaws* had all the ingredients to make it number one: action, suspense, drama, and that music—the music was horrifying. *Boom, boom, boom*—the incessant rhythm of the tuba blasts grew as the great white shark swirled at warp speed to attack the dangling legs of its helpless victims. And just when you thought your heart couldn't take another *boom*, Speilberg graciously gave the much-needed comic relief of Roy Scheider demonstrating his overwhelming fear of the ocean and its creatures within at just the appropriate time.

Driving home from the theatre, I felt great on the inside. I felt great because I knew it was because of me that all those folks saw *Jaws* at the Park Terrace. All of a sudden I giggled; then I started laughing uncontrollably.

Doneata looked at me and said, "Okay, let's have it. What's so funny?"

"Honey, I got to thinking: if those seven hundred people at the theatre tonight had any idea about how *Jaws* ended up playing in the Park Terrace and not in some other theatre in Charlotte, well, they would never, never in a hundred years believe how it happened."

Doneata nodded her head in agreement as she smiled rather sheepishly and said, "Larry Vaughn, you're one crazy film buyer in one crazy business, but I love you anyway."

My mind drifted back to an event that had occurred a few weeks earlier. We were having a very important split meeting on a Thursday afternoon in John Huff's office. John Huff was the V.P. and Head Film Buyer at ABC. (This particular split meeting was held before the Supreme Court ruled that theatres' splitting of motion pictures was illegal.) So this afternoon, several film buyers who represented all the theatre circuits in Charlotte met together to discuss splitting the upcoming summer's movies among ourselves rather than bidding against each other for the right to play a particular movie. The reason for this strategy was that negotiating among ourselves about who would play a given film was always much less expensive than bidding against each other for the right to play a particular film.

Well, this was going to be a very interesting split meeting because every film buyer in the room desperately wanted *Jaws* to play in his company's theatre. We spent the better part of an hour trying to decide which circuit was going to play *Jaws* and what it would take to satisfy the other circuits that didn't get to play it. We went around and around and got absolutely nowhere. No one was willing to back off on this mega-picture. Every buyer in the room that day wanted to play *Jaws* in his theatre—period! And if he didn't get it, it could very well mean a tough and extremely expensive bidding war.

After trying for the better part of the afternoon to put a round peg in a square hole, everyone became frustrated and tired; an uneasy silence fell over the room. I was the first to break the silence. "Mr. Huff, may I make a suggestion?" With his elbow resting on the arm of his chair and his chin resting in the palm of his hand, Huff nonchalantly bobbled his head up and down as if to say, "Why not?"

I cleared my throat and began speaking: "Listen, men, you can't horse-trade when you have only one thoroughbred and a bunch of donkeys. I believe we all realize that's what we have here. We all know *Jaws* is at the very least the biggest picture of the year. Maybe it's the biggest picture ever made. And what's left in the pot after *Jaws*—a bunch of donkeys, or should I say, little pictures. So, gentlemen, let's forget trying to horse-trade. We're a group of professional men that strive, sometimes under the most unusual circumstances, to make the best decision for our respective companies. In a situation like this, where we have one picture far superior to every other picture, I suggest an alternative for your consideration."

I paused a moment, then continued: "Gentlemen, shall we cut high card and winner take all?"

That unexpected suggestion seemed to have every bit the effect of a slap in the face, or you might say a wake-up call, to those weary, tired men in the room. I could tell each man was thinking about the suggestion that I had just made. Heads were turning, eyes were wandering from man to man as each film buyer examined his thoughts against the others' facial expressions.

Huff broke the silence. "Well, why not? Does anyone have a better suggestion?"

One by one, each man cast his vote to cut high card for the right to play *Jaws*.

Loosening his tie, Huff said, "I guess we need a deck of cards?"

One of the other guys quickly spoke up. "It has to be a new deck of cards, never before opened."

Huff buzzed his secretary, "Mary, please have one of the girls go over to the drugstore to pick up a deck of playing cards, pronto!"

While we were waiting on the cards, one of the men asked, "What are the rules?"

Huff said, "Rules? We're not going to play poker. We don't need any rules. We'll have someone shuffle the cards; then we'll each pick one. Whoever draws the highest card wins, everyone else loses. Of course, we all know that an ace is the highest card in the deck and a deuce, or two, is the lowest." He then looked over at me as if to say, "Rules! What a dumb question!"

Huff's secretary brought the deck of cards into the room and handed them to him. On her way out of the office, she glanced my way. I noticed a rather peculiar smile on her face, as if she wanted to say, "What are you men up to now?"

Huff asked, "Okay, who does the shuffling?"

One of the men not noted for his card-playing abilities was picked to shuffle the cards. After shuffling the deck, he placed it on the corner of Huff's desk. One by one each man walked to the edge of the desk to make a draw. One man would walk over and draw quickly; another would act very cautious, as if there was a snake under the top card. Each of us knew this was a million-dollar draw.

Huff and I were the last to take a card. Huff pushed his large leather chair back from his desk, dropped his arms by his side, and then very calmly lifted his right arm and motioned for me to step forward. He lifted his eyebrows. I noticed a look of concern on his face.

He said, "Mr. Vaughn . . ."

I thought to myself, "What happened to 'Larry'?"

Huff continued, "Since this was your bright idea, I think it's only right for you to have the honor of drawing for ABC."

I smiled on the outside but was quite restless on the inside. As I reached for the deck, I said, "My pleasure." I picked a card and cupped it in the palm of my hand. Immediately, I raised my hand up to where only I could see the card. I studied it for a moment and then glanced toward Huff.

Acting somewhat irritated at me, he said, "Well, get on with it! Let's have a look at it!"

In a Frisbee-like manner, I tossed the card toward the center of the desk. I then watched each man's expression as he saw the ace glide to its resting place atop the large mahogany desk. Immediately, Huff released a huge sigh of frustration as the other men frowned, shook their heads in disbelief, and mumbled to themselves as they walked slowly back to their seats. Huff was the first to speak. "This business is bad for the heart."

Someone echoed right back, "You ain't got no heart."

Huff said, "Well, if and when there's a *Jaws II,* Larry will draw for ABC."

———

Driving home from the theatre, I heard Doneata's voice. "Larry, Larry, you're not listening to me."

"I'm sorry, honey," I mumbled.

"Larry, what were you thinking?"

"I was just reminiscing about *Jaws* and the luck of the draw." We stopped for a red light. While we waited for the light to change, Doneata pointed across the dark, empty street.

"Honey, look at that old lady standing over there by the bus stop. She shouldn't be out here by herself so late at night. It's not safe for a woman to be out this time of night, especially in the downtown area."

I took a long look at the old, silver-haired lady. She looked tired standing there waiting for the bus to come and take her home. I wondered if there would be anyone at home to meet her, or if home was just a dark, lonely, empty apartment. "Doneata, do you know whom that old lady reminds me of?"

"I knew you were going to ask that question. Yes, darling, she reminds you of your mother."

As we continued our drive down Independence Boulevard, Doneata leaned over and put her head on my shoulder. Tired from a long day, she dozed off as I started to let my thoughts wander. That old lady standing at the bus stop brought back memories of years gone by. How many times had I seen my mother stand at the bus stop and wait for the bus to take her to work in the early hours of the morning; and then, in the late hours of the evening, I would watch the bus drop her off.

I thought to myself, "If people knew the story of my childhood and my young adult years, they would probably find my story just as unbelievable and shocking as, say, the idea that businessmen would cut high card to play *Jaws* in a Charlotte movie theatre. . . ."

Two

The Lie

I was too young to remember what happened that day; and if the truth were known, I wasn't even in the room when my father died. However, throughout my early years, I heard my mother, Mary, tell the story so many times that it seems like I was very much there—that I was very much a part of it all. But I was only twenty-three months old.

We were living in Cordele, Georgia. My father, Andrew Jackson Vaughn, named after the famous general of the great Confederate army, was a tall, attractive thirty-eight-year-old man with a zest for life. Mother loved to show me pictures and then tell me how dashing, stunning, and good-looking he was. She commented quite often on how he liked to dress: white, heavily starched shirts; pin-striped suits; wing-tipped black and brown leather shoes; wide, expensive ties coupled with a gold tie pin and chain—an attire which complemented his rather long, jet black hair which was always parted perfectly down the middle.

But the thing my mother appreciated most about my father was his genuine love for her and me, their son. Her voice still echoes in my mind today. "Oh Larry, if your father had only lived; he loved us so much. We would have never gone without; he wanted so much for you to become a doctor."

It was Thanksgiving Day, 1948. Dad, not wanting to break his daily breakfast routine, even if it was "Turkey Day," still had to have his Coca-Cola and Baby Ruth candy bar for breakfast. Mom had long since given up on trying to break him from that indulgence. With this day being a holiday, she even served her knight in shining armor his indulgence in bed.

I was told the three of us had a wonderful Thanksgiving afternoon. Dad and Mom spent the better part of the sunny but rather chilly day in the back yard playing with me. Mom said that Dad had spent too much money on toys for me—toys that I was too young even to play with. What can a twenty-three-month-old child do with a football, basketball, baseball, and glove? Mom said that all I could do was look at them, but my dad seemed to enjoy just watching me look at the toys.

The traditional Thanksgiving dinner consisted of just us three: Dad, Mom, and me. My grandfather, the distinguished L. L. Blackman, a wealthy Georgia pecan farmer, basically disowned Mom when her mother died. I can recall seeing the old gentleman only once, and that was years later. I remember, even then, he wasn't very friendly. I don't know anything about my father's family. Mother never talked about them, and I never thought to ask.

After Mom and Dad finished off the last of the turkey and dressing, Dad suggested the three of us take a nap before enjoying the apple pie. Mom wholeheartedly agreed. She took me to my room and put me down in my crib with some of my favorite toys while Dad started his evening ritual of clearing off the table. Mom returned to the kitchen just in time to stop Dad and usher him into the bedroom. She said, "Honey, the dishes can wait; we need a break."

After resting a few minutes, Dad became very quiet and started feeling bad. Mom thought he had just eaten too much turkey and would feel better shortly. Dad was one of those guys who were never sick. Outside of an occasional cough or cold, he was considered to be in good health; but as the evening wore on, he started feeling worse. At 8:00 p.m., Dad asked Mom to call our family physician, Dr. Wooten.

Being a small town, Cordele didn't have that many medical doctors. Our doctor, the good Dr. Wooten, was loved by all who knew him—and everyone knew him. It didn't take a lot of prodding for him to grab his little black bag and make a house call to any of his patients when the need arose, even if it was Thanksgiving night.

Dr. Wooten arrived at 8:30. Mother greeted him at the door, thanked him for coming over, and then ushered him into the house. They made small talk for a minute in the parlor; then Mom said, "Well, I guess you're not here to see me but my husband."

As they walked into the bedroom, Dad sat up in bed, looked at the doctor, and said, "Dr. Wooten, it's my heart." At that moment, my father died from a massive heart attack.

Mary Blackman had grown up enjoying the finer things in life. Being an only child does have its advantages, especially when you're the daughter of a rather wealthy, prominent businessman. Mary was one of the select few in high school who had her own car, and her car was not just transportation but a beautiful late-model brown Cadillac.

Mary was a popular young lady, especially with the boys. They not only liked to look at her car, but they also liked to look at her. Mary was very attractive with her natural tan complexion, dark brown eyes, and warm, pleasant smile. Her face was round and her long hair was a beautiful gingerbread brown.

In school, Mary was known more for being runner-up in the high school beauty pageant than for her academic achievements. Books and studying were always a struggle for her. Her father would often say, "Mary, you must get a good education if you are going to succeed in this life. Nothing ever comes easy."

Mary would reply, "Dad, I just want to get married and be a loving wife and mother; you don't need a lot of education to be a homemaker." Neither of the two really understood the thinking of the other.

My mother was always very vague when talking about my grandmother. My grandfather was most certainly the individual that made the long-lasting impression in her life. He was the strong, firm final authority in the home. However, Mom commented often how Grandfather's interests lay more in his work and his lifelong association with the Shriners than in his wife or his daughter.

I don't remember how or when my grandmother died. Mom had very little to say about it. She did tell me that my grandfather remarried and that he married a girl young enough to be his daughter. As a matter of fact, Mom said she went to high school with the girl!

After my grandfather married this young lady, he and Mom grew further apart. What really severed the relationship—that is, what relationship they had left—is when Mom told him that she wanted to marry Jack Vaughn. My grandfather emphatically forbade the marriage. Mom never told me why, but my grandfather did not like Jack Vaughn. He told my mom that if she married Jack Vaughn, he would take her out of his will, and she would never again be welcome in his home.

That is exactly what happened. Mom loved Jack and was unhappy at home. So, she went against the demands of her father and married Jack Vaughn, and she paid the price. My grandfather, true to his word, disowned her, took her out of his will, and to my knowledge only once did the two ever speak or even see each other again.

At the time of my father's death, he was in the process of having his attorney draw up important legal documents regarding his partnership with another local businessman. It never happened. When my father died, Mom ended up with poor legal counsel, no life insurance, and a lot of personal and business debt. She ended up with what she later considered to be a less-than-fair settlement from my father's business partner. Then the strangest thing happened: we left Cordele.

Rather than stay in familiar surroundings, her hometown, where she had loved ones—folks she had known all her life, Mom left with just me and our suitcase. She told no one where she was going. Because of my age, I cannot remember where we went. All I know is that we moved, and we moved quite often, usually at a moment's notice.

Three

Ernest Watson

My personal memories begin around the age of six. I remember my mother and I moved to Athens, Georgia. She no longer looked like the high school beauty queen I remembered seeing in her old photographs. Now she was a rather portly, tired, forty-five-year-old, prematurely gray widow who worked many long, hard hours standing on her feet in a downtown clothing store, trying to make enough money to support us.

I remember very well those early days in Athens. Mother and I shared a room on the second floor of a boarding house. It was one of those old, large two-story homes with a wraparound porch and was located in one of the older sections of Athens. The only privacy we had was in our room. Our furniture was old and worn: a desk, chair, dresser, mirror, and a double bed. There were several other rooms on the floor, all occupied by single women. At the top of the stairs at the end of the hall was the bathroom. It had to be shared by everyone on the floor. As I recall, that was the busiest room in the house. At that time, I was the only child living in the boarding house.

Meals were served on the first floor at fixed times of the day. There was always much conversation at the dinner table, as the men boarders who lived on the first floor met with the women boarders from the second floor.

It was that same year that I started school. Mother enrolled me in an elementary school not too far from our boarding house. While I was in school, she kept herself busy working various part-time jobs in the neighborhood.

That's when he came. His name was Ernest Watson. I don't remember how or where he met my mother, but they started dating and married shortly thereafter. He had two grown children: a son, Farrell, who lived at home; and a daughter, Regina, who was married and lived in another city with her husband. I don't know what happened to Ernest Watson's first wife.

Mother changed her last name to his: it was now Mary B. Watson. My name, however, stayed the same. Mother wanted me to keep the name Vaughn in memory of my father, and so did I.

Ernest Watson was nothing like Jack Vaughn. Where my father had been a polished, reserved gentleman, Ernest was a hard man, a man who had lived a hard life. He was a rugged trucker, and he smoked Camel cigarettes one after the other—over a carton a week. I was always a little afraid of him; his language was as rough as he was, and he always had bad breath. I think he enjoyed drinking his liquor. When he told me to do something, I did it, immediately, for my own sake.

Ernest's son, Farrell, was nothing like his father. He was a tall, slim, red-headed, freckle-faced, seventeen-year-old Georgia boy. Farrell was very polite, with good manners; he was a thinker and a rather quiet young man. From day one, Farrell was nice to me. Even though he was much older than I, we enjoyed being with each other. I really felt like I had gotten a big brother out of this new relationship. I hoped Farrell and I were going to be lifelong brothers and friends.

Mother's marriage to Ernest ended shortly thereafter. I came home one day and found Ernest in our kitchen in the arms of our next-door neighbor's wife. He threatened me severely, telling me that if I knew what was good for me I would not say a word to my mother about what I had seen that afternoon. I loved my mother very much, and I didn't like seeing Ernest kiss and hug our neighbor's wife. I knew Ernest would get mad, but I decided that as soon as Mother came home I would tell her about what I saw Ernest doing that afternoon.

Immediately, Mother went straight into the kitchen to question Ernest about the afternoon. In anger he called me into the kitchen, denied everything, and in one swift blow slapped me. The blow put me across the room. I ended up on the floor, on my side, leaning against the wall. Blood was starting to flow from my swollen lip and bruised nose. I was afraid to move; surprisingly, my fear was not of Ernest: it was of my mother.

I saw a side of my mother that I had never seen before. She looked over at me, not saying a word. She just stood there a few seconds; then she slowly looked away. Next, she very calmly walked over to the kitchen counter, picked up a very long, very thick cutting knife, and turned and looked at Ernest. This big, rugged man's man was frozen in his tracks.

Mother said nothing as she walked across the room that night, but her eyes were saying a lot.

She put the knife firmly under Ernest's chin. I kept waiting for the blood to flow; then she said to him, "If you ever touch my son again, I will kill you."

I think Ernest and I both knew that was no bluff. Mom then gently laid the knife down, walked over to me, helped me up, and we left the room. It took her only a few minutes to pack our bags and call a cab; then we were gone.

Farrell took the news hard. He wanted the marriage to work, for all the obvious reasons. He knew in their brief time together that Mother had been good for his father. He promised to keep in touch and visit often. However, Mother knew all of his free time was going to a certain young lady he seemed to be seeing a lot of lately.

Mother rented us a room in an old, second-rate motel. She said the first thing we had to do was find a place to live. I agreed with her; I wasn't impressed at all with our present living arrangements. It looked like the motel had been closed for a long time, and someone had forgotten to notify us of the closing.

After looking at several boarding house rooms, small efficiency apartments, and even one place that looked like a skinny barn, Mom, against my plea not to do it, rented the barn. I couldn't believe it! I was truly embarrassed! I even cried. I didn't want to live in a barn.

In actuality, the skinny old barn wasn't really a barn at all. It was an old two-story, three-room house located behind a brick home at the far end of the property; the outside of it was awful to look at. I don't know how long it had been there, but it looked like it should have been condemned. It had rotten wood everywhere, windows with large holes in the screens, and a roof that needed fresh patches on the old patches.

Once you walked in the front door, you were in what seemed like the middle of a very small room. To the left of the room, which ended up being the den, was a bar which separated the den from the efficiency kitchen. At the end of the den was a very narrow stairway which led up to an open area that looked like it should have been an attic or a storage room, but which in actuality was the bedroom. The only door in the bedroom was the one that led to the bathroom. The bathroom was exceptionally small. It barely had enough room to turn around.

Mother assured me that everything would be okay once we moved in and got the place cleaned up. And that is exactly what we did. We spent our first weekend scrubbing and scrubbing in our little home. We could have fit all of our furniture on a pickup truck and still had some room left over, and I guess that was good since our home's square footage was not much more than that of a pickup truck.

The next item on our agenda was for Mother to find a full-time job. While Mom was married to Ernest, she worked part-time. Now, without his income, she had to work full-time to meet our financial needs. So, every morning we would be up at 7:00, eat breakfast by 7:30; and she would leave by 7:45 to walk two blocks to the street corner where she could catch the bus to go downtown to look for work. I had to walk several blocks to the new elementary school that I attended.

Mother found employment downtown in a clothing store. Her position was saleslady in the women's wear department. I liked her working downtown because every Friday after school I got to take the bus downtown and have dinner with her at my favorite restaurant, the Varsity. Then I would go to a movie at the Palace Theatre, while she worked until 9:00 p.m. Saturdays were even better. We would ride the bus downtown together at 9:00 a.m. She would drop me off at the theatre where I would go to the 10:00 a.m. kids' show. I would watch either a Roy Rogers or Gene Autrey western, or maybe the latest Tarzan movie. Then at noon, I would meet Mom for lunch at the Varsity.

The Varsity was a fast-food restaurant before fast-food restaurants were widely known. It was located right across the street from the University of Georgia and had what I thought were surely the best hamburgers and hot dogs in the world. Mother and I ate there at least once every Friday and Saturday.

After lunch, Mother would have to go back to work, and I would go to another theatre and watch their Saturday double feature, two movies for the price of one, while waiting for Mother to get off work. At 5:00 I would meet her; we would have dinner out and go to the evening movie at the third, and last, movie theatre in town. That was what we did every weekend until the illness came.

Mother made an appointment for me to see the doctor. She knew something was going on in my body. I had a fever, tired easily, and stayed pale. After a physical and tests, the doctor diagnosed me with rheumatic fever. He told Mother I should recover fully, but I must stay in bed for the entire summer.

When we returned home from the doctor's office, she broke the news to me. We talked about it, and then she surprised me with a very special gift: a brand-new RCA color television. This was our first television. I didn't even know anybody that actually had a color television. I thought, "Here we are living in this barn, but we're probably the only family in the neighborhood with a color television."

I was ecstatic! If the truth were known, our television payment was probably more than our barn payment.

Mother took my mattress off my bed from the upstairs bedroom that we shared and placed it on the floor downstairs. This was to be my new living quarters for the next twelve weeks. I had all my army men, toy trucks, and my new color television. I thought, "What more could I possibly need?"

It was a long, boring summer. Outside of a couple of visits from Farrell, I was alone most of the day. My color television was a great pacifier, but back then, there were only a few shows televised in color, maybe six or seven a week. I couldn't wait until fall. I was sick of staying in that shack, on the floor, in that tiny room. I wanted to get back into school, go out and play, go to the Varsity, eat lots of burgers and fries; and most of all, I wanted to go back to the movies. I loved going to the picture show.

The doctor was right: I recovered fully. It was great to get back into the old routine. I told Mother that never again would I ever complain about the long walk to school, those long rides on the bus, the long waits for her to get off work, or anything else ever again.

As expected, Farrell and his sweetheart, Kathy, were married. They rented a small home in town, and it wasn't too long before they were blessed with a beautiful baby girl. Because of his busy schedule with work and his new family, I didn't get to see much of him, but I enjoyed those times when he would drop by to take me out for a quick burger. His friendship was the only thing good that I ever saw out of Mom's marriage to Ernest Watson.

One day while at school, my teacher asked me some questions about my home life. She wanted to know if I walked to and from school every day by myself. She asked about the weather: how I got to school when it rained or when it was very cold outside. She wanted to know who was at home when I returned home from school every day. She even asked about my meals, what kind of food I ate. Plus, she wanted to know who stayed home with me when I was absent because of sickness. She asked a lot of questions. I was glad that I knew the answers to all those questions, and I answered every one that she asked.

I told her that I always walked to school—that's the only way to get there when you don't have a car. After school, I stayed home by myself, from 3:00 until 6:00, until Mother finished her work. The food part was easy: we ate sandwiches during the week and burgers on the weekend. As for being sick, I told my teacher I was old enough to stay by myself when I was sick. I had done that for an entire summer before.

What I thought would please Mother disturbed her greatly. She got very upset with me for volunteering to answer those questions the teacher asked me. I knew I had done wrong, because she was so upset with me. I told Mother I was sorry, and that I would never, ever say anything to my teacher again, but nothing seemed to help. Mother was worried, and I didn't know what she was so worried about.

Shortly thereafter, Mother said that we were going to move away.

I asked her, "Where are we moving?"

She said that she did not want anyone to know and that she would tell me when we got there. I asked her how we were going to get there. She said we would go on the Greyhound bus. "But what about our furniture and our color television?"

She told me that everything that we couldn't carry with us would stay here in Athens. I started crying. I didn't want to leave. I liked the barn, my school, and my friends.

Farrell came over and took what little furniture we had and left. I'm not sure, but I think he sold all of the furniture for Mother. Everything happened so fast, it was like one big blur. One day we were there, the next day we were gone.

Four

Greenville

I was quiet on the bus. Mother started to talk to me. She told me how much she loved me. She said that I was her whole life. She shared with me how she was always afraid that she would become ill, and the authorities would take me away from her. She said she worried every single day of her life, afraid that she would lose me. Then, she told me she would never, ever marry again, that no man would ever have the opportunity again to hit me or to hurt her.

Then she talked about my father. She said, "If only your father hadn't died; he loved us so much. We would have never gone without; he wanted so much for you to be a doctor." I felt sorry for mother. I kissed her, then I hugged her. I told her I was glad we were moving, and I promised her that I would never, ever leave her.

We got off the bus in Greenville, South Carolina. Mother had a taxi take us to a very nice hotel, the Ottaray, which was located right at the top of the hill on Main Street. This was the nicest hotel I had ever seen. I wondered if the selling of all our household goods and our color television made it possible for us to stay in such a nice hotel.

We checked into the most beautiful hotel room; everything in it was wonderful: nice polished furniture, a big wooden bed with the fluffiest mattress and pillows that I had ever seen. The room even smelled good. But, the best thing of all was our bathroom. We had our own private bathroom, and it even had a tub.

Mom said, "I take claim to the tub first, but you may pick which side of the bed you want to sleep on."

I thought, "That's fair. I want the side that faces the window."

Our big, wide window with its frilly drapes overlooked Main Street. I could look across the street and see a movie theatre and all sorts of nice stores. Mother told me if I looked really hard I could see Shirby Vogue.

I asked her, "What's Shirby Vogue?"

She replied, very casually, "It's only a fur store."

I asked Mother, "Can we stay here in Greenville forever? I love this town and our wonderful room."

We had dinner downstairs in the hotel restaurant. It was a grand experience. The people were all so quiet, the waiters so polite; everyone was so kind to us. And the food was delicious! It was there that Mother told me about her new job at Shirby Vogue.

Mother informed me that while in Athens she had applied to an out-of-town newspaper advertisement for the position of saleswoman at Shirby Vogue, Greenville's very exclusive ladies hat and fur store. She said she couldn't believe it when the management actually hired her for the sales position.

I said, "Mom, you mean we are going to stay here forever? And we can live here in this hotel?"

She replied, "Yes, we can stay in Greenville forever, but we can stay only a few days in the hotel. Tomorrow we must start looking for a permanent place to live."

I will never forget those wonderful days we stayed in the Ottaray Hotel. Mom worked during the day and went through the apartment rental ads in the evening. While she worked, I stayed in the room and took daily walks up and down Main Street, mostly window-shopping in all the stores. It was fun to be in a new town, staying in a nice hotel, eating out—and best of all, going to the movies in the evenings.

After a couple of days, Mother found a small duplex for us to rent over in the Sans Souci section of Greenville. The house was much nicer than anything we had lived in before. It was located in a nice, established neighborhood, with lots of kids to play with.

Our side of the little white house was small, but very nice. We had a small front yard and a nice-sized back yard. There were beautiful, green full hedges located on both sides of the front porch. The back yard had a nice tree, perfect for climbing in. I don't remember too much about the interior of the house. I remember it was clean, and it most certainly met all of our needs.

Shirby Vogue must have been a well-paying company, because Mom kept spending money. She bought some used, but nice, furniture. It was fun to watch her get so excited over decorating our new little home. In those days she was so happy. I remember thinking, "We have everything we could possibly need—except, we don't have a color television." I dared not mention that to Mom, because I knew we would never again be able to afford one.

We had been in Greenville only a few months, when Mother came home from work one afternoon, extremely upset. She took me into the kitchen, sat me down, and told me, in tears, that Farrell's wife, Kathy, had called her at work to tell her that Farrell had been in a bad automobile accident.

I asked Mother if Farrell would be okay.

She said, "I don't know. We must go and see him right away."

It seemed to take forever; but finally, the big Greyhound rolled into the terminal in Athens. Mother and I went straight to the hospital. The receptionist at the nurses' station took us to the intensive care waiting room. As soon as Kathy saw Mom, she started crying. Mother quickly went over to Kathy, put her arms around her, and held her. Then Mother cried with her.

Standing there, I realized that Farrell might die. Kathy's eyes told the whole story. They were so swollen that I wondered how she could even see. Could it really be this bad? So, Farrell is in the hospital. The hospital is where people get help when they're sick, and that's where people go to get well.

After Mother and Kathy regained their composure, Kathy proceeded to tell Mother everything that had been happening between her and Farrell. Kathy was hurting badly, but not just because her husband was very sick in the hospital. With tears in her eyes, Kathy told Mother about her recent discovery that Farrell was having an affair with another woman.

Before his accident, Farrell was admitted into the hospital with pneumonia. While in the hospital, he told Kathy that he was going to break off the relationship with the other woman and get his life and marriage back together. Kathy loved Farrell and told him she was willing to forgive him for his unfaithfulness.

The night before he was to be discharged from the hospital, Farrell slipped out of the hospital to meet with the other woman. Kathy was unaware that Farrell had planned to meet the woman that night, but Kathy felt that Farrell was meeting the woman to tell her of his decision to stay with his family. Farrell and the woman went for a drive in her car. Farrell was behind the wheel.

The police report said that Farrell was driving too fast in the rain when he rounded a curve, swerved over the yellow line onto the other side of the road, and hit, head on, another car full of college girls, students at the University of Georgia. Four girls died that night: the girl with Farrell and all three of the college girls in the other car.

Farrell was still in the coma that he went into following the accident. The doctor asked Mother and me to talk to Farrell when we went into his room. The doctor was hoping that if Farrell heard our voices, he might come out of the coma.

At thirteen years old, I wasn't emotionally ready to see what I saw when I went into that hospital room that night. If the doctor hadn't been there, I would never have known that the swollen, blue, broken, and bruised individual lying there on that bed was the Farrell I had come to know and love. I walked over to him, careful not to interrupt the flow of the tubes going from the hospital's monitors into his body. Then, I looked at his terribly swollen head, and I wondered why the doctor failed to mention anything about having to sew Farrell's chin back onto his face.

I did exactly what the doctor asked me to do. I leaned over right next to Farrell's left ear and talked gently to him. I told him that I wanted him to get well, that Kathy and their daughter needed him, and that everything would be okay. I told him how much I missed seeing him, that I loved him, and that he would always be my big brother; then I left the room.

I never saw Farrell again. He died a few days later. It's probably just as well. The doctors said that if he had lived, he most likely would have had severe brain damage. And legally, he was responsible for the deaths of four people. As for Kathy, I don't know what happened to her or her daughter. After the funeral they moved, and we never heard from them again.

The bus ride back to Greenville reminded me of that earlier bus ride Mother and I had taken from Athens to Greenville. Like the trip before, there was a lot of thinking, but very little talking.

I knew what was on Mother's mind, and I really didn't want to ask. But I asked her anyway. "Are you okay, Mom? Are you feeling all right?"

She replied, "Yes, I'm fine. I was just thinking about you and me. I must take good care of myself, so no one will ever have reason to take you away from me." Her next statement I could recite by heart: "If only your father hadn't died; he loved us so much. We would have never gone without; he wanted so much for you to be a doctor." Without trying to, I think Mother was teaching me how to worry.

It was that same year that Mother lost her job at Shirby Vogue. I don't know what happened. She came home one day and said she was no longer employed there. Then she told me we would have to make arrangements to move to a less expensive place to live. I really hated to hear her say that because I liked where we were living. I enjoyed our home and the children I played with in the neighborhood.

Mother went to work at Greene's 5 & 10 Cent Store on Main Street. It was located just a couple of blocks from Shirby Vogue. Her salary at Greene's wasn't much money at all. It was sad to see her go from a well-paying job to a minimum wage job. I believe at the time she was making less than a dollar an hour. She worked as a saleslady, roaming as needed, from one department within the store to another.

We moved across town to a large boarding house on 5 Cateechee Avenue. It was a huge, green two-story house. I believe there were four apartments in the house. The owner, a retired, sweet old lady named Mrs. Martin, lived in the downstairs apartment on the left side of the house. Mother rented the other downstairs apartment located on the right side of the house. There were two families—a single businessman and an Air Force serviceman, his wife, and two small children—who lived in the remaining two upstairs apartments. Unfortunately, the family with children lived directly over Mom and me.

The house had a huge screened-in wooden front porch which went all the way across the front of the house. The right side of the front yard had a very large oak tree, which gave shade to the entire front of the house. Adjacent to the far left side of the front yard was a small, white

The boarding house at 5 Cateechee Avenue is now a restaurant

office building which Mrs. Martin also owned and rented to an insulation company.

The back yard was long and very narrow, not picturesque at all. At the end of the property was the side wall of a Winn Dixie grocery store. At best, the building was no more than fifty feet from the house.

On the right side of the house was a very small driveway. At the end of the driveway was a small, freestanding old wooden garage. The garage was not big enough to park a car in; it was used mostly by Mrs. Martin as additional storage space.

Our apartment had two large rooms: the living room and the bedroom. It had a very small kitchen and bath area. The refrigerator was on the back porch. The back porch was completely enclosed but not insulated. It was a very narrow porch, but big enough, I thought, to put a single bed, along with the refrigerator.

At fourteen, I wanted my own bedroom. I told Mother I would take the back porch and make it into a bedroom. Her concern was the weather. Without insulation, she felt it would be too cold in the winter for me to sleep out on the porch. But, she was in agreement that I did need my own room. So, she agreed to give the porch a try.

Then I thought I would press my luck and ask Mother for a set of bunk beds. We had to buy me a bed anyway, so why not buy bunk beds?

She liked the idea. She said, "Later on, if you have a friend over to spend the night, you will have a place for him to sleep."

Our first year in the house was a lonely one. Mother seemed to work all the time. She rode the city bus to and from work. That in itself caused her to be away from home several extra hours a week. She had to leave early in the morning to be sure to get to work on time, and she was always delayed in coming home because of the inconsistency of the bus schedule.

Mother decided not to notify the proper authorities at the school board of our move from Sans Souci to the Augusta Road area. By using our old address, I was able to continue my ninth grade education at Sans Souci Junior High.

Part of the time, I rode my bicycle to school. The distance must have been ten miles or better, but I enjoyed biking when the weather permitted. My second means of transportation to school was the city bus system.

I was home every day by 3:30 p.m. Mother usually didn't get home until 6:30 p.m. or later. After homework, I usually spent my free time playing in the yard; occasionally I would go next door to Mrs. Martin's apartment. She was a lonely widow with a lot of free time on her hands.

She loved to play canasta. She asked me if I knew how to play. I told her no, but I would love for her to teach me the rules. I believe that was exactly what she wanted to hear. She taught me how to play the game. Thereafter, we had many wonderful afternoons together playing canasta.

The weekends were always tough for Mother. She had to work on Friday nights until 9:00 and from 9:00 until 6:00 on Saturdays. To help keep me out of mischief, she went deeper in debt and bought another color television set. Even though color televisions had come way down in price from the one we had years earlier, I knew that we really couldn't afford this one any more than we could have afforded the one she bought years earlier.

I spent my Friday nights and Saturdays watching television, playing canasta with Mrs. Martin, and going to the neighborhood movie theatre.

Sunday was Mother's one and only day off. We both enjoyed that special day of rest. We would sleep in until 10:00 a.m. or later. Then, mother would cook her one meal of the week: country-style steak, mashed potatoes, brown gravy, fried okra, crowder peas, and corn bread. Weather permitting, we would put a card table up and have our lunch on it out on the front porch. It was fun to eat out on the porch, sort of like a mini picnic. Sometimes Mrs. Martin would come out and sit and talk with us while we were having lunch.

The rest of the day was more rest and relaxation, with Sunday evening being given completely to television. That's when we watched Bonanza, the best western on TV.

Because of her busy schedule, Mother had only two close friends. One was our landlord, Mrs. Martin, and the other was our neighbor, Mrs. Mobley. Mrs. Mobley was about Mother's age. I don't remember where she worked, or why she didn't have a husband, but I do remember she had one of her three children, Linda, her teenage daughter, living at home. Her other daughter and son were married and out on their own.

I think Mother and Mrs. Mobley would have liked for Linda and me to enjoy being around each other more than we seemed to. I liked Linda just fine. She was a cute girl with a really good personality, but I wasn't into girls. Linda thought I was a nice boy with a good personality, but she wasn't into boys. For that reason, Linda and I were together when we, more or less, had to be.

In August of 1960, I enrolled as a sophomore at Greenville Senior High School. This was the year that was to be a turning point in my life. Unfortunately, in many ways it was a turning point in the wrong direction.

That same month Mother was fired from Greene's 5 & 10. I'm not sure exactly what happened between her and the management. I believe while working at the snack bar, Mother gave a friend a sandwich without charging her for the sandwich. When the news got back to the powers that be, Mother was fired for breaking company policy against giving away food.

We had no cash, no savings, and we had bills to be paid. I remember Mother went over to speak with Mrs. Martin about our $50 monthly rent payment that was due. Between tears, Mother told Mrs. Martin that we were completely out of money and had no means to pay the rent. Mother told her she did not know what we were going to do for even the basics: food, rent, and utilities. Mrs. Martin graciously gave Mother an extension on the rent due and even lent her enough money for us to buy groceries.

The little bit of cash we had went fast. Mother and I walked up to the neighborhood cleaners to pick up our laundry. Because of unpaid laundry bills, everything we had in the laundry was put on hold by the management. During the walk home, Mother was crying and very depressed. The dress she had to have for a job interview at Roses 5 & 10 was in the laundry. The manager at the laundry absolutely refused to give her the dress or any other articles of clothing until the complete bill was paid in full. Later that afternoon, Mother started crying uncontrollably.

Mother went back to see Mrs. Martin. Thankfully, that dear, sweet woman bailed us out a second time. We got the laundry out of hock and had enough cash left over to get through until the end of the month. I hated to see my mother get so upset. I was afraid she might have a heart attack. The sad thing was that even if she got the job at Roses, I knew she wouldn't make enough money for us to live on, let alone to get us out of debt. It was time for me to get a job and go to work.

Mother and I had a meeting with my counselor at Greenville High about my going to work. Mother was honest and thorough in explaining our financial needs to the counselor. The lady seemed to understand the seriousness of the situation and enrolled me that day into the Distributive Education Program. Then she proceeded to find me a part-time job.

I went to work for Latham Brokerage Company, where I stocked grocery shelves three days a week in the Kash and Karry grocery store. At fifteen years of age, I was making as much money an hour, $1.10, as my mother was making at age fifty-four. Because of my work permit, I was able to get out of school every day at 12:30. I told my counselor that I loved my job, but I still needed to work more hours.

One afternoon my counselor called me and asked me if I would be interested in working on the weekends in a movie theatre. I couldn't believe what that lady had just asked me. I said very emphatically, "Yes! Yes! Yes! I would love to."

She said, "Well, wait a minute. You haven't heard what the job pays. It's only 50 cents an hour."

I said, "Great! I'll take it!"

She said, "Well, don't you want to know which theatre you'll be working in?"

I told her, "It doesn't matter. I've always wanted to work in a movie theatre. I love the movies!"

"Fine. Be at the Plaza Theatre this Friday evening at 6:00 p.m."

At 5:00 p.m. Friday afternoon, I hit the shower. I did the best I could to make my 6-foot 2-inch, 135-pound body look presentable. I wanted so much to impress the theatre's management and staff that I probably went overboard on the hair spray and the cologne. It didn't take long to decide what to wear that night; I owned only one sports coat and one tie.

The theatre was only a ten-minute walk from my house, but just to be safe, I left twenty minutes early. When I arrived at the theatre, I introduced myself to the young girl in the box office, and she told me to go on in and that the manager was expecting me.

It was a wonderful night at the movies. The theatre was playing a Jackie Gleason film, *Papa's Delicate Condition*. I spent the whole evening learning how to usher, sweep, mop, clean a commode, tear a ticket, greet someone, thank someone, make popcorn, butter popcorn, serve a Coke, and say "Good night" and "Thank you very much for coming."

The whole night was a marvelous experience. I got off at 10:00 and made only $2.00 for the night's work, but if the truth were known, I would have gladly paid $2.00 to enjoy the experience of actually working in a movie theatre.

That night when I got home, I couldn't stop talking. After a while Mother said, "Larry, we must go to bed." However, I was so wound up, I knew that I wouldn't be able to sleep. I spent the better part of the night tossing and tumbling, counting the hours until I could go to work at the Plaza again.

My love for the movie theatre only grew more intense. I was miserable working at the Brokerage Company, even though I made twice as much an hour there as I did at the theatre.

Our financial problems were still severe at home. My small salary from the theatre along with my Brokerage Company job didn't produce enough money to give Mother the financial support she needed. But then something good happened: I got a morning newspaper route.

Delivering the *Greenville News* gave me an additional $20.00 a week in income, and the only thing the paper route affected was my sleep. I had to get up 364 days a year at 5:00 a.m. in order to have all the papers delivered by the 7:00 a.m. deadline. During those days, there was no scheduled delivery on Christmas Day. That's the one day of the year that I got to sleep in.

There were two problems with my morning paper route: It was very difficult for me to get up at 5:00 a.m. on those mornings after getting off work at the theatre at 11:30 p.m.; and during the winter, it was extremely hard to go out into the cold weather at 5:00 a.m.

In cold weather, the only way I found to stay warm while sleeping on the back porch was to boil hot water and put the boiling water in a water bottle. I would then wrap a towel around the bottle and place it under the covers in the center of my bed. Just before getting into bed, I would move the hot water bottle to the foot of the bed. It worked. I stayed warm throughout the night, but when I had to get up at 5:00 a.m., the temperature inside my room was the same as the outside temperature. I often thought, "Surely, I am going to die from pneumonia."

The money I was bringing home from my three jobs was helping enormously in bringing our past bills current. I averaged $8.00 a week at the theatre, $10.00 at the Brokerage Company, and $20.00 from my morning newspaper route. That $38.00, along with Mother's $44.00, took the financial pressure off at home. Mother was finally out from under all the financial pressure she had been under for such a long time.

Five

Victor

I was never very active when it came to P.E. class or participation in any of the high school athletic programs. I went to P.E. and did what was required of me in order to get a passing grade. I usually felt sort of uncomfortable in P.E. I always had concerns that I would not do well and be looked down on by my fellow students and my teachers. Basically, I tried to maintain a low profile in P.E.—do whatever was required of me and do no more.

One day during P.E., while standing beside the basketball court, I noticed another young man standing a few feet away from me. He looked like an all-right guy, somebody I might enjoy talking with. I walked over to him and introduced myself. "Hi, I'm Larry, Larry Vaughn. What's your name?"

He answered, "My name is Victor, Victor Young."

We talked a while. It didn't take long at all for us to become friends. Victor and I were a lot alike. I don't mean in looks. Where I was 6 feet 2 inches, 135 pounds, and all skin and bones, Victor was about 5 feet 10 inches and weighed 165 pounds. I had a narrow face and big ears; Victor had a round face and small ears. He thought he was good looking; I always told him he looked okay at best. But the girls saw something in him that I didn't; they were always giving him all the attention.

When I met Victor, he had only two shirts to his name. He lived in a small wooden house in an older neighborhood with his mother, father, and younger sister. By the way they lived, you would never have guessed that his father had a good job with the post office. Their home and its furnishings were second-rate at best. Victor and I often wondered what his father did with all his money.

Victor's mother was a dear lady, but the years that I knew her she always struggled with emotional problems. Before I knew the Young family, Mrs. Young had spent some ten years in the state mental hospital. I never knew any of the specifics about why she was in there, but I knew enough to know that she still struggled with her illness. Victor's sister, Che Che, was a sweet girl. She kept herself busy with her responsibilities in the home and her schoolwork.

Even though Victor had a family, he was very much a loner, more so even than I. His home seemed to have no rules. Victor could come and go as his heart desired. Many times he would spend the night over at my house. I was always the one to have to remind him to call home and let his family know where he was staying. Victor was accountable to no one. At sixteen, he might as well have been out of his house, living on his own.

During those early days of our friendship, Victor asked me one day, "Have you ever played a pinball machine?"

I replied, "No." I didn't even know what a pinball machine was!

He went on, "Well, there are pinball machines, and then there are pinball machines." He vocally emphasized the latter one. He went on to ask, "You mean, you have never even played a pinball machine for fun?"

I replied, "No."

He asked me, "Do you like to play pool?"

I answered, "I don't know. I have never played pool."

Then he asked me, "Would you like to go to a place where they have real pinball machines and pool tables?"

I replied, "Yeah, I guess so."

That afternoon, Victor introduced me to a place that literally changed my life for years to come. I went to a pool hall, The Brown Derby. The Brown Derby was located on a side street about three blocks from downtown's Main Street. If you walked by The Derby, you would not be able to see inside the building because of its dark, smoked-glass windows and closed blinds.

Once you entered in through The Derby's narrow doorway, you would find located to your right the bar, its eight stools, and the counter area. Behind the counter was a grill for cooking burgers and sandwiches. Beside the grill was a cooler which stayed full to the brim with a variety of iced beers and soft drinks. Gus, the manager, guaranteed that if you drank enough beer it would most certainly take your mind off of whatever ailed you. Directly at the end of the bar were four pinball machines sitting one beside the other. Looking past the pinball machines you could see three pool tables. Across the room were six more pool tables which went from the back wall of the building all the way to the front door.

There were heavy wooden chairs lined up against the wall on both sides of the room. This is where the spectators and the gamblers would sit when watching those pool games of special interest. Each table had a freestanding, green lamp hanging directly above the center of the table. When a table was in use, the lamp was on. When the lamp was off, the table sat idle.

Most of the time there were at least three employees present. Gus, a young Greek, was the manager. Gus was in his early to mid twenties, tall and dark complected, with a pointed nose, dark brown eyes, and jet-black hair. He spent most of his time answering the phone and working the cash register. It was Gus's uncle Charlie who actually owned The Brown Derby, but you wouldn't know it by Charlie's barhopping and cooking on the grill. Charlie looked to be in his mid sixties. A jovial man, white headed, somewhat overweight, Charlie seemed to know everyone.

Then there was Shorty, the little old man who spent the better part of his life with his beloved alcohol. He was a frail man, a long-time alcoholic and chain smoker. It looked like he had long since given up on his appearance: his gray hair was unwashed, uncombed, and greasy. His clothes were outdated, wrinkled, and excessively worn. At this time in his life, all he was capable of doing was racking the balls in place before or after each player's pool game. Occasionally, Shorty would be called on by Gus or Charlie to man the broom and dustpan when cigarette butts started gathering on the pool hall's floor.

The air was thick and cloudy—cigarette smoke was everywhere. My first thought after looking the place over was, "How could a person possibly eat food in all this cigarette smoke?"

Victor went immediately over to one of the pinball machines. He said that this was no ordinary pinball machine. "You play this baby to win money." He put a nickel in, and while he played, he explained the process involved in playing a machine. "With each game you have five balls. The object is to get at least three balls to line up in a row. You then are a winner. You win more if you can line up four balls in a row, and the jackpot is to line up all five balls in a row."

Victor went on to say, "When you win, you push the little silver button that says 'R' for rack. It totals up the number of games you have won. You can then either keep playing using those games in lieu of money, or call Gus, and he will cash them in and give you a nickel for each game collected."

Victor didn't win that first game; so he started a new game. But this time, he asked Gus for a $2.00 roll of nickels and proceeded to put all forty nickels, one behind the other, into the machine before he played the first ball. I asked him why he was putting all the nickels in the machine at one time on one game when it took only one nickel to play a game.

He said, "I am building my odds." Victor went on to explain, "When you put a nickel in, you will win $3.75 if you line up all five balls in a row, but if you increase your odds by adding lots of nickels, you could win $30.00 if you lined up the same five balls in a row."

Victor went on to explain further: "There are pinball machines that take only dimes; others take only quarters. On a quarter machine you can feed it ten or twenty dollars' worth of quarters in a single game, but if you're hot, you might win $150.00 or better." He looked at me and commented, "Larry, it's exciting! Do you want to try it?"

I said, "Win $150.00! That's a month's pay." I spent the afternoon and several dollars getting familiar with the art of playing pinball. This was a totally different world I had been introduced to, and I loved it! I asked Victor, "Where do you get your money? You don't work, do you?"

His reply was, "What money? I'm broke, man." He went on to tell me how his dad periodically gave him a few dollars to spend, but most of the time he was broke.

I asked Victor, "Would you like to have a part-time job at the Plaza? It only pays fifty cents an hour."

"Sure, why not? They have some cute girls working there."

I assured Victor I would talk with Mr. Todd about a position for him. I also told Victor he should try to get a morning paper route. Victor applied to the *Greenville News* and within a few weeks got a route near mine. Mr. Todd also hired him to work on Friday and Saturday nights during the busy times at the Plaza.

Victor and I walked to school together every day. Once I left my house, I had about a ten-minute walk on Augusta Road to the corner at Church Street where I would meet Victor. Then, together we had another twenty-minute walk to Greenville High.

He asked me one day, "Larry, have you ever skipped school?"

I said, "No, it's never crossed my mind."

He said, "Let's do it sometime. We can go downtown to The Brown Derby and play the machines." After further discussion, we decided to do it that day and for many days thereafter.

I loved going to The Brown Derby. It was there that I was taught how to play pool. I spent many long hours on the pool table trying to grasp the basics in the art of shooting pool. However, with me, pool was always second to playing the pinball machines. The machines were where I would spend the majority of my time and money.

It was during this time that I started smoking. Victor smoked Winston cigarettes and suggested that I might like to try one. I didn't think much of the first few cigarettes that I smoked. After inhaling the cigarette, I felt sick at my stomach and dizzy. That sick sensation soon passed after smoking several more cigarettes. Within a month, I was a full-fledged cigarette smoker, smoking anywhere from half a pack to a pack a day.

At first Mother objected to my smoking cigarettes, but I reminded her that even she smoked on occasion. I promised her I wouldn't take advantage of the situation; I would smoke only a few cigarettes a day. She was pleased that, if I was going to smoke, at least I discussed it with her, and I did not smoke behind her back. From that day on I was never honest with my mother about how many cigarettes I was really smoking in a given day.

I talked to Mr. Todd, the manager at the Plaza, about the possibility of my working additional days each week. In the back of my mind, what I wanted to do was to get enough hours in at the theatre so that I could quit my job at the Brokerage Company. I knew I would have to work twice as long at the Plaza to make what I was making at the Brokerage Company, but I was willing to do just that if the hours at the Plaza would be there. Mr. Todd liked my spirit, and especially my willingness to work anytime and do anything. He told me that he would work with me and see to it that I got additional work in the future.

The remainder of my sophomore year at Greenville Senior High went by very quickly. For the first time in my life, I barely passed the grade. Where the year before at Sans Souci, I made the B honor role in the ninth grade, this year I was gathering D's instead of B's.

I wasn't spending anywhere near the time at home that I had the year before. Instead of playing canasta with Mrs. Martin, I was giving her excuses about why I didn't have the time to spend with her. I always felt bad about abandoning Mrs. Martin—she was such a nice old lady. But once you play a game for money, it is no longer any fun to play a game for fun. Mother was very much aware that I was spending a lot of time at The Brown Derby, but she knew I was with Victor, and she thought Victor was such a nice boy. As a matter of fact, Victor stayed at my house more that year than he stayed at his own home.

I couldn't keep the poor grades or skipping school from Mother. She got really upset with me about the school calling her at work. This went on for quite some time: she and I batting back and forth the issue of my staying home. Some days she would just give in to me and let me stay home as sick, knowing in her heart that I wasn't sick and that as soon as she left for work, I would be back out on the street.

Mother decided to take the TV out of our living room and place it in her bedroom. She said, "Since you're never here, why should I leave the TV in the living room? I'd prefer to watch it in bed in my room."

That same year Mr. Todd gave me the additional hours I needed to work. I quit my job at Latham Brokerage and concentrated on my morning paper route, my wonderful job at the Plaza Theatre, and The Brown Derby.

In August of 1962, at the age of sixteen, I started into the eleventh grade at Greenville Senior High. I wasn't excited at all about the upcoming school year. I felt I didn't need an education; I only needed money, and lots of it!

Victor and I spent the past summer living and working together doing the same routine. We worked mostly nights at the Plaza, from 6 p.m. until 11 p.m. After work, we would go out to the Waffle House and have some bacon and eggs before ending up over at my place. We usually got to bed around 1:00 a.m. We would then drag our weary bones out of bed at 5:00 a.m. just in time to help each other get the papers delivered by 7:00 a.m. Then, we would go back to my place and sleep from 7:30 until noon. The afternoons were spent at The Brown Derby; Victor would shoot pool with some of the locals while I was playing the pinball machines. The Brown Derby is where we would lose the few dollars we were getting up so early to make.

I saw very little of my mother during those days. She would work all day, ride the bus home, eat a sandwich, and watch TV until Johnny Carson said it was time to say "Good night," which happened nightly, Monday through Friday, at 1:00 a.m.

I saved nothing. I spent my money as fast as I made it, sometimes even before I made it. I had established a line of credit at The Brown Derby. Gus knew that The Brown Derby was my home away from home; and with my thirst for gambling, I was a safe loan as long as he didn't allow me to accumulate too much debt with him. Robbing Peter to pay Paul became a way of life with me.

Every Friday, I gave Mother the cash she needed from me to help meet our financial commitments. Sometimes I would have to borrow from Gus enough money to pay Mother. Other times when I was already indebted to Gus with a large loan, I would then take my collections from my paper route customers and give that money to Mother and fall behind on paying my paper bill.

Six

The Break

Mr. Todd took a personal interest in me. He was a middle-aged man in his early fifties. There were very few times when you would find him without a Winston cigarette hanging out the corner of his mouth. He had a pencil-thin mustache and always wore a brown hat with a wide rim around it. His hat was similar to the one Humphrey Bogart wore in *Casablanca* and *The Maltese Falcon*. I always thought that style of hat looked better on Bogart than it did on Mr. Todd. He was also a sweater man. The only time he wore a sports coat was on Friday and Saturday nights. He only wore it then because of the crowds, and being the manager, he was expected to.

Mr. Todd had a wife and two sons. His sons were in and out of the theatre, always helping themselves to free Cokes and hot popcorn. His wife seldom came around except to drop off the boys for an occasional movie.

Mr. Todd asked me one day, "Larry, how would you like for Alvin to train you to operate the projectors?"

I replied, "Mr. Todd, are you serious?" He went on to tell me that Jim, the relief projectionist, had given notice, and I could have the job if I were willing to train for it. I couldn't believe what I had just been told. I said, "Yes sir, I would love to train to become a projectionist."

He went on to say, "Okay, here's what you have to do: spend four weeks upstairs in the booth learning the fundamentals. While you're learning the projectors and the booth equipment, you will also have to prepare to go before the Greenville County Board of Electrical Examiners and pass their strict test before you can obtain your Class D electrician's license. After that has been done, you're in business at $3.50 an hour."

I got to thinking, "I'll work two days a week, at 10 hours a day, which will give me a total of 20 hours a week at $3.50 an hour, that's $70 just for two days work. Yes sirree, happy days are here again!" Mom and I celebrated the wonderful news by walking up to the Pantry Restaurant and having a great home-cooked meal.

Alvin Wade had been the projectionist at the Plaza forever. Alvin was a short, stocky man in his mid fifties, who had spent his entire life behind the scenes working in projection booths. A projectionist's greatest concern is that when he makes a mistake, the entire audience knows about it. The projectionist's work, be it good or bad, whatever is done behind the scenes in the projection booth manifests itself while the movie is playing on the theatre's big silver screen.

For this reason, Mr. Todd had installed a buzzer downstairs at the head of the aisle leading into the auditorium. The purpose of the buzzer was for the employee on duty to alert the projectionist of any problems on the screen. One buzz meant to raise the volume on the sound, two buzzes to lower the volume, three buzzes to check the focus on the screen.

Quite often Alvin would drink alcohol while working in the projection booth. Being alone in the projection booth for ten hours a day doing the same thing at the same time, over and over every day, would sometimes get the best of him. That's when he would start dipping into his pint bottle of gin. Not long thereafter, the buzzer downstairs would get a good workout as the mistakes in the projection booth would start to fly.

I've seen Alvin inadvertently put the last reel, which is the last twenty minutes, of a movie in the middle of the movie, instead of putting it in its proper place at the end. The audience would be watching a movie, then right in the middle of the movie the scene would change, and a few minutes later "The End" would flash up on the screen. That meant refund city!

The craziest thing he used to do was get high on the bottle, and while he had the first reel of the film on the screen, he would lose the second reel of the film, or even put a reel of a completely different movie on right in the middle of the first movie. Alvin would have up to three movies in the booth at one time, and when he started drinking, anything could and would go wrong.

Where most projectionists would have been long gone, Alvin's relationship with Mr. Todd protected him from getting fired. They had been together a long time, and though he never said it, I think Mr. Todd felt sorry for Alvin and put up with his mistakes far more than most employers would have or should have.

Alvin and Mr. Todd were in total agreement that I was the young man for the job. Alvin, like Mr. Todd, liked me very much. Alvin liked the attention and interest that I had shown him since day one. I was always asking him questions about all the movies he had seen, the projection booth, and the various experiences he had had in the movie business down through the years.

The three of us met, and I agreed to all their conditions. When I wasn't working downstairs as an usher, I would be in training upstairs in the booth. I would take notes, listen to all of Alvin's instructions, and study daily for the County Electrical Exam, which I must pass before I could be allowed alone in the booth.

Mr. Todd cautioned me, "Larry, it's all for naught if you can't pass the exam. You must have a license to operate these projectors."

I assured him, "Mr. Todd, it will be a piece of cake. Don't you gentlemen worry about a thing." They liked my confidence; now I had to deliver.

Mr. Todd took me aside downstairs after the meeting and said, "You know, Larry, not just anybody could train under and later work with Alvin. You have been here long enough to know what I am talking about, but I think you have the temperament to be able to work for and put up with Alvin and his ways. Do your very best, and let's talk if you have a problem."

I knew exactly what Mr. Todd was referring to—Alvin's drinking. I told him I wanted this opportunity more than I had ever wanted anything in my life, and I would make it work.

During those weeks in training, I spent very little time at The Brown Derby. Sure, Victor and I would skip a day of school every now and then and go to The Derby to spend some money and have a little fun, but for the most part my mind and body were consumed with the Plaza Theater. I was very much aware that I had an exam coming up, an exam which I must not fail.

In six weeks I had the projection booth down to a fine art. Alvin might as well have been on vacation. I was doing it all: check in a feature film, build the show, clean the projectors, thread the projectors, splice a film, curtain lights up, curtain lights down, light the lamp house, change the carbons, sweep the floor, make the changeover, you name it: if it concerned the projection booth, I could do it! The only thing left was the exam.

I went downtown to the Greenville County Courthouse to a small room on the first floor and took the Class D Electrician's Exam. I don't remember how many questions I missed that day, but I remember I missed only a few. I believe I left with an A or B+ on the exam. One thing I know for sure, I left with an Electrician's Class D card and license in my back pocket, and that's what really mattered to me.

I decided to celebrate my new position by buying myself a motorcycle. I went over to the Harley-Davidson store and bought, on credit, a brand-new Harley. It wasn't one of those big ones like you see on the street today; it was rather small, but it more than met my needs. Mother had the usual motherly concern about my owning a motorcycle—that I might wreck the thing and break my neck. I told Mother what she wanted to hear, and it seemed to satisfy her.

I barely passed the eleventh grade with a bunch of D's and maybe a C. Academically, I was going nowhere. I remember one of my teacher's commenting before class one day, "Students, has anyone noticed who is with us today? Mr. Vaughn is back. Everyone be sure and speak to him before he leaves. Who knows when we'll see him again!" The class got a good chuckle out of her snide remark, but her point was well taken. I seldom made it to school two days in a row.

It was during that summer that I started venturing out to other places besides The Brown Derby to have some fun. Now that I had a motorcycle, I didn't have to depend on my feet or the bus system to take me where I wanted to go. I found several new places to spend my money. I found a hamburger joint that went by the name of Cudd's Drive-In. Cudd's stayed open until 2:00 a.m. It wasn't Cudd's greasy burgers that got my attention, but his new twenty-five-cent pinball machine.

It was a good thing that I was making more than fifty cents an hour, because I was spending a lot more money than fifty cents at Cudd's. Every night after the Plaza closed, I would hop on my cycle and head for Cudd's. It was nothing for me to drop fifty to seventy-five dollars into the quarter pinball machine in one sitting, and many nights I would win fifty, a hundred, or even more.

I was starting to gamble so much that it didn't even bother me whether I won or lost. I was there for the thrill of the game. I knew if I won tonight, so what? I would give it all back tomorrow, and vice versa. If I lost tonight, no big deal! I'd win it back tomorrow.

I quit my morning paper route. It was all but impossible to stay up half the night, sleep a couple of hours, then get up and deliver those papers. With the $85 a week I was making by ushering and running the projectors at the Plaza, the $20 to $25 I was making on the paper route seemed not as important to me as getting that uninterrupted sleep that my body so badly needed.

Victor quit his paper route shortly after I did. He landed a good job working after school stocking grocery shelves with a brokerage company. He continued to work at the Plaza, but he dropped his hours back to weekends only in order to make a few bucks and keep his theatre pass. All employees were issued a season pass good not only to the Plaza but to the opposition theatres in town as well. The pass was a great perk to have, especially if you enjoyed going to movies.

I was now going into what was supposed to be my last year of high school. I was a seventeen-year-old senior with only ten months of school left. I had no idea about what I was going to do after high school. If I didn't go straight into college, I knew Uncle Sam would like very much for me to have an all-expense-paid trip to Vietnam, courtesy of the United States Army. I knew on my eighteenth birthday I would have to register with the local draft board.

Mother lost her job at Roses 5 & 10. I don't know the specifics about why she was let go, but she came home one day out of work. At least, this time, we didn't have to worry about losing our apartment or how we would be able to put food on the table.

Mother wasn't out of work long at all. She found a position with another five-and-ten cent store, the W. T. Grant company out on Wade Hampton Boulevard. They hired her to work in their downstairs drapery department. The downside was that she was back to riding the bus to work. At her former company, Roses, she could walk the fifteen minutes from our home to the store, which was located in the Lewis Plaza Shopping Center.

My focus most of my senior year was on my work and my gambling. I went through the motions of going to school, but I put zero energy into my studies. That year I became very "street-smart." I learned there are many ways to make a fast buck; you don't have to restrict your pleasure to just pinball machines and pool tables—not when you have basketball games, football games, and other sports games being played year-round and on a daily basis.

That was the year I failed the twelfth grade. You can only fool around so long and not have to pay the price. I most certainly pushed my teachers beyond the limit. The school principal told me, "We have decided to let you fail the twelfth grade and return next year to repeat the twelfth grade, if you so desire. However, we are going to see to it that

Victor Young graduates, as we do not want the two of you back at Greenville High together next year."

That's what happened: Victor graduated, and I didn't.

Seven

The Fever

Victor and I didn't spend much time together that year. For the first time since the day we met, we started going in two separate directions. Victor and I had been so close for three years that when anyone saw one of us, he would see the other, but now we were starting to veer apart. Victor stayed busy pursuing his objectives, while I was pursuing mine.

I had ahead of me another year of school, my work at the theatre, and my love for gambling. Victor was working full-time at the brokerage company, spending only a couple of nights a week at the theatre; and after he bought his car, he wanted to spend his free time dating.

Victor bought an old 1951, pale-green, worn-out Ford. It was one of those heavy, ugly old Fords that were built like a tank. He bought the car and almost set a record for the number of failed attempts to obtain a motor vehicle license. I believe he got his license on his fourteenth effort.

Victor liked dating the girls that worked at the theatre. He was always wanting me to get off work early and for the two of us to take a couple of the girls out and have some fun. I wanted him to forget the girls and for the two of us to go to The Brown Derby like we had always done before.

When Victor and I did go out together, we would usually get into a heated argument over my wanting to gamble the night away. He would agree to go to The Derby, but he wanted to shoot pool for only an hour or so, then leave. He got upset with me because I would start playing a pinball machine and refuse to leave until The Derby's 11:00 p.m. closing.

After The Derby closed, Victor would want to go out and cruise the town, or maybe go to the Waffle House and get a bite to eat. That was not what I wanted to do. I wanted to go to Cudd's, or somewhere else that had pinball machines, a place that stayed open until 2:00 a.m. where we could stay late and play.

Victor and I were continuing to grow further and further apart. Late one evening, he dropped by the Plaza and said to me, "After the theatre closes, Larry, let's go out for some bacon and eggs."

"Good idea," I said, "give me about twenty minutes."

We drove in his car to the Waffle House. From the moment the waitress brought the coffee, it was quite obvious Victor was there to talk more than he was to eat. He had something to say. Without interrupting him, I let him speak his mind. He said, "Larry, I would like to talk to you about your future. I have concerns about where I see you going in life. You're like the brother that I never had, and it bothers me watching what is happening to you. I know I'm responsible for introducing you to a lot of things that I probably should not have: pinball machines, The Brown Derby, skipping school, smoking, and even some other bad habits, but what I don't understand is why it is that you have to go to the extreme in every single thing that you do."

He continued, "You do absolutely nothing in moderation. You can't even smoke in moderation. You smoke at least twice as many cigarettes in a day as I do. Let me tell you what Gus told me. He said, 'Nobody shoots pinball machines like Larry does.' Gus said you're the best on a machine that he has seen; you win more money and lose more money than anybody he knows. Larry, you know, Gus knows a lot of people.

"Frankly speaking, Larry, I think you're obsessed with yourself and your pleasures. It always has to be Larry's way or no way at all. All you want to do is gamble and work at a job that is eventually going to take you nowhere. So, you got lucky and started making some money running the projectors. Is that really what you want to do with the next twenty years of your life—sit upstairs in some dark booth by yourself ten long hours a day, five days a week, watching the same old movies over and over again? And where can you go from the booth? I'll tell you where, nowhere. You can forget about becoming a theatre manager anytime soon. Mr. Todd is going to be around for a long time. Face it, Larry, your obsession with the Plaza and gambling is a dead-end street, a street that is taking you nowhere."

I lit another cigarette before giving Victor a reply. I said to him, "You have got to feel much better now that you have gotten that off your chest." We both chuckled. Then I leaned over, put both my elbows on the table, and looked at Victor, staring straight into his eyes. I said, "Let me tell you a fact, old friend; there is a difference between you and me. I know exactly what I want out of this life, and I'm going after it, full-speed ahead. I am going to be a gambler, a successful gambler—that is a fact. That is the purpose for my life. I like nothing better than a good bet, and it doesn't matter what I bet on. Money and guts are the only two tools I must have to be successful in my quest to become a professional gambler. The guts I already have; now I need the money. If I can obtain the cash needed by being in an environment that I love, then what's wrong with that? In your opinion, I'm in a dead-end job. I couldn't disagree with you more. I have found a wonderful joy in the theatre business, an enjoyment that I have never experienced before, and I plan on staying in the theatre business, even if the only job available is mopping floors for the remainder of my life.

"Now as to the difference between you and me, let me explain to you how I think we differ. Victor, you want to count the cost in something before you are willing to do it; I don't. I've seen you lose good money when you should have won big money, but you were playing too conservatively to win. You're very conservative with your money and in your decision making. I'm not. I want to live wide open, and let the chips fall where they may. If I can't gamble beyond my means, then there is no satisfaction in my gambling. My adrenaline will only start pumping after I have crossed that imaginary line of danger. And, as for smoking, I might just start smoking two packs of cigarettes a day if I so desire. Who cares? I don't."

Victor lit a cigarette, inhaled a deep breath, blew out his air of frustration, and said, "You're crazy." We both laughed and decided it was time to go to bed. We realized that night that we were still good friends, but we were both very much aware that Larry Vaughn had no intention of changing his bad habits for Victor, or for anyone else.

A few days later, I almost killed myself one afternoon while taking a joy ride on my motorcycle. I was riding down 291 Bypass, which is one of the busiest streets in Greenville, when all of a sudden my front wheel hit a deep hole in the highway. My motorcycle flipped over in midair with me on it. In actuality, I ended up underneath the motorcycle. I just about scraped all the skin off of my backside trying to get the cycle to lie down and stop dragging me down the highway. In a desperate attempt to avoid hitting me, cars were slamming on their brakes, skidding and sliding all over the highway.

When the dust settled, I staggered to my feet. I was rather embarrassed to be standing there with my pants in many small pieces scattered down the highway a quarter of a mile behind me. With no broken bones but bruised all over, I decided to sell that motorcycle as soon as possible and buy a car.

I bought a 1957 Plymouth for $125 and got my license on the first try. It was good for Mother and me to finally have our first car together. Even though she didn't drive, it helped her greatly that year for me to be able to take her to and from work when my schedule permitted.

Mother came home one day and informed me that she wanted to take a bus trip by herself to Redondo Beach, California, and visit her good friend Mrs. Mobley and her daughter Linda. The Mobleys had recently moved to California. Mother had mentioned several times about how much she missed them. Mother's only concern about taking the trip was that I would be left at home by myself for two weeks. I told her that I would be perfectly all right. I encouraged Mother to go and visit the Mobleys. I knew how much Mother enjoyed them, and I thought the trip would do her good. However, for some reason, which I kept to myself, I didn't really like the idea of Mother's going that far away from me, nor the fact that I would be left home alone for two weeks.

I drove Mother to the Greyhound Bus Station and stayed with her until the station official announced that the bus would be boarding momentarily. We walked out to the bus together. I kissed Mother, hugged her, and told her how much I loved her. Then, I slipped some extra spending money into her purse and told her to have a wonderful time in California with the Mobleys and not worry about me.

She said, "Larry, I wish you were going with me, but I know you can't take off from work right now."

She hugged me one more time, then smiled at me as she boarded the bus. I stood waving until the bus was out of sight.

The hardest thing I had to get used to during those two weeks while Mother was in California was my coming home to a dark, empty house every night. I must admit, I did not like coming home when no one else was there. Sometimes, people tend to take things and other people for granted. Mother had always been in her bedroom when I came home, either having just gone to sleep or watching the last few minutes of Johnny Carson. Every night, when I came home, I would slip into her room, and if she was awake we would sit and talk a few minutes. If she were asleep, I would reach over and kiss her on the forehead. She would usually wake up just enough to tell me that she loved me.

I really didn't do anything differently those two weeks that Mother was in California than I would have had Mother been home. I had become a totally independent young man, just like Victor was when I first met him. I now had a free rein twenty-four hours a day, seven days a week. I could do whatever my heart desired, whenever I desired to do it.

It was good to see Mother's smiling face as she stepped down from the Greyhound that Saturday evening. We hugged each other. Then, I got her bags, and we went to the Waffle House for some bacon, eggs, and conversation.

Mother had pictures and stories to tell about her wonderful experience in California with the Mobleys. It sounded like the Mobleys had gone out of their way to see to it that Mother saw and did everything. I was pleased that they had shown Mother such a good time. She was tired but happy. The trip had been a good one for her.

In May of 1964, after four long years, I finally graduated from Greenville Senior High School. I believe my report card that year had all D's with the exception of one C. My biggest immediate concern was my upcoming eligibility for the draft. I knew I must continue my education, or I most certainly would be heading for Vietnam.

Mr. Todd was also concerned about my military status. He said, "Larry, what do you want to do? Would you like to go into the military?"

I told him, "Mr. Todd, I really think I would enjoy being in the service. No, I'm not nuts about going to Vietnam, but a two-year break in the routine might be good for me. Victor wants me to join the Marines with him. My biggest concern right now is leaving my mother. She is a constant worrier. She worries about everything. When I was young, she worried herself sick about someone being able to take me away from her. Now that I'm of age, she doesn't worry about losing me anymore, but she worries about everything else. She has worried so much that I think she has given *me* an ulcer. I think my being in the military would be very hard on my mother."

Mr. Todd said, "I understand all that, but what do you intend to do about the draft?"

I answered, "I have a plan. I am going over to Greenville Tech and take a course in something, anything that will give me a deferment for a year. Then, during that year while in school, I will try to get into the Army Reserves or the National Guard."

Mr. Todd commented, "If that comes about and you get your deferment, there is a job opportunity for you in Clemson working two days a week running the projectors in our company's other theatre, The Clemson Theatre. Larry, working the projection booth two days a week in two theatres will give you a very good paycheck."

———

I asked the young man sitting at the information desk a question. "Can you tell me, of all the courses offered at Greenville Tech, which one-year course demands the best pay upon completion?"

Without any hesitation the young man said, "Yes, I can tell you: welding."

I repeated his answer, "Welding?"

He replied, "That's right, welding. Certified welders do very well."

I said, "Okay, I would like to enroll in the fall welding class."

The welding class was for fifty weeks: six hours a day, five days a week, working with blueprints, math, and fire—lots of fire. There must have been six or eight other men in the welding class, along with myself. The instructor, an older gentleman who had been in construction and welding for many years, was very knowledgeable and patient when teaching us. He seemed to enjoy teaching young men about those things that he knew best. The other students, like myself, were all fresh out of high school.

Our instructor demanded that we all stay very busy and attentive while being taught the many facets of welding. All the men in the class (except yours truly) were looking forward to getting their certification and starting out making top dollar welding in construction companies. The only thing I was looking forward to was getting into the Reserves and getting away from welding. I hated everything about welding!

Victor joined the Marines. He went to Parris Island, South Carolina, for his basic training and then to Camp Lejeune, North Carolina, for advanced training. Shortly thereafter, he went to Vietnam and stayed over there for his twelve-month tour of duty. He wasn't awarded the Bronze Star, but he did receive the Purple Heart when some enemy shrapnel caught him in his hip.

While attending Greenville Tech, I was fortunate enough to get into the National Guard. It so happened the unit I joined from Williamston, South Carolina, was in need of an individual with projection and welding skills. With my qualifications, the position worked out perfect for me. What's ironic is that I was never called upon to use either my welding or projection ability. After my advance training, the powers that be had me operating a switchboard in the command headquarters.

I graduated from Greenville Tech certified in both arc and gas welding. On graduation day, I was offered several well-paying jobs from both local and national companies. Immediately, I turned them all down and walked over to the trash can. I then proceeded to place my diploma and certification papers into the trash before leaving the grounds. I promised myself, "Outside of orders given by my superiors in the National Guard, I will never, ever, strike another arc or weld two pieces of metal together again."

That year went by so very fast. I was going to Greenville Tech, working in Clemson two days a week, spending another two days a week in the projection booth at the Plaza, and the remainder of the time working downstairs at the Plaza—I kept busy. I also had to spend one weekend each month at the National Guard Reserve Center.

With my active schedule, I still found time to work in an occasional evening on the pinball machines. However, playing the machines didn't seem to mean as much to me as it had a year earlier. Maybe it's because I had started spending a lot of time and money betting on college and professional football and basketball games.

It was easy and very convenient to place a sports bet. I was introduced to a gentleman, by a mutual friend, who placed bets for a living. I could call him any time, day or night, and get the line or the spread on a game. The line or spread means that when a game is being played, the oddsmakers are picking, in their opinion, the best team to win the game, and they even tell you by how many points they think that team will win.

Then, the next decision was mine: if I wanted to place a bet, I could do it right there over the phone. I could either choose the team that was supposed to win and give the points; or if I thought too many points were being given, I could take the underdog with the points. It was a simple matter of picking and choosing. There was a small charge for the gentleman handling the gambling transaction. I might bet fifty dollars on a basketball game. If I lost, all I lost was the fifty; but if I won, I might collect only forty-five dollars. Everybody has to make some money to make the bet work.

I could not attempt to guess how many sports bets I have made down through the years. I used to study teams so much that I knew everything about the coaches and the players. That's what I would do during those long days in the projection booth, study the charts on upcoming games of interest, so that I would know how to place my bets on the upcoming games.

I sold the old Plymouth and bought a late model, two-seater MG sports car. It was a beautiful convertible car: metallic green, black leather interior, five-speed transmission, with chrome wire wheels. It was a fun car. Mother thought it was a bit much. I think she would have preferred my driving a big, four-door sedan. But she even seemed to have fun riding around town in the MG, especially with the top down.

I received orders in August of 1965 that I was to report within thirty days to report within thirty days to Fort Jackson, South Carolina, for my six months of basic training. A month's notice didn't give me much time to tie up all the loose ends at home. Mother was my only genuine concern. She was having a hard time with my going away for that length of time.

I told her, "Mother, this is what we were hoping for: that I could get into the Guard, go to Fort Jackson, which is only a hundred miles away from home, then have my advance training, hopefully, at Fort Stewart, Georgia, and be back home within a year. Isn't that better than being drafted into the Army for two years, with one of those years, most likely, being spent in Vietnam?"

She apologized for being so despondent.

I assured her, "Mother, you know I will find a way to come home as often as I can."

While I was away on active duty, both Mr. Todd and Mr. Mosley, the manager at The Clemson, hired part-time projectionists to take over my duties at their theatres. Both men assured me that when I returned home, my job would be waiting for me.

Boot camp was most certainly a new experience for me. When I arrived at Fort Jackson, I was out of shape, both physically and mentally. I was used to being the independent one: the man that answers to no one, the guy that does what he wants, when he wants, where he wants, and only if he wants. That attitude was good for all of about five minutes.

The first thing they did was completely shave my head, and from there it got worse. I was up every day at 5:00 a.m. for exercises: jumping jacks, pushups, all sorts of physical workouts. It seemed like all we did every day was exercise, march, run, wait in line to eat, do hand-to-hand combat, and listen to the drill instructor tell us how disgusting we were as human beings living on this earth.

For the previous two years, I had had a lot of stomach problems, problems that I never shared with the Army doctors because I did not want to say anything that would disqualify me from being accepted into the National Guard. Before joining the Guard, I had been to the doctor several times with severe pain in my stomach. After drinking the hospital's barium cocktail and having my stomach x-rayed, I was diagnosed with an ulcer. In boot camp my stomach seemed to hurt all the time.

Every night after dinner, I took two cartons of milk from the mess hall to my barracks with me. I cracked open the window that was located directly across from my bunk and placed the two cartons of milk in the bottom of the window frame. During the night when my stomach started hurting, I got up and drank some of the milk which relieved the pain, and then I tried to go back to sleep. I usually had to do this several times a night, at least five to six nights a week.

My barracks upstairs had twenty bunk beds—a total of forty men on the floor. Of the forty men, I think two were from South Carolina: John Miller, another reservist from Anderson, and me. It seemed like everybody else was from New York or the surrounding area.

When you're living with forty men, twenty-four hours a day, seven days a week, you really get to know one another. You learn what each man likes or dislikes—what makes him tick. During our break or free time, the men would do a variety of things: some would read and write letters to their loved ones, others would use that time for getting a little extra sleep. There were always those guys who wanted to play a little basketball or touch football.

Then, there was a poker game. It doesn't take a Rhodes scholar to guess which group I ended up in; the poker game is where I spent all my free time.

Payday comes only once a month in the Army. I will never forget my first paycheck at Fort Jackson. It was a Friday afternoon. I had a month's pay and the weekend off. Late that afternoon I went over to the PX. I needed to buy a new watch, because I had broken my other one. I bought a beautiful sterling silver, square-faced, Waltham wristwatch. I paid only $35 for it, but it would easily have sold for at least $75 to $80 in a civilian jewelry store.

Later that night, I dropped by the latrine to see how the weekend card game was going. The action looked great. I decided I would wait around until a seat came open, and then I would play a while. Around 2:00 in the morning a player called it quits. I replaced him at his seat.

The first hand that I was dealt was a very expensive hand for me to play out. I put every dollar I possessed—I'm talking about my whole month's paycheck less the cost of my watch—and I still didn't have enough cash to play the hand out!

I told the other players, "Look, fellows, I'm busted. All my cash is on the table, but I want to play this hand out. Last night I bought this Waltham watch at the PX; it's brand new. Will you allow me to put the watch into the bet to cover my remaining part of the bet?"

Each man examined the watch; then they agreed to let me substitute the watch in lieu of the remaining cash that I needed. The hand I was holding was strong enough to win nine out of ten times. Unfortunately, this was that tenth time. I lost the hand.

I got up from the game and went to my bunk. I lay there thinking, "I have the rest of the weekend with no money, no place to go, and I don't even have a watch to tell me what time it is. And how am I going to make it for another month without even cigarette money." That was the longest single month of my life. I was able to borrow a few bucks from one of the guys, enough cash to keep me in cigarettes and toothpaste until payday.

When payday finally came, I paid my debts from the weeks before, and from there I went straight to the monthly poker game. That night, I fared much better than I had the month before. No, I didn't win back the paycheck that I lost earlier, but I did win enough money to buy me another Waltham watch with a few bucks left over.

I learned there are two types of individuals who play cards for money. One is called a poker player. When playing cards, a poker player plays by the book. If the book says the player should fold his hand early on because the odds are too great against his winning the hand, then he will do so. If the book says stay in and see another card because the odds are in his favor, then he will do just that. A poker player is conservative in his way of thinking. Many poker players have read all the books on the do's and the don'ts of cards, and they know exactly how they are to respond as each card is being played.

The second type person who plays cards for money is called a gambler. A gambler knows the statistics of winning and losing just as well as the poker player, but he gives very little attention to the stats. His intention is to build the pot and get a lot of money into the particular hand that is being played. Then, he bets on what is called "the come." That means he is betting on those cards that have yet to be played. In other words, when a gambler wins, he wins a lot of money because he has forced all the other players to keep putting additional money into the game as the game goes along. The flip side is that when a gambler loses, he also loses a lot of money. As a rule, conservative poker players don't enjoy playing cards with gamblers. The poker players' concern is that if they lose, they lose a lot of money; but if they win, they can thank the gambler for helping them to win much more money than they would have ever invested in the game on their own.

I was a full-fledged gambler, and I made no bones about it. Anybody who played with me knew that when it came to a bet, there wasn't a conservative bone in my 135-pound body. I won more money by bluffing with losing cards, causing the winning player to fold his hand, than I did by winning the hand with good cards. The only part of basic training that I truly enjoyed was those late-night poker games in the latrine. The reason we played cards in the latrine is that it was the only room in the building that had lights on throughout the night.

Mother received a phone call from "Jane Dodd." Jane introduced herself as the older sister of one of the cashiers at the Plaza. Jane was a single girl who lived alone in an apartment and was a recent graduate of Greenville Tech. Jane asked my mother, "Mrs. Watson, would you like for me to drive you to Fort Jackson one Sunday afternoon to visit your son, Larry? I have my own car and the free time to take you, if you want to go." Mother accepted Jane's most generous offer, and the two of them came and spent several hours with me one Sunday afternoon.

Everybody that knew Jane Dodd liked her. She was a quiet girl, known for her warm, sincere personality. She had a fair complexion, freckles on her round, pretty face, and she wore her dark brown hair short, cut at the neck.

It was great finally to have contact with the outside world. I could tell Mother's being able to see me was very good for her. It was also nice having Jane there. The three of us spent the entire afternoon talking and picnicking. As they prepared to leave for Greenville, I told Jane how much I appreciated her taking the time out of her weekend to drive my mother to Fort Jackson to see me.

Jane said, "I didn't come here just for your mother; I also wanted to see you."

I finally completed the required six months of basic training at Fort Jackson. I was surprised upon opening my orders to find that I was to report to Fort Bragg, North Carolina, not Fort Stewart, Georgia, for my advanced training. Because my Guard unit was a communication unit, it was necessary for me to complete my training at Fort Bragg. Because Fort Bragg was the home of the 82nd Airborne Division, a paratrooper unit, the

Larry's mother with him at Fort Jackson

training was certainly much more physical than it was at Fort Jackson. However, this time I thought I was in condition to meet their strenuous physical requirements.

I remember my first run at Fort Bragg. The wake-up call came very early in the morning, around 4:30 a.m. The sergeant had all of us outside doing calisthenics before the sun even came up. After a strong physical workout, we were told to dress out in full combat gear. That meant we were to have our helmets, backpacks, and rifle for the next exercise. He then proceeded to take us on a five-mile run.

I got about three miles into the run and had to stop. I was exhausted. Trying to run that far in combat boots with all that gear on, plus carrying my rifle, was too much for me. I used the steel liner of my helmet as a chair to sit on and sat down on it beside the road. Soldiers kept running by looking down at me as I just sat there. I knew I could only go on if I could muster up a second wind. Sitting there, I began to wonder why no one else had fallen out of the run besides me.

One of the sergeants came running up to me just as I was about to stand up and said, "What's wrong, soldier?"

I said, "Nothing, Sarg. I'll double-time and catch up with my company." I finally caught up with my company and fell in at the back of the formation. At the end of the run, the sergeant said nothing to me about my falling out of the run. I thought, "Whew, I'm not in trouble."

Later that afternoon after all the work of the day was done I went to my bunk. I thought, "No staying up late tonight; I'm going to put my weary, tired bones to rest at 8:00 p.m."

It was about that time that the sergeant stopped by to see me. He said, "Private Vaughn, you did something today that paratroopers don't do. You fell out of formation during an exercise, and because of that unacceptable act, you will report to KP in exactly six hours. Your duty of KP will be from 00:30 until 23:00 tomorrow night, unless the cook wants to keep you longer. If you don't perform on KP any better than you did on your exercise today, I'll have you back on KP this weekend and every weekend as long as you're fortunate enough to be in this man's Army. Do you read me?"

I quickly replied, "Yes sir, I'll report to the mess hall at 00:30 as instructed, sir."

I thought it best that I not remind the sergeant that I wasn't a paratrooper. I was just a National Guardsman who had the misfortune of being stationed with a bunch of overzealous paratroopers.

I made sure the mess sergeant was very pleased with my twenty-two-and-a-half hours of KP duty. It was the longest day of my life. I knew then why none of the other soldiers had fallen out of formation during the five-mile run the day before. I promised myself, "I might die during a run, but I will never, ever fall out of a run again."

Most of the men in my barracks were all experienced Vietnam veterans. Many of them had been to Vietnam with the 101st Airborne Division, and upon completion of that tour of duty, they had now been assigned stateside duty at Fort Bragg. It didn't take long at all for me to find my seat at the high-stakes card table. I spent all my free time playing cards in the barracks with those physically fit men of steel known as high-rolling, card-loving paratroopers.

During the three months that I was stationed at Fort Bragg, I made several weekend trips home. I started dating Jane Dodd. I enjoyed being with Jane. She was several years older than the young girls I was used to being around at the theatre. Jane was career minded. She had a good job working as a computer programmer but was always wanting and getting more responsibility at work. She was smart, especially in mathematics. Mother thought the world of her. She and Jane had become the best of friends. They spent a lot of time together while I was away at camp. Mother kept telling me, "She's the one, Larry. I think you ought to marry that girl. She would be very good for you."

Eight

Changes

It was wonderful to be back home in Greenville. It felt great to have my active duty behind me. Now I could concentrate on my future, get back to work, spend some time with Jane, and start making some important decisions.

Mr. Todd called me before I had a chance to call him. After a brief time of small talk, he said, "Larry, have you heard the news?"

I said, "What news?"

He went on to explain. "Mr. Heffner is going to build a new theatre right here in Greenville, and I am going to be the manager of it." Mr. Todd went on to say, "It's not going to be just another theatre, but a show place. Mr. Heffner said it is going to be the most luxurious theatre in the entire Southeastern United States. He has named it The Astro.

I congratulated Mr. Todd on his well-earned promotion. Then he informed me that Mr. Heffner wanted to talk with me about taking the position of manager at the Plaza. I couldn't believe what I heard. "Are you serious? Mr. Heffner is offering me the manager's job at the Plaza?"

Mr. Todd said, "That's right. You're first on his list."

Outside of saying an occasional hello to Mr. Heffner when he and his family would come to a movie at the Plaza, I had never really talked to the man. I knew a lot about Mr. Heffner from things Mr. Todd had told me about him. Mr. Heffner came from a very wealthy family. He was married to a very nice lady. The Heffners had several children, ranging in ages from a young child to two teenagers and an adult daughter. They resided in Greenville in one of the exclusive country club neighborhoods. Mr. Heffner divided his time between his two bowling centers, one in Greenville and the other one in Asheville, and his two theatres in Greenville and Clemson. Mr. Todd said Mr. Heffner's true love was the theatre business.

I went over to his office and met with him. Mr. Heffner wasn't a very large man at all. He had a very slim build; he reminded me of the movie star and singer Bing Crosby. I wondered if he was hard of hearing, because throughout our conversation he seemed to talk quite loudly. After listening to him for a few minutes, I could tell he was a very intelligent man. He seemed to be knowledgeable about everything we discussed that day. I would guess his age at that time to be in his early to mid fifties.

Mr. Heffner told me, "Larry, I've had my eye on you for a long time. Mr. Todd has kept me abreast of your progress at the Plaza. He tells me you are willing to do anything when it comes to that theatre. Well, my question to you is, can you manage the Plaza and manage it well?"

Before I had a chance to answer his question, he went on to say, "The key to being a good theatre manager is to never ask or expect more out of your employees than you yourself are willing to give. Listen to your employees, train them well, teach them to love their work, and most important of all, you must know and love your job. Larry, you must be dedicated to the company if you are going to work for me."

I could tell by the way that man was looking at me that he knew my thoughts even before I said them. It was impossible for me to hide my emotions. I responded with excitement in my voice. "Mr. Heffner, this is exactly what I have always wanted, my own theatre. I'll do my very best to make you proud of me. Thank you so very much for this opportunity."

After that day, Mr. Heffner and I became very close. I spent a lot of time at his office each week working with him on newspaper and radio advertisements. Mr. Heffner had a remarkable imagination; he spent several weeks teaching me all the different facets of motion picture advertising. At the close of a meeting, he would give me a rather brief idea about how he would like to see another film advertised. Then I would leave with that idea, think about it, build on it, and meet with him later for further discussion.

After a few months, it was remarkable how Mr. Heffner was using my thoughts and my suggestions instead of his thoughts and his suggestions about the best possible way to market a film.

One afternoon, Mr. Heffner said to me, "Larry, you have a great creative ability, and I intend to make use of it. In the future you will be responsible for all three of our theatres' newspaper and radio advertising." He went on to say, "Along with that responsibility comes a lot of hard work and a good raise."

At twenty-one, I was probably the youngest theatre and advertising manager in South Carolina. I was making good money in the industry that I had always loved the most.

I wanted to share my good news with Mother and Jane. That night the three of us went out to dinner. I told them about my meeting with Mr. Heffner, trying to remember it word for word, as I wanted to leave nothing out. Then I looked directly at Mother and said, "To celebrate my good fortune, Mother, I am going to buy you your own home."

Mom said, "Oh no, you're not! You're going to save your money for your own home."

Jane and I laughed at Mother, knowing that she wanted her own home more than anything in the world.

I replied, "Mother, I've already picked out the house for you. Do you remember that cute little white house three houses down from us that's for sale?"

She said, "Yes."

I said, "Well, it's yours, if you want it."

Mother and I met the realtor at the house. Right away, I started getting upset with Mother when the three of us were walking through the house. Mother was so excited she couldn't stop talking. She told the realtor, "Oh I can do this here, that there, and won't this look good if I do such and such."

I pulled Mother off to the side and warned her, "If you don't stop making such a fuss over this place, I'm going to have to pay top dollar to buy it for you."

Mother gave me that little cheesy smile of hers, then nodded her head in agreement. She said, "I'm sorry, I'll be good."

I said, "You're always good—just be quiet."

To be as old as it was, the house was in good condition. It needed a coat of paint on the inside, but the outside looked just fine. It was a nice-looking white, wooden house—two bedrooms, one bath, small kitchen, dining room, living room, and a small Florida room. It also had a large, unfinished basement. The front yard was small, but it had a very long and deep back yard. On the left side of the house was a gravel driveway which led to a freestanding white wooden garage located at the rear of the house.

That evening, I put a contract on that cute little white house on Cateechee Avenue. I gave Mother a hug and a kiss and said, "Congratulations, you now have your retirement home." Six weeks later, the loan

Larry Vaughn purchased his first house at age twenty-one

was approved and Mother was about to become a full-fledged home owner, and I was now in debt for thirty years.

Mother wanted to move in and fix up the house as we went along. I told her if she would only wait one month I could have some of the kids from the theatre come over and paint the inside of the house while I was away at Fort Stewart for my two weeks of summer camp. I promised Mother, "We'll move in the week after I get back from camp."

I left for my annual two weeks of summer camp at Fort Stewart on a Saturday morning at the end of June. It was exhausting trying to get everything done that had to be done before the convoy left that day. It was only when I was actually driving down the highway that I finally felt like all the bases had been covered. The theatre was taken care of, and Mr. Heffner and Mr. Todd would oversee all the advertising. And as for Mother, she was too preoccupied with making decorating plans in her new home to be missing me. Mother was counting down the days until we could move out of that small apartment in the boarding house that we had lived in for so many years to her new little dream home. I lit a cigarette, inhaled a deep breath, and held it; then I exhaled the smoke. I relaxed a moment and then thought, "I have two weeks free; it's poker time."

The worst part about going to Fort Stewart in the middle of the summer is the mosquitoes. The mosquitoes were so big at Fort Stewart that they looked like some of the Army's helicopters. Insect repellent was a must if you planned on coming home alive. Our battalion always had the misfortune of staying miles deep in the woods, right in the middle of mosquito city and near absolutely nothing else. That year was no different.

I was one of the chosen few who got authorization to drive his own car to camp that year. It was nice to have my own vehicle and not have to ride that long distance in a military jeep or truck. One of my reserve buddies, Hank Medlin, rode along with me. We made several stops along the way but still made it to camp by midafternoon. The convoy arrived around 5:30 p.m. By the time we got our communication equipment unpacked, in place, and had dinner, the day for the most part was over. The men that rode in the convoy seemed extremely tired from the long ride in those very uncomfortable military vehicles. I never remember having a comfortable ride in any army vehicle, be it a jeep or truck. The ride was always so bumpy. I often wondered, "Why is it all military vehicles seem to be issued with worn-out shocks?"

I lay in my bunk that night thinking ahead to the next Thursday, which would be the Fourth of July. I knew Thursday there would be a big card game taking place, and I looked forward to being an important player in that card game.

I finished my shift on the switchboard at noon on Wednesday. Most of the men had taken a jump-start on the Fourth and had already started the celebration. When I got back to my bunk, the poker game was well underway. There was still one seat open, and that seat was for me.

Except for a quick trip to the latrine, I never left my seat from 1:00 Wednesday afternoon until the call came at 3:00 Thursday afternoon. When you're playing in a high-stakes game, that's the way you play. You do not leave the table. You drink a lot of coffee, eat a sandwich for energy, stand up and stretch during the deal; but you don't leave the game.

I heard someone yelling, "Vaughn, PFC Vaughn, has anyone seen Vaughn?"

One of the guys watching us yelled back, "Moneybags is over here."

The sergeant came over to the game and said, "Vaughn, the captain wants to see you pronto in the command tent."

I was up around seven hundred dollars and I thought, "Just my luck. I'm on a roll, and he has to call me." I played out the hand and then assured the guys I would be back shortly.

While taking the brief walk over to the command tent, I was trying to figure out why the captain would want to see me. I was supposed to be off duty for another twenty-four hours. I looked a mess. I was un-shaven; my uniform was all wrinkled—I had been wearing it for two days—my hair was oily, and I needed a bath. I decided the captain's calling me couldn't be good news. I must have done or said something wrong the last time I was on duty.

I walked into the headquarters tent. I saw Captain Conner standing at the far end of the tent talking to one of his lieutenants. He looked over at me, said something to the lieutenant, and then immediately started walking toward me. I snapped to attention and said, "Sir. PFC Vaughn reporting as ordered."

Captain Conner looked directly into my eyes; then he dropped his eyelids, tilted his head forward toward me, and said very quietly, "At ease, Vaughn. Please sit down."

My heart was starting to beat fast, and I didn't even know why. I knew bad news was about to come. Captain Conner went on to say, "Private Vaughn, I received a call a few minutes ago from headquarters. A short while ago, they were notified by the Red Cross that your mother is in critical condition in Greenville General Hospital. The only other pertinent information I have is that the doctors suspect she has had some form of hemorrhage in her brain. I have cut you special orders; you are to return home immediately."

I ran back to the barracks and took a fast—very fast—shower and shave. I put on my civilian clothes, grabbed a pack of cigarettes, and without telling anyone any specifics, I was gone. I averaged a speed of over ninety miles an hour trying to get home that day. With the excessive speed I was driving on those old country roads, it's a miracle I didn't kill myself or someone else that day.

Up until that day, I had never had a religious bone in my body. The only time I remember even going to church was to see this attractive young lady that worked at the Plaza. At seventeen, I had a terrible crush on her: her name was Frankie Taylor. One Sunday morning I got up, put on my suit, and went to her church. I stood at the back of the church until she and her family came in and were seated. I then proceeded to sit down in the row directly behind her where I foolishly looked at the back of her head for the better part of an hour or so. That just about sums up my experience in church.

Those hours I spent alone in my car, I was trying desperately to take away the long distance, shorten the amount of driving time, and get to the hospital as quickly as possible, knowing inside that every second counted. "I must get there before it's too late." I thought, "I must pray. I will pray, right now. God, please, don't let Mother die, not now. She has so much to live for: her new home, me. Please, God, don't let her die."

I pulled up to the front door of the hospital at 7:30 p.m. I left my car half-parked, keys in the ignition at the entrance. I ran to the information desk and asked for directions to Mary Watson's room. The receptionist directed me to the intensive care section.

As I opened the door of her room, the reality of death encompassed me. It was hard to see Mother lying there in that dreary, miserable hospital room. She was very pale, almost gray looking, in a deep coma. I leaned over and kissed her cheek. Then I whispered to her, "Mother, it's Larry. I'm here; you must wake up. I love you, Mother, so very much. I need you; please don't leave me now." I squeezed her hand and waited.

We had a total of fifteen minutes together before Mother died. Even though she never came out of the coma, I always felt like she hung on to life for those few extra minutes until I could get there to see her and to be with her one more time. The death certificate stated my mother died of a hemorrhage to the brain at 7:45 p.m. on Thursday evening, July 4, 1968, at the age of 61 years.

Victor had completed his tour of duty in Vietnam. He was currently stationed at Camp Lejeune, North Carolina. Victor arrived home Friday evening for the funeral, which had been scheduled for late Saturday afternoon. Mrs. Mobley was unable to come, as she was in bed recovering from a bout with the flu; but she was thoughtful enough to allow Linda to make the flight in her place. Linda arrived on Saturday afternoon a couple of hours before the service.

It was Jane who found Mother the day she became ill. Jane dropped by the house to make her routine check on Mom, just to see how she was doing. When there was no reply to her knock on the door, Jane went on in as she had done many times before. She found Mother unconscious, lying on the kitchen floor. Jane called an ambulance and stayed at the hospital with Mother until I got there.

The service was held at Jones Funeral Home. I thought, "Mother would have been pleased with the arrangements." I purchased a very expensive silver casket with all the trimmings. Jane went shopping for me and found Mother a beautiful new dress to be buried in. A preacher from one of the local Baptist churches that Mother had occasionally visited spoke at the service. There were more people at the service than I thought would have been there. Mrs. Martin, Mr. Todd and his family, many of my employees, Mother's store manager, Mr. Williams, plus several ladies that Mother had worked with down through the years. Yes, I thought everything was done that could be done—Mother would have been pleased.

After the funeral, Victor got angry with some of the things the minister had said during the service. Victor said, "Larry, the way that preacher was talking, he insinuated several times that your mother wasn't a Christian. I think I'll go straighten that man out."

I told Victor, "Knock it off. I heard the man; the service was fine. It's over; leave it alone!"

On Sunday we all went our separate ways. Victor had to report back to Camp Lejeune; Linda was scheduled to fly back to California. Jane was needed desperately at her office because their computers were down. And I had to get back to Fort Stewart. Because of Mother's death, the Guard had offered to let me stay home and make up the remainder of my lost active duty time later in the year with another reserve unit. I thought it best to go on back to Fort Stewart and get the remainder of my summer camp behind me.

Everything looked so different that Sunday afternoon, driving back on that lonely highway to Fort Stewart. How could everything happen so fast? The hospital, Mother's death, the decisions, the funeral, all of it happened in only three days. Now, here I was back on this highway, the same highway that just four days earlier I needed so badly. The highway that was going to get me home, to bring me together with my mother, was now nothing but an empty highway—a highway that was very much like me. I pulled my car off to the side of the road, parked, and cried.

After a while, I regained my composure. I started the engine and continued my journey to Fort Stewart. I lit a cigarette as I thought to myself, "I must shake this depression and live with the facts. Mother is dead, and I will never see her again, that's a fact. Even though there is so much I wish I could change, undo, and say to Mother, I can't. It's too late; that's a fact. At least I bought her a home; she was happy with the possibility of retiring in her own place, and that's a fact. And the fact that concerns me the most right now is that I miss her and that at twenty-one years of age, I am all alone."

When I walked into the tent, the expressions on the men's faces said it all. I knew then they had been told the news of my mother's death. While I was unpacking, each man came over and offered his condolence. I thanked them individually for their kind words. Then I walked over to the poker game that I had left that Thursday afternoon. It was still being played. There was one empty seat at the table. I sat down, laid $500 on the table, and asked, "How high are stakes this late in the game?" I played throughout the night until 6:30 Monday morning, not really caring whether I won or lost. I ended up about $1,600 ahead.

Nine

The Metal Box

The second week at Fort Stewart had gone by rather quickly. It felt good to have another year of National Guard summer camp now behind me. I was glad when I saw the sign along the highway announcing only twenty more miles to Greenville.

It was exactly one week to the day since my mother had been buried. A large part of me dreaded going back to that apartment that was filled with all the memories of those last years with my mother. I decided the very first thing I would do is go ahead and move out of that apartment and into the house. Yes, that would be the best thing to do, get away from the apartment and its painful memories as soon as possible.

I drove straight to the Plaza. After greeting the employees, I went into my office where my assistant manager, Scott Bolton, brought me up to date on everything that had happened at the theatre during my two weeks of absence. Before discussing business, Scott asked me, "Larry, have you talked to Mrs. Martin since you've been back?"

I replied, "No, why? Is something wrong? Is she okay?"

Scott said, "Larry, I think she's okay, but she has called for you twice this week. She said it is very important that she see you as soon as you return home. She made me promise her that when I saw you, first thing, I would have you give her a call."

I looked at my watch; it was 9:10 p.m. "Hmm, she's probably still up. I'll give her a ring." I dialed the number, and she picked up on the third ring.

"Hello, Mrs. Martin?"

"Yes?"

"Hi, Larry here, how are you?"

"Oh, Larry, I am so glad you called. Where are you?"

"I'm at the Plaza. I have been in town only a short while."

"Larry, can you come over and see me? I have something very important to talk with you about."

"Will it keep until the morning? I could come over around ten."

"Well, I guess so, but I must talk with you first thing in the morning. No later than ten."

"I promise; I'll see you then."

I hung up wondering what was on her mind—probably something to do with when I was going to evacuate the apartment.

When I walked into the apartment that evening, I couldn't believe what I saw. It was almost completely empty. The only furnishings left were a bed, the kitchen table, a chair, a few dishes, the coffee pot and my clothes. Everything else was gone. The apartment had been cleaned thoroughly. There was a note on the kitchen table. It was from Jane.

Dear Larry,

    I didn't want you to have to come home and deal with having to move furniture and cleaning the apartment. Everything but what you see here has been moved to your new home. Let me know when you want the remaining furniture moved. I have a friend who has a pickup truck and will be glad to move it for you. Remember, you still have to have the power turned on at the house. The water was turned on last week.

                        Miss you,
                        Jane

I thought, "Jane is a lifesaver. She gets a steak dinner for this one."

I knocked on Mrs. Martin's door at 10:00 a.m. sharp. Mrs. Martin, still in her granny housecoat and floppy bedroom shoes, greeted me with a warm, gentle hug and kiss. She then told me to make myself at home in the living room. She said, "I will be back in a jiffy; the coffee has almost finished perking, and I've made some blueberry muffins that will go great with my homemade apple jelly."

That Sunday morning, I sat in Mrs. Martin's living room thinking about the years gone by, of the hours upon hours that dear old lady and I had entertained one another in that very room playing canasta. Then, I thought of how this dear, sweet old lady had met such a financial need, not once, but twice in Mother's life. I hoped whatever Mrs. Martin's need was that day, I would be more than able to meet it for her.

Mrs. Martin returned shortly as promised, with a pot of hot coffee, delicious blueberry muffins fresh out of the oven, and homemade apple jelly. We each ate a muffin, drank some coffee, and had a brief time of small talk. She excused herself from the room and returned a moment later with a small, black metal box. I had never seen the box before. It looked to be old, maybe like one of those black metal boxes that your grandfather would have kept important documents in for safekeeping.

Mrs. Martin sat down beside me and placed the black box on her lap, and without realizing it, started gently tapping the top of the box with her fingers as she spoke. She said, "Larry, this box was entrusted to me many years ago by your mother to give to you, only in the event of her death." Mrs. Martin then, using both her hands handed the box to me.

I laid the box on my lap. Then I asked Mrs. Martin, "Do you know what's in here?"

She said, "I have some knowledge about the information in that box." Immediately she stood up and said, "Larry, this box might be something you want to sort through on your own. I'm going to get dressed. You're welcome to stay here in the living room, or you might want to go through the box in the privacy of your own home."

I felt like she wanted me to leave. I thanked her for the coffee, muffins, and for being such a wonderful friend to my mother and me. Then, I went next door to unlock the box.

I walked across the porch to my apartment. I went inside and sat down at the kitchen table. I lit a cigarette, gently laid the box on the table and stared at it, as if I were waiting on it to speak to me or open itself up. I waited a few minutes before unlocking the box, trying to anticipate what might be inside. My mind drew a complete blank. I took the key and placed it in the hole.

When I opened the lid of the box, lying on top of the pile of papers was an envelope addressed to me in Mother's handwriting with the instruction, "To be opened first." Beneath the envelope were several old, faded documents, an insurance policy, and a very old, faded letter from a lawyer. I opened Mother's envelope. Inside was a handwritten letter from her addressed to me. I set the box and its contents back on the table, then proceeded to read the letter carefully.

> My Dearest Larry,
>
> While I was alive, I could never bring myself to tell you what you are about to find out. I hope you won't be too upset with me. Larry, Jack and I adopted you when you were eight months old. Your mother by birth died when you were six months old. You have a brother, Buddy, who is ten months older than you are. Your father didn't want the responsibility of raising you or your brother after your mother died, so he adopted each of you into separate homes. Your brother has known from an early age that he was adopted. Three years ago your brother hired a private investigator to try to

find you. The investigator did his job well. The investigator arrived at our home one evening wanting to meet with you. Fortunately for me, you were at work at that time. I pleaded with him to leave because you did not know of your adoption. I explained to him that I wanted your adoption to be kept private until after my death. Right there in our living room, the investigator called your brother and explained the situation to him and asked your brother for further instructions. The investigator then handed me the phone, and I had a long talk with your brother. After hearing my plea, your brother agreed to honor my request and remain silent until after my death. I know what I did was probably wrong; if so, please forgive me for not wanting to share you with anyone.

Your name at birth was Larry David Stembridge. Your father's name is Harold Stembridge. Not long after your mother's death, Harold remarried; he now has a wife, three daughters, and a son. They live in Montgomery, Alabama. Your brother, Buddy, has always known he was adopted. Buddy has spent several summers with your father and his family in Alabama. Buddy has wonderful parents, the Pooles. They live in Fort Valley, Georgia. Mr. Poole is in the grocery business. He owns and operates his own grocery store.

Buddy is the only member of your family that has ever tried to contact you. Your father has never expressed any interest in wanting to see you. I still thought you might want his telephone number. Your father's address and phone number are on the attached sheet of paper. You will note I have also included your brother's address and phone number.

Larry, you were my whole life, and I wanted nothing to separate us from each other. I was afraid that if you knew you had a brother and other family members you might want to establish a relationship with them and not continue to live with me. Please forgive me for my selfishness; I just couldn't take a chance on losing you to your brother or other family members.

As you read the legal documents, you

Harold and Willie Stembridge

64

*In the metal box Larry found this photograph of himself
and his older brother, Buddy*

will see why, for years, I worried about losing you. Jack died before the adoption papers were ever finalized. What followed after Jack's death was a lot of litigation and court hearings. It was much harder back then for a single woman to adopt a child than it is today. In fear of losing you, I kept moving from town to town and from job to job. Down through the years, I made a lot of mistakes and have done a lot of things wrong. I do hope even through this deep, dark secret, you will know just how much I loved you.

The only person who knows of this is Mrs. Martin. She has been a good friend to me. Please don't harbor any resentment toward her for not telling you, as I made her promise to say nothing until after my death.

In the box is a Metropolitan Life Insurance Policy in the amount of $5,000. That should more than cover my burial services.

Larry, I wish things had been different. If only your father hadn't died; he loved us so much. We would have never gone without; he wanted so much for you to be a doctor. We would have had a wonderful life.

I will love you always,
Your Loving Mother

I reread the letter several times before putting it down. I would have given anything if Mother could have been there that moment, for just a moment, for me to tell her how much I loved and appreciated what she had done for me. It hurt deeply that she wasn't there and that I couldn't put my arms around my mother just one more time to tell her how all her fear was for nothing.

I always thought Mother went through all her suffering and poverty because of my father's untimely death. That was just how life left her, a widow, having to support herself and her small child. I thought her moving from town to town, job to job, standing on her worn, tired feet, day after day, eight hours a day was not by choice, but because she had to for survival. But no, she didn't have to place any of those hardships on herself at all. They were all by choice. She wanted to fight for the right to keep her adopted child, and she was willing to give, not only the best years, but the remaining years of her life for me. I thought, "Mother, I wish you could see what I had engraved on your gravestone: 'Mary B. Watson, a wonderful Mother.' "

I spent several minutes going through the other documents in the box. I found my original birth certificate, a few photographs, some legal documents pertaining to my adoption, and a letter from Mother's lawyer responding to some concerns Mother had during the probation period of the adoption. After a few minutes, I carefully placed all the papers back in the metal box, closed the lid, and locked it. I then took a shower and shaved, dressed, and went to the theatre.

That Sunday evening I wanted to be home from work by 8:30, as I had two important phone calls I needed to make. I was home by 9:00 p.m., which was good for me. I put on some coffee and opened a fresh pack of cigarettes. I waited on the coffee to perk before making the call. I thought, "Whom should I call first: my father or my brother? I think I'll have some fun and call my father first."

A lady answered the phone, "Hello?"

"May I please speak to Harold Stembridge?"

"Just a moment please."

After a brief pause, I heard his voice. "Hello?"

"Harold? Harold Stembridge?"

"Yes."

"Harold, how are you?"

"Just fine, thank you. How are you?"

"Oh, I'm doing okay. It's been a while since I've seen you, and I just wanted to check in and see how you and the family have been doing."

There was a pause on the line. Then Harold said, "Your voice sounds familiar, but I can't remember the name."

"Oh, I'm sorry, it has been a while. It's Larry, Larry Vaughn."

"Who?"

"Larry, Larry David Vaughn, formerly Larry David Stembridge. You remember me, don't you? I'm your son!"

There was a moment of total silence, then Harold very emphatically said, "Oh, that Larry Vaughn, of course. Larry, how have you been?"

"Just fine, thank you for asking."

"Larry, it has been so long."

"Yes sir, over twenty years to be exact."

"Well, what has been going on with you? Where do you live?"

I tried to put twenty years into a five-minute telephone conversation. I could tell I had totally blind-sided this man; and he, being in shock, was grasping very little of what I had to say. He was fumbling through his words, and I sensed a feeling of embarrassment in his voice. I then tried to calm him down. I told him I understood completely about why he had to put my brother and me up for adoption after Mother's death. Those words seemed to make him feel better. At the close of the conversation, he invited me to come and spend some time with him, his wife, and the stepbrother and stepsisters I had never met. I told him I would get back with him again. That was the last conversation I had with my father for several years.

A lady answered the phone. "Hello?"

"Is this Mrs. Poole?"

"Yes, it is."

"Mrs. Poole, my name is Larry David Vaughn; I am your brother-in-law."

I then heard a loud scream over the phone. Many more screams followed. Her screaming caused me to drop the receiver, but I could still hear her screaming as the receiver lay there on the floor. Tears filled my eyes as I picked up the receiver and asked, "Mrs. Poole, are you okay?"

She didn't reply to my question. I could hear her crying, "Buddy, Buddy, come quickly! It's Larry, your brother, on the phone." She then said, "Oh, Larry, I can't believe this is happening." Then she whispered, "Here comes Buddy."

His very first words were, "Hello, little brother, it's good to hear from you."

We talked for the better part of an hour. It was a wonderful time of sharing with each other those things that had happened in each of our lives since our separation twenty years earlier. I thanked Buddy for honoring my mother's request three years earlier and not forcing the issue on wanting to make contact with me.

He replied, "Little brother, I wanted to see you real bad, but not bad enough to hurt your mother."

Buddy and I promised each other that we would get together in the very near future.

Then I made my last call of the night. I called Jane. I read Mother's letter to her. Then I asked Jane, "Did you have any idea?"

"No, she never said a word."

We talked a while; then I told her good night and went to bed.

A couple of days later, Jane had her friend finish moving my furniture out of the apartment into the house. I enjoyed having my own home, but I didn't enjoy coming home to an empty house every night.

The following weekend my brother, Buddy, and his wife, Ann, and their young daughter, Pam, came to visit me. I invited Jane to come over and meet them. The four of us plus Pam spent the entire day together just talking, getting to know one another, and, of course, eating. The girls had fun listening to Buddy and me fill in the blanks of being apart for over twenty years.

Buddy was only ten months older, but he acted like he was years my senior. To Buddy, I was his little brother, and that was final. Our resemblance was amazing; we did look very much like brothers.

Buddy commented, "Little brother, how come you got all the looks?"

I disagreed with him. I thought we were both handsome, except I was about three inches taller than Buddy, and maybe twenty pounds lighter.

I said to Buddy, "Let's you and me take a walk." We told the girls to stay out of trouble, that we would be back in a little while. We started to walk around the block. Buddy opened up the conversation. He talked about how as a teenager he would go to Alabama and spend his summers with our father. But as he grew older, he saw very little of our dad. He felt like because of the distance and their busy schedules, the two of them grew further apart.

I asked Buddy, "Did our father ever say anything about me?"

He said, "No, he never talked about you or your whereabouts."

Buddy and I talked about our common interests. We both pulled for the same professional football team, the Oakland Raiders. Buddy enjoyed gambling, not to the extreme I did, but he liked to make a good wager on a game every now and then. Buddy, like me, was a hard worker. He had been the backbone of his father's small grocery business. We talked for a few more minutes then returned to the house.

Late that Sunday afternoon, the Poole family loaded their car, said their good-byes, and headed back to Georgia. It had been a good weekend for all. I was glad to have met my brother and his family. I wanted to be sure to maintain our relationship with one another in the years ahead.

The $5,000 insurance check came in from Metropolitan Life. Financially, I was in good shape. I was making a good salary working for Mr. Heffner. I had already paid off all the funeral expenses with part of the $1,600 I had won playing poker at summer camp. I decided, "What better time than now to buy a new car?" I knew if I didn't spend the money on something, I would throw it away on sports bets or cards.

I bought a brand-new 1968 Jaguar XKE, 2+2 Coupe, right off the showroom floor at Judson T. Minyard's Motors. I paid $7,500 for the car. It was fire engine red with a black leather interior and a chrome high-performance engine. When I pulled up to a red light, heads always turned in awe at the beauty of that splendid machine.

It was about six weeks after my mother's death that Jane and I married. The wedding took place in the living room of her parents' small country home. If she had only been patient, Jane could have, most certainly, done better than to marry me. She knew going in what kind of a man I was. I told her I would always be dedicated to two things: my theatre and my love of gambling. But she, like myself, did not like living alone and was willing to take her chances. Our honeymoon was supposed to have been a week in Florida, but I cut it short by several days because I wanted to get back to Greenville to play in a high-stakes poker game. Our marriage had few expectations on either side. We each, more or less, had our own life to live. Therefore, after a period of time our marriage ended in divorce.

Ten

Introduction to Hollywood

I received a call one day to come over to Mr. Heffner's office right away. I dropped what I was doing and got there in about fifteen minutes. When I opened the door, Mr. Heffner was standing there in the foyer waiting on me. He said very calmly, "Larry, come in my office and shut the door." I knew by the silence something serious was going on.

Mr. Heffner continued, "Sam Todd has had a heart attack. Stop worrying! I just left his wife at the hospital. Sam is going to be okay, but he won't be back to work for quite some time. What I want you to do is manage the Astro. In the future, you'll work out of there."

What was a bad break for Mr. Todd turned into a golden opportunity for me. Mr. Todd was transferred back to the Plaza, where things were slower and where he wouldn't have to work as hard or be under so much stress. I ended up being the manager of one of the best grossing theatres in the entire Southeast.

I was making a lot of money. I had a strong weekly salary and a good expense account. I received a commission on both concession and ticket sales, and whenever I made a picture do exceptionally well at the box office, Mr. Heffner would give me another raise.

Mr. Heffner continued to give me more authority within the company. We met one afternoon. He said, "Larry, I think it's time you start traveling; I want to take you to Charlotte, introduce you to some of the film exchanges, and show you what really goes on in the film business. Make arrangements to be away from your theatre next Tuesday and Wednesday. We're going to Charlotte."

That next Tuesday, Mr. Heffner and I left Greenville at 9:00 a.m. for our trip to Charlotte. While driving up, Mr. Heffner gave me the agenda.

"We are staying downtown at The Golden Eagle Motor Lodge," he told me. "When we get to Charlotte, you'll drop me off at the room. I need to make some calls. I want you to take $200 and go over to the liquor store. Be sure to buy a bottle of everything on this list. Oh, and don't forget to pick up four decks of playing cards." He handed me a shopping list along with the $200. He went on to say, "I hear you like to gamble almost as much as I do—is that true?"

I answered him very emphatically, "Yes, sir. I just can't afford to gamble at the level that you are known to."

Mr. Todd had told me many stories about Mr. Heffner and his love of gambling. Mr. Todd had said that Mr. Heffner was always going back and forth to Las Vegas just to gamble, and Mr. Heffner was even personal friends with Howard Hughes.

I asked Mr. Todd, "You mean the real Howard Hughes, the richest man in the world?"

Mr. Todd nodded and went on to say, "That's right, I've been in Mr. Heffner's office and seen personal stationery on his desk from Howard Hughes." To say the least, at twenty-two years old, I was very impressed with Mr. Michael Heffner.

I dropped Mr. Heffner off at the Golden Eagle, and then I went shopping. When I returned to the room, we set up the portable bar and card table. Mr. Heffner had invited several film executives to drop by our hotel room to meet me, have a cocktail or two, and play poker.

Little did I know that the men I met that afternoon would play such an important role in my life in the years ahead. I met the branch managers from several film companies: Warner Brothers, Twentieth Century Fox, Columbia Pictures, Paramount Pictures, MGM, the Walt Disney Company, and more. They all came out when Michael Heffner came to town. Michael had the reputation of being a big spender, wheeler-dealer, man of much action. I found out quickly that when Michael is in town, it is not business as usual—it's party time!

The card game and drinking started around 1:30 that afternoon and went right through the night until around 7:30 the next morning. I don't even remember if I won or lost. I wanted so much to be accepted by everyone in the room that I couldn't really concentrate on the thrill of the game. The next morning we all went out for breakfast and Rolaids.

On the drive back to Greenville, Mr. Heffner said, "Larry, for a first timer, you handled yourself very well with the boys in Charlotte. They like you; I can tell. Larry, you have the opportunity to go a long way in this business. Just be sure to stick close to me."

When he said that, I thought to myself, "Glue, that's how close I plan on sticking to you, like glue."

There were many, many more trips that I took with Mr. Heffner. We went everywhere together: New York, Hollywood, Las Vegas, Atlanta. He showed me the motion picture industry from a first-class seat. We made a great one-two punch together. I had the creative advertising abilities, and Mr. Heffner, the film-buying expertise. He had the connections and know-how to make the deal to get the important motion pictures to play in his theatres in the highly competitive theatre market.

He called me over to his office one afternoon. "Here," he said, "read this." It was a private invitation to a Producer's showing of Mario Puzzo's *The Godfather,* to be held in the Director's Screening Room in Beverly Hills, California. Mr. Heffner said, "Let's you and me go out to Beverly Hills and see the film, meet with some of the studio top brass, and then drop by Vegas for a couple of days on the way home."

"Sounds great! I'm looking forward to it," I replied. "Especially the Vegas part."

He laughed, then said, "Take cash, and lots of it."

We had two first-class tickets from the Greenville/Spartanburg Airport to Los Angeles International Airport. On the flight out, we had several hours to think, talk, and play gin rummy. We talked about my future.

Mr. Heffner said, "Larry, you will be making many trips in the future without my being with you. I want you always to travel first class. Never go tourist. If we can't afford to send you first class, then you just stay at home. Also, when you take these film people out, you are representing me: you are always to take them to the very best restaurants and buy them only the very best liquor. See to it that the film executives always have an evening to remember, and don't you ever be concerned about my questioning your expense account, because I won't. I have complete trust and confidence in you and in your ability to represent Star Enterprises. I just want to be absolutely sure you know the rules I expect you to play by."

The stewardess brought us a cocktail. Then Mr. Heffner said, "Enough of the shoptalk—let's play some gin rummy."

Mr. Heffner was an excellent gin rummy player. I wasn't. But I was a good student, and he was teaching me the game well.

We had reservations in what was considered by most to be the hotel of choice in Beverly Hills: The Beverly Wilshire Hotel. It was an absolutely elegant hotel. The Beverly Wilshire is where many of the rich and famous choose to stay.

After checking in, Mr. Heffner said, "We must go to The Brown Derby for lunch. It's one of the very best restaurants in all of California." The two hours we spent at The Brown Derby was a wonderful experience.

The screening was at 6:30 p.m. We went into the theatre, and I felt like someone had just dropped me into a fantasy world, a world full of movie stars. Stars were everywhere. I couldn't get over being in a room full of so many celebrities at one time. I whispered to Mr. Heffner, "There's Ali McGraw, Ryan O'Neal—"

Mr. Heffner chuckled. "You'd better get used to seeing stars, Larry. This is just the beginning."

After the screening, Mr. Heffner and I had an invitation from Paramount Pictures to attend a private cocktail party with the cast and director of *The Godfather,* along with other studio VIP's in one of the private rooms at one of the hotels located near the theatre.

It was a wonderful evening. Mr. Heffner knew no stranger. He was gracious to introduce me to so many familiar faces—faces that I had seen so many times on the silver screen. It was indeed a night to remember. The most memorable part of the evening was the two-hour conversation Mr. Heffner and I had with Jack Lemmon. I listened to these two men talk about what was right and what was wrong with the motion picture industry. Each had his own thoughts and arguments, but I could see the mutual respect they had for one another. As the night wore on, I realized just how intelligent Michael Heffner was and how respected by even the Hollywood elite.

We spent the majority of the following day at the Paramount Pictures Studio. After spending the morning visiting the distribution arm of the studio, we had lunch with several stars: Leonard Nimoy, Walter Matthau, and William Shatner. After lunch we went over to one of the sound stages and watched a few minutes of a film in production.

When we boarded the plane for the short flight from Los Angeles to Las Vegas, Mr. Heffner quipped, "Well, now that the work's over, we can go to Vegas and have some real fun."

I thought, "Work? This has been the most wonderful week of my life." I must admit, I was exhausted but not from work. I was worn out from trying to keep up with Mr. Heffner. He had only one speed, and that was wide open.

A chauffeured limousine was awaiting our arrival at the airport. The chauffeur greeted Mr. Heffner and me, then proceeded to put our luggage into the trunk of the limousine. I noticed Mr. Heffner never gave instructions to the chauffeur about where to take us. We got into the limousine and were whisked away to the hotel without any further ado. On this trip, I believe we stayed at The Sands.

It was around 2:00 in the afternoon when we arrived at the check-in counter. Mr. Heffner went up to the receptionists and introduced himself. Upon hearing his name, the lady was quick to greet him, as if she were expecting him. She then apologized that our suite was not ready for us. She explained that the delay was because of a celebrity, some musician I had never heard of, who was late checking out of the suite. Not wanting to rush the musician out of the suite was creating a small inconvenience on our end.

Mr. Heffner said, "Honey, I didn't come here to rest. I came here to gamble." He motioned toward me and continued, "My partner and I will be in the casino. Don't you concern yourself about when we get into that room. Have our bags put in the room after it has been cleaned." He then turned to me and said, "I am going to the craps table. Do you want to take a piece of the action?"

I said, "Sure, I'm in for ten percent."

That was the first casino I had ever been in. Mr. Heffner stopped and explained to me how a casino works: "Larry, it's beautiful in here. There must be a million light bulbs in the ceiling. Over there are the slot machines, often called 'one-armed bandits.' You will hear them being fed coins twenty-four hours a day. Beyond the slots are the poker tables. There's always a game being played, and there's always a seat open at at least one of the tables. To your right, see all those tables? They're blackjack tables. Blackjack is one of the fastest card games you can play, and as far as the amount of the bet in the casino, the sky is the limit.

"Look to your left. Those four tables are craps tables. That's my game; I'm a crapshooter. See those girls walking around taking drink orders? Drinks are free in here. You can drink all the liquor your stomach desires for free, as long as you're gambling. And last, but hopefully not least, those windows behind the slot machines are where you cash in your winnings, if you're lucky enough to win. You will notice there are no windows in the casino, nor clocks. It can be 3:00 p.m. or 3:00 a.m. in a casino; you can never tell the difference. Management goes out of its way to try to make you forget about time. They figure the longer they can keep you and the drunker they can get you, then the more money you will spend. There, now you know what I know. I'll see you later."

Mr. Heffner went toward the craps table; I went over to the blackjack table. I stayed about an hour and lost over $200. I walked over to see how Mr. Heffner was doing. I was impressed at the way the man gambled. I saw him lose $5,000 in less than five minutes. I noticed when he needed chips, he didn't take cash out of his wallet. All he did was lift one arm into the air in the direction of the Pit Boss. The Pit Boss is the man in charge of the table. The Pit Boss in turn would motion for a young lady to take a small chalkboard over to Mr. Heffner. Mr. Heffner then would jot down a number on the board. The lady showed that number to the Pit Boss who then gave Mr. Heffner that amount in chips.

I thought, "Hmm—an open line of credit!" I hesitated to ask, but I did anyway, "How are we doing?"

"Well, let's see, you're in for ten percent, right?"

"Yes, sir."

"At the moment I'm down $8,000, which means you're down $800."

I took a walk, as I didn't want to distract him from what he was doing, even though at the time all he was doing was losing money.

When we walked into our suite that evening, I was flat broke. I thought to myself, "Great! I have two more days here and not a nickel to my name."

Mr. Heffner interrupted my depression when he said, "Larry, I'm going to take you to one of the best restaurants in all of Las Vegas tonight. We're going to have a dinner fit for a king."

And we did. I don't remember what I ate, but a better meal I have never had. When it came time to pay the very expensive dinner bill, the waiter informed Mr. Heffner there was no charge for the dinner and drinks, as everything was compliments of the Casino Boss. The Casino Boss was the equivalent of a General Manager in most other lines of work. Mr. Heffner thanked the waiter, and then proceeded to tip him $50 for his services.

When we got back to the suite, Mr. Heffner said, "Larry, I've got to get some sleep before I can go back to the casino. I know we took a beating on the tables today. Don't worry; we'll come back strong tomorrow. If you want to go back downstairs and play some more tonight, my wallet is on the dresser in the other bedroom. Take whatever cash you need. There's plenty there, but don't wake me up when you come in."

My mind was willing, but my body wasn't. I also was exhausted. I went straight to sleep.

We stayed in Las Vegas two more days. It was a financial roller coaster. I was up, and I was down. During those two days my adrenaline got a complete workout. After all was said and done, I left winning back $275 of the $2,000 that I had taken on the trip with me. But I had a wonderful trip with no regrets.

Eleven

The Sale

Anticipating a busy day at the office, I got to the theatre exceptionally early one Tuesday morning. As I walked in the door, the telephone was ringing. I answered, "Good morning, Astro Theatre."

"Larry, hello."

"Mr. Heffner?" I asked.

He said, "Would it be possible for you to drop what you're doing and come over here right away?"

I answered, "Yes, sir. I'll be right over." I thought to myself, "Good thing I got in early today. It sounds like something big is up."

I walked into Mr. Heffner's office and without looking up he said, "Close the door and please sit down." Mr. Heffner stood up, pushed his chair back from his desk, slowly walked around his desk, and sat down on the sofa directly across from me. He said, "Larry, I don't know how to tell you this; I guess I just have to say it: I have sold the company to Martin Theaters."

I just sat there in shock, and my body went numb. After a few moments Mr. Heffner said, "Larry, you know how much I love this business, but Martin Theaters offered me a price that I cannot, in my right mind, turn down. They are going to take over operations within sixty days."

Mr. Heffner went on to say, "Let me tell you about Martin Theaters. They are based in Columbus, Georgia. They own and operate several hundred theatres all over the Southeastern United States. All of the major film companies have the utmost respect for Martin Theaters. They will be an excellent company for you to work for. They know all about your marketing and management abilities. They have assured me that they want you to be an important part of their management team."

I said, "Mr. Heffner, this is one of the saddest days of my life. I'm sure everything that you have just said is true, but without you, this business won't be the same for me. I do want to thank you for putting in a kind word for me with the folks at Martin. You have taught me a lot about the theatre business. Many men have spent their entire life in this industry and haven't been exposed to it the way that I have been exposed to it because of my association with you. For that alone, I shall always be indebted to you."

In sixty days, I was newly employed by Martin Theaters as manager of their Astro Theatre in Greenville, South Carolina. I hit it off very well with their home office personnel in Columbus, Georgia.

That year I entered a promotion on Paramount Pictures teenage film, *Friends,* and was awarded Martin Theaters' top honor: Showman of the Year. This was an annual award given to the manager who put together the most successful advertising campaign on a motion picture. I was pleased to have been awarded the plaque and check for $500 during my first year with the company.

Frank Brady, President of Martin Theaters, felt my marketing abilities were being limited by living in Greenville. He wanted me to move to Columbus and take over the newly created position of assistant to the vice president in charge of Advertising and Marketing. After spending two days at the home office, I turned down the promotion. I wanted to stay in Greenville, mainly because of all my gambling buddies.

After I declined the Columbus advertising position, Mr. Kurtz, the executive vice president of the company, made a trip to Greenville with another proposal for me. He discussed the possibility of expanding my areas of responsibility within the Carolinas. I was offered the job of Area Director for all North and South Carolina, which meant I would be responsible for all the company's present and future theatres within the two states.

Mr. Kurtz explained, "Larry, now you can have your cake and eat it too. You don't want to leave Greenville. Well, with this position you won't have to. You will travel a good bit, but you can live here. What do you think?"

I told him I liked the idea and asked him to let me think about it over the weekend.

He said, "Fine, I'll be expecting to hear from you first thing Monday morning."

The very next night Mr. Heffner called me at my office. He called from his hotel room in Las Vegas.

"Larry, what's going on between you and Martin?"

I filled him in the best I could.

He said, "Larry, listen to me. Don't make any commitments to them before I get home. I will be home Saturday. Then you and I will have time to talk."

I responded, "With all due respect, Mr. Heffner, what do you and I have to talk about?"

"You're coming back to work for me" was his reply. "Don't ask any more questions; you're gonna love it. I'll call you as soon as I get home. Okay?"

I said, "Yes, sir. Have a great time in Vegas, and thanks for the call."

I wondered what in the world Mr. Heffner was talking about.

I met Mr. Heffner at his office late that Saturday night. He laid his new project out on the table. "Larry, the name of the company will be Ideas, Inc. We will sell campaigns to all the major studios on their yet-to-be-released feature films."

I interrupted him. "Mr. Heffner, I have a question. How are we going to get past their marketing people? They all have huge marketing departments with state-of-the-art equipment and very qualified people who make big bucks to do just that—sell their films. Why should they pay twice?"

"Larry, I can open the doors of opportunity. I can go straight past their advertising departments to the heads of the studios, and you can put together, better than their advertising people can, the idea or campaign that will make the picture work. Well, what do you say? Do you want to take a gamble, or not?"

I thought a minute; then I answered, "Mr. Heffner, Martin Theaters has been very good to me. In less than a year I received the top award in their company. In addition, they have offered me two very important promotions. They like me very much. They have gone out of their way to make me happy with their company. But, Mr. Heffner, you have always treated me like a son. I'll do anything you ask me to do, even if I have my doubts about whether it will work. I'll give Martin my notice Monday."

That's exactly what I did. Monday I called Mr. Kurtz, the executive vice president of Martin Theaters, and said, "Thanks, but, no thanks." I left them within the month.

I moved into the office across the hall from Mr. Heffner in his office building. The first project we developed came from a television movie. ABC had a Tuesday night at the movie film, *Brian's Song*, which was a wonderful story about the relationship between two professional foot-ball players for the Chicago Bears: Brian Piccolo and Gayle Sayers. The movie was a real tear-jerker. Piccolo developed cancer at the height of his career, and his best friend, Sayers, stood beside him until his un-timely death.

On Wednesday after the Tuesday night movie, I went into the office and asked Mr. Heffner, "Did you happen to see *Brian's Song* last night?"

His reply was, "Larry, I saw it. That is a wonderful movie! My whole family, including yours truly, cried throughout it."

We got to talking. "Columbia Pictures dropped the ball on *Brian's Song*," I observed. "It should have never been made for TV; it's too good a movie."

Mr. Heffner started walking in fast little circles, scratching his chin. I knew his wheels were just a-churning.

He stopped, looked up at me, gave me a great big smile and said, "Larry, let's go to New York and try to buy the rights to *Brian's Song*, and then we'll sell it to theatres across the country. So what, if it's already played on free TV. We'll make the public want to pay to see it again and again."

I agreed. "Mr. Heffner, that is an excellent idea."

Mr. Heffner picked up the telephone and called Norman Jactor's office at Columbia Pictures in New York. "Hello, Norman? Michael Heffner here. How's everything going in the Big Apple? I saw a wonderful movie last night on the tube. Yes, it most certainly was a tear-jerker."

Mr. Heffner put his hand over the receiver and whispered to me, "Norman said the ratings last night went through the roof." Then he winked and went back to the conversation.

"Norman, I need to see you right away. When is your first open appointment? No, I can't wait until then. It must be this week. I would rather discuss it in person. Okay, Friday is fine. I'll see you at 2:00 p.m."

We walked into Columbia Pictures' New York office at 1:45 Friday afternoon. I don't remember Mr. Jactor's title, but from the location and size of his office, he most certainly had to be one of the senior officers at Columbia Pictures. When explaining to Mr. Jactor the concept of our newly formed company, Mr. Heffner was more than gracious in intro-ducing me as the "Idea" behind Ideas, Inc. Finally Mr. Heffner got around to the purpose of our visit.

"Norman, Ideas, Inc. wants to buy the distribution rights for *Brian's Song*. We want to play it in theatres."

Mr. Jactor laughed, "Michael, you got it all backwards. Major motion pictures play in theatres first, then they play on free TV."

Mr. Heffner shot back, "Norman, I think *Brian's Song* is a major motion picture that should have never been released to TV first, and if you will sell me the rights to the film, Larry and I are going to make moviegoers pay to see it again at the theatre where it should have been seen in the first place."

I could tell Mr. Jactor was taken back. He was trying to figure out if we knew something that he didn't.

He thought a few minutes, then he answered, "Michael, I can't just sell you the film; it doesn't work that way."

Mr. Heffner asked, "Then what can you do? I'm talking about paying Columbia Pictures a good, fair price for the opportunity to do something that, to my knowledge, hasn't been done before."

Mr. Jactor asked, "How long are you two going to be in town?"

Mr. Heffner responded, "How long do we need to be here?"

Jactor was quiet a minute, then he said, "Excuse me. I'll be back in a few minutes." He left the room.

Mr. Heffner looked over at me and winked. "Larry, old Norman is behind the eight ball. He doesn't know what to do. If he lets us have the movie and we make a big movie out of it, he'll be accused of giving the picture away. If he doesn't take my offer of found money and the movie doesn't get the opportunity to flop in a theatrical run, he made a big mistake by not taking the cash to the bank. Relax, Larry, I've got a feeling he's going to work with us." Mr. Heffner was having a good time. I could tell this was all just a game with him.

Mr. Jactor returned about an hour later. He apologized for being gone so long, but now he was ready to talk. He said, "Michael, let's try an experiment. You can take the film and play it throughout the Carolinas. We'll give you five percent of the total gross of the film, plus pay all of your company's expenses. If it works, we'll expand to other parts of the country. If not, we'll shelve the project and take a small loss."

Mr. Heffner accepted. "Norman, It's a deal. I will need three 35-mm theatrical prints within six weeks." We all shook hands, and Mr. Heffner and I left.

On the plane home Mr. Heffner said, "You best get busy Monday. You must overcome the fact that the movie played on free TV. Turn it around somehow and use it to our advantage. I want you on the road with this picture. In every city that we open *Brian's Song,* you are to be there. That's enough shoptalk. You know by now what you need to do—let's play some gin rummy."

Brian's Song was a moderate success in the Carolinas. I spent two months touring with the film, making sure all the bases were covered in each town that it played in. Ideas, Inc. made a nice profit off the two state playdates, but the numbers weren't strong enough to impress the top brass at Columbia Pictures to broaden the engagements beyond the Carolinas. After one more try, we were turned down a second time on our offer for Ideas, Inc. to purchase the sole distribution rights to *Brian's Song*.

Mr. Heffner and I planned a trip to California to introduce the major studios to Ideas, Inc. We stayed once again at the Beverly Wilshire. We spent the days and nights meeting with senior level executives at all the studios, showing them some of our successful campaigns from the past. Everyone seemed impressed with our work, but everyone also expressed concern about how their own marketing departments would fit in with a so-called joint marketing venture with Ideas, Inc. That had been my greatest concern all along.

On that trip I learned, once again, that you should never underestimate Michael Heffner. One evening we were down at the hotel lounge around midnight. I was worn out from a long day of tooting my own horn to the Hollywood elite. I told Mr. Heffner, "I've had it; I'm going to bed." He said good night and that he would be up later.

I went to the room, got in bed, and was half asleep when Mr. Heffner started banging on the door. "Larry, Larry, you in there?" In undershorts and T-shirt I stumbled to the door. I opened the door to find Mr. Heffner standing there with another gentleman. They walked into my room.

Mr. Heffner said, "Larry, do you know who this is?"

I looked at the man, extended my hand, and said, "No, sir."

The gentleman introduced himself. "Hello, Larry, I am Frank Yablans."

I said, "Mr. Yablans, would you excuse me while I put some clothes on? I had just turned in for the night."

Mr. Heffner spoke up. "Fooey with clothes, Larry. I told Frank all about your work; where is your briefcase?"

Frank Yablans was not only one of the most respected producers in Hollywood, but in all of the world. His motion pictures were household names, literally, around the world. Besides being a celebrated producer and director, he was also currently president of Paramount Pictures.

And there I was, undressed, hair messed up, sitting on the side of my wrinkled bed telling *the* Frank Yablans how great I was.

I went from top to bottom. It took a good twenty minutes to show him my stuff. He listened, asked questions, made several positive comments about my campaigns; then he said, "Fellows, I'm sold! Your work is very good, but you have to sell my marketing guys. Here, write this name and number down. Call Mr. Jackson's secretary tomorrow and make an appointment to see him. Be sure to tell her I told you to call."

We chatted a few more minutes; then Mr. Yablans left the room. I looked at Mr. Heffner and said, "Boss, if you ever pull a stunt like that on me again, I'll shoot you!"

He laughed and said, "At least you could have put some clothes on."

I slammed the door as he whisked out of the room. Needless to say, I was so wound up from the last hour's events that I slept very little that night.

The next day we went over to the studio, met with Mr. Jackson, showed him our work, and left. I told Mr. Heffner, "That guy will hire us to work in his department for him, but he will never use our independent service."

Mr. Heffner said nothing, but his silence told me he agreed with what I had just said.

Twelve

Doneata

Things were very slow at the office once Mr. Heffner and I returned from California. I was in a situation where I found myself with very little work to do. With no projects in the works, I spent the majority of the day piddling and looking for things to do. Mr. Heffner was concerned that I was getting bored. He came into my office one morning, sat down, and said, "Larry, we need to have a chat."

I looked up from my desk, took a sip of coffee, and replied, "What's up?"

He continued, "Larry, I know you're used to having several irons in the fire at one time, and now, all of a sudden, you find yourself with nothing to do. I'm here to tell you to enjoy the free time; eventually we will get some work, but for now I want you to take it easy. Why not have a period of R & R, being that there is absolutely nothing going on right now."

He went on to say, "If you don't have anything to do at the office, don't come in here just to be seen. Take the day off. Take the week off. Go play golf; and when things pick up, I'll get my work out of you then. I'm not concerned about your schedule; and if I'm not concerned, then why should you be concerned?"

I took Mr. Heffner's advice. I started playing golf four to five days a week. I would drop by the office every morning to check the mail—what mail I had. Then I would head for the golf course. In the afternoons, I would drop back by the office and spend a few minutes there. Finally, I would go home, shower, and go out on the town.

Just about every night I would go downtown to a private club called The Amvets and gamble the night away. There were two rooms in The Amvets. The interior of the club was decorated in all black: the bar, its stools, the tables and chairs. Overall, The Amvets had a very dark appearance to it. The main room was long and narrow. That room had a large bar with around a dozen bar stools. Behind the bar, running the entire length of the bar, was a very large mirror. At the end of the bar were several tables and chairs and a small dance floor. Back in the late sixties, most of the private clubs in Greenville had brown bagging, which meant you had to bring your own bottle of liquor to the club if you wanted to have an alcoholic drink. I spent very little time, if any, in that room.

The Amvets had a small room located off to the left of the bar area, and only the select few were even aware of its existence. The entrance door was always closed to that room. Most of the time, an employee was posted at the door to admit only those individuals with a clearance to enter. That room is where I spent many long hours, several nights a week.

There were two tables in the room: a poker table and a blackjack table. I spent the majority of my time at the blackjack table. Blackjack can have up to seven players at one time. There were many nights that I would cover the seven open player places. I would play all seven hands at one time. At The Amvets, the maximum bet was only $5, but when you play seven hands at one time it quickly jumps to $35 a round. You could play a round in five minutes or less.

I didn't gamble at The Amvets on the weekends. My weekends were spent playing in private card games in homes, with men who enjoyed playing for much higher stakes.

Victor had completed his tour of duty with the Marine Corps. He was now living at home, waiting on August to roll around so he could start his freshman year at the University of South Carolina. Victor decided that since Uncle Sam was willing to foot the bill, he might as well get a college education.

I received a call from Victor one day.

"Hi, Larry, what are you up to?"

"Hello, Victor, it's good to hear your voice. I'm up to absolutely no good, as usual. But some things never change."

Victor replied, "When was the last time we went out together and had some fun?"

I paused and then responded, "I don't know; it's been a while."

Victor went on, "Larry, do you remember Kathy Simpson?"

I said, "Kathy Simpson? Sure, a blonde. You used to date her some."

"That's right," Victor explained. "I ran into Kathy at the McAlister Square Mall last week. We talked about going out this weekend. Then

Kathy suggested double-dating. Kathy has a friend named Doneata Eubanks that she would like to bring along. Kathy said that Doneata is a real sweet girl and pretty too. She asked me if I knew of anyone that I could bring along to be Doneata's date. Well, your name popped into my mind. So I thought I would give you a ring and see if you're available."

"Victor, count me in. Call me next week with the time and place."

Victor and I met at my office about an hour before we were to pick up the girls. It was good to see Victor again. We filled in the gaps of time about what each of us had been doing since the last time we were together. Then, we left in his car to pick up the girls and go out to dinner.

I really enjoyed the time I spent with Victor, Kathy, and especially Doneata that night. I was amazed to find out that Doneata had grown up living only two streets from my home on Cateechee Avenue. As a matter of fact, I was their morning paper boy. On warm mornings, when delivering my papers, I used to lie down in the gully beside their front yard and take a break. That was the halfway point of my paper route. In all the years of living on Cateechee Avenue, I never remembered seeing Doneata. She commented about how many times she used to walk past my house on her way to do grocery shopping for her mother.

I thought, "Amazing, I never remembered seeing her."

During the dinner, Doneata showed me a photograph of her two-year-old son, David. He was a real cute two year old. She went on to tell me, "I have been divorced for over a year. My husband abandoned my son and me shortly after he was born."

I thought, "Her husband is a foolish man." I was already wanting to know Doneata and her young son better.

At the close of the evening, I asked Doneata if it would be possible for me to see her again. I told her I really enjoyed the time we spent together, and that I would really like to meet her son.

She was noncommittal. She said, "I have a very busy schedule right now, but maybe sometime in the future we can have dinner together again."

That was not what I wanted to hear Doneata say. I thought to myself, "I am going to have to work overtime on this girl."

After several calls and much persistence on my part, Doneata agreed to go out to dinner with me. We spent the entire evening talking with one another. I asked her to tell me about her family.

She took a deep breath and said, "Well, I have a mother, father, two brothers, and a sister. I am the oldest of the children."

I asked, "Any pets?"

She laughed, and said, "No pets."

I went on to say, "Tell me about your parents."

She said, "Where do you want me to start?"

I replied, "Let's start with your father."

"My father is a rather quiet, simple man. A man of very few words. He has spent his whole life standing on his feet, working twelve-hour days in one of the mills here in Greenville. He minds his own business, stays to himself, and when at home he's usually in the bedroom with Mother, or on his cot in her bedroom getting some sleep. Sorry I can't paint a more exciting picture of my father, but there's really nothing more to tell."

I then asked, "Tell me about your mother."

Doneata, then took another deep breath and said, "My mother is, or maybe I should say, was, the politician and entrepreneur of the family. Let me try to explain; Mother has known governors, both past and present; lawyers, the good ones as well as the bad ones; senators; etc. You might say Mother has traveled in some most unusual circles."

I asked, "How did she come to know the political elite?"

Doneata replied, "Through her various business dealings. Mother has had her finger in many pots down through the years. At one time, she owned a lot of property in Greenville and its surrounding area."

I asked, "What happened?"

Doneata went on to explain, "When I was eleven years old, Mother was involved in a very bad car accident, an accident which left her in and out of the hospital for years. Mother has had so many operations on her back that her poor back looks like a road map."

I then asked, "Is it because of the wreck that she lost control of her business and investments?"

Doneata said, "The extended hospital stays, along with being confined to the bed at home and all the years of pain medication Mother was on, put a big toll on her being able to maintain control of her business investments."

"Couldn't your father keep a watch over her business affairs?"

"No, I told you that Father was never a businessman."

"Okay, tell me about your brothers and your sister."

Doneata said, "The three of them live at home along with my parents, my child, and me."

"Sounds like a full house," I commented.

She agreed, "It is." Doneata went on to say, "Delaine is twenty, very intelligent. He stays busy running errands for Mother and doing odd jobs. He is also in college. My sister, Mentora, and my younger brother, Homer, are both students at Greenville High School. Mentora is a wonderful sister; I love her dearly. And Homer is a very special brother. He has a good heart. I also love Homer very much."

Doneata said, "That's all you're going to get out of me. If you don't mind, I have a couple of questions for you."

I smiled and said, "Shoot."

She continued, "Kathy has told me some most remarkable stories about you. What I would like to know is, are they true?"

I smiled and asked, "During this interrogation will I be allowed to plead the fifth?"

Doneata said, "Absolutely not."

I sat back and said, "All right, fire away."

"Larry, are you as big a gambler as Kathy says you are?"

"Yes."

"Have you spent the majority of your life in the movie business?"

"Yes."

"Is the company you're now working for—Ideas, Inc.—a legitimate company, or is it a front for some sort of gambling syndicate?"

I took a double take at her to see if she was serious. I believe she was very serious. I responded, "What! Of course Ideas, Inc. is a legitimate company. Why would you ask such a question?"

"Because Kathy told me that Victor told her all you do during the day is gamble on the golf course. Then at night, you live on the gambling tables in private clubs."

I replied, "With a friend like Victor, who needs an enemy? Doneata, it's not really as bad as it sounds."

She said, "Good, I have the time. Please straighten me out with the facts."

I thought a moment; then I said, "Well, the gambling, golf, and night club activities are all true, but as far as my work, I am very good at what I do."

She said, "Again, exactly what is it that you do?"

I said, "I think I am an idea man. I come up with creative ways to sell motion pictures to the public. It is my job to give the public a desire to see a certain film."

Doneata said, "Larry, I have been trying to find something that you and I have in common, but there is nothing there."

I said, "What are you talking about? I think we have a lot in common."

"Listen, Larry, you're a gambler. My family has never had a deck of playing cards in our home. You have been brought up in the theatre business. Did you know that I have been to a movie theatre only once in my entire life, and I was there for all of fifteen minutes before I left? And, as for gambling, I have never so much as bet a penny on anything."

I quickly stated, "Doneata, all of this is wonderful news!"

She said, "How do you figure?"

I replied confidently, "Haven't you ever heard that opposites attract? It's absolutely wonderful that we have nothing in common. We must have been made for each other!"

Doneata did not look convinced. She spoke again, "Kathy also warned me that Victor told her you're nuts! I believe Victor is right on that account too."

I took Doneata home feeling like I had lost instead of gained ground in developing my relationship with her. I decided I'd best come up with another strategy before it was too late and I lost her, even though I didn't yet have her.

I started sending Doneata flowers—I mean lots of flowers—trying to win her over. Then after sending dozens of roses, roses of all colors, for several weeks with no response, I decided to make the call. Doneata answered the phone and said, "Hello?"

"Doneata. Hi, Doneata, Larry here; did you get my flowers?"

She replied, "Which ones? It looks like a florist shop over here."

I explained, "My flowers are the ones with the smiley face on the card."

She said, "They all have a smiley face on the card; and, by the way, my mother is very upset with you. She has instructed the family not to accept any more flowers with a smiley face on the card."

Then she hung up the phone. I thought, "I'm calling her back." But the line was busy. For over one hour I kept calling, but all I kept getting was a busy signal. I finally dialed the operator and asked the operator if she would mind checking the line, as I had been getting a busy signal for over an hour. The operator came back shortly to inform me that the receiver was off the hook at their home. I thought a few moments and knew I had to do something about this situation.

I went to my old friend, Scott Bolton, and asked him if would he do something rather strange for me without asking any questions. Scott thought the world of me. He said, "Sure, Larry, as long as you'll come and visit me if I land in jail."

I said, "Scott it's nothing like that, I promise." I went on to say, "Here's what you are to do: go to this address and knock on the door. Tell whoever comes to the door that you are from the telephone company, and their phone has been reported off the receiver. Then, tell them they must put the phone back on the receiver immediately, as you are having other problems in the neighborhood with phones and this phone's being off the receiver might be what's causing the other problems."

Scott said, "Do you want me to steal a phone truck to make it look real?"

I said, "Don't be silly; just do as instructed and make it look real."

It worked. As soon as Scott left their house, the phone was back on the hook, and I had Doneata on the line. I wouldn't let her hang up until she promised to go out to dinner with me the following Friday night.

The following Friday, I picked Doneata up early at 5:00 p.m. and drove her to Atlanta, Georgia, for dinner in a restaurant located high above the city. It was that night that I told her I loved her and that one day she and I would be married because I was going to come up with an idea, a way to make her learn to love me.

Thirteen

Starting Over

In 1971, if given the option, I'm sure many men would have enjoyed the opportunity of trading places with me. I was a twenty-five-year-old man making a very good salary, working for a wonderful man, living under absolutely no pressure or stress, working maybe five hours a week, and playing golf as often as my heart desired. However, on the inside, I was a miserable man. Yes, I was miserable because of my lack of self-accomplishment with my work. Ideas, Inc. was a company going nowhere, a company that might as well have been closed.

I could see that even Mr. Heffner was becoming disenchanted with Ideas, Inc. His enthusiasm for the company wasn't there anymore. I felt as if, when at the office, Mr. Heffner put most of his time and energy into his two bowling centers. I also noticed he was making more frequent trips to Las Vegas for gambling and relaxation. I was beginning to wonder if maybe Ideas, Inc. hadn't come along ten years too late; it seemed like Mr. Heffner had lost the drive that it would take to make Ideas, Inc. work—that is, if there had ever been a chance for it to work.

I went in to see him early one Friday morning. "Mr. Heffner, if you have a few minutes, I would like to talk with you about something that is bothering me."

"Of course, come in, Larry. Do you want to shut the door?"

"Yes, thank you, sir. Mr. Heffner, I think it best that I come right to the point. I am very concerned about the future of Ideas, Inc. As a matter of fact, I think we should fold the company, and I should move on to something else."

Mr. Heffner shot right back at me, "Larry, we have already had this conversation once, haven't we? I told you that it doesn't bother me that we're slow right now and that it shouldn't bother you."

I interrupted him, "But that's just the point, Mr. Heffner. It is bothering me that I don't have anything to do! I feel like I'm stealing from you, dropping by every Friday and picking up a paycheck for work that hasn't been done."

He replied, "That's nonsense. What in the world has gotten into you, Larry?"

"I'll tell you what's wrong with me. I have come to the realization that Ideas, Inc. is not going to make it, and that it's time for me to make some other arrangements for employment."

Mr. Heffner thought a few minutes; then he switched gears. "Larry, you might be right. When we started Ideas, Inc., I thought we could find a way around the studios' advertising and marketing departments. It's like running into a brick wall trying to get past those guys."

I added, "That was the only concern I had from the beginning. I knew it would be a fight for us to get our foot in the door. No one wants to be told that someone else can do his job better than he can."

"Larry, what would you think about shifting your responsibilities from Ideas, Inc. into the bowling business?"

"Mr. Heffner, nothing personal, but I don't like bowling. I want to go back into the theatre business."

"Larry, would you like for me to make a call to Martin Theaters and see what I can do to get you back on with them?"

"No, sir. After the way I treated Mr. Kurtz, I know he doesn't want to hire me back. Would you if you were Mr. Kurtz?"

Mr. Heffner frowned and then pointed his finger up toward the ceiling, "Larry, don't forget that I am still one of the major stockholders in that company, and that I carry a lot of weight."

"That's true, you do. But, Mr. Heffner, I have no intention of asking Martin Theaters to take me back."

He was quiet a few minutes. Then he asked, "Larry, have you ever met Dick Huffman?"

"No sir, I haven't had the pleasure. Of course, I know all about Dick Huffman, but I have never had the pleasure of meeting him."

"Would you like for me to give him a ring?"

"Yes, I would like very much for you to call him."

Dick Huffman was Vice President of ABC Southeastern Theatres, located in Charlotte, North Carolina. ABC not only owned the television network, but at that time ABC operated one of the largest theatre circuits in the United States. They had hundreds of theatres in most of the major markets in the country.

Mr. Heffner called Dick Huffman and made an appointment for Mr. Huffman and me to have lunch together the following week in Charlotte. I was looking forward to meeting this fine gentleman of the film industry. I had heard many good things about him, not just from local industry people, but from several senior executives in California during some of those times when I was out on the West Coast on business.

I arrived at his office at 11:45 a.m. I was led into Mr. Huffman's secretary's office by the receptionist. The young lady said, "Mrs. McClelland, this is Mr. Larry Vaughn from Greenville, South Carolina."

"Hello, Mr. Vaughn, I am Mr. Huffman's secretary. Please call me Mary. Mr. Huffman is expecting you. I will tell him that you are here."

Mr. Huffman came out to greet me; then we went into his office. He had a very impressive corner office, located on the seventh floor of the Northwestern Bank Building in downtown Charlotte. It was a very large office with two large sofas and several very comfortable chairs. He had a very large mahogany desk with a high-back leather chair. His office was very open, with two walls being all glass from the floor to the ceiling. The view was of downtown Charlotte. I thought to myself, "It must be beautiful in here at night."

He interrupted my thoughts. "Larry, how was your drive up?"

"Very nice, Mr. Huffman. It is a beautiful day for a drive."

He grabbed his coat and said, "Do you like barbecue?"

"Yes sir, very much." He smiled a very warm, personable smile and said, "Good, I know just where I want to take you."

It took us about twenty minutes to drive to the restaurant. Most of the conversation on the way to the restaurant was related to shoptalk: which movies have performed well at the box office this year and what the upcoming season was beginning to look like.

The restaurant was one of those local, well-known barbecue houses. It was very busy once we got inside, but we seemed to find the perfect table nestled over in a corner out of the way.

I thought, "This is good. We can eat and have our conversation without being disturbed by all the hustle and bustle of the crowd."

Mr. Huffman was an older man. I would guess at that time he was in his late fifties or early sixties. He looked a lot like former President Ronald Reagan did during his White House years.

We had a delicious barbecue plate with all the trimmings. While eating, our conversation was mostly talk about the motion picture industry: its strengths, weaknesses, what concerns we saw in the industry in the days ahead. I enjoyed listening to his thoughts and comments.

Mr. Huffman seemed to be very knowledgeable of the industry as a whole.

He finally got around to talking about me. "Larry, Michael tells me you're unhappy with the advertising company and would like to get back into the theatre business."

"Mr. Huffman, it's not that I'm unhappy with our advertising company; it's just that I don't see a future for the company. Mr. Heffner is keeping himself very busy with his bowling centers and other activities. I have to depend on his relationship with Hollywood to open the door of opportunity for Ideas, Inc. to have a chance to work. Right now, I don't see that happening. Rather than waste another year of my life and more of Mr. Heffner's money, I say it's time for me to go back to work. I'm tired of playing golf and looking for things to do at the office."

"Larry, I heard through the pipeline that you turned down a good position with Frank Brady to go back to work for Michael."

"Yes, sir, I did. I had mixed emotions at the time, but I guess it was easier to say no to Martin than it was to Michael Heffner."

Mr. Huffman smiled and nodded his head as if to say he knew exactly what I was talking about. He thought a moment and then said what he had been preparing himself to say. "Larry, you most certainly have an impressive résumé. To be only twenty-five years old, you've worn a lot of different hats in the theatre business. I believe you have a thorough knowledge of every department except film buying. Is that correct?"

"That's correct. I know nothing about film buying. The reason for that is that during the nine years I worked for Mr. Heffner, he personally did all the film buying for his company. And of course, Martin Theaters has its own film department."

Mr. Huffman commented, "I'm glad Michael was opposition to us in only one town. He was a heck of a film buyer. I heard that ABC never even had a chance to play *Patton* in Greenville. Rumor has it that Michael won *Patton* playing gin rummy with the Fox boys here in Charlotte."

I smiled but made no comment.

"Larry, I would like very much to have you come aboard our team; but, unfortunately, with your qualifications, I have nowhere to put you. Every department here in Charlotte is covered with very good men, each doing an exceptional job in their given area of responsibility. At this time I don't have any district manager positions open. Our district managers are all dedicated, hard-working, long-time employees of ABC; plus, we like to promote our district managers from within. It's good for the morale of the men out in the field to see us promote from within." He sighed and then continued, "Unfortunately, for you and me, I don't have a position available at this time where your talents could be utilized to the fullest."

I thought to myself, "Okay, Larry, how badly do you want to get back into the theatre business? Go ahead and ask the man the question." I collected my thoughts and said, "Mr. Huffman, what about my managing a theatre? Would there be an opening for a manager?"

His reply was quick. "Larry, we don't pay our managers a salary anywhere near what you are accustomed to making. If you managed any one of our theatres, you would be looking at a 50 percent or more pay cut."

"Do you presently have a management position open?"

He thought a minute, "Larry, with your past experience, are you absolutely sure you want to go back to managing a theatre, especially a theatre with a very small grossing potential?"

"Mr. Huffman, may I ask in which city this theatre is located?"

He paused a moment, then he said, "Would you be willing to relocate to Raleigh, North Carolina? If so, we have a single-screen theatre, The Cardinal, that we could let you manage."

I thought a few moments; starting over at twenty-five was not so bad. I answered, "Mr. Huffman, I would love to manage The Cardinal Theater. When may I start work?"

Driving back to Greenville, I had mixed emotions about whether or not I had done the right thing taking the theatre manager's job in Raleigh. I could have always contacted one of the major studios about employment and switched from exhibition to distribution. However, that would most likely mean a move to California, where the cost of living is sky-high, and everything else I care about is so far away. I thought, "No, it doesn't matter that I am back managing a little theatre. This is only a small detour in my climb to the top in the wonderful world of the motion picture industry."

I met with Mr. Heffner and gave him the gist of my meeting with Dick Huffman.

He said, "Larry, you've made the right move. You'll go straight to the top at ABC. You won't be in Raleigh any time at all. Remember my words; you'll go straight to the top."

I thanked him for his vote of confidence and gave him my two-week notice, which was just a formality since there was absolutely no work for me to do those last two weeks. Then, I left his office.

I had dinner with Doneata that night. We talked much more than we ate. I told her, "I am about to go through a rebuilding program, sort of like a boxer does when he loses a fight. I am starting back where I was five years ago. I am going to manage a small, single-screen theatre in Raleigh, North Carolina. I won't be making much money at all. As a matter of fact, my salary is going to be less than half of the salary that I have been making with Mr. Heffner. Well, Doneata, what have you got to say about all of that?"

"Larry, my concern is not with your work, but your gambling. Your love of gambling scares me to death. The way you gamble, it really doesn't matter if you make $200 or $2,000 a week. Your conception of money is that money is only a tool, a tool that enables you to be able to do what you really love, and that is to gamble. Until you deal with that issue, what does it matter where you work, how much you work, or what you make for doing your work."

I quickly replied, "Doneata, I love you very much, but I am what I am. However, I don't want to lose you. I am going to make a serious effort to work on my bad habits. Will you and your son come to Raleigh with me?"

Dave Garvin was the district manager for Raleigh and the surrounding areas. He was a very tall, thin, middle-aged gentleman. He looked a lot like the actor James Stewart, except Mr. Garvin always wore wire-rimmed glasses. He had the reputation of being the mastermind of the company's Friday and Saturday night late show business. I was told going in, "You can get on Mr. Garvin's good side very easily; just do good business on your late shows."

My first experience with Mr. Garvin was in a meeting of all the managers in his district. There must have been around twenty men in the meeting. I had been with the company only a month. Mr. Garvin was demanding more business on the late shows. He said, "You men need to concentrate more on these late shows. It's extra income for you. We need to put some new life into them. I have called this meeting for the specific purpose of late shows. Now, let's hear some new, fresh ideas. Then, he looked directly at me and said, "Mr. Vaughn, I hear you're supposed to be such a hotshot when it comes to advertising. Well, what thoughts do you have for us?"

Without putting any serious thought into what I was about to say, I replied, "Mr. Garvin, I have noticed the theatres play double-feature late shows: comedies, westerns, rock films, war movies, action films, etc.

Well, what would you think about maybe playing two opposite types of films together, like maybe *Love Story* and *Night of the Living Dead*?"

Mr. Garvin straightened his body, leaned his head forward, squinted his eyes and looking straight at me, he opened his mouth; he then dropped his jaw and stared at me for what seemed like forever. Finally he said, "Mister, we have work to do here. We don't have time to listen to foolishness. If you can't say anything intelligent, then keep your mouth shut until you can think of something intelligent to say."

That was it! He embarrassed me to the point that I was speechless. At break, one of the other managers said, "Mr. Garvin can be quite crude at times. You just have to overlook him."

I thought to myself, "Mr. Garvin will eat his words before this month is over."

After the meeting I went straight to my office. I called Joe Johnson, my theatre booker in Charlotte. I asked him a question, "Joe can you get me a print of *Love Story* and *Night of the Living Dead* for a late show in four weeks?"

Joe answered, "Sure, there are plenty of prints around. But Larry, you need to be aware that both those films have already played numerous times in the Raleigh area. Last time they played at the Cardinal, they didn't do any business. Larry, are you sure you want to play them again?"

I said, "Yes, please book them for me to play the first weekend of next month."

"Okay, Larry, if that's what you want to do. Which one do you want to play first?"

I responded, "Joe you have misunderstood me. I want to play them as a double feature, together, the first weekend of next month."

"Larry, you're going to do what?"

"I'm playing them together, as a double feature, if that is okay with you and the powers that be."

That night I worked up the campaign. The radio spot went like so: *[Background piano music—theme song to* Love Story*]* "Ladies and gentlemen, this Friday and Saturday night, The Cardinal Theater is proud to present, for the first time ever on the same program, Ali McGraw and Ryan O'Neal in Eric Segal's classic, *Love Story*. And on the same program—" *[piano music abruptly stops and suddenly you hear an absolutely terrible, long scream]* "the greatest horror movie ever made, *Night of the Living Dead*." *[more munchy sound effects]* "That's right ladies and gentlemen, both *Love Story* *[piano music]* and *Night of the Living Dead* *[screaming]* together, for the first time on the same program. Be sure to be at the Cardinal Theater this

Friday and Saturday night. It's the place where love ends [piano music], and horror begins [a terrible scream]."

When the spot played on the radio, the disc jockeys went crazy. One DJ commented, "Well, it's quite obvious that the Cardinal Theater has two different managers, and one doesn't have the foggiest idea what the other one is doing."

My *Love Story* and *Night of the Living Dead* combo was a huge success. My two nights gross was head and shoulders above any other late show gross in the entire company.

Monday morning I received the call I had been waiting for since Saturday night.

"Larry."

"Good morning, Mr. Garvin."

"Congratulations on the wonderful success of your late shows this past weekend."

"Thank you, Mr. Garvin."

"Larry, I owe you an apology for what I said to you in the manager's meeting. It's just that—well, I could never imagine such a combo working. Please forgive me for what I said. I shall not take your suggestions so lightly in the future."

I accepted Mr. Garvin's apology. After that day he and I became very good friends.

Word got out into the field that Mr. Huffman had developed serious health problems and would be stepping down from the controls of the Charlotte office. Harvey Garland, President of ABC Theaters, had made a decision to replace Mr. Huffman with John Huff, another vice president out of the Atlanta, Georgia, office. Huff had the reputation of being a hard-nosed businessman, a hard worker, a man who had worked his way up through the ranks. He was very diversified in his capabilities: he knew all facets of theatre operations including film buying; plus, he worked his way through night school to obtain his law degree. John Huff was a man that demanded and got the necessary respect required to be effective in the task ABC had called him to do.

Mr. Garvin called me at the office one Monday morning with instructions for me to be in Charlotte the following Wednesday for a meeting with Mr. Huff.

I asked Mr. Garvin, "What does Mr. Huff want to see me about?"

Mr. Garvin said, "I'd best let him tell you that. You just be there at 10:00 a.m."

It was good to be at least familiar with the Charlotte surroundings. It was only a year earlier that I had been in the Charlotte office and met with Dick Huffman about the possibility of a position with ABC. I thought, "My, how time goes by so very fast. I have already been with ABC a year." I walked into Mrs. McClelland's office and greeted her at 10:00 a.m. She exchanged small talk with me for a few minutes. Then she told me to have a seat, that Mr. Huff was on the phone, and he was known for being long-winded at times. That day was no exception: I waited about thirty minutes before the light on his phone went dark.

She went into his office and returned almost immediately and said, "Larry, you may go on in; he is expecting you."

The office was just as I had remembered it the last time I was there. The only noted difference was that there was a different man in the room. Mr. Huff walked around his desk, extended his hand, and said, "Larry Vaughn, I've been looking forward to meeting you." He motioned to a chair, "Please sit down."

He was a much younger man than Dick Huffman. He had a medium build and a dark complexion with slick, black hair. I noted how round his dark brown eyes were. I could tell from the aroma of his cologne that it was expensive. He carried himself very well. He dressed immaculately: very expensive white dress shirt with French cuffs and expensive cuff links, which matched perfectly his gold tie pin. His suit was tailored and made of fine material.

I thought, "This guy is a dresser."

He wasn't what you would call handsome by any means, but he did have an interesting face. I thought, "I wonder if he has ever played any cards?"

After a few minutes of socializing, he asked the question, "Larry, do you have any idea about why I had you come in to see me today?"

"No sir, not a clue."

"Larry, I have a folder here given to me by Dave Garvin outlining the work that you have done during the short time that you have been in Raleigh. You do more business on your weekend late shows than a lot of our theatres do in seven days. I want you out of Raleigh and in that office right there." He pointed to the office outside of his. "I want you here in Charlotte within two weeks."

I thought to myself about what Mr. Heffner had said to me a year earlier: "You'll go straight to the top at ABC, Larry. It will be a good move for you."

Mr. Huff looked at me and said, "Well, ask me your questions?"

I thought a minute. Then I replied, "Mr. Huff, I assume I am being brought to the Charlotte office for a support position in the Advertising and Promotion Department—a position where I may be able to utilize my creative abilities throughout the circuit rather than just in Raleigh."

He leaned back in his chair, looked at me, and frowned as if I had said something wrong. Then he remarked, "Advertising, Larry? I'm not bringing you to the Charlotte office to draw ads. No, I'm going to make a film buyer out of you."

Fourteen

The Making of a Film Buyer

On Thursday night, the fourteenth of November 1974, Doneata and I were married. It was a simple wedding which took place in the Reverend O. Edmonds's parsonage, which was located beside his small country church some twenty miles outside Charlotte.

I remember it was wet both outside and inside the car that night. It was pouring down rain outside, and Doneata was sniffling and crying terribly inside the car.

I asked her, "What's wrong with you? Do you want to marry me or not?"

Her whole body shook. She replied, "I think so."

"What do you mean you think so? I told you a long time ago that I love you and that we were made for each other. Remember, we're opposites! Haven't I been good lately? It's been so long since I placed a bet on a football game that I have forgotten how."

She looked over at me with that look of disbelief, took her hanky, wiped her eyes, and said quite sarcastically, "Sure you have."

I looked at my watch and said, "Doneata, we will be there any minute now. I don't want to get married with you crying throughout the wedding. I am going to be the best thing that ever happened to you and David. I know I'm absolutely crazy on the outside, but inside I have a wonderful heart with your name written right across the middle of it. There are some things I can't promise you, but this I can: I will always love you with all my heart. Because of my love for you and David, I will always work very hard at being a good husband to you and a good father to David."

Doneata started trying to do something about her terribly smeared makeup: her mascara had blackened her cheeks and her lipstick was smeared. She momentarily gave up on the makeup and dropped her arms beside her. She sniffed, blew her nose, and looked over at me with red, teary eyes. She exhaled slowly, trying to control her emotions, and then took a deep breath. "Larry, I love you so very much. It's just that you scare me sometimes. All I have ever wanted out of life is just a normal home: a husband who would love me and be a good father to my children. I know that you love David and me very much. Well, that's not the problem."

She looked down, wiped her nose with her hanky, and stared out the window into the rain. I knew she was trying to choose the words that matched her feelings. Finally, she said, "The problem is that, well, you're not normal. I'm caught in a trap. I'm afraid to marry you, but I can't live without you. I do hope we're doing the right thing."

"Doneata, trust me. We are doing the right thing."

She was quiet a minute. Then she looked over at me and gave me the cutest smile. I knew then that she was going to be okay.

While Doneata was busy putting her face back together, I thought to myself, "Larry, she really has second thoughts; you'd best behave yourself."

In the days ahead, Mr. and Mrs. Larry Vaughn and son resided in a very nice apartment in the city of Charlotte, North Carolina.

————

True to his word, Mr. Huff gave me the office next to his. It was also a nice-sized office, somewhere around one-third the size of his. It had a nice desk, high-top black leather chair, and two guest chairs. But what I liked best about my new office was the view. Behind my desk was all smoked glass, which gave me a wonderful view of the downtown Charlotte area.

I thought it best for me to come in to the office on the Saturday morning before I was to report in to work on Monday. Saturday, with the office being closed, would be the perfect time for me to hang some pictures, straighten up my desk, and try to get a little organized before Monday came around. I unloaded my briefcase and started putting some of my personal items away. I was glad Mr. Huff's secretary, Mary, had given me a key to the office.

It took me less than an hour to get everything in place. When I felt comfortable with the way I had arranged my desk and the pictures, I stood up and walked over to the door, leaned against the wall, and looked out at the large lobby area. There was a receptionist station in the middle of the lobby, with four secretaries' stations scattered at various locations. There were four more offices like mine: two offices to the left of my office and two more offices were located directly across the lobby. I started thinking about how different it was going to be come Monday morning when the phones started ringing and all the desks would be occupied with all the employees back at work fresh from a weekend off. My thoughts drifted back to the meeting I had had just two weeks earlier with Mr. Huff. I was starting to think through everything Mr. Huff had said to me that afternoon.

"Larry, do you have any idea how many men would give their right arm to be offered a position in the Film Buying Department? This is a golden opportunity for you to learn film buying under my direction. One of the most important and, I might add, best-paid employees in the company is the Film Buyer. You can have the most beautiful theatre in Charlotte, but if you can't get the movies in your theatre that the public wants to see, what does it matter how nice your theatre is? The people won't be there. The public doesn't know ABC Theaters from CDE Theaters. They just want to go to the theatre that is playing the movie they want to see. The engine that drives this business is the picture. You must have the picture the public wants to see before you can sell a drink, a candy bar, or a box of popcorn."

He went on to say, "Film buying is extremely tough and demanding work. It's a highly competitive business that takes an individual who must have special abilities in order to get the product into the theatres in a timely and cost-effective manner. You must have excellent communication skills. A film buyer has to be able to communicate with a variety of individuals. You will work daily with people who are as different from one another as day is from night. Yes, as a film buyer you are going to be dealing with many different personalities and egos. There are times that you will have to push, or you'll get run over. But a good film buyer knows when to push and when to back off. You cannot be afraid to take chances, or you won't last a month working in the Film Department.

"Film buying is very much like gambling, except you're gambling with someone else's money." When he said that, unbeknown to him, he struck a nerve with me.

He went on, "It's nothing to bid a guarantee of $35,000 to $40,000 in a theatre on a picture and lose that picture to the opposition theatre. You then say, 'Well, maybe I should have put up more money to get the picture.' However, what if the picture you lost for $40,000 opens in the other guy's theatre and he only ends up grossing $20,000. See, you won by not playing the picture, and the other guy lost when he got the picture he wanted because he had to pay too much money for the picture."

I interrupted Mr. Huff and asked, "Does that happen often?"

"Unfortunately, quite often. Film buying is a very expensive guessing game. No one is an expert when it comes to figuring out what the public wants to see."

I commented, "I guess the film companies are the ones that are making all the money."

"Not so! They spend a fortune before the picture ever opens. Sure they pick up what we call 'blood money' in these towns where we have heavy bidding, but the film company needs the picture to work across the board—I mean everywhere—for them to see a profit."

I said, "I have another question. You said the film companies do well in towns where we have heavy bidding. How many towns do we bid in?"

"Not that many in the South, mostly in the Carolinas. By the way, Larry, in this office we have three other Film Buyers: Dan Gattis, Tony Rhead, and Joe Johnson. You will be the fourth, and of course I am the Head Film Buyer. All your bids will go by my desk before being submitted to the film companies."

"My bids? So I will be responsible for some bid towns."

"Larry, you will be responsible for the majority of our bid towns. I am giving you the Carolinas."

"Mr. Huff, with all due respect, why would you give the new guy on the block the Charlotte territory?"

"Several reasons: You aren't afraid to take chances; you proved that by going to Raleigh. And you know how to sell a picture. Subsequently, I think you will be good at guessing just how well a picture will do in a given market. Plus, you worked all those years for Michael Heffner. Michael used to be one of the best film buyers around. You could not have worked as closely with Michael as you did all those years and not have picked up some of his ways."

I looked at my watch. Saturday morning was almost gone, and there I was daydreaming the day away. I called Doneata and told her to have David ready in twenty minutes, because the three of us were going out to lunch.

In 1974, Charlotte was a key exchange center for both exhibition, (the theatre circuits) and distribution (the film companies). All the major film companies had branch offices in Charlotte. Several of their offices were located in the same building as ABC's. I already knew most of the branch managers from my Michael Heffner days. In earlier years, Mr. Heffner and I at one time or another had wined, dined, and played cards with all the Charlotte branch managers.

Monday morning I walked into my new office to find two large books placed right in the center of my desk. The first thought that came to my mind was, "Now, those books weren't there Saturday." One book was labeled "North Carolina," the other, "South Carolina." They were my booking books. Little did I know that during the months ahead those two books were going to become very good friends of mine as I would be living and working out of them not five, but six to seven days a week.

That first Monday in the office was like a whirlwind. Mr. Huff wanted me to be everywhere at once. He wanted me to learn film buying from personal experience. He said, "These are your theatres. If you have a question ask. Someone around here will be able to answer the question for you. However, as of right now, the film buying of these theatres is your responsibility."

I knew as much about the actual process of film buying as Mr. Huff knew about building an atomic bomb, but that's the way he taught me. It was all trial and error with a lot, I mean a lot, of questions thrown in between. What helped me get through that first day was the many calls I received from the various branch managers in town welcoming me into the mad world of film buying.

Within a short period of time, Mr. Huff and I were working very well together. He spent a lot of time with me, teaching me the many facets of film buying. I could certainly tell that he was also a lawyer, as he was always questioning me about how I came up with figures for this or reasons for that. He was a very inquisitive man. It didn't take long at all for us to build up a mutual respect for each other. He even gave me a nickname: "Superbooker."

One of John Huff's favorite things to do outside of work was to play tennis. It got to be more frequent than occasional that he would call me into his office on a Friday morning and say, "Larry, what plans do you and the family have for tomorrow?"

My reply the first few times was, "Oh, nothing special."

He would then suggest, "Why don't you and the family come over and spend the afternoon with my wife and me? The girls can talk, and you and I will go play some tennis. After tennis I'll put some steaks on the grill."

"Sounds fine to me. What time do you want us to be there?"

"Around 2:00 p.m. Oh, Larry, since you're coming over, be sure to bring your booking books. We might want to do some work after dinner."

I learned quickly that his word "might" meant "will!" I always ended up working several hours late at night at his house on the weekends. Finally, I learned to say, "Sorry, Mr. Huff, I won't be able to play tennis this weekend; the family and I have made other plans."

The Film Department was most certainly in a world all to itself. During those first few months at ABC, I learned why Mr. Heffner, when I worked for him, never allowed me to get into the film buying process. Film buying is where the action is. John Huff was right: the engine that drives the business is the picture, and the excitement comes from trying to get the picture, especially the picture that everybody else wants. And since the bidding process was so much like gambling, I was able to enjoy my two favorite activities, films and betting, and still keep my promise to Doneata. She didn't seem to mind so much that I would cut for high cards at the office to book a film; but I was able to enjoy the thrill of risking everything—using someone else's money!

The next year went by very fast. Mr. Huff kept me running at the office. I averaged a good ten hours a day. Prior to John Huff's arrival in Charlotte, ABC didn't have a reputation of being the big spenders when it came to bidding for films. However, John Huff was a lot like me when it came to spending money; he went after all the so-called important pictures, especially when it came to the big pictures. He made a lot of costly mistakes, but ABC became a tough circuit for the opposition to go up against when it came to buying film for their theatres. Working beside John Huff was a great film buying experience for me.

––––––––

On a cold, windy afternoon in November of 1975, I received a call at the office from Doneata.

"Hi, honey, what are you doing?"

"You only get one guess," I replied.

"Trying to make Huff-n-Puff happy?" (Huff-n-Puff was a private nickname that Doneata and I had given to Mr. Huff.)

"Bingo, you're right on target, sweetheart. How is your day going?"

"Great. I just wanted to call you and tell you that I have gotten a baby sitter for tonight, and you and I are going out to dinner. Also, I have a present that I am going to give you tonight."

I thought, "A present for me tonight; it can't be our anniversary; that was last week." I responded to her, "Doneata, you'd better not be out spending a lot of money on me. Remember, Christmas is only a month away."

"You'll see, just don't work late tonight. Tell Huff-n-Puff that tonight you've got better things to do."

"Okay, I won't work late. I'll be home by 6:30. Bye for now. Love you!"

Doneata made reservations at a little Italian restaurant that we both enjoyed going to on special occasions. The menu was a bit pricey, but the atmosphere and food were wonderful. It was the perfect place to go for a nice evening out. I questioned myself about why I didn't consider going there a week earlier for our anniversary dinner.

The waiter seated us in our own private booth, not too far from the warmth of the fireplace.

Doneata said, "Don't ask for your present until after dinner because you can't have it until then."

"Okay, but may I at least see the box?" I asked.

"Absolutely not."

"Okay! I was just checking."

The waiter came and took our order. We had a wonderful time of food and conversation. After the waiter took away our empty plates and returned with two hot cups of coffee, I whispered to Doneata, "I want my present."

She said, "Honey, I'm sorry, but you still have to wait."

"Oh no, you can't go changing the rules on me now. Where is it?"

She took her finger and put it right in my face. Then she curled it, motioning for me to come closer to her. I leaned over, we were almost nose to nose, and she said, "You can't have our baby until June 29."

That was the most wonderful moment of my life. Doneata and I were going to have a baby. I was so glad she told me about our baby after dinner. If she had told me earlier, before dinner, I would have been too excited to eat a bite.

The holidays flew right by. Before I knew it, it was January of 1976. Everything was going great at work. There were a lot of movies out doing good business, and Huff seemed very pleased with the job that I was doing.

On the home front, Doneata was sick in the mornings and stayed tired a lot, but she seemed very happy. She was so excited about our having a baby. David seemed at times to be struggling with his health. He too was tired a lot, and his color didn't look quite right. His complexion looked gray to me. I didn't think that he acted well. Sharing my concerns, Doneata took David to the doctor for a checkup. The doctor found David to be anemic and suggested David start taking a strong multivitamin.

One afternoon in mid February, Walter Powell from New World Pictures dropped by my office to chat. Walter was an older man who had been in the film industry most of his life. He was the guy that knew "who's who" and "what's what" in the film business. In his lifetime, he had worked for several of the major film companies. I liked talking to Walter; he always had an interesting story to tell if someone had the time to listen.

He tapped on my door, which was already open, and said, "You busy?"

"Walter, I'm always busy, but that means nothing. Come in and have a seat. Tell me, what's going on in the industry? Any juicy gossip?"

"Larry, do you mind if I close your door?"

I thought that was strange, Walter had never asked to close my door before. I said, "No, go ahead."

Walter closed the door, sat down, and looked at me. He said, "Larry, I have a question for you. How happy are you here at ABC?"

I stopped whatever it was that I was doing and looked at Walter, wondering about the seriousness of his question. I could tell from the expression on his face that he was wanting to go somewhere with that question. I pushed my chair back from my desk, crossed my legs, leaned back, and put my hands behind my neck. "Well, let me see, Walter. I really haven't thought that much about it, but with all things considered, I guess I'm happy here. Huff is demanding as all get out, but he's been fair to me. Why do you ask, Walter?"

Walter leaned over and spoke very softly. "Larry, I know a man who is looking for somebody, and that somebody could be you. Larry, this is a big job. I'm talking about a big job. Are you interested?"

I thought a minute: "A big job. The only big job in this office is Huff's, and he's not going anywhere anytime soon. Doneata is pregnant. I could always use more money; I'd best hear Walter out."

I replied, "Talk to me, Walter; your time is my time, but let's not talk here. Let's meet later."

Walter and I met later that afternoon in his office, which was located down the hall from mine.

"Okay, Walter, curiosity killed the cat, and it's really bugging me. You need to fill in the blanks for me."

"Larry, do you know the name Eddie Stern?"

"Eddie Stern? No, I don't believe I do."

"How about Wometco Enterprises? Does that ring a bell?"

"Yeah, sure. I've heard of Wometco. They own WLOS-TV in Asheville. They're big in the vending machine business, especially in the South. I believe Wometco is also a big distributor for Coca-Cola, and I know because they are opposition to ABC in South Florida; Wometco has the best-grossing theatres in Florida. Walter, did I tell you anything that you didn't know?"

"I don't believe that you did, but you left out that Wometco owns and operates all the theatres in the state of Alaska as well as the number one track of theatres in Puerto Rico. Plus, they operate theatres in Freeport and Nassau in the Grand Bahamas. In addition to that, Wometco owns the number one television station in Miami as well as The Miami Seaquarium."

"Very good, Walter. I'm impressed with your knowledge of Wometco, but what does any of this mean to me?"

Walter said, "Larry, this morning I had a phone conversation with Eddie Stern. Eddie is the Vice President and Head Film Buyer for Wometco. Eddie's been at Wometco forever: some thirty years or better. Eddie is in the big leagues; the only game he knows how to play is hard ball. On any given weekend, any one of Wometco's theatres in Miami will out-gross what all of your theatres in the Carolinas combined will gross."

I interrupted Walter. "Now, you wouldn't tend to exaggerate a little bit, would you?"

"Well, maybe a little. But I've seen one Wometco theatre take in $125,000 just on a weekend."

"Well, Walter, maybe you aren't exaggerating that much." We both laughed.

"Larry, Eddie had a specific purpose in calling me. He's looking for a man to bring into his department. He asked me if I knew of anyone that I could recommend to him. The first person that came to my mind was you."

"Walter, I appreciate that. I am honored that my name would even come to your mind. Tell me, did you give Eddie Stern my name?"

"Yes, I talked to him a good ten minutes about you."

"And?"

"He asked me to speak with you and find out if you would be interested in talking with him. If so, I'll call Eddie back, give him your home phone number, and you will hear from him tonight."

"That fast?"

"That's the way Eddie operates."

I was interested, so I asked Walter, "Tell me more about Eddie, the person."

"Well, there's only one Eddie Stern. He's probably in his early sixties, but he doesn't look a day over fifty-five. He has the reputation of being a jet setter. He and his wife, Jerry, travel all over the world. He does very little business with the local boys. His negotiations are done with the home-office people. Some of the branch managers don't think too much of Eddie because he is known to leapfrog over them and deal directly with the president or senior vice president of the various companies. He is well educated, a very polished man. He has done a great job for Wometco the past thirty years or so that he has been there. He also has the reputation of being a very hard man to work for. Well, what do you think? Do you want me to have him call you?"

"Yes, Walter, I would like that very much." Then I added, almost as an afterthought, "By the way, Walter, don't they have dog racing in Miami?"

When I got home from work, I told Doneata all about my conversation with Walter Powell. She said, "You mean this man is going to call you tonight."

"I guess so. That's what I understood Walter to say."

We looked at each other, and I said, "Miami is not that far away."

Doneata smiled and said, "I go where you go."

"You got that right honey, but I don't know, even if he offers me the job, that we should go."

She said, "At least we don't have to make that decision right now."

The telephone rang at 9:30. I picked it up on the third ring and said, "Hello."

"Larry Vaughn?" the voice on the other end of the phone queried.

"Yes, sir."

"Hi, Larry, Eddie Stern here. I believe Walter Powell informed you that I would be calling tonight."

"Yes, sir, he did. I have been looking forward to hearing from you."

"Larry, Walter tells me that you have done a good job for those folks at ABC."

"Well, I try. Some days are better than other days."

"I know exactly what you mean. Listen, Larry, I would like to have you come down and spend a day with me."

"Yes, sir, that can be arranged."

"How about this weekend?"

"Yes, sir, Saturday or Sunday will be fine."

"Good, let's plan on Sunday. I will have Freida, my secretary, phone you tomorrow evening with your ticket and flight schedule information. Larry, I am looking forward to seeing you come Sunday. Have a nice evening."

"Thank you, Mr. Stern. I too am looking forward to meeting you."

Doneata and David took me to the airport Sunday morning.

"Larry, now you promise me that you won't make a decision today while you're with Mr. Stern. I know how you are, and I want us to talk before you give him a firm answer."

"Honey, don't you think another minute about it; I promise. I'll leave him on the hook—if he offers me a hook."

Doneata pulled our Grand Prix up to the airport's passenger drop-off. I got out of the car, looked in the back seat at David. He was sound asleep. I reached over and gave him a peck on the cheek; then I gave Doneata a kiss, a hug, and a pat on the tummy, and told her that I loved her.

The "fasten your seat belt" sign came on as the jet started making its descent toward Miami. I had never been to Miami before, so I really didn't know what to expect as far as the people or the lay of the land. I noticed some five minutes before we landed how dense the area below was. There were a lot of people down there, and I wasn't even in Miami yet. I got to thinking, "I hope I dressed appropriately." I was wearing a pair of tan slacks, a very expensive pullover collared sweater, and brown Balley loafers. My clothes were nice enough, but I was dressed casually; still, it was Sunday, and I was not on real "business."

The flight was right on time. I left the plane and walked through the doorway into the waiting area and heard a man say, "Larry, good morning. Eddie Stern."

"Good morning, Mr. Stern. You recognized me before I recognized you."

"Well, there aren't that many 6-foot 2-inch, 135-pound men sporting a mustache and long black hair around here!"

"Yes, sir, I guess you're right."

"Larry, let's go this way. I got lucky and found a parking space out front."

We got into his Cadillac and made the fifteen-minute drive from the airport to Wometco's downtown headquarters. Mr. Stern did all the talking: he was telling me all about the city, the people, and how Miami had changed during his thirty years of living there.

While he was talking I thought to myself, "Cary Grant—Cary Grant! That's who this guy reminds me of. Mr. Stern is a very handsome man, lots of class, and he carries himself like he is a somebody. How old did Walter say he was—in his sixties? He sure doesn't look, talk, or act like it."

We pulled up to the downtown office building where Mr. Stern parked the car in his assigned space.

We got out of the car, and he began explaining the company to me. "Larry, Wometco owns this entire block of buildings. That big pink building on your right is our television station. In that building is also the corporate headquarters; that's where Colonel Wolfson, our founder and CEO, has his offices. You see that door going into the back of the building? That's my screening room. And that building down on the corner is the Wometco Film Lab. This building that we're going into is all offices. The theatre division occupies the entire second floor."

"Mr. Stern, I have a question."

"Well, I will answer it only if you promise to stop calling me Mr. Stern. Call me Eddie."

"Eddie, my question is, why are all these buildings painted pink?"

"Larry, everything Wometco owns is painted pink. That's Mrs. Wolfson's favorite color."

"Are all the theatres painted pink?"

"Larry, if Wometco owns it—it's pink."

He then gave me that look as if to say, "What are you gonna do?"

We got off the elevator on the second floor. Eddie continued giving me the tour.

"This is Stanley Stern's office. No relation to me, just same last name. Stanley is the Senior Vice President of the Entertainment Division."

We continued down the hall, and Eddie continued his commentary.

"Larry, on your left is our Art Department. We have two men and a young lady who work full-time in there. Here's the Film Buying Department on your right; we'll come back there later. The next office on your left is Marvin Reed's. Marvin is our Director of Advertising and Marketing. Those other two desks are for Marvin's secretaries. This office on your right is Jack Mitchell's. Jack is our Vice President and General Manager. Marvin and theatre operations answer to Jack. Now, let's look at the Film Buying Department."

Eddie opened the door to the receptionist's area. There were two desks along with some guest chairs.

"Larry, if you come aboard, this will be your secretary's desk; her name is Betty Woodall. Betty has been with the company a long time. She is in her early fifties: kind of set in her ways, but a good secretary. The other desk is Ofelia Manning's. Ofelia is a young Cuban girl, recently married to a Miami police officer. She has two small children from a previous marriage. She's good on the phones. Ofelia also doubles as a secretary for my booker, Dick Fries. Dick has been with the company, oh, maybe ten years. Dick's a good detail man. If you come with us, this will be your office: nice desk, very comfortable chair, but sorry, Larry, no window. Dick's office is to the left of this office."

We walked back out into the receptionist's area. Then Eddie went into his secretary's office.

"This is Frieda's desk. She has been here forever and a day. I'm not sure who bosses whom when it comes to Frieda. She tries to run everything, even me."

The phone started ringing, and Eddie said, "That's my private line."

He opened the door leading into his office and made a dash across the room. I walked to the doorway to take a peek into his office. Eddie had the largest office and largest desk that I had ever seen. His desktop was beautiful, made of mahogany. The desk was a little larger than a king-size bed, except it was pear shaped, with the large end facing Eddie. He had two large sofas, a television set, a refrigerator, three lamps, a stereo, and a double closet. There were three black leather chairs placed around the desk. I assumed they were there for meetings.

There were two phones on his desk, and one additional phone was placed at the end of each sofa. There was a side door leading out into the hall that could be opened only from the inside. There were pictures of Eddie and movie stars everywhere: on his desk, the walls, the side tables. Eddie motioned for me to come into the room and sit down. He put his hand over the phone and said, "I must take this call. It's Joseph E. Levine."

I looked around the room trying to figure where I should sit. I choose one of the sofas. I saw an ashtray and held up a cigarette for Eddie's approval before lighting. He nodded okay; then I lit up. I sat there thinking, "Here I am in Miami waiting on this guy to get off the phone, and who's he talking to—Joseph E. Levine! Now, let me see. What all has Joseph E. Levine done outside of making Dustin Hoffman a star by giving him the lead in his film *The Graduate*? He also made—"

Eddie put the receiver back into its cradle. "I'm sorry, Larry, that was an old friend of mine, Joe Levine. When my wife, Jerry, and I married a few years ago we went to England on our honeymoon. Joe gave us his Rolls Royce and chauffeur to use while we were there. He is such a nice guy, and talented too."

We chatted a few minutes; then Eddie said, "Let's get the business out of the way; then we'll go to lunch. Let me see, I need to have you back at the airport by 3:15 for your 4:00 flight. I know about your work history; tell me about your family."

I proceeded to tell him all about Doneata, David, and our child that was due in June. After I talked several minutes, I said, "That brings you up to date with the Vaughn household."

Eddie went on to say, "Larry, I am looking for a good, qualified assistant: a man that can help me run this department. My needs are twofold: One, this man must be able to work alongside me and do things exactly like I want them done; two, during my absence this man must be able to take charge of the department and make decisions as needed. I'm no spring chicken; Jerry and I are planning to do a lot of traveling in the years ahead, but I'm not planning on retiring any time soon. The Colonel is in his sixties and going strong. As long as he's here, I plan to be here. Outside of the Colonel, I am the final authority in the Film Department. I don't discuss my business with the other guys; Film operates autonomously from the other departments within the company. Now, Larry, I have checked you out thoroughly, and I might add that you're the man I want for the job. I have never been one to quibble over money; so let's just say that if you come to work for me, I'll double your present salary."

I just sat there. I thought to myself, "Larry, don't let him know that your blood is trying to pop out of your veins. Don't let him know that you want to jump up and shout, 'Whoopee!' Keep cool, Larry! Now is not the time to blow it."

I cleared my throat and said, "Eddie, I like what I have seen of Wometco so far, and I also like what I've heard you say. May I have some time to think about your most generous proposal?"

"Absolutely. Go back to Charlotte and talk it over with Doneata and call me Tuesday night after 8:30, but before 10:00."

I thought to myself, "No! Don't make me wait until Tuesday to say 'yes, yes, yes.' I could call you ten minutes after the plane touches down in Charlotte today."

I replied very casually, "Tuesday evening will be just fine, Eddie. Let's have some lunch."

I told Doneata the whole story. I tried not to leave out one single word. When I finished she said, so sadly, "Tuesday night, honey, why didn't you tell him yes today?"

Before I could react she said, "You know I'm just teasing. Oh, Larry, this is all so exciting!"

We both agreed that this was the opportunity of a lifetime.

"Doneata, first thing Wednesday I will give ABC my notice."

Tuesday night at 8:45, I called Eddie.

"Hello?"

"Hi Eddie! Larry Vaughn here."

"Larry, how are you? I was expecting your call."

After a few moments of small talk, I said, "Eddie, I have talked it over with Doneata, and if you still want me, I'm yours."

"Larry, that is wonderful news. That's exactly what I was hoping to hear. How much notice do you need to give ABC?"

"Eddie, because of my present responsibilities at ABC, I would like to give them a four-week notice, but only if the four weeks can work on your end."

He thought a minute. Then he said, "Well, you and Doneata will probably need two or three weekends to come down here and look for a place to live; four weeks will be okay."

"Great! I shall give ABC my notice first thing in the morning."

"Larry, keep all your receipts and fly back and forth as often as needed. Let me know what the charges are for breaking your apartment lease. Remember, the company will take care of your moving expenses. I must run, Larry; one of my favorite shows is coming on TV."

I told him good night, and that was the end of the much-anticipated conversation.

Wednesday morning I told Mrs. McClelland to tell Mr. Huff when he got off the phone I would like to talk to him for a few minutes on a private matter. About an hour later she told me to go into his office.

"Good morning, Mr. Huff."

"Good morning, Superbooker! What's up?"

"Well, Mr. Huff, I guess there's no other way to say it than just to say it." He looked up from his papers. "Mr. Huff, I am going to be leaving the company. I am prepared to give you a four-week notice—that is, if you want me to stay on that long. I thought four weeks would give you the time needed to shift those responsibilities I currently have to other individuals within the company."

Mr. Huff said, "May I ask where you are going?"

117

"I have taken a position in the Film Department at Wometco Enterprises."

"Eddie Stern? You're leaving me to go to work for Eddie Stern? You won't last three months!"

"Mr. Huff, that remains to be seen."

"Have you checked Eddie out? He needs a revolving door in his office: that's how fast Eddie Stern goes through assistants."

"Mr. Huff, all this is really quite unnecessary; I have already accepted the job."

"Larry, you should have talked with me first. I think you're making a big mistake. Besides all that, I don't think you're ready for the Miami market; they play hardball down there."

"So I've been told."

"I guess he's going to pay you twice what you're making here."

I thought to myself, "Bingo! You're right on the money." But, I made no comment.

"Larry, is it a done deal?"

"Yes, sir. It's a done deal."

Fifteen

Two Years

It was a long four weeks at the office. Even though Mr. Huff kept me extremely busy tying up all the loose ends before my scheduled departure, the days at the office seemed more or less to drag by. The long days were probably caused by the apprehension of my wanting to get into my new responsibilities at Wometco.

At home it was just the opposite. Considering we had only four weeks, Doneata and I were playing beat the clock trying to get everything done. Two of our four weekends were spent in Miami trying to find a place to live.

Eddie went out of his way to help us find the right apartment. He supplied us with a car, a map, and even made several appointments for us to look at apartments. We decided to rent an apartment at Kingston Square, which was located about a mile from the Dadeland Mall. At that time Dadeland Mall was one of the busiest shopping centers in Florida. Across the street from the mall, Wometco had their flagship theatre, The Dadeland Twin. It was the best-grossing theatre in Florida.

During those two trips to Miami, Doneata and I spent our evenings with Eddie and Jerry. They were gracious enough to invite us to their Coral Gables condo for cocktails. Afterward, the four of us would go out to one of Miami's many fine restaurants. We enjoyed each other's company; Doneata and I had the opportunity to get to know the Sterns much better. It was especially good for Doneata to spend some time with Jerry. They hit it off right from the start.

When we returned to Charlotte, Doneata had her hands full trying to get everything packed, make all the necessary phone calls, and keep her strength up as the birth of our baby was just a few months away.

It was good to see the Mayflower moving van pull out of our driveway heading south—south toward Miami.

Kingston Square was one of the nicest apartment complexes in Miami. I thought, "Since it's only money, we might as well live high on the hog." The complex was completely enclosed with a six-foot white wall surrounding it. At the entrance was a guardhouse, which seemed to be there more for appearance than for guarding, since there was seldom a guard present.

There were about ten octagon-shaped buildings located within the complex. The buildings were beautifully designed. They were white with large brown shutters over each window. Every apartment had its own patio. Each building had eight families, four on each floor. There were two very large swimming pools along with a children's pool on the grounds. The landscaping was immaculate. Palm trees were everywhere. Although I had never seen Hawaii, I thought, "Surely, Hawaii can't be any prettier than this." The complex was completely surrounded by a paved road. It was exactly eight-tenths of a mile around, from start to finish. That road was used daily by the many joggers who lived in the complex.

We had to settle for a first-floor, two-bedroom apartment because there were no three-bedroom apartments available. We were promised a three-bedroom apartment as soon as one became vacant; however, Doneata and I dreaded the thought of having to move again.

For a two-bedroom apartment, it was very spacious. We had a large master bedroom and bath area; the second bedroom was much smaller, but we thought David and the baby could manage. It would be a tight fit for them for only a short while. Down the hallway was another full bath for David. We had a very large living room and dining room. The kitchen was small, but the appliances were all top quality. Located at the front of the living room was our patio. The patio was the perfect size for me to read the paper and cook out.

On my first Monday I made it a point to be at work by 8:00 a.m. The office didn't open until 9:00 a.m, but I wanted to get there early and get unpacked before anyone came in. Upon my arrival I was surprised to find Eddie already at work. I walked into his office and said, "Good morning, Eddie. Here I am."

He looked up from his papers, gave me a warm smile and greeting; then he asked me to sit down. We chatted for about fifteen minutes; then Eddie said, "Come on, I want you to meet Stanley."

We walked down to the end of the hall and entered Stanley Stern's office. Stanley was sitting at his desk reading the morning edition of the *Miami Herald*. When Stanley stood up, I noticed he had an impressive appearance: he was tall and rather handsome. He was like Eddie in his expensive style of dress. I would guess Stanley at that time to be in his early sixties. He had a dark complexion. I thought, "Stanley must spend a lot of time out in the sun."

Eddie spoke, "Stanley, I want to introduce you to Larry Vaughn."

"Hello, Larry. I am certainly glad you're here. Our booking department has been running on empty for over a month now. Maybe you can get us some pictures. We sure need the business."

We all laughed; then Eddie said, "Stanley, you'd best be kind, or I'll start telling Larry some secrets on you." Eddie gave me the short version of how Stanley started with the company some forty years ago as an usher, and how Stanley had worked himself up through the ranks into the office of Senior Vice President in charge of the entire Entertainment Division at Wometco.

As we left his office, Stanley said, "Larry, one day I am going to get into film buying. Then maybe I can have a big office like Eddie's."

Eddie replied, "Larry, I get the office, but guess who gets the money." We left on that note.

Next we went to Jack Mitchell's office. Jack too was reading the *Herald*. Eddie commented, "Don't you guys ever do anything around here but read the *Herald*?"

Jack looked up and smiled. "Good morning, Mr. Stern. I was just reading through the society section to see how your and Jerry's weekend went."

Eddie pointed his finger at Jack as if to say, "Behave."

"Jack, I would like to introduce you to my new assistant, Larry Vaughn."

Jack got up from behind his desk and gave me a very sincere, warm welcome. Eddie gave me a brief work history on Jack. "Jack, how long have you been with the company?"

"Almost ten years, Eddie."

"Larry, Jack has been in and out of the theatre business. He spent several years in the hotel business, and since joining Wometco he has done an exceptionally good job for the company. The Colonel and Stanley think a lot of Jack: he's a good General Manager. Oops, we'd best go, Larry." Eddie pointed toward Jack's head. "Look! Jack's head is starting to swell!"

We all laughed; then Eddie and I went next door.

Marvin Reed broke the chain when we walked into his office. Marvin was drinking a cup of coffee, but he was not reading the newspaper.

Eddie said, "Good morning, Marvin. Say hello to Larry Vaughn; Larry's my new assistant."

"Hi, Larry; I've heard all about you. Welcome to south Florida. Now maybe Mr. Stern here will stop being so grumpy. You know, Larry, Eddie's had to work these last couple of months, and Eddie's not used to having to work."

Eddie said, "Come on! Can't anybody around here say anything good about me?"

Marvin started laughing; I could tell Marvin had ribbed Eddie before. Marvin reminded me of my deceased half-brother Farrell, except Marvin was a much older man than Farrell had been when he died. Marvin looked to be in his late forties or early fifties. Marvin was red headed, freckle faced, and had a fair complexion.

I asked him, "Marvin, are you by any chance from Georgia?"

"I most certainly am. Did my Southern accent give me away?"

"Yeah, I guess that's what it is. You remind me of someone I used to know who happened to be from Georgia."

I knew right away that I was going to like Marvin Reed. We chatted for a few moments; then Eddie and I left.

When we returned to our offices, everyone was busy at his respective work stations. Eddie introduced me to my secretary, Betty Woodall. Betty was exactly as Eddie had described her. She was a widow and looked to be in her early fifties—a rather portly, polite, gray-headed lady.

I thought, "I bet Betty could tell me some interesting stories. In her many years at her desk, she has watched all of Eddie's assistants come and go."

I was only able to say "hello" to Ofelia, for she was already busy answering the phones.

Eddie interrupted my chain of thought. "Dick Fries, I would like for you to meet Larry Vaughn."

"Larry, pleased to meet you."

I could tell Eddie was tiring from all the introductions; he motioned for me to come into his office.

"Likewise, Dick; we'll chat later."

On the way into his office, we stopped at Freida's desk.

"Miss Goldberg, meet Mr. Vaughn."

Freida looked up from her typewriter, smiled, extended her right hand, and said, "Welcome to Wometco, Mr. Vaughn. May I ask a favor of you?"

I said, "Of course."

She continued, "Please don't wait until 4:30 to have me type your bids. I like to leave at 5:00."

Eddie raised his eyebrows, wrinkled his forehead, then looked at me and said, "You're meeting Freida on one of her better days."

Freida gave us an artificial frown; then she went back to her typing.

We went into his office and sat down. Eddie picked up the phone tapped a couple of numbers and said, "Hello, Sarah, please tell the Colonel that whenever he has a free minute I would like to bring Larry Vaughn over to meet him."

While walking across the parking lot to Colonel Wolfson's office, Eddie stopped me and introduced me to two other gentlemen. "Larry, I would like for you to meet Arthur Hertz and Michael Brown. Arthur is the Chief Financial Officer for the company, and Michael is one of Wometco's vice presidents."

We talked briefly; then Eddie and I continued on our way. "Larry, those two guys are the money men. They are the very best when it comes to moving money. Art has had the Colonel's ear for many years. He has been very instrumental in making Wometco as diversified and prosperous a company as it is today."

The Colonel's secretary, Sarah—another senior employee who had worked for Wometco more than forty years—sent us in to meet with the Colonel.

Eddie said, "Good morning, Colonel Wolfson, I would like to introduce you to my new assistant, Larry Vaughn."

"Larry, Eddie has told me all about you; please sit down." The Colonel spent several minutes asking me about my background and the various companies that I had worked for. He then asked several questions about my family. He wanted to know where we were living in Miami and if I thought my family would be happy living in south Florida. He then went on to say that Wometco, even though it had several thousand employees, was one big family and that his door would always be open to me for any need that I might have—be it business or personal. I thought that a very kind and unusual statement for the man to make considering that he really didn't know me and that this was my first day at work.

The Colonel then asked Eddie, "How were the numbers over the weekend?" As the two of them started talking business that gave me the opportunity to look around the old gentleman's office. Colonel Wolfson's office was quite impressive. The walls were all beautifully polished wood. There were pictures throughout the room with the Colonel and famous people, from U.S. presidents to movie stars. This old gentleman had most certainly made the rounds. At the far end of his office, mounted in the ceiling, were four television monitors. Each monitor was tuned in to one of the three major television networks, and the fourth monitor was a continuous update about how the stock market was faring. Located directly below the television monitors was a very large, plush leather sofa that covered the entire back wall of his office. The guest chairs were comfortable, all made with upgraded leather. The ceiling had several huge skylights that gave the dark, paneled room the necessary light. Indeed, it was a very impressive office with several sculptures, paintings, and plaques of appreciation and recognition scattered throughout.

I looked over at the Colonel. He had to be at least in his late sixties. He seemed to be a most gracious man. Even though his eyes looked tired, his mind seemed to be very sharp as he talked with Eddie about the weekend's receipts. I thought to myself, "Everyone that works for the Colonel stays with him forever. The average age of an employee around here must be the late fifties. If you can get on here, you're in forever—unless, you're Eddie Stern's assistant. That's where I've been told the revolving door is always in use."

When we left the Colonel's office, Eddie stopped me in the parking lot and said, "Larry, you heard what the Colonel said about his door's always being open to you, for either business or personal needs."

"Yes, sir."

"Well, he meant just that. Colonel Wolfson wants his employees to be happy. If you ever have any needs, he wants to be aware of them. That's the way the Colonel is."

I thought to myself, "I can't wait to tell Doneata about this most remarkable day."

That evening I went home exhausted. I was not necessarily tired from the amount of work I had done, but mostly from the stress of an all-new environment. During dinner I brought Doneata up to date with all the people I had met during the day.

She said, "Larry, do you really think you're going to like working for Eddie Stern?"

"Honey, I'm going to love it. These are good people. I can tell."

———

Our first three weeks in Miami were wonderful. Doneata felt like she was on vacation. Every afternoon she would take David up to the pool; he would swim and play while Doneata socialized with our neighbors.

Mel and Sally Rosen lived directly across the hall from us. Mel was a medical student at the University of Miami.

I was having a great time both at work and at home. Things couldn't have been better at the office. I was really enjoying learning to buy film in a top ten market from a man who had spent his whole life doing it. Eddie Stern was one smooth operator; he had a style all his own, and I enjoyed watching this man do what he did best: buy film. I thought to myself, "After working for Michael Heffner, Dick Huffman, John Huff, and now Eddie Stern, I have no excuses; I should be a master craftsman when it comes to the film business."

Every day someone different was inviting me out to lunch. The two men I really enjoyed getting to know were Jack Mitchell and Marvin Reed. I knew the three of us were going to become the best of friends. One day, Jack, Marvin and I went out to lunch.

Jack smiled and asked, "Larry, do you know what the three of us, you, Marvin and I, have in common?"

I answered, "No, what?"

"On the management level, we're the only Gentiles working at Wometco."

I questioned, "Gentiles, what do you mean?"

"You know, Christians. We're the only Christians. Everyone else in management is Jewish."

I thought a minute, then replied, "Well, Jack what does all that mean?"

"Larry, what it means is that they, the Jewish people, are God's chosen people and we're not."

I responded, "Well, that's no big deal to me. I've never had any interest in religious matters. It doesn't matter to me if someone is Jewish, or—what did you call us, Gentiles?"

Jack continued, "Well, for the record, I'm Catholic, and Marvin here is a Baptist. Marvin even goes to church every Sunday. I should go to Mass, but most of the time I don't."

I said, "Jack, I appreciate your telling me all of this; however, church and religion are not my thing. Nonetheless, if I ever need prayer I will have you, Marvin, and Eddie each pray for me. That way I'll have all the bases covered." We laughed and dropped the conversation at that.

On the drive back to the office from lunch I was quiet, thinking about a conversation I had a few days before with Doneata.

"Larry, would you mind if David and I visit that church up on the corner one Sunday morning?"

"Why would you want to do something like that?"

"Oh, I'm not sure; I just think I would like to visit it, that's all."

"Doneata, if you want to visit it, that's fine, and it's okay to take David with you. But don't ask me to go. And don't go bringing any of those strange Christians around our home."

I thought to myself, "Funny how that subject has come up twice in one week."

Eddie wasted no time in getting me out of the office and into the film companies. He wanted me to travel first thing and meet with all the film distributors, reintroducing myself as Larry Vaughn of Wometco Enterprises. I spent my second week with Wometco doing just that: wining and dining the film distributors, telling them how pleased I was to be a part of the Wometco team.

It was late one Saturday afternoon when David and I decided to take an afternoon swim in the pool near our apartment. He was in the water having a good time while I enjoyed relaxing in the chaise longue by the pool. He splashed some water my way and said, "Dad, when are you coming in?"

"Give me ten more minutes; then I'll jump in."

Larry Vaughn and Dudley Moore in a casual meeting in Las Vegas

"Okay, but hurry up. I want you to come in and play with me."

It wasn't five minutes before David got out of the pool complaining about his arm being hurt. Then he started crying. It was obvious he was in a lot of pain. I took him home to have Doneata look at his arm.

After examining David's arm Doneata said, "Let's see if Mel is home. If so, we can have Mel look at David's arm. Doneata stepped across the hall and tapped on the Rosens' door. Sally answered the door, and Doneata explained the situation to her.

Sally said, "Mel is at the hospital, but he should be home by 8:00. I'll have him drop over as soon as he comes home."

Mel came over first thing. "Hi, Doneata. Hi, Larry. Let me see David's arm." Mel spent a few minutes examining David, and then said, "Has either of you noticed this lump on David's shoulder?"

Neither of us had noticed the lump earlier. Doneata replied, "Mel, I don't think the lump was there an hour ago."

Mel checked out David thoroughly. Then he said, "I think you need to take David to the Emergency Room and have a pediatrician look at his arm."

I said, "Mel, are you sure it can't wait until Monday?"

"Larry, I told you last week that David doesn't look right; that was before this problem came up with his arm. I really believe he needs to be seen by a pediatrician. If he were my child, I would take him on over to the Emergency Room."

We thanked Mel for his advice and acted accordingly. We took David within the hour to South Miami Hospital.

When we got to the hospital, there was very little activity going on in the Emergency Room. I filled out the necessary forms while the nurse was taking David's temperature and checking his blood pressure. We had to wait only a few minutes before the orthopedic doctor came in to examine David.

"Good evening, folks, I understand we have a swimmer here with a damaged wing."

David started telling the doctor about his aches and pains. After examining David, he said, "Mr. and Mrs. Vaughn, I will need to have an x-ray taken of David's shoulder and arm. Business is slow tonight; so it shouldn't take but a few minutes."

While David was in x-ray, another doctor dropped by to talk with us.

"Hello, Mr. and Mrs. Vaughn, I'm Dr. Flicker, the pediatrician on call tonight. How is your son doing?"

We brought Dr. Flicker up to date, and then he asked, "Would you mind if I also take a look at your son after he comes out of x-ray?"

I said, "No, that is fine with us."

Dr. Flicker also gave David a thorough examination. Then both doctors went and looked at the x-rays.

After looking at the x-rays, the two doctors came back to David's room. The orthopedic doctor said, "Nothing showed up on the x-rays—no broken bones. Looks like our young swimmer is going to live."

Doneata then commented to the doctors about how pale David had looked the last few weeks.

The orthopedic doctor commented, "You might want to put the child on a good, strong multivitamin."

Doneata said, "I took him to the doctor last month in Charlotte, and he put David on vitamins. He's been taking them daily since that time."

Dr. Flicker asked the orthopedic doctor, "Have you ordered any blood work?"

"Blood work? No, I don't think we need blood work done at this time."

I interrupted. "Doctors, since nothing is broken, would it be okay for us to go ahead and take David home? We could make an appointment for him to see one of you next week for a follow-up visit."

The orthopedic doctor was the first to speak. "That sounds good to me; however, you should keep David out of the pool and off the playground until that lump goes down."

Dr. Flicker looked at him and said, "I disagree completely. I think we should admit David to the hospital and let him stay here overnight where we can keep a close watch on him. As far as blood work, I want to know what, if anything, is going on in the child's body."

Then the orthopedic doctor replied, "If you want to do some blood work, that's fine; but I do think you're overreacting by wanting to admit the child into the hospital."

I looked at the two of them and said, "Okay, doctors, whose advice are my wife and I to take? It's now so late, I personally like the idea of taking David home tonight. Doneata could have him in Dr. Flicker's office first thing Monday morning. That would be less wear and tear on my wife and me. However, we don't want to make the wrong decision."

Dr. Flicker spoke up, "Mr. and Mrs. Vaughn, if I didn't think it extremely important that we admit your son, I wouldn't press so hard to do so. I don't want to alarm you, but I think something is going on in

David's body. I want to keep him right here where I can watch him until I get the results from his blood work back."

I looked over at the other doctor. He was quiet; he was backing away from the issue. I asked Dr. Flicker, "What are you looking for? What concerns do you have?"

"Mr. Vaughn, until I see his blood work there's no reason to get into any specific areas of concern. Please admit him. We'll watch him tonight, get our test results tomorrow afternoon, and talk when we have additional information."

"Okay, my wife and I will admit him per your instructions."

At 7:30 Sunday evening, Dr. Flicker took Doneata and me into a small corner room at the hospital. I could tell by the way Dr. Flicker was acting that he was a very disturbed man. I thought to myself, "I hope he is just having a bad day, and his looks are no reflection of the report he has received on my son's condition."

He greeted us and asked Doneata about how she was holding up being so close to her due date. Then he went right into his report. "Mr. and Mrs. Vaughn, I have all the test results back." He was quiet a moment, held his head down, pressed his lips together, shook his head as if in despair, and then said, "Mr. and Mrs. Vaughn, I am so sorry to have to be the one to tell you that your son has leukemia."

Doneata looked directly at me. She started crying, and I started shaking. I said, "Dr. Flicker, are you absolutely sure?"

"I'm sorry, there is absolutely no doubt—it's leukemia. We need to make plans to transfer David to Jackson Memorial Hospital first thing in the morning. He cannot stay here at South Miami Hospital; they don't have the personnel or equipment needed to treat him long-term here. I'll be back in a few minutes, and we'll talk more in detail."

Dr. Flicker left the room, and Doneata and I both cried. I put my arms around her, and we just held each other.

She said, "Leukemia. Why does it have to be leukemia?" We were both very emotional. I appreciated Dr. Flicker's giving us that time to be alone together. I thought, "Our paradise, our new life, our dreams, everything has suddenly become unimportant. David had been diagnosed with leukemia, a deadly killer."

Sunday evening I called Eddie and gave him the news. He couldn't believe it. "Larry, are you absolutely sure it's leukemia?"

"Yes, sir. They did a bone marrow Sunday afternoon. It's leukemia—acute lymphatic leukemia."

"Larry, don't worry about the office. Call me when you have the boy in his room at Jackson."

"Thanks, Eddie. You'll hear from me no later than midafternoon Monday."

"Larry, if you need anything, I mean anything, I want and expect to be your first call."

"Thanks again, Eddie. I really appreciate your concern."

Monday afternoon Doneata and I met with David's two doctors, Flicker and Paul. Little did we know that day that these two men were going to become household names in our home for years to come.

Dr. Flicker did most of the talking. "Mr. and Mrs. Vaughn, we would like to discuss with the two of you the method of treatment we suggest using on David." He went on to explain those things we could expect to happen to both David and us in the months ahead. David was going to have to spend several weeks in Jackson Memorial Hospital. They were going to start chemotherapy and radiation treatments immediately.

Then Dr. Flicker warned Doneata and me, "The months ahead are going to be extremely tough on the family as a whole, especially on you, Mrs. Vaughn, in your present condition."

After the doctors filled in all the blanks and told us pretty much what was to be expected, I asked, "Doctors, I have one question. I know everyone is different, but since you are the doctors and you see this type situation, I assume quite often, I want a straightforward answer out of you. How long do you think our son has to live?"

The doctors looked at each other. Then Dr. Flicker said, "Larry and Doneata, I can't tell you for sure how long David will live, no one can. But I'll try to give you an answer based on what I have seen and experienced. Some of the children with leukemia live only a few weeks, others for a number of months. But looking at David and his present condition, if I were you. . . . " He paused momentarily, then continued. "I would be thinking about having David with me for maybe two years."

As Doneata started to cry, I walked over to the two young doctors and said to them, "I know this meeting has also been very hard on the two of you. I would like to thank each one of you for being so sensitive to my wife and me while presenting the facts to us about David's sickness. I also appreciate your being completely honest with us. Dr. Flicker, you have got to be very tired after spending so many long hours with us at South Miami Hospital Saturday night and the better part of your day with us on Sunday. I do hope you will be able to get some time off soon."

We shook hands, and they left the room.

After that hard meeting with our doctors, Doneata and I went straight to see David in his new room. When we first walked into the room, we thought we were in the wrong room. There were toys and stuffed animals everywhere. It looked like someone had brought all the toys from the hospital's playroom and put them in David's room. He was sitting up in bed having a wonderful time playing with his new cars, trucks, and all sorts of gadgets.

I asked, "David, where did all these toys come from?"

He said, "They came from your new boss, Mr. Stern, and his wife."

I showed Doneata the card, "Get well soon. With love, Aunt Jerry and Uncle Eddie." And then, Doneata started to cry again.

Later that night, after we finally got David to sleep, Doneata and I left the hospital for the thirty-minute drive home. We got in the car, and she started crying. I put my arm around her shoulder and said, "Sweetheart, there is another family member that you are going to have to give some consideration to. You know whom I'm talking about: our baby. I know it's going to be hard, but you must find some way not to get yourself so upset."

"Larry, two years! That's all we have, two years."

"No, that's all they think we have. Maybe they will find a cure between now and then. David is a fighter. It's way too early for us to give up on him."

The next day I went in to the office at 8:30. The support I was given from Colonel Wolfson, Eddie, Stanley, Jack, and Marvin was overwhelming. Each of these men and their families were ready to do whatever they could to help Doneata and me during our time of need.

At 10:00 a.m., Betty buzzed me. "Mr. Stanley Stern wants to see you in his office right now."

"Okay, Betty. I'm on my way." As I was taking the short walk down the hall, I thought, "I just talked with Stanley an hour ago; I wonder what's come up so soon."

"Yes, sir, you called."

"Have a seat, Larry, I want to talk with you." Stanley got up from behind his desk, walked over to the door, and said to Martha, his secretary, "Hold my calls, unless it's the Colonel." He then closed the door and walked over and sat down in the other guest chair directly beside me. He turned his chair so he could have eye contact with me; then he said, "Larry, do you mind if I pry into your personal life a little?"

I didn't know where Stanley was heading with that question, but I said, "No, Stanley, not at all."

"Okay, tell me about your medical insurance. Since you've only been here three weeks, are you still covered with ABC?"

"As a matter of a fact, I am still covered with ABC."

"Good. How much does the major medical pay before it maxes out?"

"Fifty thousand dollars."

Stanley answered, "That's no good. You'll go through $50,000 in six months. Leukemia is one of the most expensive types of cancer to treat." He thought a few minutes. Then he said, "Larry give me a name of someone at ABC that I could talk with about backing your termination date at ABC up to a week earlier. If ABC will cooperate, then I will be in a position to enroll you under our executive plan. You and each of your dependents will have individual coverage of up to $1,000,000. That should take care of a big part of your financial concerns. Now, whom should I talk with at ABC?"

"His name is Huff, John Huff."

Stanley reached over, made a fist, hit me lightly on the knee, and said, "We may have to pay you an extra week's salary, but I guess you could live with that."

As I walked to the door I stopped, looked back at Stanley, and said, "Stanley, I can't believe how good you folks have been to my family and me. We have been here less than a month and you, Eddie, the Colonel, and the rest of the company have been so kind to us. In only three weeks you folks haven't had the time needed to really get to know me."

Stanley interrupted me, "Larry, we know all we need to know about you. I have a feeling you're going to be with Wometco for a long time."

———

I found the best therapy for me was to get heavily involved in my work during the day. The busier I was at the office, the less time I had to think about what was happening just a few blocks away at Jackson Memorial Hospital.

Those next few weeks were terrible. Doneata might as well have been living at the hospital. The only time she left David's side was when I was there. I was working from 8:30 until 5:00. Then after work I would go straight to the hospital for several hours, home by midnight, and up at 7:00 to start doing it all over again. Doneata and I continually stayed tired, depressed, and frustrated.

I started thinking about what the counselor at the hospital told us the day after David was diagnosed with leukemia.

"Mr. and Mrs. Vaughn, we do recommend that you as a husband and a wife receive counseling because of what your family is about to go through." She then went on to give us facts and figures about the divorce rate among families that go through this type of hardship. We didn't take her advice, but I was now starting to understand exactly what the counselor was trying to tell us. I noticed I was chain-smoking during the day and drinking more liquor at night. I was trying desperately to escape from the pressures that seemed to be choking the very life out of me by pouring all my energies into working, smoking, and drinking.

After three months we got some wonderful news. David's cancer had gone into remission! Shortly thereafter we got to take David home from "The Zoo." That's the nickname the three of us had given to Jackson Memorial Hospital.

On June 29, Doneata checked into Mercy Hospital for a much happier occasion. Doneata gave birth to our child: a 6-pound, 15-ounce, absolutely beautiful petite baby girl. We named her Mentora Mary after two very special ladies: Mentora after Doneata's grandmother; and Mary, of course, after my mother.

Sunshine and joy were starting to come back into the Vaughn family home.

Sixteen

Going Overboard

Because of her jaundice condition, Mentora was not allowed to leave the hospital with her mother. Mentora had to remain at Mercy Hospital two additional days. If Doneata and I had any idea as to how much Mentora would cry when we finally brought her home, we would have most certainly appreciated those days of peace and quiet much more than we did.

When I left for work in the mornings, the last thing I would hear as I walked out the door was Mentora screaming; and the first thing I would hear when I came home in the evenings was Mentora screaming.

Sally used to come over at dinner time and say, "I'll take the beautiful little monster for a stroll so the three of you can at least enjoy your dinner."

Yes, Mentora was a beautiful baby, but her disposition was next to impossible to live with. She just about drove our family and our neighbors crazy during that first year.

One afternoon, Doneata lost it. After spending all day at Jackson Memorial Hospital with David waiting for hours to see a doctor and having to listen to David scream as the doctors performed a very painful bone marrow and spinal tap on his lower back, she then had to contend with Mentora, who was known for her eight hours of nonstop screaming and crying. Well, the pressure got to be too much. When Doneata finally got home late that afternoon, she immediately put Mentora down in her crib and David on the sofa, and then she walked outside and straight to the pool. There, fully dressed, she casually walked off the side of the pool into the six-foot deep section of water. All the neighbors around the pool totally ignored Doneata's unusual behavior. They knew she was totally stressed out. Later, some neighbors told us that, after Doneata left the pool area, they all applauded.

———

135

Things were going very well at the office. We were having a big summer at the movies; all of our theatres were doing exceptionally well. I loved coming in to the office every morning and looking at the box office receipts from the day before. Wometco had the premiere track of theatres in the south Florida area. All the film companies were pleased to play their movie in a Wometco theatre because of the grossing potential of the theatres. When I worked at ABC, their largest auditoriums would seat 600 to 700 people. Wometco's large auditoriums seated anywhere from 1,000 to 1,550 people.

Competitionwise, Miami was a hot spot for the big national theatre circuits. The top three major circuits in the country, General Cinema Corporation, Loews, and ABC Theaters, all had a strong presence in the Miami market. My job was to see to it that Wometco got the lion's share of the big pictures, especially in Miami since Miami was Colonel Wolfson's back yard.

Eddie called me in to his office one morning. "Larry, how long have you been working for the company?"

"Let me think, Eddie. I came in March; it's now July. That's about five months."

"Good, I think you've caught on very quickly to how we play the game down here. Larry, Jerry and I want to take a trip in the fall. We want to travel to China and some other places. I will need to be out of the office for three months. The Booking Department will be your responsibility."

"Eddie, that's great! A trip to China."

"Well, Jerry has been wanting to go; so I thought the fall would be as good a time as any for us to get away."

"Eddie, I'm looking forward to the challenge. I assure you that you need not be concerned about anything at the office during your absence."

"That's good, Larry. You will have my itinerary, but I don't expect us to talk more than once or twice while I'm away. No point in my going away if I can't get away. However, if any fires get started, I expect you to reach me before the building burns down."

I thought a minute. Then I asked, "Eddie, whom do I report to during your absence?"

"Well, the boys will all be around: Stanley and Jack as far as I know will be in and out, and the Colonel is there if and when you need him. However, I would prefer your keeping the other guys out of my department while I'm gone."

"What about the bids? Who will approve my bids?"

"Larry, that's what I hired you for. You have forgotten more about bidding than those other guys will ever know about bidding. You approve your own bids. Just work them up, sign them, and send them out. Miss Goldberg will be more than happy to type them for you." We both chuckled at that thought.

"Well, Eddie, I hope I don't make any costly mistakes."

"You will; that's part of being a film buyer. Just buy us several good pictures at the right price to help make up for your mistakes. And don't let General Cinema, Loews, and your former buddies at ABC take all the marbles. Make them pay for what marbles they get! As far as traveling, while I'm away, take what trips you think are necessary. I would rather have you close to home while I'm gone, but you may travel as needed."

I went back to my office thinking, "This is going to be a wonderful experience for me to show not only Eddie but everyone—the Colonel, Jack Mitchell, Marvin Reed, Distribution, and even my former boss, John Huff—the job I can do in a big market when left on my own."

The Wometco screening room is where Eddie and I would watch movies. The film companies would send us, on a regular basis, prints of yet-to-be-released motion pictures for our own personal viewing. Most of the prints would be what was called "a work print," meaning the print came to us directly from the lab at the studio. The prints sometimes came in very rough condition: there might be discoloration in the film, no mention of title or cast, maybe a scene would be left out completely and the screen would have "airplane crash" written where a plane was supposed to crash. Nonetheless, the print gave us an idea of what the finished picture was going to look like.

Quite often Jack and Marvin would attend a screening if their schedule permitted and the movie was one they had interest in seeing. Dick Fries, the booker in our office, would occasionally join us when time permitted. The time we normally screened movies was during lunch. Many days we would look at two movies if needed. We have watched up to three movies in one day. We would normally screen two or three days a week. Sometimes we would screen in the evenings if things were too busy at the office during the day. I averaged watching somewhere between 200 to 250 movies a year.

During that first year in Miami I did very little gambling. Sure, Doneata and I went to the dog track and the horse track a few times, but it was none of the serious gambling like I used to do in years gone by. It's not that I didn't still have the desire to gamble. The desire was very

Larry, Marvin Reed, and Jack Mitchell at a dinner at the Fountainbleau

much there, but for the first time in many years other things in my life were taking priority over gambling.

My adrenaline got more than a good workout when Eddie and Jerry were away on their China trip. When it came to bidding for products, I was throwing money around like it was play money. Sure I made some great deals for the company, but I also bought my share of turkeys. I remember putting up a total of $285,000 on one picture to play in several Wometco Theatres in the Miami area. Well, I was awarded the picture in every single theatre that I bid to play the picture in. That's usually a bad sign in itself. I always hated to be awarded a picture in every theatre. My reasoning was simple: if I were awarded the picture everywhere, then I either put up too much money for it or none of the other circuits wanted to play the picture. I liked to win a few and lose a few. When it came to bidding, I found the statement "misery loves company" to be very true. This particular picture, a Mel Brooks film, was a big disappointment and only grossed, in all our theatres combined, a little over $100,000. That meant Wometco had to eat the other $185,000. That's part of playing what's called hardball.

Sometimes I got lucky by doing a favor for someone, and that favor ended up making me look like a genius. Twentieth Century Fox came out with one of the so-called space fantasy films. The picture was screened for all the film buyers around the country, and nobody liked the picture. It was labeled a big risk: a question-mark film. It was what

138

film buyers would call "two weeks and out," which meant it was a little picture that would play two weeks in theatres and then be gone. Fox wanted to open the film in June while the kids were out of school, but film buyers were concerned about the picture's playing in June. By opening the picture in June, it would be going head to head with the other studios' big summer releases. Film buyers were afraid the picture would get lost in the crowd of much-bigger, more-popular films. No one wanted to give up valuable summer play time to play the space film.

I received a call from Charlie Jones. Charlie was the Branch Manager for Twentieth Century Fox Film Corporation. I had known Charlie from my Michael Heffner days. Charlie was one of Michael's best friends when Michael was active in the business. The three of us had played poker in Charlotte on several occasions.

Charlie started the conversation. "Larry, old buddy, old pal, you have got to help me out on this space picture. The home office will have my head on a platter if I open this picture in Miami without proper theatre representation. You and I both know Miami is a highly visible and very important market. Now, Larry, what can you do for me?"

I said, "Charlie, I don't want to leave you hanging, but I already have my theatres booked with other very important pictures. But somehow I'll work out three or four playdates for you so you can get the picture played off in Miami."

Charlie said, "Larry, I knew you wouldn't let me down. Remember, I owe you one. Thanks for helping me get this picture set in Miami."

The name of that little "space fantasy" film that no theatre circuit wanted to play was *Star Wars*. *Star Wars* went on to set industry records in every theatre it played in. I sure was proud of my four playdates in Miami. I wished I had been a better friend to Charlie Jones and had given him fourteen playdates instead of only four.

I might also add that Charlie Jones didn't have to worry about getting playdates in Miami or anywhere else when the bids went out on *The Empire Strikes Back*, which was the sequel to *Star Wars*. After the overwhelming success of *Star Wars*, every film buyer in the country wanted to play *The Empire Strikes Back*. I was fortunate enough to open *Empire* exclusively in Miami. That privilege didn't come cheap. I bid $175,000 in one theatre and $125,000 in another—that was a lot of money in 1980.

I was right about my hunch that Marvin and I were going to become good friends. We started spending a lot of time together. Sometimes we would car-pool to work together; other days we would bus in and out together. Marvin and his wife, Sadie, lived only a couple of miles from Dadeland. He was the guy I went to lunch with most of the time.

———

That first year in Miami was very hard for David, both physically and mentally. He was a six-year-old boy who spent every weekday being taken by his mother and baby sister back and forth to Jackson Memorial Hospital for chemotherapy and radiation treatments. Most of the time when David was at home he was tired, weak, and sick, mainly because of the high doses of medication he was taking to fight off the deadly cancer cells.

Three weeks after David started chemotherapy, he lost all of his hair. Yes, he was completely bald. Baldness was extremely hard for David to accept; children, without realizing it, can be so cruel. David got to the point where he didn't want to leave the apartment. He would rather stay inside the apartment where he was safe from the ridicule of the neighborhood children than go to Burger King or even out to play.

Doneata and I decided the best thing to do would be to have David fitted with a wig. We took him out and bought the most natural looking wig that we could find. Unfortunately, a wig doesn't stay on a six-year-old boy who wants to run and play like it does on an adult. David's wig fell off several times and always at what seemed like the most inappropriate time. The wig ended up resting on David's closet shelf.

Every Friday night I had a date with my best girl, Doneata. That was the one night a week that she could get away from the children and all the responsibilities associated with the home. Quite often we would go over to Victoria Station, a restaurant located across from one of the runways at Miami International Airport. When we weren't at Victoria Station, we would go over on Key Biscayne to The Rusty Pelican. It was a seafood restaurant located right on the bay overlooking the Miami skyline. That was where we would talk, relax, and try to unwind from the many pressures of the week.

This particular Friday evening, Doneata and I were sitting in a booth located by the window at The Rusty Pelican. It was a beautiful night. From our seat we could see the gentle ripples on the water outside as they splashed up against the rocks beside the weather-beaten building. The sun was almost down; only a dim ray of red light reflected itself as it glided across the top of the water. Across the way, the tall glass skyscrapers were starting to light up. Miami nightlife was on the way.

I asked Doneata, "Why so quiet? What are you thinking about?"

"You don't want to know," she responded.

"If I didn't want to know, I wouldn't have asked. Now tell me, what are you in such deep thought about?"

"God. I'm thinking about God, Larry."

I thought to myself, "She's right! I don't want to know what she is thinking about. Foolish me, why did I ask?" I took a sip of my drink, lit a cigarette, and then said, "Okay, Doneata, tell me your thoughts about God."

"Larry, I don't want to talk about anything that will upset you; this is our time together."

"Doneata, if it's on your mind, it might as well come out of your mouth. Now talk to me before I do get upset."

"Well, Larry, do you remember the church you told me that David and I could visit several months ago."

"The big one down on the corner?"

"Yes, Grace Church. Well, when I visited the church that Sunday, I filled out one of their visitor cards and dropped the card into the offering plate."

"Why did you do that?"

"I don't know. It seemed like the right thing to do at the time."

"Did you put any money in the offering plate?"

"No, I don't believe I did."

"Good. Go on tell me more."

She took a deep breath and continued. "About a week after David and I visited the church on Sunday, a lady came to visit me."

I interrupted, "You haven't been back to the church since that one time, have you?"

"No, just once. But this lady, her name is Wanda, Wanda Glass, has come by to see me nearly every Thursday since my visit."

"I thought you weren't home every Thursday."

"Well, when I'm not at home, she leaves her card in the crack of the door as a way of letting me know she has been there."

"How long ago was it that you visited the church?"

"Oh, I don't know—several months maybe. It's been close to a year."

I thought to myself, "This Wanda sure is a persistent woman." Then I said to Doneata, "What else?"

"Wanda calls me sometimes, and we talk."

"Let me guess what you two talk about: Church, going to church. How you, David, Mentora, and probably I need to be in church. Am I right?"

"Larry, Wanda doesn't say a whole lot about her church. What she has been talking to me about most is God and His Son, Jesus Christ."

"Doneata, did I ever tell you about the party I was invited to in Greenville, and the bad experience I had with one of those gung-ho Christians?"

"Honey, you have told me a lot of stories, but that one I don't remember."

"Well, it's so stupid that I have tried to forget it. But, let me tell you what happened. Before we met, I was invited to dinner at a friend's home. A lot of people had been invited to this particular dinner. I forgot exactly how many people were there, maybe twenty to thirty. I don't really remember. The person that invited me asked me if I would mind bringing a large bag of ice, as he knew I had access to all the ice I needed from the commercial ice machine at any one of my theatres. So, I brought a large bag of crushed ice, enough ice to take care of fifty people or more.

"Everyone is sitting down at this dinner having a good time of food and conversation. Of all people to be stuck with at my table is a guy that's on fire for the church. This guy dominated the entire discussion at the table. He spent the whole dinner telling everyone about his ministry, as if I cared one *iota* about his ministry.

Doneata asked, "Was he a preacher?"

"I don't know. I think he said he was going overseas to preach or something. I remembered thinking, 'The way this guy is so gung ho, he should be going into the Marines.' Anyway, I finally got to answer one of his questions. He stops talking about himself long enough to ask me exactly what it is I do. I told him I was in the theatre business. You would have thought that I had said, 'I'm a hit man for the Mafia.'

"He proceeded to tell me about how all movies are evil, how movies corrupt peoples' minds, and how he personally would have absolutely nothing to do with a movie theatre or anything from a movie theatre. I said, 'Friend, do you know where the ice in all that ice tea you have been drinking tonight came from? One of my theatres.' When I said that, I thought he was going to throw up right there on the spot. He got straight up from the table, went to the sink, and poured his ice tea down the drain. Needless to say, the party was getting pretty much out of hand by that time.

"I went out on the back porch and lit up a cigarette; he came out behind me. He told me in so many words that I was totally lost and going straight to hell, if I didn't change my ways."

Doneata interrupted me. "And what did you say to him?"

"Honey, you really don't want to know."

Doneata said, "I knew I shouldn't have brought up the subject."

"Doneata, it doesn't bother me at all to talk religion. It's just that it's a subject that I have very little, if any, interest in. I don't mind your thinking about God and having a lady friend who is a Christian, as long as you don't go overboard with it."

"Larry, I have already gone overboard."

"What do you mean?"

"Larry, this morning, after you went to work, I went into the bathroom and locked the door. I then got on my knees and cried out to God. I gave up the struggle that has been going on in my soul for some time now. This morning I asked Jesus Christ to come into my life, to forgive me of my sins, and to make me a new creature in Him."

I just stared at Doneata a few minutes. Then I said, "How is this, your being a Christian, going to affect our future relationship with each other?"

She answered, "Larry, what do you mean affect our future relationship? You're my husband, and I love you dearly. My being a Christian wife is only going to make things better between you and me."

"Okay, we'll see. Furthermore, I don't want you trying to convert me or bring any of those weird Christian people around our home."

"Darling, I won't. I promise. Larry, the only request I have is that the children and I be allowed to go to church on Sunday mornings."

I thought and then asked, "Is that all?"

"Yes darling, that's all."

"Okay, but that's it, period. And I won't budge an inch on anything else. I'll never change. Never, do you understand?"

Doneata smiled and said, "Yes darling, that is fine. I love you just the way you are."

As we left the restaurant, I thought to myself, "Doneata has had a tough year. I guess she feels she needs religion in her life. As David gets better, this will probably pass."

The following Monday morning I was busy at my desk going over the receipts from the weekend when Marvin popped his head into my office. "You screening today?"

"Nope."

"Let's do lunch. I'm in the mood for some Cuban food."

"Sounds fine with me, Marvin. Buzz me whenever you're ready."

At 12:30, Marvin and I walked to one of our favorite downtown Cuban restaurants. I ordered my favorite Cuban dish, a minute steak, which is a very thin strip of beef that has been grilled in onions and peppers and comes piled high with French fries. Marvin got his usual black beans and rice with fried bananas on the side.

While waiting for our food to come, I asked, "Marvin, will you give me some of your beans and rice if I give you some of my steak?"

"No."

"Why not?"

"The last time we shared food, you gave me a little tiny piece of steak, and I gave you half my plate of beans and rice."

"Are you sure I did that?"

"I'm positive, and I won't let you do it to me again."

"Tell you what I'll do, Marvin; I'll let you cut off a piece of my steak, however much you think is fair, before I get my beans and rice."

"Nope."

"There's no way you'll consider sharing your beans and rice with me?"

"Yes, there is a way that we can share."

"How?"

"I'll give you some of my beans and rice if you'll let me be the one that separates both your steak and my beans and rice. Also, you have to throw in half your French fries."

"What? Half my French fries too? No deal. If you wanted French fries you should have ordered French fries. That's too much food for me to give away for just some beans and rice!"

"Okay! I'll throw in one of my fried bananas."

"Marvin, you have yourself a deal."

The waitress arrived with our much-anticipated—and talked about—lunch. While eating, we started talking about the past weekend.

"Larry, how is David doing?" Marvin asked.

"All things considered, he had a good weekend. David is so happy to have his hair back. I believe being bald was harder on David in some ways than having to deal with the pain and sickness associated with the treatment of his leukemia."

"I'm glad your boy is doing better. How about Mentora? Is she still giving her lungs a good workout?"

"Marvin, that girl has the worst disposition and attitude that I have ever seen. If she wasn't so pretty, I'd give her to you and Sadie."

"We'll take her only if you supply the ear plugs too." Marvin broke out in laughter. His freckles deepened beneath the pink flush of his rosy cheeks. "You know what's wrong with Mentora, don't you, Larry? She looks just like you, and when you were a baby, that's probably the way you acted."

"You mean what goes around, comes around?"

Marvin gave me that great-big Georgia smile and said, "That's right!"

"Well, if that's the case, then one day Miss Mentora will get herself married. Oh, and I can't wait to see her have to put up with her little terror of a baby." We both laughed.

Marvin continued, "And Doneata, what's she up to these days?"

I thought to myself, "Marvin is a Christian, but he's not crazy like some of these Christians I've been around. I wonder if I should tell him that Doneata is now a Christian? Maybe Doneata is going to be like Marvin. I think I'll tell him."

"Marvin, you're a Christian, right?" I could tell by the expression on Marvin's face that my question surprised him.

"Yes, Larry, I've been a Christian for many years."

"Well, I remember Jack's telling me that you went to church every Sunday and that you are a Baptist, right?"

"I've always been a Baptist. Sadie and I go to church every Sunday at that big Baptist church down on Kendall Drive near the Kendall Shopping Center."

"Well, the reason I brought up this subject is that you asked about Doneata." Marvin had a puzzled look on his face. "Friday night I took Doneata over to The Rusty Pelican for dinner. During dinner, she informed me that she had made, I believe she said something like, a profession of faith in Jesus Christ. Well anyway, I'm not exactly sure how she worded it. The bottom line is she is now a Christian."

Marvin had his mouth wide open while I was talking. He closed his mouth, gave me a big smile, and said, "Larry, this is wonderful news about Doneata. I can't wait to tell Sadie. She will be so happy to hear that Doneata is now a Christian." He paused a minute, got a serious look on his face, and said, "Larry, how do you feel about Doneata's becoming a Christian?"

"Marvin, to be quite frank with you, I have never cared to be around Christian people. Most of the experiences that I have had with Christians have not been good. Now, you are different. If Jack hadn't told me that you were a Christian, I wouldn't have even suspected that you were one. You don't force your Christianity on other people. You're like—well, you're like a regular guy."

Marvin nodded his head in agreement with what I was saying. Then he said, "Larry, I think there is a time and a place for everything. At work I try to work and on Sunday I go to worship. I try to keep a balance in my life; however, there are some Christians who don't."

I looked at my watch and said, "Speaking of balance, we'd best get back to work; it's almost 1:30."

When I got back to my desk, there was a stack of phone calls to be returned. In thumbing through the pile, I saw that Walter Powell had called. Immediately, I buzzed Betty and asked her to put Walter first on the list of calls to be returned.

Within a few seconds, Betty buzzed me: "Mr. Powell is on line two."

"Good afternoon, Walter, how have you been?"

"Larry, I'm doing great. I hope you are."

"Yes, Walter. Things couldn't be better."

"I have been watching the numbers down in Miami; looks like Wometco is having a big year."

"Well, the business is very good, but film rental is too high. You know as much as anyone, Walter, that theatre circuits are in the popcorn and candy business. All the ticket sales goes to the film companies."

"Larry, that's the nature of the beast. You gotta have the picture to sell the concessions."

"Yeah, I think someone else has made that statement before. Walter, is this a social call, or do we have some business to tend to?"

"No business to discuss. I was just checking up on you. I wanted to make sure you're still happy with Wometco."

"Walter, let me tell you something. I have had the opportunity to work for some of the very best men in the business; however, Eddie Stern and Wometco are what I have always wanted. I have the second-best job in the business, and I have no interest in going anywhere else."

"Larry, you said you have the second-best job. Who has the best?"

"Why, Walter, I thought you knew everything! Eddie Stern has the best job in the industry."

Walter chuckled as he said, "You're absolutely right, Larry. Maybe one day that big desk and office will be yours."

"Walter, I'm in no hurry at all. As a matter of fact, I am as happy as a lark right where I am."

"Okay, I gotta run."

"Have a good day, Walter."

"Larry, let's try to have dinner together sometime soon." With that, the conversation ended.

Several weeks had gone by since Doneata had informed me about her becoming a Christian. I must admit that I liked some of the changes I had seen in Doneata. She wasn't as fussy as she used to be, not that she was ever hard to live with; but it just seemed like she was going out of her way to be more patient and kind with the children and me.

There were several things that she was doing that did bug me. At times she would leave these little Bible leaflets throughout the house: in the bathroom, by the end table at the bed, by my chair in the living room, and even in the seat of my car. The biggest aggravation was when she would change the radio station in my car from talk radio to one of those Christian stations and leave the radio on the Christian station after she finished using the car. That got my attention in a very negative way. I also got upset with Doneata about placing her Christian books—books she always seemed to be buying—out on the table in the den.

I talked to Doneata about every single one of those irritations, and she didn't even get mad. She just said, "You're right, honey; I'm sorry. I'll be sure to keep my Christian literature picked up, my books in the bedroom, and turn the radio back to the station you had it on when I leave the car."

She was so apologetic, I felt bad about complaining to her. Yes, most of the changes in Doneata I liked, but I wondered how long it would stay this way before she started wanting to pressure me to give up my smoking, gambling, drinking, and other sinful ways.

———

In the months ahead, everything seemed more or less to stabilize in the Vaughn home. Maybe it was just because Doneata and I were finally acclimated to our circumstances and surroundings: David had leukemia; Mentora was a strong-willed child; Miami was beautiful but offered a totally different lifestyle from living in the Carolinas, and Wometco was a great company to work for. Still, Wometco was a company that demanded a strong level of performance in a highly competitive theatre market. And I also was very much aware that I was now married to a woman that claimed to be a Christian.

It was during that period of time that I became ill. No, I wasn't sick in the bed with a fever, nor did I miss any work, but I just didn't feel well. During a period of about three weeks, I lost about fifteen pounds. I had no appetite and very little energy. Doneata thought it was time for me to get a checkup, but I wanted to hold off on the checkup until my Wometco company physical came due in a few weeks.

One morning Doneata commented to me as I was leaving for work, "Larry, you've lost so much weight, and you're dark under your eyes. You really should see a doctor."

"Honey, we'll talk about it when I get home tonight. You know, you don't look so good yourself."

"I know. I feel like I'm coming down with something."

"Well, you'd better rest today. Let the house go and just take it easy." I gave her a kiss and left.

That particular day, Marvin was out of town on business. The day before I had made arrangements with Ofelia for her to pick me up at Dadeland and give me a ride to the office. I never liked to drive downtown by myself because, by law, a single driver was not allowed to drive on U.S. Highway 1 in the car-pool lane. If I didn't use the car-pool lane going from Dadeland to downtown Miami, it took an extra thirty minutes to get to the office.

We were driving down U.S. Highway 1 when, all of a sudden, a car plowed into the back of Ofelia's car. She slammed on the brakes as we started spinning across the highway. Another car hit us on my side of the car. I was sitting in the front passenger seat, but when we finally came to a stop, I was lying on the floor behind the front passenger seat. I was sore but didn't feel too bad, and no one else was injured.

After a two-hour delay with the policeman, we hobbled on in to work. I went into Eddie's office to give him an update. While I was standing there talking to him, he said, "Larry, take off your coat. I want to look at your side."

Unbeknown to me at the time, I had done a number on my right side. My side was bruised, swollen, and bleeding.

Eddie said, "That's it! We're going to the hospital."

"Freida, call Dr. Ipp. Tell him I have an emergency, and ask him where I can meet him."

Within a minute, Freida came into the office and said, "Dr. Ipp is over at the Miami Heart Institute. His nurse said he can wait for you there in the Emergency Room."

Eddie said, "Call the nurse back and tell her I'm on my way."

It took Eddie about fifteen minutes to make the drive to the Miami Heart Institute. We met Eddie's personal physician, Dr. Ipp, in the Emergency Room. Dr. Ipp not only looked at my side but, after making a brief examination, started asking me several questions about my general health. I guess he noticed how pale and sallow I was looking. He said, "Mr. Vaughn, I want to put a dressing on your side, and while I have you here, I think it would be a good idea to go ahead and admit you and have some tests run. You are showing some unusual symptoms that we need to look at."

I was never given the opportunity to speak. Eddie said, "That's fine. Go ahead and admit Larry; I'll call the office."

I interrupted: "Mr. Stern, don't I have any say in this matter?"

"No, you don't! Just lie there and be quiet."

I replied very emphatically, "Yes, sir!"

My room looked more like a hotel room than a hospital room. The furnishings were very nice. There was a large wooden dresser across one wall with a large antique mirror just above the dresser. To the left of the bed was a night table with a Victorian lamp. There was also a very nice overstuffed love seat and a huge brown overstuffed leather chair with an ottoman located in the corner. Were it not for the hospital bed I was lying on, I would have never known I was even in the hospital; even the bed had a nice quilted bedspread on it. I thought, "If I have to be in the hospital, the Miami Heart Institute is the hospital to be in."

Dr. Ipp was a senior gentleman. He was at least in his mid to late sixties, a heavyset, balding man who wore thick glasses and had a double chin. I didn't have to know anything about his medical credentials. If he was Eddie and Jerry's doctor, that was good enough for me because Jerry was very concerned about medical care.

Doneata finally came to see me. She did not look well herself. I was very concerned about her. We talked about the accident, and everything Dr. Ipp had said.

Doneata commented, "I'm glad you're in here. I'm tired of worrying about you." After convincing her that I was going to be fine, I made her go home to rest.

Dr. Ipp wasted no time in drawing blood and having me go through a battery of tests. The tests were very tiring, and some of them were quite unpleasant to go through. I thought about David, and how he must have felt having to go through similar types of testing all the time.

Doneata called me early the next morning and informed me that she was unable to get out of bed. I suggested that she get one of our neighbors to help out on the home front until she recovered. "She must have some sort of virus or something," I thought. "I feel so helpless. Mentora needs attention, and David is always in need of special care. I sure hope our neighbors come to the rescue."

Dr. Ipp came in to see me around 4:30 that afternoon. "Hello, Mr. Vaughn. Let's have a look at that side." As he was taking the dressing off he asked, "Mr. Vaughn, have you been out of the country recently?"

"No, sir."

"Think now, be sure."

"Dr. Ipp, I've never been outside the United States—not for one day."

"Okay, just checking."

"Why?"

"Oh, it's too early for you to start in with a lot of questions. I don't know anything right now. I probably won't have any answers for at least a couple of days. This side is healing well; I'm glad we got you in here when we did. Mr. Vaughn, get some rest. We'll talk tomorrow."

At 9:00 that evening, since I hadn't heard from Doneata, I decided to give her a ring. After talking with Doneata I realized that she was very sick and that it was more than a twenty-four-hour virus. I encouraged her to rest and to see a doctor tomorrow. I again assured her that I was fine. What disturbed me the most about this whole situation was when Doneata informed me that Wanda Glass was helping out at home. I thought, "Wanda—that's Doneata's Christian friend. Why couldn't Sally or Wylene have helped out? I knew some sort of payback would be in order, and I didn't want to be indebted to a Christian."

I ended up spending ten long days in the Miami Heart Institute. Dr. Ipp never really diagnosed what was wrong with me. He did have a theory; he seemed to think that somehow I had picked up a foreign virus, most likely from someone who had recently been overseas. It took time for the virus to work its way through my body. He felt, after thorough testing, the worst was behind me, and I was now on the road to recovery.

During those ten days at the Miami Heart Institute, I was able to see Doneata only that first day. The rest of the time she had been at home sick in bed. While I was in the hospital, Doneata and I talked daily. Doneata kept me up to date with the events at home and how, thanks to the Glass family, all our immediate needs were being met. As I feared, I owed a debt of gratitude to her friend Wanda and her family.

Eddie checked me out of the hospital and drove me home.

"Larry, Dr. Ipp said you should not work for a couple of more days. I don't want to see you at the office until we have talked, say, in three days. You understand?"

"Eddie, before I came with the company everyone told me how hard you were to work for. When am I going to see that hard side of you?"

Eddie pressed his lips together, then turned his head my way wrinkling his forehead as if offended and said, "Larry, my boy, you must not believe everything you hear. I've been good for you just as you've been good for me."

I smiled to myself as I looked out the window, counting the palm trees as we drove by.

Seventeen

The Payoff

It was wonderful to be back at home with the family. It was my intent to spend the next few days just lounging around the apartment enjoying Doneata and the children. Doneata still hadn't completely recovered from her illness; however, she was feeling a whole lot better than she had felt earlier in the week.

The very first thing on my agenda was to send a bouquet of flowers to the Glass family. I knew I must do something to show my appreciation for all they had done. I was hoping flowers would be a proper way of saying, "Thank you for your kindness," without having to have any personal contact with them. I ordered the bouquet first thing.

Doneata did not cook during the next week because the women from the church continued to bring over our evening meal every night.

I asked Doneata, "Did you ask Wanda to have meals brought to our home?"

"No, honey. Wanda told me the women in her church wanted to do this for us. She promised the ladies would bring the meals to the door, but they would not stay and talk."

I thought to myself, "Those people from that church sure are giving us a lot of attention, seeing that they do not even know us. Moreover, they're even playing by my rules! Hmm."

I noticed Doneata was standing firm in her new role as a Christian wife and mother. I really liked the new Doneata. She was continually going out of her way to be sensitive to my needs, as well as the children's.

The next week I started feeling guilty that I had not called the Glass family personally to thank them for all they had done for my family during my hospital stay. I thought to myself, "So what's the big deal in making a phone call? What I should do is take them out to dinner. And yet, I don't want to do dinner because I know what Charles will want to talk about: religion. However, they did bail us out of a deep hole. Is that what you would call it—a deep hole? Or would a hard time sound better? A word really doesn't fit these past few weeks. A big blur, that's what it's been to me. Yeah, that would make a lot of sense: 'Mr. Glass and family, thank you for bailing me out of a big blur. Please don't use your religion to fix the blur or use your prayers to fill the hole. Just leave us alone so I can quit feeling indebted to you.' I'm sure that would go off really well. Anyway, a phone call of thanks is most certainly in order. I am grateful for all they have done. Yes, I will call Charles and Wanda and thank them for their kindness to my family."

That evening I went into the bedroom to call Charles.

"Hello!" answered a female voice.

"Wanda?"

"Yes."

"Good evening, this is Larry Vaughn calling."

"Hello, Larry, how are you feeling?"

"Just fine, thank you. Daily I'm getting back to my old self."

"Well that's wonderful! We have been praying that both you and Doneata will have a quick and complete recovery."

I thought, "There they go, filling the hole with prayers." Wanda was saying something. "I'm sorry, what did you say?"

"Larry, thank you so very much for the flowers. We have enjoyed them all week; they have been the centerpiece of our living room table."

"Wanda, the flowers are the very least that I could do for all that you all have done for us. The purpose of this call is to thank you and your family for the overwhelming support you all have shown to my family during our time of illness. I can't believe all the delicious meals you've sent to us."

"Larry, those meals last week were not just from my family; they were also from concerned and caring families in our church."

"So I hear. Wanda, I would appreciate very much if you would pass on my expression of thanks to the other families involved."

"Yes, Larry, I'll be sure to do just that."

"Larry, here is Charles. Would you like to speak to him?"

"Oh, why, yes."

"Hello, Larry Vaughn."

"Hi, Charles. Charles, I was just telling Wanda how much I appreciate all you and your family have done for the Vaughn family the past couple of weeks."

"Larry, we are glad we were able to help meet a need in your home."

("There," I thought. "He used 'need.' ")

Charles was still speaking. "You know, my wife thinks a lot of Doneata and your children. Those two ladies are developing quite a friendship."

"Uh huh, yes, you're right."

"Larry, let me ask you a question. Would you mind if I dropped by to meet you? From everything Wanda has told me about you, I feel like I already know you."

(I thought to myself, "Yeah, I bet you have heard all about me. Me and my 'need' for salvation. Isn't that what Doneata called it? Well, I'll go ahead and let the guy drop by and give me his spiel; I owe him that much.")

"That would be fine, Charles. I also would like to meet you."

"Larry, would Tuesday night be okay with you? Say around 7:30?"

"Yes, Charles, I'm looking forward to seeing you then."

Charles arrived at the apartment at 7:30 sharp. I don't know exactly what I was expecting Charles to look like, but he didn't look like what I would have thought. He was a young man in his mid-to-late thirties, dressed very neatly and conservatively. His speech and mannerisms were very professional—I could tell this man was an executive. Charles's black hair looked like it had just been combed. He wore his hair with a perfect part on the right side; then it was combed over and went up in the front. I noticed Charles had brought his Bible with him—the Bible I expected him to bring. Doneata brought us some coffee and cake; then she left the room.

I started the conversation. "Charles tell me about yourself."

"Well, let me see, Larry. You know I have a wonderful wife, Wanda. I also have three children: two beautiful girls and a very handsome son. Of course, the three of them got their good looks from their mother."

We laughed. "I work for Eastern Airlines. I spend a lot of time in the air going back and forth from Miami to our New York offices."

I asked, "Are you a pilot?"

"No, sometimes I wish I were. I'm the treasurer of the airline."

I thought, "Charles is a professional all right."

"Outside of my work and my family, I am very active in my church. I teach a Sunday school class for young married men."

We talked for a good forty-five minutes. Charles asked me all about myself. I tried to sugar-coat some of my experiences in life the best I could so that he wouldn't think of me as being too much of a heathen. I left out a lot of details, but for the most part I painted a fairly accurate picture of myself.

At 8:30 Charles said, "Larry, where has the last hour gone?"

I thought to myself, "It has gone fast. I have actually enjoyed talking to this guy. He's not just a somebody—he's an officer at Eastern Airlines. I'm impressed that Charles has taken the time to come and visit with me."

"Charles, they say, times flies when you're having fun. I guess we've been having fun."

"Larry, may I ask a favor of you?"

I thought, "This is it—the payoff. He'll want me to go to his church one time and get it over with."

"Yes, sir—shoot."

"I would be honored if you would consider visiting my Sunday school class. There are only eight other men in the class, and they are all young married men like yourself. We have a time of Bible study; it lasts about forty-five minutes."

I asked, "What are the women doing while this class is going on?"

"Starting out everyone meets together in a large room for about fifteen minutes. We have a brief time of announcements, a song, and a prayer. Then we divide up by age, with the men going one way and the women another way."

"Charles, let me think about your offer. You know, I'm not really into going to church."

"Larry, I'm not asking you to go to church. I'm only asking you to visit my Sunday school class. You could leave as soon as the class was over."

"Charles, let me think about it. You just might have a visitor Sunday."

"Larry, that would make my day." Then, almost as an afterthought, Charles asked, "Larry, before I go, would you mind if I close out our time together in prayer?"

"No."

Charles then proceeded to pray a prayer of thanksgiving to God for having brought the two of us together. Charles also thanked God for answering prayers in meeting the health needs of our family.

When he left, I went into the bedroom. Doneata had just gotten out of the shower.

"Well, honey, how did it go with Charles?"

"I like him, Doneata; he's a nice guy. You know he brought his Bible, but he didn't even open it up. We just talked the whole hour. I did let him close in prayer, but that was no big deal. He asked me if I would come to his Sunday school class next Sunday."

"And what did you say?"

"I told him I would let him know. Doneata, if I go to Sunday school, you can forget about my staying for church, because I won't!"

"Honey, if you decide to go, the kids and I will leave after Sunday school with you."

———

It was great to get back to work. My first week back turned out to be very hectic—trying to catch up on the accumulation of paperwork that had developed and returning over two weeks' worth of telephone calls. Eddie too was doing double time trying to get everything off his desk because he and Jerry were planning on taking a trip to Nassau the following week.

Eddie called me into his office to inform me that during his absence his old friend, Joseph E. Levine, would be in Fort Lauderdale meeting with the press and giving interviews on his upcoming Anthony Hopkins film, *Magic*.

Eddie told me, "Larry, you be sure to plan on spending some time with Mr. Levine. He will be staying at the Jockey Club. Whatever Joe needs from you, give it to him. As you know, he's a close personal friend of mine."

Jack Mitchell then dropped in to see me. "Larry, it's good to have you back at your desk."

"It's good to be back at my desk. Oh, Jack, Doneata and I really appreciate how you and Ann kept tabs on us the last couple of weeks. Tell Ann I'm still enjoying her homemade pimento cheese. She should open a sandwich shop—that stuff tastes great."

"Larry, I received a call from Columbia Pictures Publicity. Suzanne Pleshette is going to be in Fort Lauderdale next week promoting her new picture." Jack thought a minute, then said, "What's wrong with me? I can't think of the title. Anyway, Miss Pleshette requested that Wometco have its Film Buyer come to the meeting along with Marvin and me. Since Eddie will be out of town, you be sure to make yourself available."

"That's fine, Jack. I'm looking forward to meeting Miss Pleshette." I thought, "Next week is going to be a very stressful week, especially if the week starts on Sunday with my going to Charles's Sunday school class!"

I told Doneata Saturday evening that I would plan on attending Sunday school on Sunday. She got excited and said, "Oh, Larry, that is wonderful! I am thrilled that you're going to go."

I thought, "It sure doesn't take much to make Doneata happy these days."

We walked into the adult Sunday school department right before the bell rang. I had planned it that way. Charles and Wanda were holding seats for Doneata and me. I was glad to see that we were sitting toward the back.

The first part went pretty much the way Charles had said it would. A young man welcomed everyone, especially the visitors. Charles introduced Doneata and me to the other husbands and wives. Then they had some announcements, took prayer requests, and one of the men prayed. We then separated into our individual classrooms.

After Charles closed the door to his room, he introduced me to the other seven men who were present. He proceeded to tell the men that my family and I had moved to Miami a little over a year ago from Charlotte, North Carolina. He said that I was currently employed as the Assistant Film Buyer in the theatre division of Wometco Enterprises. I watched the men's facial expressions carefully. That statement Charles had just made did not seem to offend anyone. Then Charles moved right into the lesson.

I was really too uncomfortable to actually understand anything Charles had to say. I brought a Bible that we had lying around the house with me, but it took me forever to find where anything was. Charles would say turn to Acts, and I would watch the other men find Acts in their Bibles before I could even get my Bible open. No one seemed to notice my ignorance; however, my ignorance most certainly bothered me. I tried to listen while I was there so I wouldn't waste my time, and I hoped that by listening time would go by faster. I was glad when the bell rang, for I knew that the class would end in a matter of minutes.

After the class Charles thanked me for coming. He asked, "Larry, would I be pushing it to ask if I might drop by again this Tuesday evening to visit with you?"

Without giving much thought to what he had just said, I replied, "Sure, Charles, will you be coming at the same time?"

"Larry, if it's okay on your end."

I nodded in approval.

He extended his hand saying, "Good. I'll see you Tuesday at 7:30."

———

Charles tapped on the door at 7:30. I greeted him, and we went straight to the dining room table for a cup of fresh-brewed coffee and a piece of Doneata's homemade lemon pie. After some small talk, Charles wanted to get serious. I let him talk.

"Larry, have you ever had any interest at all in going to church, God, or being around Christian people?"

"No interest at all, Charles. I have never felt a need for God or His people in my life. The only reason you are welcomed back in my home tonight is because I like and respect you. Plus, I can tell you are an okay guy."

"Larry, let me ask you a question. Do you believe the Bible is the inspired Word of God? That there is only one God, and that He has a Son, whose name is Jesus Christ. Or do you believe in some other religion? Or is it that you just believe in nothing."

"Charles, to be perfectly honest with you, I have never given much thought as to what I believe. I think I believe mostly in myself."

"Well that's a start. Tell me what you believe about yourself."

"You really want to hear this?"

"Larry, if I didn't want to hear it, I wouldn't have asked."

"Okay. I believe I am very good at what I do. Because I am good at what I do, one day in the not-too-distant future I am going to be rich and able to give my family whatever their hearts desire. Charles, I grew up in poverty. I am now sitting on the crest of wealth. I am pleased with myself. I am a self-made man. I know all that sounds a bit arrogant, but you asked for it. I believe different people at different times in their lives need God. For example, it happened to my wife recently. Doneata was going through so much with David's leukemia and our daughter, Mentora, that she needed something extra to draw on. Instead of turning to alcohol or something else, she chose religion."

Charles listened to me ramble on a few more minutes about how independent I was, and then he asked me, "Larry what about after this life has been lived. Say, God allows you to live sixty more years, and everything you have just predicted comes true. What about your soul when you die? What is going to become of it?"

I smirked at the question and said, "Charles sixty years is a long way off. Who knows what will happen between now and then."

Charles went on to say, "Okay, Larry, let's say you don't have sixty years. Let's say your death will be tomorrow. Now what about your soul? Where is it going to spend eternity?"

I didn't respond to his question.

"Larry, everything that you say you have at your fingertips I now have. I have wealth, power, a big home, a beautiful wife, and three wonderful children. Did you know that if God so willed it, I may never see my family again. I could have a heart attack on the way home tonight; or my wife and children could be killed in an automobile accident as we speak. I could lose my job tomorrow, and my house could burn down tonight. The only thing I have that can never be taken away from me is my salvation—yes, my salvation in Jesus Christ. And better yet Larry: if I do die of a heart attack or my loved ones are killed, one day we will all be reunited together to spend eternity with one another in heaven, because my household and I have all accepted Jesus Christ as our personal Savior.

"Larry, do you know how I know all that to be true? Because that's what God's Word says is true."

He held his Bible reverently in the palms of his hands. I thought, "He acts as if he held some precious jewel or that all the knowledge of the world rested in its pages."

He continued speaking, "Larry, inside the covers of this old, worn book are sixty-six books that were written by many different men, men who were all writing under the inspiration of the Holy Spirit. See, the Holy Spirit guided the men about what to write. Many unsaved men have become Christian men of God while trying to find error in this book."

He looked up from his Bible and fixed his eyes on mine; then he continued. "No, it doesn't matter what you have done or said. Jesus is willing to forgive you of your sins if you will only ask Him to forgive your sins and put your complete trust in Him as your Lord and Savior."

Charles then proceeded to read me some Scripture verses pertaining to salvation. Then Charles asked me, "Larry sometime during the next week will you read seven verses from the Gospel of Luke for me? It shouldn't take you but just a few minutes to read through them."

I asked him what they referred to.

"It's the story of a farmer who had great wealth: wealth like you and I have talked about tonight. I believe it to be a good analogy about the way we are to view our wealth today. Here, write it down: Luke chapter 12, verses 15 through 21. Will you do that for me?"

"Okay, I guess."

Charles closed our time together in prayer. He asked God to use the time we had together that night in my life and to give me a desire to know more about spiritual matters. He again thanked God for bringing the two of us together.

After Charles left, I went immediately into my bedroom and opened my Bible to Luke 12. I started reading at verse 15:

> And he said unto them, Take heed, and beware of covetousness: for a man's life consisteth not in the abundance of the things which he possesseth. And he spake a parable unto them, saying, The ground of a certain rich man brought forth plentifully: And he thought within himself, saying, What shall I do, because I have no room where to bestow my fruits? And he said, This will I do: I will pull down my barns, and build greater; and there will I bestow all my fruits and my goods. And I will say to my soul, Soul, thou hast much goods laid up for many years; take thine ease, eat, drink, and be merry. But God said unto him, Thou fool, this night thy soul shall be required of thee: then whose shall those things be, which thou hast provided? So is he that layeth up treasure for himself, and is not rich toward God.

I turned out the light and lay there in the darkness of my room; for the first time in my life, I was concerned about what would happen to my soul if I died.

The next week I took Doneata with me to Fort Lauderdale to the Jockey Club to meet the famous director Joseph E. Levine. It was a wonderful experience to meet the grand old filmmaker and hear some of his stories. He had a large, beautiful ocean-front suite. I spent most of my time drinking expensive liquor, eating the delicious hors d'oeuvres, and talking films with Mr. Levine. After a couple of hours, I looked over at Doneata and motioned for her to get ready to leave.

Doneata and I went over to Mr. Levine and told him how much we enjoyed meeting him. I also told him how I was looking forward to opening his film, *Magic,* during the weeks ahead.

He said, "Larry, may I ask a special favor of you?"

"Yes, sir! You name it."

"Larry, I would appreciate very much if you would let me phone you at your home during the opening weekend, and maybe you could give me some numbers on how my film is doing."

"Mr. Levine, it will be my pleasure. If you prefer, I shall be pleased to gather together the numbers and call you when I have all the information in hand."

"Oh Larry, that would be just wonderful, if you're sure it won't be too much of an inconvenience."

Larry, Doneata, and Joseph E. Levine

"It will be my pleasure, Mr. Levine. Besides, Eddie Stern has given me strict instructions to give Joe Levine anything he wants. And I don't want to get in the doghouse with Eddie."

"No, you don't, Larry. I've been there before."

We both laughed at the thought of upsetting Eddie Stern.

That Friday afternoon, Jack, Marvin, and I drove up to Fort Lauderdale to meet with Miss Suzanne Pleshette aboard a luxury yacht that was docked in one of the marinas. The three of us were becoming like The Three Musketeers, as we really enjoyed each other's company.

I noticed that Jack, who was driving, kept looking through his rear-view mirror at me. Then he would look at Marvin through the corner of his eyes. His grip tightened on the steering wheel, and again he looked back at me. I knew that something was up.

As we entered the marina, Jack got very serious for a moment and said, "As soon as we get aboard the yacht, I would appreciate very much if the two of you would give me some breathing room around Miss Pleshette."

He paused, licked his lips, glanced in his rear-view mirror quickly, and then continued. "I have always wanted to meet her. She is one of my favorite actresses, and I love her television program, *The Bob Newhart Show*."

Marvin thought a moment; then in a very professional manner looked over at Jack, snapped his fingers, and said very emphatically, "Jack, as soon as we get on board, would you like for Larry and me to jump off the side of the yacht and take a swim in the ocean. Would that give you enough breathing room with Miss Pleshette?"

I always loved to hear Marvin get going. He would get so tickled that his face would turn red and his eyes would start watering. Marvin was laughing; then I started laughing. I wasn't laughing at what Marvin said but at the way Marvin reacted to what he had just said. Jack was shaking his head from side to side. I noticed that his grip on the steering wheel was less aggressive. I knew he felt better since he had told us what was on his mind. He had that look on his face as if to say, "Marvin is crazy."

Jack said, "Larry, whose idea was it to bring this guy along with us anyway?"

"It was yours, Jack—don't you remember? You're supposed to be Marvin's boss."

We walked up the ramp to the deck of the yacht. The captain was standing there all decked out in white, waiting to greet us. Jack introduced himself, Marvin, and me. The captain then ushered us into a very nice sitting room. The room was quite large to be on a yacht; however, I thought the yacht looked more like a small ship. Inside the room was a very nice off-white sofa, which could easily seat up to four. Across from the sofa in the corner of the room was a fully stocked bar. I saw another person all decked in white standing in the other corner of the room holding a large silver tray filled with hors d'oeuvres for our enjoyment. There were two more chairs in the room. The chairs were placed directly in front of the sofa.

Marvin and I wanted to be sure to let Jack take the lead, since this was a meeting of special interest to the old fellow. Miss Pleshette walked into the room. Jack walked toward her to greet her. He extended his hand.

"Hello, Miss Pleshette. I'm Jack Mitchell, Vice President and General Manager of Wometco Theaters. It is a pleasure to meet you."

"Hello, Jack. It is very nice to meet you too. I have heard many good things about Wometco Theatres. I understand Wometco has some great grossing theatres." Then Miss Pleshette looked straight past Jack toward Marvin and me and said in a very sweet, curious voice, "Jack, which one of these gentlemen is your film buyer? That's the man I'm looking forward to spending some time with."

Jack Mitchell, Susanne Pleshette, and Larry Vaughn

As soon as Miss Pleshette made that statement, Marvin got all choked up. He started coughing, and his face got very red. Then before I knew it, he was laughing along with his coughing. Marvin tried to stop, but he couldn't control his laughing. Marvin Reed had just totally embarrassed himself.

Miss Pleshette got a very inquisitive look on her face, leaned over toward Jack's ear, and in a loud whisper asked, "Jack, what's wrong with that man? Did I say something funny?"

Jack replied, "No, ma'am. That's Marvin Reed. Marvin was our Director of Advertising. He's one of those guys who thinks everything is funny."

Then I smiled, wondering whether Marvin caught the "was" in Jack's statement. Miss Pleshette gave Jack a look as if to say, "Okay, I understand; you don't want to let me in on your private joke." While Marvin was trying to regain his composure, I walked over to Miss Pleshette and introduced myself as Larry Vaughn, Wometco's Assistant Film Buyer.

We stayed on the yacht for about an hour and a half. We had a wonderful time talking with Miss Pleshette. She told us about her upcoming movie and made me promise to give Columbia Pictures, who was releasing the film, several playdates on the film. Before we left, she had her publicity agent take several photographs of us as a group as well as some individual photographs. She promised to have the photographs delivered to our home office within three weeks. On the day the photographs arrived, one photograph of Miss Pleshette and Jack was proudly hung on Jack's office wall. Whenever I saw the picture, I thought of the "was" in Jack's address to Marvin and wondered how Miss Pleshette would have reacted if Marvin and I had really jumped into the ocean.

––––––––

I kept going to Charles's Sunday school class. The more I visited the class, the more comfortable I felt being around the other men in the class. Charles was faithful in keeping tabs on me. He continued to try to meet with me on Tuesday evenings when our schedules permitted. Tuesday nights were the times that Charles and I would have some rather straightforward discussions about what the Bible had to say about man, man's sin, Jesus Christ, and the work Christ had done on my behalf when He went to the cross for me. I never said a whole lot to Charles, but for the first time in my life I was beginning to think about things other than my gambling, smoking, drinking, and work. I was finding myself thinking quite often about God and His Son, Jesus Christ.

Charles called me one evening at home to tell me about the new preacher that would be preaching the following Sunday. "Larry, I know you have never stayed after Sunday school for church, but I just want to let you know that our new preacher, Pastor "Henry Hemstead," will be in the pulpit this Sunday. We're all so excited that we finally have a pastor that I wanted to share the good news with you. Larry, don't give me an answer now, just think about it. It would be wonderful to see you and your family in church this special Sunday."

I told Charles I would think about it and thanked him for the call. I'm one of those guys who really hate to say no when someone I respect asks me to do something special for him. Because of my friendship with Charles, I told Doneata to plan on staying for church the next Sunday because the new preacher would be there, and I wanted to hear what he had to say.

"Grace Church" had a large, beautiful auditorium. The choir area could easily seat 75 to 100 people. Behind the choir loft was a large, open space. Doneata explained that that is where people are baptized after salvation.

"Baptized?" I thought. "What would people want to be dunked in water for?" I wondered if Charles had been baptized. I guessed he had been at some time or another since he has salvation, or was saved—however they say it. Anyway, I knew I wouldn't ever be baptized, since I'd never be saved. I'd just take my bath at home! I looked up and saw a large balcony area and behind the balcony a booth from which I assumed someone controlled the lights, camera, and action. I guessed the church would seat about 700. We sat about halfway down on the left side of the auditorium.

One of the deacons introduced the new pastor to the congregation. What caught my attention was his appearance. He was wearing brown alligator shoes and an off-white, western-cut, tight-fitting tailored suit. His shirt was expensive; I noticed it had large French cuffs. His tie was silk. I thought, "That tie is a bit much for a preacher to wear, but I guess it goes perfectly with his western attire." He had long blonde hair that he combed straight back without a part in it. He was a big man but not overweight. I would guess him to be in his early forties. He had the chest of an athlete and probably a thirty-six-inch waist. With no disrespect to a south Dallas used car salesman, that's what the preacher reminded me of. I wondered, "Now what kind of a car is the preacher driving? I would bet cold hard cash that he drives either a Lincoln or a Cadillac."

He preached about twenty minutes. During his message he kept walking very fast across the stage, going back and forth. He had the audience laughing and crying. Everyone but me seemed to be having a good time. I thought to myself, "This guy is not a preacher; he's an entertainer." The total service lasted about forty minutes. The last twenty minutes was given to what Doneata called an "invitation."

As we left the church, I told Doneata, "Let's go by the pastor's parking space. I'm sure he has an assigned space."

Doneata asked, "Why do you want to do that?"

"Oh, I don't know; I'm just curious about something."

"Larry, his is the first space on the left side of the building."

If I had made a bet, I would have won. The preacher drove a shiny, two-toned red-and-white Eldorado Cadillac.

The experience I had that Sunday with the new preacher turned me off from ever wanting to go back to Sunday school or church. I thought, "I have seen enough movies to know how a preacher is supposed to look, dress, and act." I went to church that day expecting to meet a preacher that looked and acted like Spencer Tracy or maybe Gary Cooper. However, what I found was someone who looked and acted like Elvis!

After that day it seemed like every Sunday morning I woke up in a bad mood. I went through the apartment making excess noise, looking for things to complain about. I found myself continually being short and rude with Doneata and especially with the children. Half the time I ended up staying home from church.

One Sunday I decided I would go to church. While getting dressed, for no reason in particular, I became exceptionally rude with the family. Doneata came into the bedroom, shut the door, and said, "Larry, why don't you just stay home from church. No one is forcing you to go to Sunday school or church. As a matter of fact, it would be best if you didn't go in the disposition that you're in."

I shot back at her very sarcastically, "Well, sweetheart, that's just fine with me. You and the kids go play church—I'm going up to the pool to get some sun and read the paper. When you get home, I might be here or I might not." On that note I changed clothes, took the newspaper, and left.

When I got up to the pool, no one was there. It seemed that on Sundays when the Christians were at church, everyone else chose to sleep in. I sat down at one of the empty tables and lit a cigarette. I looked around; it was a beautiful day. It was too bad I felt so miserable. I tried reading the paper, but I couldn't. I was too upset to concentrate. I was miserable on the inside. I tried to analyze the situation, "What's wrong with me? Every weekend is a bad weekend. I wish I had to work on Sundays. I have always been a black-and-white kind of guy. So let me look at the problem: put the facts right here on the table and make a decision that will take care of the problem before I let the problem ruin another beautiful weekend.

"First of all, Doneata is a Christian. Is that a problem? No, not really. She doesn't push her Christianity off on me. Sure she would like for me to go to church with her and the children, but that's not really the problem. Doneata accepts me just the way I am as long as I'm not angry and rude to her and the children—like I have been lately. Doneata never complains about any of my bad habits. Doneata is not the problem.

"Secondly, I'm not a Christian. Is that a problem? It never has been a problem before. But now for some reason I am allowing it to become a problem. The pressure to be a Christian is not being applied on me by anyone other than myself. The question is why am I doing this to myself? I must be honest with myself: Do I want to accept Jesus Christ as my Lord and Savior the way Charles has been talking about? I don't think so. Why not? I don't know. I'm just not ready to make a commitment like that—not today anyway. I'll mark that down as a possible problem.

"Thirdly, I need to make a firm decision about whether or not I should continue going to Sunday school and church with the family. What exactly do I want to do? If the truth were known, I think I want to go to church. Yes, that's it. I know I want to go to both Sunday school and church. But why do I want to? That's when I seem to be at my worst —when it's time to make the decision to go or not to go to church. I just need to make one final decision and stick with it and forget about my feelings. If by chance the Bible is truth and everything else is a lie, then it would behoove me to spend more time in the study of God's Word. It just bothers me that I have to hear it from someone who looks and acts like Elvis. I think my indecision about whether or not to go to church has been the problem. That problem is solved—I'm going."

I left the pool and went home and started trying to figure out a way to get out of the doghouse with Doneata and the children. When they returned home from church, I had lunch on the table and a new countenance about me. I apologized for my conduct earlier in the day. We ended up having a good Sunday afternoon together as a family. Doneata knew something had happened, but I thought I would let time instead of my words show her the change.

For the next few weeks I went to Sunday school and church every Sunday. It was nice not to have to make a decision about whether or not to go. That decision had been dealt with weeks earlier. I enjoyed Charles's Sunday school class very much. I stayed busy every week taking notes and asking questions. I ended up talking as much as anyone in the class.

I was still uncomfortable with Pastor Hemstead. I guess there are some people who just rub you the wrong way, and he always rubbed me the wrong way. I remember one Sunday morning Pastor Hemstead from the pulpit made the statement, "I have noticed how hard it is for you people to get to church on time on Sunday. It amazes me that you men can get to the office on time Monday through Friday, but when it comes to getting to church on time on Sunday, well, that's another story."

That particular Sunday we were late to church because right as we were about to leave home Mentora spit up on my shirt, and I had to change shirts before we could leave. On the way out of church I stopped to speak with Pastor Hemstead. I said, "You know, Pastor Hemstead, you're right in what you said about men not getting to church on time. I can get to work on time Monday through Friday with no problem, but

I admit I do struggle to get to church on time on Sunday. Do you know what the difference is?"

He took a hard look and said, "No, tell me."

"Well, the difference is this: on Monday through Friday I don't have to make sure my wife's up and get the children up, bathed, dressed, fed, and in the car to ride with me to be at the office by 8:30. If I did, I'd probably be late for work too." The good Pastor Hemstead gave me his artificial smile, and I left. I thought, "That smile of his annoys me greatly. I'd like to knock his teeth in just once. Now, now, Larry, it's not good to think such of a pastor. Behave yourself."

———

Overall things were going well in the Vaughn household. Doneata had the home on a schedule that was working. David still had to have his weekly trips back and forth to Jackson; however, physically David was doing much better than a lot of the other kids with leukemia were doing. That was one of the sad parts about taking those trips to Jackson Memorial Hospital. Occasionally, David would have a brief time away from Jackson. When Doneata returned to Jackson with David to resume his treatments, she would notice a child was missing. When Doneata asked one of the nurses about the child, she would be told the child went out of remission and died shortly thereafter. We saw many families fall apart as they watched their children die during those years David was being treated at Jackson Memorial Hospital.

It was business as usual at Wometco. Eddie and I stayed busy working on bids, trying to figure how much such-and-such a picture was going to do in a given market. Florida had what was called "blind bidding," which meant a film company could offer their picture out on bid before it was ever made. Many times a company would bid a picture while it was still in production. That meant all we had to go by was a title, cast, producer, director, and a synopsis of the film. We would have to put up several hundred thousand dollars on a picture, say three to six months before the picture was to open. When we finally had the opportunity to see the picture that we had put up so much money on, it might very well have been a dud—a big disappointment.

On some bid applications the film company would include in the application what was called a forty-eight-hour escape clause, which meant the theatre circuit that was awarded the picture could cancel the bid within forty-eight hours after the picture had been made available for trade screening. If that happened, then all the theatre circuits would then have the opportunity to rebid, or negotiate for the opportunity to play the picture. However, this clause was omitted from the majority of the films being offered on bid.

On the flip side, we made some cheap deals when bidding for the rights to play what looked like little films. I remember one picture in particular: It was the story of an alien who came to earth, spent some time with some kids, and then found a way to return home. The name of that little hidden jewel was *E.T.*

Yes, Eddie and I had a good time working together. He would want to put the farm up on some crazy hunch, and I would try to talk him out of it or vice versa. We complemented each other. I enjoyed working under a man who could lay out, sight unseen, hundreds of thousands of dollars for a picture, go home and sleep like a baby, and wait several months to see if he won or lost. Eddie had a saying, "If Wometco can find somebody who can run Film Buying better than I can, then why are they paying me all this money and not him?" Eddie believed that too. Humility wasn't one of Eddie's stronger suits.

Late one Friday afternoon I received a call from Paramount Pictures. I was told the director, John Frankenheimer, would be in Miami on the following Saturday morning. Mr. Frankenheimer was coming to Miami for the specific purpose of showing his much anticipated terrorist film *Black Sunday* to Joe Robbie. Mr. Robbie was at that time the owner of the Miami Dolphins. The closing scene of the film was shot at the Orange Bowl during a Miami Dolphins game. Paramount wanted to rent our 163rd Street Theatre for the private showing. I approved and made the necessary arrangements for them to rent the theatre.

Saturday morning I was at the theatre. I wanted to see the picture since it was filmed in Miami at the Orange Bowl. *Black Sunday* had all the makings of a big picture: a big-name director—Frankenheimer—a big name star—Robert Shaw—and was filmed in our own backyard, Miami. After seeing *Black Sunday,* I thought it was everything it was built up to be. Paramount even wanted the Film Buyers to see it before they bid for it in order to whet their appetite. Yes, *Black Sunday* was going to be a very big picture.

Eddie was out of town the Saturday morning we screened *Black Sunday*. When Eddie returned to Miami, I filled him in on the picture. "Eddie, this is going to be the big one of the season, especially in Miami. I want to go after it in our big theatre, The Miracle in Coral Gables."

"Larry, what kind of a figure do you have in mind?"

"Eddie, I want to tie it up; the other guys are going to have their tongue hanging out for this one."

"Larry, how much?"

"In the Miracle with 1,500 seats, I want to guarantee $150,000."

"Ouch, Larry! That is a lot of dough. Do you really think we need to go that strong?"

"Yes, sir, I do."

He paused a moment, frowned and said, "Go ahead, it's only money. Send your bid in to Paramount."

Black Sunday opened to be the disappointment of the year. The picture grossed in Coral Gables maybe $35,000. That's the bad news. The good news is Wometco never had the opportunity to play the picture in the Miracle Theatre. We lost *Black Sunday* on bid to General Cinema. I am glad to say that their film buyer thought more of *Black Sunday* than I did. After *Black Sunday* opened so disappointingly, I thought to myself, "Larry, you just dodged a $150,000 bullet with your name on it. Somebody up there must be watching out for you."

––––––

It was a brisk Sunday morning in February of 1978 when the alarm clock started ringing at 7:00. I reached over to cut it off, hoping to silence the alarm before it had time to wake up Doneata. I got up, went straight to the kitchen, and started making a pot of strong coffee. While the coffee was perking, I lit a cigarette and went outside for the newspaper. It was chilly and cool this morning; the weather felt good. I was looking forward to a good day of church, roast, and relaxation. At 7:30 I had everyone out of bed and at the breakfast table. I commented, "Let's move right along. We don't want to be late to church. I want to leave by 9:00 sharp."

That morning at church everything went as expected: Charles had prepared a good message that was applicable for us men to use in our everyday walk, and Pastor Hemstead had a good twenty-minute message and his usual twenty-minute invitation.

On the way out of church Doneata said, "Mentora and I have to stop by the ladies room." While waiting on them, I casually walked over to the display table in the lobby and picked up one of the many tracts that were lying there on the table. Without thinking, I put the tract in my shirt pocket, and then I just stood there in the lobby waiting on Doneata and Mentora.

When we arrived home, I was met with the wonderful aroma of the roast cooking in the oven. Sunday lunch was always my favorite meal of the week. Doneata would always do most of the cooking for Sunday on Saturday afternoon. By Sunday I was always starving just thinking about the mashed potatoes, field peas, sliced tomatoes with mayonnaise, homemade rolls, and, of course, the rump roast. While Doneata finished preparing the meal, I went into the bedroom and changed clothes. When I took my cigarettes out of my shirt pocket, I noticed the tract that I had picked up earlier at church. I placed it along with my cigarettes on the dresser. A few minutes later Doneata was calling everyone to the dinner table. We had a wonderful Sunday lunch with Doneata's specially prepared roast and all the trimmings.

After lunch Doneata went to our bedroom for her Sunday afternoon nap. David was outside playing with some of the neighborhood kids. Mentora was in her crib either resting or sleeping; at least for the time being she was quiet. I slipped into our bedroom to get my cigarettes. Trying not to wake up Doneata, I quietly walked over to the dresser and picked up my pack of cigarettes. Once again I noticed the tract from church. I picked it up as I left the room. I went into the living room and sat down on the sofa. My stomach was full from the feast I had recently been served. I lit a cigarette and leaned back on the sofa enjoying the rest and tranquillity.

A few minutes later I looked at the tract I had tossed on the table. It was a small blue tract. On the front of it was the picture of a dove in flight. I picked it up and started to read through it. It was entitled "How to Be Born Again." It took only a few minutes for me to read through it in its entirety. After I read it, I started reading it again. That little tract asked a very personal question that I had been asked before, but for some unknown reason, at this moment in time, it had my undivided attention. "Have you been born again? Have you experienced the spiritual rebirth Jesus said was absolutely necessary for entrance into heaven? This is the one thing, according to the Word of God, that will determine your eternal destiny."

I knew at that very moment what I had always known to be true: that I was an unsaved man. I knew that if I died that day I would spend eternity in hell where the worm never dies. I felt like there was a war going on inside my body—a war for my soul. I knew the only way to end that war was for me to forget God and continue to live in my sin, or to confess to God that I was a sinner in desperate need of salvation. I continued reading from the tract: "The moment we open our hearts to the Lord Jesus and place our complete trust in Him—and Him alone—as our Savior, God promises to forgive our sins, save our soul, and reserve us a home in heaven."

I sat there on my sofa with tears streaming down my face wondering, "Why has it taken me so long to understand what a wretch I have been." I realized at that moment that I was going full speed on a one-way road to hell, and that the only person standing between me and eternal damnation was Jesus Christ the Righteous One.

I got up from the sofa and went to the corner of the living room. I got down on my knees and started crying uncontrollably. After a few moments I prayed a prayer: "Heavenly Father, I would like to ask you to forgive me for living my life in complete rebellion to you. I have done so many terrible things in my life that I am amazed that you would even consider having me in your kingdom. I confess before you at this time that I have faithfully served Satan, the liar and the deceiver, all my life, and I know that I deserve damnation along with him. But I thank you for your Word, for the truths that are found in it, and I thank you for your Son, Jesus Christ. At this time I am asking you to forgive me of my sins as I receive your Son as my Lord and Savior. I do believe He died for me and was raised again to give me new spiritual life. Thank you God for saving me."

I went into the bedroom and woke Doneata up from her nap. I told her the good news.

"Doneata, your husband has become born again." We held each other and cried as each of us gave God the glory for saving my soul.

Eighteen

Shallow Faith

I slept very little the next few days—or should I say weeks. I was so excited to be a Christian that I wanted the whole world to know. I called Charles and told him the good news.

He said, "Larry, I felt like it was only a matter of time before you gave up the struggle. I knew God was dealing with you. My family and I praise the Lord for answering this wonderful prayer. You are now my brother, my brother in Christ.

Monday morning first thing, I went over to Marvin's office. "Good morning, Marvin, how are you doing?"

"It's about time you get to work. I'm already on my second pot of coffee."

"Marvin, I'm glad that it's you that has to be here early on Mondays and not me. Marvin, is Jack in his office?"

"Yeah, but you'd better not go over there right now. Jack and Stanley have been behind closed doors for about half an hour."

"What's up?" I asked.

"I don't know. I'll find out after Stanley leaves."

"Okay, listen I'm not screening today. Let's get Jack and have some Cuban food for lunch."

"Fine by me."

"Marvin, when you see Jack, be sure to mention lunch. I have something I want to tell the two of you."

"Is everything okay?"

"Yeah, this is not bad news; it's good news. I'll tell you and Jack all about it at lunch. Buzz me when you're ready to go."

I walked over to Eddie's office to see how his morning was going. "Good morning, Eddie, how was your weekend?"

"Larry, Jerry and I had a wonderful weekend. We took some old friends out to dinner Saturday night, and yesterday we were invited out to dinner by Judy and Malcolm Schwartz."

"Schwartz—he is your dentist, isn't he?"

"Yes, he is. You know, for some reason I always feel a little self-conscious around Malcolm." Eddie laughed. "I feel like he's always looking at my teeth, but Malcolm and Judy are very nice people." Eddie paused, then asked me, "Larry, did you and the family have a good weekend?"

"We sure did. Eddie before we get busy let me tell you what happened to me this weekend."

He looked up from his receipts, gave me a pleasant smile, and said, "Sit down, and tell me about it."

"Eddie, yesterday the most wonderful thing happened to me: I became a Christian."

Eddie had one of those "you-don't-say" expressions on his face. "You did?"

"Yes, sir. I most certainly did. Right in my living room at home I asked God to forgive me for my life of sin and rebellion to Him. I accepted His Son, Jesus Christ, as my Lord and Savior."

Eddie seemed interested. He went on to say, "Larry, did you know I used to have a leadership position in the Presbyterian church."

I was really taken back. I replied, "No, Eddie, I thought you were Jewish."

"I am, but my first wife was from the Carolinas, and she was a Christian. I used to go with her and our children when the children were little to the Presbyterian church. There was a period of time where I was quite active in the Presbyterian church."

"Well, Eddie, why do you now go to the synagogue and practice the Jewish faith?"

"Because I divorced the Christian girl and married a Jewish lady." Eddie gave me a silly grin and laughed when he said, "I guess you might say the woman that I am married to has a lot to do with what religion I believe. Larry, did you know that in our home Jerry and I celebrate both Christmas and the Jewish Holy Days?"

"How do you do that?"

"I put up a small Christmas tree on the entrance table in our foyer every Christmas while Jerry takes care of the Jewish preparations. Well, Larry, I am glad you and the family have found yourself a church."

Freida stuck her head in the door, looking haughtily at both of us like we were cheating the company out of valuable time and money. "Mr.

Stern, do you want to talk with Colonel Wolfson? He is waiting on line two." I felt that was my cue to get to work.

Jack, Marvin, and I left for lunch at 12:30. While walking down Miami Avenue, I noticed Jack's thoughts seemed to be a thousand miles away. I asked, "Jack, how's your day going?"

"Larry, they have me wearing too many hats around here. Stanley informed me this morning that I have to be in Japan in two weeks. It seems like our wax museum over there needs an overhaul, and guess who gets the project?"

I spoke up, "I didn't even know we had a wax museum in Japan."

"Larry, the company has so much going on that I can't keep up with what we have just bought or just sold. The museum we have had for some time now. I guess Eddie or Stanley failed to mention it to you."

I thought to myself, "I wonder if Walter Powell knows Wometco operates a wax museum in Japan." Then I responded to Jack, "How long are you expected to be over there?"

"Three weeks—three long weeks."

We got to the restaurant and placed our orders. Marvin said, "Okay, Larry, give us this good news you were talking about. I need to hear it; I'm having a miserable day."

Jack interrupted. "You're having a miserable day? I need to go to Japan like I need a hole in my head. I don't know how I am going to get all the work done that needs to be done."

I said, "Fellas, take it easy. That's why you two get paid the big bucks, because you're so good at what you do."

Marvin said, "Oh, shut up! You and Eddie make all the money, and Jack and I do all the work!"

Jack chimed in, "You're right, Marvin. We should have been film buyers instead of gophers."

"Well, I had something important that I wanted to share with my two best friends, but now I'm not going to do it because you have hurt my feelings."

Marvin stood up reached into his back pocket and took out his handkerchief. He started pretending to wipe tears out of his eyes; then he reached over and put both his hands on my shoulders. "I'm so sorry."

I looked around the room and wondered what all the other people must have been thinking right then; but of course Marvin was never one to care what other people thought. The food came. Marvin divided the beans, rice, bananas, steak, and fries among the three of us, and we started to eat.

While eating, Jack said, "All joking aside, Larry. What did you want to tell us."

I laid my fork down, took a sip of tea and said, "The most wonderful thing happened to me yesterday. I became a born-again Christian."

That statement caught Marvin's attention. I could tell Marvin was all ears. I wasn't sure about Jack's reaction; he continued eating while I was talking. I took the next five minutes to tell them exactly how God had been working in my life and how finally Sunday I gave up control of my life and surrendered my life to Jesus Christ. When I finished talking, Marvin said, "Well, I would have never guessed that's what you wanted to tell us—not the Larry Vaughn I know. Hum, the anti-Christian, old Mr. Independent Larry Vaughn surrendering his life to Jesus Christ! Larry, I am happy for you. I can't wait to tell Sadie."

Jack chimed in, "That is good news, Larry. I'm also happy for you." Turning to Marvin, he asked, "I don't think the meat was as good today as it usually is. Marvin, was your meal okay?"

We paid the bill and went back to the office.

That afternoon I made the rounds. I told the secretaries about my salvation experience. They smiled and the general comment was, "That's good, Larry," but not one single secretary seemed particularly excited to hear that I was now a Christian man. I was so excited about my new-found faith. At the end of the day, I was disappointed at the lack of enthusiasm of my fellow employees. They would have shown more excitement if had I told them I bought a new car. I thought, "What's wrong with them? I have the greatest news in all my life to tell, and all I get from them is a 'That's nice, Larry' or an artificial smile and a 'I'm happy for you.' "

That week I spent several hours at the Bible Bookstore where I bought a nice leather Bible. I even had my name engraved on it. I also purchased some literature written for new Christians, as I was ready to start growing in my faith in Jesus Christ.

The following Sunday morning my family and I went forward during the hymn of invitation to join Grace Church. It was also at that time that I made a public profession of my faith. I was baptized on a Sunday evening a few weeks later. I thought of the old saying, "Never say never!" Sally, my Jewish next-door neighbor, along with several of my other unsaved neighbors and friends, came to see me get baptized. It was a wonderful experience that I shall never forget.

I wasn't quite as bold in sharing my new faith with the film companies. For some reason it seemed harder, and at times it even seemed inappropriate to want to mention my salvation experience to them. I thought, "At the right time I'm going to tell everyone in the motion picture industry about my faith in Jesus Christ, but I'll have to pick the right time."

Pastor Hemstead cornered me one Saturday morning during a church workday. Of course, the first thing I noticed was how the pastor was one to dress up, even for a so-called workday. He wore fresh-pressed jeans, a bit on the tight side, expensive cowboy boots, a thick black belt with a two- to three-inch thick silver buckle, and an off-white western shirt. His long blond hair was combed back with not a single strand out of place. I thought to myself, "The only thing missing is a horse named Trigger."

"Brother Vaughn, I have been wanting to talk to you."

"Pastor, we can talk now, or if you prefer, I would be pleased to take you out to lunch one day next week."

He smiled at me while taking my arm.

"I've seen that smile before," I thought. "I need to try to appreciate it a little more—the smile, that is. Yes, as a Christian now, I should like my pastor's insincere smile. However, if I told myself I liked it—well, to be frank—I'd be telling a lie. Okay, I'll acknowledge his smile. Now, don't look at his smile anymore—concentrate on his eyes."

He was speaking, "No, it won't take long. Why don't the two of us go over there and sit on the bench and talk a few minutes."

"Okay." We walked over to a small bench located beside the playground area.

We made small talk a few minutes before he got around to what he was really wanting to say.

"Brother Vaughn, you know you are now a Christian man."

"Yes, sir."

"Well, the Bible tells us that once we become born again those old things—our old nature—dies, and all things become new."

"Yes, sir."

"Brother Vaughn, are those old things dying with you?"

"Yes, sir. I think so. My language is certainly cleaned up. I used to swear all the time at work, but I don't anymore. Well, I have slipped on occasion, but immediately I confess it to the Lord and ask Him to help me out in that area."

"What about your cigarette smoking? Are you trying to do anything about stopping?"

"Pastor Hemstead, I have tried to stop smoking on and off for the better part of three years now. It seems that whenever I try to cut back on my smoking I get nervous and actually smoke more."

"Brother Vaughn, your smoking is a terrible witness to other Christians and to those people who are unsaved who know that you are a Christian. You should really pray about that and stop that filthy habit."

I didn't like what he just said, but my reply was, "Yes, sir."

He crossed his leg, wiped some dust off of the top of his pointed-toe boot, and said, "Brother Vaughn, you're not going to like what I am about to say, but as your pastor and because I love you and want God's best for you, I am going to say it anyway."

I interrupted him, "Pastor, I might be young in my faith, but I'm a big boy. I can take it—shoot."

As he started to talk, I felt a gust of wind lift my hair from its resting position. I put my fingers through my hair. I then looked at Pastor's hair. "Amazing," I thought. "Not one of his hairs moved against the force of the wind. I'm sure my hair's windblown, but he still looks like he just walked out of a barbershop. I wonder what he uses on his hair. Probably some sort of maximum-strength hair spray or some cement gel. I bet it takes him longer than his wife to get dressed in the mornings. Now, now, Larry, first it was his smile, now his hair. Okay, just look at him in the eyes. For some reason his eyes are not as interesting as his smile and hair."

Pastor Hemstead looked at me as if to read my reaction to what he just said.

"I'm sorry. What did you say?" I responded.

"I think you should quit your job and get in another line of work. Christian men have no business messing with movies."

I thought, "What! I must have missed something while thinking about his hair." I stood up and said, "Thank you, Pastor Hemstead, for your suggestions. Is there anything else?"

He then stood and replied, "No, Brother Vaughn, that has been weighing very heavy on my heart, and I wanted to share it with you."

"Well, I guess I'd better get back to those weeds because I'll have to be leaving in a little while. I'll see you tomorrow, Pastor Hemstead."

For some reason weeds sounded wonderful. I thought, "At least weeds are susceptible to the wind. I don't like things being so fixed that even the wind is unable to play its natural role."

I got off to myself and started sinning in my heart. I was thinking terrible things about Pastor Hemstead. I knew he was right about the smoking: smoking had been bothering me ever since I became a Christian. I used to worry about what cigarettes were doing to my lungs; now it concerned me about what cigarettes were doing to my witness. As far as his statement that Christian men have no business messing with movies, well, I felt he had no business messing with my business! For the rest of the day I struggled with the conversation I had had with the good Pastor Hemstead.

The following Friday night I went by our Dadeland theatre to see how business was going. I brought Doneata with me, since we had gone out to dinner earlier. I parked my car and noticed a long line of people outside the theatre waiting to get in to see the 10:00 p.m. showing of an R-rated movie that I was playing. As I walked past the line going up to the entrance of the theatre, I saw a familiar face: the good Pastor Hemstead and his wife.

I stopped dead in my tracks and asked, "Pastor and Mrs. Hemstead, how are you doing?"

They weren't even embarrassed for me to find them standing there. There they were waiting to go in and see an R-rated movie.

He said, "Hello, Brother and Mrs. Vaughn. We have heard that the acting is so good in this film that we thought we would take a night out and see the movie that everyone is talking about."

I thought to myself, "You hypocrite! or, what is the word? Pharisee? This film is known for its raunchy scenes." Doneata and I left and went on into the theatre. I wasn't about to let the good Pastor and his wife in for free.

On the way home I told Doneata about the conversation I had with Pastor Hemstead a week earlier on the church workday. I said, "Doneata, I may be young in the faith, but I've had that preacher pegged right from day one. He's a three-dollar bill."

"Larry, you shouldn't say such a thing about Pastor Hemstead."

"Doneata, I know men, and I've been around a lot of men like him. I might add that he's one of the worst kind of men—he's a hypocrite. But don't you worry or fret, Doneata. I'm just blowing off steam. I've got a full-time job trying to take care of Larry Vaughn and family. As for your Pastor Hemstead, men like him eventually lose control and expose themselves for what they really are."

Within six months, Pastor Hemstead got caught in some indiscretions with several women in the church. The deacon board asked him to resign, and he left the church.

At work I started noticing things that before salvation I had never given any serious thought to. One problem I was having was in the screening room. All my life I watched movies. I have seen everything from A to Z: One's imagination can most certainly fill in the blanks on what these eyes have seen and ears have heard in my years in the motion picture industry.

For me to grab a sandwich and a Coke and prepare myself to watch two or three movies on a given afternoon was just business as usual. Some of the movies I was now screening were starting to take my breath away. I would leave the screening room feeling like I needed to take a bath because of what I had just sat through. I thought to myself, "I must be more careful with the type of movies I screen."

————

Eddie called me into his office one afternoon. "Larry, can you free yourself up to be in Atlanta next Friday afternoon? Warner Brothers is having a private dinner and a producer's screening of a yet-to-be-released Burt Reynolds film. Warner is having some of their home office executives fly in from L.A. for the event. I'm not sure, but I think Burt Reynolds is scheduled to be at the dinner. I think it important that you plan to be there to represent Wometco."

"Sure, Eddie. Tell you what I'll do; I'll plan on going up Wednesday afternoon. I'll make some appointments with some of the other distributors for Wednesday night, Thursday, and Friday afternoon. Then Friday night I'll attend the dinner and the movie and return to Miami on Saturday morning."

"Sounds good to me."

I immediately went back to my office and called Roger Hill. Roger was the Jacksonville Branch Manager for Warner Brothers. Roger was a young man in his late twenties. He was built sort of like me: tall, skinny, and black headed except he wore big, thick glasses. Soaking wet he probably weighed no more than 140 pounds. Although I had never met her, I understood Roger had a very pretty wife, who was liked by all that knew her. Everyone said, "Roger and his wife make a real cute couple." The rumor had it that Warner Brothers had big plans in the future for Roger, and he was noted for being a very intelligent, level-headed, hard-working company man. He had a very good personality; Roger was a people person. I liked Roger as a person and had the utmost respect for him as a businessman.

His secretary put him on the phone, and he answered, "Hello!"

"Hi, Roger, I wanted to touch base with you about next week."

"Larry, are you talking about the Burt Reynolds's dinner?"

"Yeah, I'll be there."

"Listen, Larry, here's what the two of us are going to do. Of course, we'll have to go to the dinner, but let's not eat anything. Knowing Warner Brothers they will probably serve steak and lobster. Larry, you can get steak and lobster in Miami. I want to take you to the best hamburger joint in the world. It's located right across the street from Georgia Tech. The name of it is The Varsity."

When Roger said, "The Varsity," a memory from years gone by flashed across my mind: The Varsity in Athens, Georgia, where my mother and I used to eat two meals every weekend.

I went on to say, "Roger, I have eaten at The Varsity probably more times than you have. Except I used to go to The Varsity in Athens which was located across the street from The University of Georgia."

"Well, I don't have to waste any more time selling you on The Varsity. Are you game to do it?"

"Absolutely."

"Great, Larry! We'll have a wonderful time, and you'd better eat a light lunch."

Sitting in my seat on the jet bound for Atlanta, I started to let my mind wander. Looking out the window, I started to think about the past few weeks. The church is upside-down. The men wanted Pastor Hemstead to leave, and the women wanted him to stay. I thought to myself, "What a mess. Here I am a new Christian, and my church is without a pastor and in the process of a split. What would the odds be on my joining a church with problems like that? Now that I am a Christian, I have got to get the family back regular at church. I don't think we have been but once in the last month. That's not right. This Hemstead mess is no real excuse for us to stay at home. However, I think Doneata and I were right in considering leaving the church. I wonder how those families that left are doing with the church that started up in the Wests' home? I'm glad I'm on this plane going to Atlanta. This is going to be a fun trip. I'll make those important church-related decisions when I get back to Miami. Right now, I'm going to unwind and enjoy my trip."

While in Atlanta, I always stayed at either the Ritz Carlton Hotel or the Terrace Garden Inn. Both hotels were located in Buckhead. I would usually rotate according to what was going on and who was in town. It's funny how some guys had only one hotel they would stay in, and that was it. So, if they'd rather stay at the Ritz, that's where I would stay; or if they liked the Terrace, then I would stay there. I preferred the Terrace because it had an indoor jogging track, and I was starting to get into running. However, the Ritz Carlton was the hotel of choice in the Atlanta area. On this particular trip I stayed at the Terrace Garden.

I spent Wednesday through Friday afternoon wining and dining film executives from Fox, Paramount, Buena Vista, Columbia Pictures, MGM, and Universal. Late Friday afternoon Roger picked me up at the hotel, and we rode together to the restaurant. Roger was like a little kid talking about our slipping off later to The Varsity.

"Now remember, Vaughn, no eating at the dinner. Just pick through your salad and no more than two bites of your dinner."

"Can I have some popcorn during the movie?"

"Absolutely not! You are not to eat or drink anything during the screening."

"Roger, you're starting to sound like my mother. She always used to worry about my snacking and not being able to eat my dinner."

"Well, the difference between your mother and me is that she would spank you when you didn't listen. If you disobey me, I won't sell you any pictures."

We both laughed at the thought.

The dinner was a typical Warner Brothers dinner. We started out with cocktails and conversation. Everyone was introduced to each other; then we were ushered into a private room where we all sat at one huge table. Red and white wine were served with the delicious meal of Caesar salad, steak, and lobster. Roger and I didn't sit together. He sat with two other film buyers, and I sat with two of his home-office bosses. That gave me a chance to put in a good word for Roger with Corporate, not that it was really needed.

After the dinner, we all walked across the parking lot to the theatre where the screening was to be held. A section of seats was roped off for the Warner staff and their guests. After the screening Roger looked over at me and winked as if to say, "It's party time." I went over and gave my verbal report on the film to Bob Motley, the Warner Division Manager out of Dallas. Then I went outside and smoked a cigarette while waiting on Roger to get his work done.

About 10:15 Roger and I were finally on our way to The Varsity. Roger said, "I don't know about you, but I'm taking my tie off. You don't need anything but an appetite where we're going."

I did the same. During the drive to The Varsity, we talked about the film—what we thought it would do in a given market and about Warner's upcoming releases. When we got to the restaurant, Roger was ready to go; as I recall, he ate two hamburgers, one hot dog, a large order of fries, two Cokes, and some of my onion rings. I don't know where he put all that food. He sure got his money's worth. I think I had a burger, a hot dog, and some onion rings. That was a lot for me.

During the ride back to the hotel, things got quiet. I think it was because we were so full from our overindulgence of eating. After a few minutes Roger asked me, "Larry, what's this I hear going around film row that you have become a Christian? I've had two or three guys ask me, 'Roger, have you heard about Vaughn? He's gone and got religion!'"

You could have knocked me over with a feather! That was the last thing I was expecting to come out of Roger's mouth. I hesitated before I said anything. Then I said, "Yeah, I've decided it's time to settle down. I've got a wife and two kids: I've been burning the candle on both ends for a long time. I think it's time for me to get into church."

"Larry, why did you decide to become a Christian? Tell me more about it."

I was tired and full; I had probably drunk too much wine earlier. I didn't want to talk about things of God. I was trying to use this trip to get away from the church and church-related problems in Miami. I responded, "Roger, sometime I'll tell you all about what I believe and why I believe in what I believe, but, not now. I'm too tired to get into anything heavy tonight." We dropped the discussion at that and returned to the hotel. I went to my room thinking that was probably one of the worst testimonies on record that I had just presented to Roger Hill. I must sit down with Roger soon and share with him my faith in Jesus Christ.

I never saw Roger Hill after that night. Shortly thereafter Roger was critically burned in a hotel fire in Boston. He spent his last few days on this earth in an intensive care room, where his body was charred black beyond recognition. When I heard the news, my thoughts went straight back to that night in Atlanta driving on I-85, and Roger asking me to share with him my faith. Yes, I remember it well: I was too tired—I was too full—I was too carnal to care! As soon as I heard the news, I called Roger's office and asked his secretary if there was any way the hospital would allow visitors. She told me that only the immediate family were allowed to be with him, and that in his condition he was not expected to live very long.

After I talked with Roger's secretary, I got up from my desk and told Betty I had to run an errand. I took a walk over to Biscayne Bay, which was about ten minutes from our office. I sat on a bench overlooking the bay, and I cried out to God asking Him to forgive me for being such a poor witness that night in Atlanta. I prayed that God would save Roger's soul before he died. I prayed that he would show mercy to Roger and use someone, someone with a willing heart to share the gospel, to share Christ with him before he died. I walked back to my office feeling so ashamed of myself for being so shallow in my faith.

———

Even though the family and I were absent more than present from church, we were still growing in our walk with the Lord, seeing as I was still trying to have some consistency in our daily devotions. As I read the Bible, I found that God was continually dealing with me about my cigarette smoking. I remember one afternoon when I took Mentora for a walk. During the walk, I lit up a cigarette. While I was taking a drag from the cigarette, Jim Bishop from the church drove up. Jim slowed down momentarily to chat. We made small talk for a couple of minutes. I was embarrassed for Jim to find me standing there smoking a cigarette in the presence of my daughter.

After Jim left, I thought about how Doneata used to get so upset with me when I would light up a cigarette after church while still on the church grounds. She would say, "Larry, can't you show some respect? You could at least wait until we get off the church property before you start smoking!"

I would come back at her, "Doneata," and I pointed toward the church. "See those old men standing at the front of the church smoking? If they can do it, then why can't I?"

"I'll tell you why. Since when do two wrongs make a right? Please, Larry, don't smoke on church property."

"Okay, it's no big deal to wait an extra minute or two."

That evening at home I read through 1 Corinthians 6. When I read verses 19-20, I stopped, meditated on the verses, and reread them several times: "What? know ye not that your body is the temple of the Holy Ghost *which is* in you, which ye have of God, and ye are not your own? For ye are bought with a price: therefore glorify God in your body, and in your spirit, which are God's."

I never gave any serious thought to what Pastor Hemstead had said to me about my smoking because I had no respect for him as a preacher. However, according to this verse in 1 Corinthians, not only is the local church a temple of the Holy Spirit, but so is my body. I got a sick feeling in the pit of my stomach—I recalled another time when I had that same sick feeling. Yes, it was when I was at Fort Stewart and was told my mother was ill. The scene flashed before my eyes: the captain nervously glancing into my eyes. The long trip home on that road—yes, that road. I remember now—that road represented my life at that time: empty, crooked, lonely. "Oh, God, thank you for saving me from that emptiness. But I'm now having that same feeling. But I shouldn't be. I'm saved now, a new creature. What's the verse? It's something like 'Old things are gone—' No, 'old things are passed away.' Yes, that's right. 'Old things are passed away, and all things are become new.' There's my problem. I'm still clinging to an old thing."

Next thing I knew, I found myself on the ground in a kneeling position. I started to pray: "Heavenly Father, I have been in bondage to cigarettes for many years—yes, many years. Lord, I am asking You to help me do something that I cannot do on my own. Yes, I've tried once before to stop smoking on my own, but I couldn't do it."

I thought back to that time. I was unsaved at the time. I went in to see the doctor. He told me, "Larry, you must stop smoking those cigarettes. You will not live long if you continue to smoke." He went on like doctors do, using all of those medical terms which all boiled down to, "Stop smoking if you want to live to see your daughter enter college!" I left the office and on the way home determined that I would stop smoking.

I thought, "Yeah, I had heard of people who could not stop smoking. They had tried everything, but it was all to no avail. Well, not me—not Larry Vaughn! I can do anything I set my mind to do—yes, and that includes stop smoking."

My knees were starting to hurt. I repositioned myself to release the pressure on my knees. I started to pray again, but then remembered how sure I was that day. Yes, I had gone home and had told Doneata that I was going to stop smoking. She gave me encouraging words. I did well for a few days, but finally I couldn't handle it any more. I looked for an out. I told Doneata I was going to take David to play on the railroad tracks. David loved railroad tracks. I took my cigarettes with me. Yes, David and I made many trips to the tracks.

I knew I couldn't break this habit on my own. I needed a power greater than myself to help me. I continued to pray: "I know Your Word says that my body is a temple of the Holy Ghost, and that I should glorify You with my body. I know the smoking of cigarettes displeases You greatly, as I feel in my spirit the wrong that I am doing every time I smoke a cigarette. Father, my flesh is weak, but my spirit is willing. Please help me overcome this bad habit, which is poor witness of my new life with Christ."

That was the night our great God performed a miracle in my life. I stopped smoking. Did I lose the desire to smoke? No, I didn't. But through His grace I overcame the desire and did not give in to those temptations that had been a part of my life for so many years.

Nancy West telephoned Doneata early one Monday morning to tell her about the church she and her family had visited the day before. The Wests had recently left Grace over the Hemstead issue. Brian and Nancy had two sons, Corey and Kelly. The Wests were a young couple in their early thirties. They were very serious about their relationship with the Lord. They seemed to try very hard to live by biblical standards. Brian and Nancy had been an encouragement to us as we saw how the Lord was working in their lives and in the lives of their children.

Nancy was not one to show her emotion, but this time was an exception. Nancy was so excited she could hardly get the words out. "Doneata, Brian and I have found a church that we really like. We visited "Parker Road" yesterday for the first time. We even went back to their evening service last night. It was a wonderful experience."

She continued, "Now Doneata, let me warn you. Parker Road is not like Grace Church. Their denomination has the reputation of being conservative and Reformed in their theology."

Doneata stopped her in mid-sentence. "Nancy, you need to step down on my level. What do you mean by conservative and Reformed in their theology?"

"Doneata, we'll have to get with our husbands later. Brian can explain the difference between the two denominations better than I can. You and your family must visit Parker Road next Sunday. Knowing Larry the way I do, I'd be surprised if he doesn't really like Parker Road."

"Nancy, this is perfect timing. Larry has been saying every day that we have got to get back into church. I know he'll want to visit Parker Road."

The next Sunday my family and I visited Parker Road. We arrived at the church about ten minutes before the morning service was to start. We sat about halfway down on the left side of the auditorium The church building itself was new and beautiful. It wasn't as large as Grace; the auditorium could probably seat 250 to 300 at best.

Nancy was right when she said I would like Parker Road. I appreciated the entire service: the order of the service, the music, the preaching of the Word, and the people. After the service, we stopped and talked briefly with the pastor. His name was "Terry Yaegar." Pastor Yaegar had a quietness about him, but there was also a warmth about him that made me want to get to know him. He was in his early forties, married, with two teenage sons. I found his appearance to be more in line with that of a pastor than an entertainer. He had a nice face, brown eyes, thin lips, and a very warm, personable smile. He dressed nicely: gray suit, conservative tie, and black wing-tip shoes. I enjoyed hearing him talk. His vocabulary was perfect—he had mastered the English language. I could tell he was an educated man. That evening on the way out of church Pastor Yaegar stopped me and invited my family to come to his home for dinner on Friday night. I was pleased that he had invited us, and I accepted the invitation right there on the spot.

On the drive home from church that night I told Doneata, "Honey, this has been a wonderful Lord's Day. You know what I like about Pastor Yaegar?" I didn't give her time to respond, "I like the way he preaches. I got a lot out of both of his messages today. His preaching is more like teaching. You remember the way Pastor Hemstead used to preach at us, not really giving us biblical training? Well, Pastor Yaegar has points I can follow, and he uses the Scriptures as his basis for what he says. Did you notice he didn't even pace the platform once! Let alone run back and forth across it, and he didn't yell one time. Also, did you notice he forgot to give an invitation at both services?"

"Larry, I am so happy that you're happy." Doneata agreed that it was a wonderful day.

Friday evening we arrived at the Yaegars' home at 6:30. Both of their sons were gone for the evening—it was just the six of us for dinner. While Doneata and "Faye" were putting the dinner on the table, Pastor Yaegar gave me the tour of his home. It was a most expressive large home, with a large lot located in one of the better neighborhoods in South Miami. I was surprised to see he had his own private tennis court in his back yard. I thought to myself, "Pastor Yaegar must have had money before he got into the ministry. A preacher's salary alone can't meet this overhead."

The dinner was delicious. Faye Yaegar was a wonderful cook. Doneata and I could tell she had really gone out of her way to make the evening special for us. During dinner Doneata and I gave the Yaegars our testimony about when we became Christians and how we were now looking for a new church home. Pastor Yaegar was fascinated with my occupation.

He said, "Larry, I have always been a big fan of spy novels—that's what I do to unwind. I have read all of Ian Fleming's books on James Bond and seen most of the films."

I commented, "Pastor, I too, am a big fan of Ian Fleming. I've read all of his books and seen all of the James Bond films." I spent most of the time at dinner answering questions about film buying and the motion picture industry. Pastor Yaegar commented to me about how he had always had a fascination with how "corporate America" operates.

After dinner we had a time of conversation and coffee. I asked Pastor Yaegar to tell me about his denomination and Reformed theology. He gave me a brief history of the denomination and spent some time explaining the two different viewpoints each denomination supports concerning man and his free will in those areas, in reference to things of God.

He said, "You have been in a denomination that teaches the Arminian view. Those believers who follow the teaching of Arminius believe a lot of the responsibility for one's salvation depends on man's own personal decision about whether or not he accepts the gospel. Arminians believe in the possibility of salvation for all. The doctrines of Arminius opposes the absolute predestination taught by Calvin and the Reformers, which the Reformed faith supports. Calvinism, on the other hand, is marked by a strong emphasis on the sovereignty of God and especially by the doctrine of predestination."

He paused for a moment, then continued. "Larry and Doneata, this is a subject that we could spend the rest of the year talking about, and you know what? We would still have questions next year. However, it is important to know what you believe, and why you believe what you believe. That is why we have an eight-week class for new members that those desiring membership must go through before they are allowed to join Parker Road. We want people to understand the teachings of the Reformed faith."

He then encouraged us to hold off on any further questions until we had time to go through the new members' class. He said, "The new members' class will answer all your questions and give you a thorough and complete introduction to the Reformed faith."

On the drive home I commented to Doneata, "This has been a very interesting evening. I'm looking forward to this new members' class just to find out more about what those folks believe the Bible has to say about man and his free will. Doneata what did you think about the evening?"

"Honey, the Yaegars are the nicest people. I just love Faye. She really went out of her way to make everything so special. Did you notice the bouquet of flowers she had on the dining room table? I also believe Pastor Yaeger is a very sincere man."

I caught a hint of something in her voice. "Doneata, do you have any reservations?"

"Well, Larry, did you notice their home? I've never seen a preacher with so much wealth." Doneata then second-guessed herself. "But there's nothing wrong with a preacher having so much—it's just that I wasn't expecting it."

"Honey, I know exactly what you're talking about. I remember the first time I saw Elvis—I mean Pastor Hemstead. I was really taken back."

We both laughed as Doneata reached over and popped me on the arm. "Larry, you had better quit making jokes about Pastor Hemstead and start praying for him. He and his family are in great need of prayer."

"Honey, you're right. I'm sorry. Grace is all torn apart, and I'm sitting here making light of it. I am ashamed of myself." I paused for a moment, then continued. "Well, Doneata, let's sum up the evening."

She smiled as if to say, "You always like to organize each event in your life, putting the positives and negatives in their proper place." I really don't know why I had the habit of summing up everything mentally and then storing it in its proper file. Doneata was now looking at me, wondering when I would give her my "outline."

Doneata glanced at me and said, "Well?"

"I like the Yaegers very much. I want to give Parker Road a serious try. Starting next Sunday, let's get involved in Sunday school and plan on attending the new members' class."

"Larry, I just want to get back in church. The last few weeks I have missed terribly our not having a place to worship."

Nineteen

A Vapor

"Larry, I need to see you in my office, right now."

"Okay, Eddie, I'll be right there." I wondered what the cause of Eddie's urgency was. When I arrived at his office, I asked, "What's doing?"

"Larry, Stanley just left my office. He informed me that Jack has a very large tumor in his right kidney. Dr. Manos suspects the tumor to be malignant."

"What? That's terrible news! When did all this come about?"

"Stanley said that late yesterday after everyone had left, Jack, on his way out stopped by the men's room and started urinating blood. This morning the hospital made some x-rays and found the tumor."

"Eddie, did Stanley say when they are going to operate?"

"Thursday morning at South Miami Hospital."

"I'll be sure to start remembering Jack and Ann in my prayers."

"Larry, he's going to need them."

I went back to my office and called Doneata. I told her to call Ann Mitchell and see if there was anything we could do. This shouldn't have come as a surprise: Jack had been pale as milk for some time now. I noticed at lunch he hadn't been acting like his old self. I just figured Jack was keeping himself stressed to the limit.

About that time Marvin came into my office. He looked tired and worried. "Have you heard about Jack?"

"Yeah, Eddie told me the news a few minutes ago."

"Larry, I just left a twenty-minute meeting with Stanley. Guess who's the new acting General Manager. Yours truly! That's right. Stanley wants me to fill in for Jack during his absence."

"Marvin, I know your desk is going to be busy for the next few weeks. I'll try not to drive you crazy making any last-minute booking changes.

Marvin, we really need to hold up Jack and Ann in prayer the next forty-eight hours."

"You're right. I haven't even told Sadie the news. I'd better go call her before she hears it from someone else. Oh, Larry, by the way, I won't be riding home with you after work. Sadie is going to pick me up. She wants me to ride with her up to North Miami to exchange a gift at Neiman Marcus."

On the way home I stopped by the hospital to visit Jack and Ann. When I walked into the room, Jack was lying there in bed with his eyes closed. No one else was in the room. I tiptoed over to the bed, bent down, and whispered in Jack's ear, "Are you dead or just sleeping?"

Somewhat startled, Jack opened his tired eyes and said, "I ain't sleeping, and I sure ain't dead! I'm just resting." He held out his hand—I bypassed it and reached over to give him a hug.

"Larry, don't you fret one little bit. I am going to beat this thing. Thursday it will all be over."

"I'm not worried about you old pal. Marvin is the one I'm concerned about. Stanley gave Marvin his marching orders today. I think Marvin is the one that's going to need a transfusion."

Jack started laughing, "This will be good experience for Marvin. That is if it doesn't kill him."

"Where's Ann?"

"She went down to the cafeteria to get something to eat. She should be back any minute now."

"Well, I'll hang around until she comes back." Just when I was about to ask Jack if I could have prayer with him, Stanley came walking into the room singing "It's cookie time."

Stanley was carrying a large, brown box with at least two dozen bags of assorted Pepperidge Farms cookies. Stanley gave Jack and me an uncharacteristically silly look, shrugged his shoulders, and said, "Jack, I forgot which was your favorite, so I bought you a box of each."

As Stanley found his resting place on the side of Jack's bed, I thought it was time I said my good-byes and headed on home.

While driving home, I was thinking just how quickly everything can change. Farrell died so young. And my mother, she died so suddenly. Roger Hill was alive in Atlanta and dead in Boston. David, he was healthy one day and diagnosed with leukemia the next. Now Jack is lying in that hospital bed about to have cancer surgery—a few days ago he seemed fine. What did I read recently in my Bible about the uncertainties of life? I think it was from the book of James. Yes that's it, James 4:14: "Whereas ye know not what shall be on the morrow. For what is your life? It is even a vapor, that appeareth for a little time, and then vanisheth away."

I thought, "That verse is so true. What is life but a vapor? I'm glad God doesn't allow me to know what's in store for tomorrow. The trials and cares of today are all I can handle. That's a good verse for me to share with the family during our devotional time tonight. Maybe I'll also share the verse with Marvin tomorrow. It disturbs me to see how he is letting things get to him the way he did at the office today."

The next morning, Marvin picked me up at 8:10 sharp. One of the many things I liked about Marvin was the fact that he was always on time. Never late, never early—that was one of Marvin's quirks. I asked him, "Did you see Jack last night?"

"No, it was too late to go by the hospital when we got back to South Miami. I talked to him though." Marvin inhaled then exhaled a deep breath. "Jack's ready for the surgery."

"How about you, Marvin? Are you doing okay?"

"Sure, I'm fine. I'm just a bit on the tired side."

"You were really upset yesterday. You shouldn't let your work get to you like it does; it's only a job, Marvin."

"Larry, to be honest with you, I didn't sleep much at all last night. I'm just stressed out."

"I understand how you feel, Marvin; but as Christian men, we need to look past our circumstances and look to the One who controls these circumstances. Last night on the way home from the hospital, I thought of a Scripture verse. It was James 4:14." I quoted the verse to Marvin; then I continued. "Marvin, that verse is for you, Jack, and me today. You need to give your work to the Lord. Ask Him to give you the strength and wisdom needed to get through today and live one day at a time."

Marvin dropped his shoulders and sighed. "Well, I guess you're right."

"Marvin, I'm not the one that's right; it's God's Word that is right." We were quiet the rest of the way to the office.

Dr. Manos came out from surgery. He addressed Ann. "As far as I can tell, the surgery looks like a total success." Ann spilled tears of joy when she heard that her loved one was going to be okay. Dr. Manos went on to say, "I took out the right kidney because the tumor was completely enclosed in it. I feel very confident that I got it all, but I still need to get some test results back to make absolutely sure the cancer hasn't spread to any other parts of his body. Ann, Jack will be in recovery for a couple of hours before being sent to his room. Why don't you and your friends go have a cup of coffee."

Doneata and I stayed at the hospital until Jack came out of recovery. I'm sure he didn't remember our being there, but Ann did; and that was reason enough for our staying there.

Jack got a clean bill of health from Dr. Manos. He was at home recuperating within a few days. The next few weeks Marvin didn't know whether he was coming or going, trying to do his work along with all of Jack's General Manager responsibilities. There were days that I couldn't even get Marvin to break long enough to go to lunch. I didn't like what I saw happening to Marvin. I could tell the responsibility that was put on his shoulders was starting to break him down.

———

That year Doneata and I decided that our family was getting too big for apartment living. We bought a nice three-bedroom, two-bath home in the Cutler Ridge area. Cutler Ridge is about ten miles south of Dadeland. The home was actually a four bedroom, but the previous owner had knocked out a wall separating the master bedroom from the fourth bedroom. The extra space gave Doneata and me a large-enough bedroom to accommodate all our bedroom furniture, plus enough room for a sitting area. The den had two glass sliding doors which led out to the pool. We had a nice large swimming pool which took up approximately one third of the space in our back yard. Around the pool was a very nice cement walk and deck with the far end large enough to accommodate a table, four chairs, and two chaise longue chairs. The back yard was completely enclosed with hedges and a chain link fence. We also had a large eat-in kitchen with a living room and dining room located off the kitchen.

Moving that far south gave me an extra fifteen minutes to drive each way to work. I would drive to our Dadeland theatre and meet Marvin in the theatre's parking lot. We would ride the city bus the additional thirty minutes to the office.

I came in from work one Tuesday afternoon and went into the bedroom to change into some shorts and a tee shirt. Doneata followed me into the bedroom and sat down on the side of the bed. I had seen that look before. I knew Doneata had something she wanted to tell me.

I said, "Honey, how has your day been?"

"Just lovely."

"Anything special doing?"

"Uh huh."

"Do you want to talk about it?"

"Uh huh."

"Shoot."

Doneata stood up walked over to me and put her arms around my neck. Then she whispered in my ear, "We're going to have a baby."

I immediately put my hands around her waist and pushed her back so I could look straight into her face. "Doneata, are you joking with me?"

"Only if Dr. Friedman is joking with me. I left his office at 3:30 today. He said, 'Doneata, you are 100 percent pregnant!' "

"Honey, that is wonderful news! I wonder if it's going to be a boy or a girl."

Doneata said, "Darling, I don't care what it is as long as it's healthy and doesn't scream all the time."

I thought a minute when she said healthy and scream. "Yes, we must pray daily that this child will be not only a healthy child but also a happy child."

We took David and Mentora out to dinner that night and shared the exciting news with them. We told them, "Before summer you are going to have a little baby sister or brother."

David asked, "Dad, does this mean that we will have to move again?"

"No, Son; we'll manage where we are."

"Good, Dad. I love our swimming pool."

———

During that period of time Eddie and I were staying very busy trying to keep the important movies in Wometco theatres. Eddie and I both felt the pressure as more theatres were continuing to be built in the south Florida area. The marketplace was so competitive that it was all we could do sometimes to keep our theatres booked with good, playable product.

When working on bids for a picture, I suggested to Eddie, "This may sound a bit bazaar, but hear me out. To ensure that we are awarded this picture in our theatres, let's guarantee to the film company what we think the picture is actually going to gross at the box office."

Eddie interrupted, "Larry, are you suggesting that going in we make it our intent to pay 100 percent film rental?"

"That's correct. But please hear me out. Say we agree the picture in question should gross say $40,000 in a particular theatre. Then that is exactly how much money we will bid for the picture. If we have guessed right, then the film company will get every dollar that we take in at the box office. If we guessed high and the film takes in only $33,000, then we have to eat the $7,000 loss. And if the picture grossed better than our expectations, then there will be a few dollars left over for Wometco."

I could tell by Eddie's squirming that he didn't like what I was saying. Eddie interrupted again. "Larry, maybe we should just close the theatres and open some grocery stores. We can't stay in business by thinking that way."

"Eddie, we will have our other auditoriums in each particular theatre working with the expectation of making money. This auditorium will be the only auditorium used in the theatre for the purpose of bringing in traffic and giving us additional concession sales. I think it would be better to have the picture with high film rental than to have an auditorium with no bodies in it."

"Larry, I've had to eat a lot of bad bids, but I have never done it intentionally. However, since there are no pictures on the market, let's try it your way on this one and see what happens."

Yes, the marketplace was extremely competitive. I felt that if I could get the picture on the screen, then at least we could sell some popcorn and Cokes. That beats the alternative of not having the picture and being left with an empty auditorium.

A few weeks later Eddie called me into his office. "Larry, I have gone over every playdate on your 100 percent guarantees, and I don't think we got hurt anywhere. The Colonel is going to raise both his eyebrows when he sees our high film rental percentage, but it ended up being the lesser evil of the two. That was a good idea you had, but let's be sure to use it sparingly."

Before I became a Christian, the part of my work I enjoyed the most was the screening of movies, but now when I went to the screening room, I would spend more time with my eyes closed than with them open. It really concerned me the types of movies I was watching in the screening room. It seemed every other word spoken in some films was a curse word, and the nudity seemed to get worse with each movie I screened.

One afternoon Marvin and I were sitting on the bus taking our daily afternoon ride to Dadeland. I started talking to Marvin about the theatre business. "Marvin, does your work ever bother you as far as your relationship with the Lord?"

Marvin closed his eyes, tilted his head, and partially opened his eyes as he turned my way and said, "Larry, what are you referring to?"

"Well, I was thinking about that movie we screened yesterday—all it was, was trash—trash from start to finish. I can't get some of those scenes out of my mind."

Marvin spoke to me as if he were talking to a child. "Larry, we don't have anything to do with the making of movies or which movies people choose to go see. If we start getting convicted about all the junk that is put into movies, we'll go crazy."

Marvin thought a minute. I could tell his wheels were spinning. "You don't allow Doneata and the kids to come to any of the screenings, do you?"

"As a general rule, no, I don't. However, I did invite Doneata to come to the screening last Thursday night when I found out Walter Matthau would be there to look at his new film. Doneata has always liked Walter Matthau; she enjoyed meeting him. He even gave her his autograph on one of his personal checks. Unfortunately, he wrote void where the amount goes."

Marvin laughed. "That's too bad. I would love to have a blank check signed by Mr. Matthau."

"Marvin tell me about your salvation experience."

When I said that, Marvin wiped his brow, took in a deep breath, and exhaled very noisily, as if to say he was frustrated and getting a headache. "Larry, what is it with you here lately? I can't ride to or from work or even go to lunch with you without you wanting to talk about the Lord."

"Okay, Marvin, don't get so touchy."

"Well, if you don't mind my being frank with you, I'm tired of your always drilling me on Bible verses and questions, questions, and more questions. If you want to continue riding to work with me and having lunch with me, then you had better find someone else to answer all your biblical questions about life, because frankly I'm tired of hearing it."

I didn't say a word; I just sat there thinking, "Marvin is either in sin or unsaved."

After a few seconds, I said, "I'm truly sorry, Marvin, that I have made you so upset with me. In the future I won't bring up the subject. Your friendship means a lot to me, and I don't want us to stop busing to work together or going to lunch together."

Marvin looked over at me; he seemed to have an expression on his face of genuine concern that I understand exactly what it was that he was trying to say. "Larry, it's just that here lately religion is all you talk about, and I get tired of hearing it all the time. And another thing, I'm tired of you coming over to my office and finding some fault in every magazine or press book on my desk. I'm just tired of it. If you ask me, you're getting legalistic."

I thought, "Legalistic? I'll have to find out what that word means."

"Larry, why don't you work on converting Jack, Stanley, and Eddie instead of me?"

When he said that, I thought to myself, "I thought you and Jack were already converted."

We were quiet the rest of the ride home. I wondered what happened to that fun-loving guy that used to keep me in stitches—that guy that reminded me so much of Farrell, my deceased half-brother. Has Marvin changed or have I changed? I knew I had to be careful with Marvin in the future or he was going to start avoiding me.

———

On the fourth of May in 1981, Doneata gave birth to a 9-pound 15½-ounce baby boy. We named him Larry David Vaughn Jr. I remember the first time I saw him; I was expecting to see a large version of what Mentora looked like when she was born, but he didn't look anything at all like Mentora did when she was born. Mentora was the most beautiful baby, but this big guy looked just like Alfred Hitchcock or maybe Winston Churchill, but nothing like Doneata or me. When we got him home, we were pleased to find our not-so-handsome baby was at least a good baby. He had three desires in this life: to be fed, changed, and left alone.

We had cake and ice cream when celebrating David's fifth anniversary from being diagnosed with leukemia. Not that the memory of that day in itself was a pleasant memory—no, quite the contrary. But the celebration was that David had hung in there, and his cancer had been in remission for five long years.

I remembered thinking back to that Monday afternoon in April of 1976. That was the day when Dr. Flicker had told Doneata and me to prepare ourselves to have David with us for maybe two years. Looking back today, Dr. Flicker's prediction would have been correct with a number of the other children who were being treated for leukemia at Jackson along with David. Many of those dear children died during those first two years.

During those five years, David was not able to attend school with any regularity. The trips back and forth to Jackson for treatments and the physical toll the chemotherapy and radiation took on his body were all his mind and body could handle. He even went completely bald for a second time. His second baldness was after all his hair had grown back, and he had a complete head of hair. One day David came into the house from playing. When he took off his baseball cap. Doneata noticed inside the rim of the cap a huge clump of David's hair. By the time I got home from work, both Doneata and David were still crying over the loss of his hair. Those were five tough years, but God gave us the grace and strength to get through them. I knew we were blessed to still have David alive and in remission from his deadly leukemia.

We had the privilege of sitting under Pastor Yaegar's ministry for only a few months. He shocked the congregation one Sunday morning by announcing that he and his family would be leaving Parker Road as the Lord was calling him to another ministry in another section of the country. Doneata and I were both saddened to hear that the Yaegars would be leaving Parker Road. The few months we spent under his ministry at Parker Road were a wonderful learning experience for us. Weekly, we were being taught the doctrines of the Reformed faith in the new members' class. Both Doneata and I were beginning to grow spiritually, and for the first time we were being fed sound doctrinal teaching from the Word of God every Sunday and Wednesday.

Within a few weeks the Pulpit Committee brought in a young man in his mid-thirties by the name of "Robert Short" to candidate for the position of minister at Parker Road. The Reverend Short was from Scotland. He was tall and fairly thin. He had a fair complexion with red hair that he wore parted on the left side, combed over the top of his head, and brushed back on both sides. He wore a perfectly manicured beard and mustache on his long, narrow face. He had a sharp Scottish accent and a very unusual laugh. He was married to a tall, very thin, rather cute, blond girl from Alabama. Her name was "Joan." Joan, like her husband, had an outgoing, warm personality. The Shorts had two small children: a daughter, "Mandy," and a son, "Sean." Everyone at Parker Road welcomed the Shorts with open arms into the church family.

Jack called a meeting in his office at 2:30 on a Friday afternoon. The purpose of the meeting was to go over playdates on a Clint Eastwood movie we were scheduled to open in several of our theatres in about four weeks. I was in the meeting along with Jack, Marvin, and two district managers: Leo Brown and Tom Jarrard. There were also several of our theatre managers present who were scheduled to play the picture in their theatres.

Jack asked me to give the group a report on the Eastwood film since I had seen it a few days earlier in Dallas. Jack also asked me to share with the men how important it was to the company that we do exceptionally well on the film. Jack didn't want me to give out any figures, and yet he wanted me to let the men know the importance of this picture. With as many playdates as we had on the film and the large guarantees, this one picture could "make or break" our month at the box office.

After I gave the guys a good pep talk and hyped the film to the point that they were all starting to get excited about playing the picture, Jack then proceeded to take out his yellow legal pad with a check list of advertising and promotion ideas. Jack had several things he wanted each man to do to ensure that we got the maximum gross out of the picture when it opened. Jack went one by one around the room, giving each man instructions about what he wanted each individual to do in preparation for the opening of the film.

When Jack got around to Marvin, he told Marvin to contact a certain radio station and try to work up a promotion on the film. Marvin was very negative on using that particular station. In fact, Marvin started using curse words when explaining to Jack the bad experience he had with the station on other promotions. Marvin even went as far as to take the Lord's name in vain in describing his displeasure with the station. I looked over at Marvin; he acted as though I wasn't even in the room. I thought to myself, "That's it. I'm going to talk to Marvin, and I don't care if he ever speaks to me again."

Later that afternoon I walked over to Marvin's office to discuss with him a different matter when he cursed again. This time it was during a phone conversation he was having with one of the managers. I thought to myself, "I wonder if he's now trying to make a statement to me. I don't know what he's doing. What happened to the Marvin that used to be disagreeable only when he didn't get his fair share of steak and French fries? And even then he did so with an air of jest."

That afternoon we rode to Dadeland together on the bus. We had very little to say to one another. Marvin spent most of the time reading his *Variety* entertainment magazine, while I sat thinking. "When am I going to have a talk with this guy?" We got off the bus and walked over to our cars. I started to say something then, but I thought, "No, the time's not right. I had better bathe this conversation in prayer before I talk to Marvin." We wished each other a good weekend and then went our separate ways.

Driving home from Dadeland I got to thinking about the night ahead. Mrs. Short had called Doneata earlier in the week and invited our family to dinner at their home Friday evening. I thought, "This is a good way to start the weekend—getting to know Pastor and Mrs. Short and their children. If first impression means anything, I think I'm going to really like the Short family."

We arrived at the Shorts' home at 6:30. I was most impressed with their home and neighborhood. It wasn't an estate home with a tennis court like the Yaegars' home, but it was a very nice home in one of the nicer areas of South Miami. I thought to myself, "Financially, preachers must do okay." After a brief time of introduction, the girls went into the kitchen, the kids went into the back yard, and the guys went into the den. Pastor Short asked me, "Brother, what would you like to drink? We have tea, soft drinks, wine, and ice-cold beer."

I replied, "Pastor, I'll have whatever you're having."

"Then you're having an ice-cold Budweiser."

I thought to myself, "So much for wondering if the pastor is a wine drinker."

As Pastor Short made his way to the refrigerator, he said, "Larry, it's Friday night. Please feel free to call me Robert."

"Okay, Robert it is." I thought to myself, "I wish I had asked for a glass of wine since I'm not a beer drinker." He returned with two beers, and we sat there and watched "Wheel of Fortune" on TV while drinking our beer.

After dinner the four of us went out on the patio while the children stayed in the den playing games. Larry Jr. was entertaining himself playing in his playpen. I had intended on asking the pastor, I mean Robert, some theological questions, but I could see that he and Joan were more interested in relaxing and getting to know our family. We ended up staying until 10:30. Much of the evening was given to my talking about the motion picture industry. Like everyone else, the Shorts seemed fascinated with the movies and movie stars. Doneata and Joan enjoyed each other almost as much as Robert and I enjoyed each other. I could tell we were going to become close friends.

After we got home and got the kids down for the night, I told Doneata about Marvin's behavior during the meeting in Jack's office earlier in the afternoon. She said, "Larry, we must pray for Marvin; he's never acted this bad since we've known him."

"Doneata, it's the office. Ever since Jack had his surgery, I've seen a big change in Marvin. I know he's under a lot of stress, but for a man who claims to know Christ, he sure doesn't act like a Christian. I don't know—maybe he's just a backslider. Anyway, I'm going to talk with him next week. Let's be sure to pray about this over the weekend."

I was sitting at my desk Monday morning looking at the box office receipts from the weekend. I really didn't have my mind on how much business the theatres were doing; my mind was on Marvin. All weekend I couldn't get him off my mind. I knew I had to talk to him, so why procrastinate any longer? I walked across the hall to his office. He was on the phone. I sat down across from him and propped my feet up on the corner of his desk. He looked up at me as if to say, "Who do you think you are?"

I yawned, stretched, and started rubbing my stomach. I whispered, "Let's do lunch today." He put his hand over the receiver and said, "I don't want no Cuban food."

"Me neither. Let's go down to Burdines."

"Okay. What time?"

"Just buzz me when you're ready to go."

He nodded in agreement; then I left. Going back to my office I thought, "Perfect timing! He's in a good mood."

Burdines was one of the major department stores in Miami. On the ground floor of their downtown store they had a restaurant called The Market Place. It was a good place to go for a piled-high turkey or pastrami sandwich.

We got to the restaurant early, just before noon. I ordered my usual smoked turkey on whole wheat with a side order of potato salad, while Marvin went with a rare roast beef on rye. We both had water with lemon and a cup of their gourmet coffee to drink. Since we were early, I was able to pick out a table for two located off to the side of the restaurant. We were sitting right beside the floor-to-ceiling glass wall which over-looked Miami Avenue. I liked being able to watch the variety of people walking up and down Miami Avenue while we were having our lunch. I thought to myself, "This is the perfect place to be seated today. We're right in the middle of everything, but there are no other tables anywhere near us. This is probably the best seat in the restaurant."

While eating our sandwiches, Marvin was telling me about the meeting he had earlier that morning with Jack. "Larry, Jack's got me running from morning to night. You won't believe the schedule I have this week. He's got me doing everything but painting the theatres."

We both laughed. It was good to be able to catch a glimpse of the old Marvin. I wondered how long Marvin was going to stay that way once I started talking to him about this luncheon's hidden agenda.

When we finished eating our lunch, I walked over and got two fresh cups of hot coffee. I said a brief prayer that the Lord would give me those words that He would have me say to Marvin and that our talk would be a good one.

I took a sip of coffee, pushed my chair back from the table, crossed my legs, and rested my elbow on the table. "Marvin there is something I must talk with you about. It has been weighing heavily on my mind all weekend, and to be perfectly honest with you, that's why I asked you to go out to lunch today."

I looked directly at Marvin, wondering how he was going to respond. Without showing any emotion Marvin looked straight at me, smiled slightly, and said, "What is it, Larry?"

"Marvin, I know you and I have had several conversations about our relationship with Christ, but I want to have one more talk with you." I looked into his face, expecting to see anger starting to build, but it wasn't there. He had a blank expression on his face as if to say, "Okay, I'll hear you out."

"Marvin, it concerns me greatly to see how you have been behaving the last few months. I guess you don't realize it, but at the office you have been a terrible witness as a Christian. Friday afternoon in Jack's office you even took our Lord's name in vain, and that wasn't a slip of the tongue as you also said several more curse words during that meeting." I looked at Marvin. He sat there looking sort of numb, but I could tell he was taking in every word I had to say.

I continued. "Marvin, do you realize that the only Christ that Eddie, Jack, Stanley, and all the other people that we work and come in contact with might see is the Christ they see in you and me?" He didn't respond; so I kept on talking. "You get upset with me every time I want to talk about spiritual things. You've even threatened to stop associating with me because of my interest in those things of God. Marvin, the way you're thinking and acting is not the normal way a Christian man thinks and acts. Marvin, you're either terribly backslidden and in deep sin, or you're unconverted and have a head knowledge but not a heart knowledge of Jesus Christ."

He still sat there with no expression, but I could tell he was still taking in every word that came out of my mouth.

"Marvin, if I were you, I would do one of two things: I would get right with my God today, or I would put my Bible in the attic and stop claiming to be something I'm not. You know, Marvin, that Jesus had some strong words to say to individuals who act like you have been acting. In Revelation 3:15-16 Jesus says, "I know thy works, that thou art neither cold nor hot: I would thou wert cold or hot. So then because thou art lukewarm, and neither cold nor hot, I will spew thee out of my mouth."

Marvin cleared his throat, pulled his chair closer to the table, then placed his arm on the table and started rubbing his wedding band with his fingers. He didn't say anything at first; then he looked at me and said, "Larry, I needed to hear that. You're right! You're absolutely right in everything you said."

Marvin then took a deep breath and exhaled the air out very loudly. "Larry, the problem is that the office is driving me crazy. I'm not sleeping at night. I'm angry; I have no peace." He paused, then continued. "Yes, I'm out of fellowship with the Lord, but, Larry—" Marvin then looked very sternly at me, "I am a Christian. I made things right with the Lord several years ago before I had my bypass heart surgery. I know Jesus is my Savior; I'm just out of fellowship."

"Marvin, you just said you know what the problem is—the office. Marvin, the office is not the problem. Your being out of fellowship with God is the problem. You can't see the forest for the trees. Look at all the ways God has blessed you. Look at your home for instance—it's beautiful. Have you ever thought that your home is much nicer and more expensive than Stanley's, Jack's, Eddie's, or mine? You and Sadie both have a clean bill of health. Financially, you've told me yourself that you're not hurting. I wish I had as much Wometco stock as you have. Why, I'd probably retire and take the family on a trip around the world." We both chuckled about that statement.

"Seriously, Marvin, the Lord has blessed you greatly, and you have been acting so unappreciative for all He has done for you. Your problem, Marvin, is that you have surrounded yourself with all these material things, and you have left God out. You can't keep adding things to things and think that is going to solve the problem. The Bible says that naked came we into the world and naked we shall leave. Marvin, you need to start thinking about those things of God and forget about these temporal pleasures of this earth. They are all going to burn up one day."

Marvin replied, "You mean when I die I won't be able to have a U-haul with all my stuff going to heaven with me?"

We both laughed, and I continued. "Marvin, do you know what I would do if my job bothered me like you say your job bothers you?"

"No, what?"

"I would make a change. I would go to Jack and tell him we have a problem and ask him if there's any way we can work it out. If not, then I would leave Wometco and find employment elsewhere."

"Who would be interested in hiring a fifty-three-year-old man who has had open-heart surgery?"

"You don't know the answer to that until you've asked."

"Larry, you've given me a lot to think about today. I'm going to go home tonight and do some serious soul searching."

"Marvin, you are not only my best friend, you are also my brother in Christ. I am so pleased we had this talk today."

"Me too. Larry, do you realize what time it is? It's 2:20!"

"Marvin, you may not have to pray about your job. You may be fired when you get back to the office."

We both laughed as we quickly cleared our empty plates off the table.

On the way back to the office Marvin told me, "Oh, by the way, I won't be busing in with you in the morning. I have to put the car in the shop at Dadeland. I'll catch the earlier bus downtown."

"Okay, I'll see you when I get to the office."

That evening I spent the better part of an hour telling Doneata all about my wonderful luncheon with Marvin. I finished by saying, "Doneata, our God is so good! It could not have been a better meeting. I know God blessed in a very special way my time with Marvin today." We stopped and gave God thanks.

The next morning I catnapped during the thirty-minute bus ride downtown. When I got off the bus at Burdines, I started the ten-minute walk to Wometco. After I got about three blocks up North Miami Avenue, I noticed two police cars and an ambulance parked alongside the street with their lights on. There was an old man who looked rather shabby sitting in the back seat of one of the police cars.

The police were using yellow tape to mark off a large section of the sidewalk. I also noticed a third car, an old model car with the front end smashed in, parked between the police cars. I thought, "That must be the car that old man was driving." As I got closer, I noticed there was a man who looked to be dead lying on the sidewalk face down without a shirt on. It looked like the police officer had partially covered the body with a piece of black plastic. There were also tire marks where a car had run up on the sidewalk. I also noticed a storefront wall was damaged and cracked from what looked like an impact of some kind. The wall had fresh blood along the side of it. I thought to myself, "Most likely, that guy lying there without a shirt on is a derelict. I'd bet he was asleep on the sidewalk and somehow that old car ran over him and threw him against the wall." It was nothing to walk around downtown and see street people lying around everywhere.

A merchant walked over, and I said, "Probably a derelict lying there." He said, "No, I don't think so. That police officer over there said the man was a businessman."

I walked across the street from the accident and went the one additional block to Wometco. I went straight to my office, turned on the light, and laid my newspaper on my desk. I thought, "I think I'll go over and see Marvin and see how last night went. I walked across the hall to his office—it was locked. I thought, "That's odd. Marvin was supposed to be here early today. He must be in Jack's office." I went on down to Jack's office and stuck my head in the door. "Hi, partner, what are you up to?"

"Good morning, Larry. I was just looking at the stock report. I sure wish I could exercise some more options. Wometco is going nowhere but up."

I interrupted him. "Jack, have you seen Marvin this morning?"

"Nope."

"That's odd. He told me yesterday that he would be in early today." I guess Jack noticed the concern on my face. "Larry, what's wrong? What are you thinking?"

"Oh, nothing important. It's just that, well, there was an accident this morning on North Miami Avenue about a block from here. I think one of the street people was killed."

"Why do you think it was a street person?"

"I could tell the guy didn't have a shirt on."

"Oh." Jack got up from behind his desk and said, "Come on. Let's walk down to the scene of the accident."

We walked outside the front door of our office building and started walking toward North Miami Avenue. I noticed Art Hertz, the Chief Financial Officer of the company, walking toward us with a very solemn look on his face. Art walked up to us and looked directly at me, but he started to talk with Jack. Art said, "Jack."

I immediately interrupted Art as I pointed toward the scene of the accident and said, "Art, that body over there isn't Marvin Reed's, is it?"

Then I wondered why I had even blurted out such a statement. I thought, "Of course it's not Marvin." Fear gripped me as Art bit his bottom lip and nodded his head in agreement. All of a sudden I felt sick and weak. I started crying.

Jack took me back to my office. He then said, "Larry, why don't you go home. I'll have one of the secretaries drive you. I would take you myself, but I have to go over and meet with Art and the Colonel to see how we are going to handle this. Someone has to tell Sadie."

"No, I don't want to go home. I'll be fine in a few minutes."

"Larry, when does Eddie get back in town?"

"This afternoon."

"He's not going to believe it."

Jack left, and I instructed the girls to hold all my calls. I picked up the phone and called Doneata. "Honey, are you sitting down? I've got some awful news to tell you." I told Doneata the whole story. She couldn't believe it. She cried throughout the entire conversation.

"Larry, yesterday, the lunch with Marvin, everything that was said. What does all this mean?"

"Honey, I don't know what to think. I'm glad Marvin and I had that time together yesterday. Maybe God was giving Marvin another chance to get his heart right before going home, or maybe God knew he wouldn't get his heart right. Maybe, oh, I don't know! Only God knows."

"Larry, why don't you let me come on down and pick you up?"

"Honey, not now, but keep yourself available. I'll phone you later."

Jack and Stanley were given the unpleasant assignment of telling Sadie Reed that her husband was dead. When Stanley and Jack walked into her office, she knew something was wrong. Sadie got up from behind her desk and asked, "Jack, Stanley, is it Marvin's heart?" Upon hearing the news, Sadie collapsed. Jack and Stanley took her home.

About an hour later I received a call from Stanley. "Larry, are you up to coming over to the Reed home? Sadie wants to see you badly."

"Yes, sir. I can be there within the hour."

When I walked into the living room, Sadie stood up and ran over to me. She put her arms around me. Then she just held me—she was crying uncontrollably. After a moment I took her by the arm and said, "Come on, Sadie, let's sit down."

"Larry, not in here. Let's go out by the pool; I have something I must ask you."

We left the other people in the living room and went out by the pool. Sadie sat down in one of her floral-covered pool chairs and motioned for me to sit down directly in front of her. She adjusted her chair to where we were facing each other. I noticed we were so close that our knees were touching. Sadie took both my hands and held them. Tears were streaming down her face, but she did not bother to wipe them away.

"Larry, I have one question to ask. You're the only person on this earth that can answer this question." Sadie paused and closed her eyes. Her lips were quivering. It was as if she were praying before she asked the question, "Larry, tell me. Larry, was my Marvin a Christian?"

I looked into her sad, bewildered eyes. I noticed how swollen her face was. She was a broken woman: a woman whose heart had just been broken in two upon hearing the news that she had lost the most precious person in her life. What could one say at a time like this? I squeezed her hand and said, "Yes, Sadie, I believe Marvin was a Christian."

I was a pallbearer at Marvin's funeral. It was one of the saddest days of my life. I heard very little that the preacher said that day. My mind kept going back to the luncheon Marvin and I had had just a few days earlier. I thought to myself, "There was something else that I was wanting to say to Marvin Monday. What was it?" I thought a minute; then it came to me. "I know; I wanted to share with Marvin that Scripture verse that I had shared with him a long time ago—the verse I gave him when Jack was having his cancer surgery. It was James 4:14. Oh, how Marvin would gladly testify to those words now if he could only speak: "Whereas ye know not what shall be on the morrow. For what is your life? It is even a vapor, that appeareth for a little time, and then vanisheth away."

Twenty

The Struggle Within

Outside of the continuous sound of thousands of coins being fed simultaneously into the slot machines and all the activity of hundreds of people gambling on the casino floor, everything seemed different to me from the last time that I was standing in the lobby of the MGM Grand Hotel in Las Vegas. The last time I was there, I was excited. I had a pocketful of money, and I was ready to go nonstop, full speed ahead. I pushed my mind and body to the very edge before I would eventually crash and have to somehow find my way back to my room to give my exhausted mind and worn-out body their much-needed and demanded time of rest.

Yes, everything seemed so different to me now. I thought, "What's wrong with me? Let me think. How can I be standing here in the center of all this beauty, all this glitz and glamour, where a fortune can be won or lost on every deal of the cards, where there's so much excitement that you can't tell day from night, where all of the pleasures of life are available for the asking, and yet have a measure of concern. Everything looks so artificial. I know what's wrong with me! I'm depressed—depressed over Marvin's death. And yet there's something else. I don't know what exactly. Something within me is unsettled. My desires are not the same anymore. Yes, I guess it's just that I'm depressed, and maybe my lunch didn't agree with me—maybe that's what the uneasiness is in my stomach."

I questioned myself: "How come I don't want to do what I have done, and done well, for so many years? Go gamble to the limit, and have some real fun! Burn the candle at both ends. Could it be that after all these years I am losing my interest in gambling? Don't I want to know if I still have the touch? Can I still bring an audience of fifteen to twenty people to the blackjack table just to watch me gamble? What is it Victor and

Charlie Jones used to say? 'Vaughn, you don't have blood in your veins—you have ice water!' Let me think back: what's the most money I have ever bet on one hand? I believe it was across the street at Caesar's Palace. Yes it was. It was on good-old Caesar's blackjack table. I bet $3,500 and held on 17. I made the dealer take a card on his 16. Unfortunately for me, he hit a 3 for 19 and won. So what! I was playing with their money. I had already won over $7,000, playing blackjack earlier that evening."

I stopped reminiscing about days gone by. Without going to the blackjack tables, I left the casino and walked over to the elevator. "I think I'll go up to my room and take a bath. Maybe I'll gamble a little bit just for fun, nothing serious, after my dinner with Paramount Pictures tonight."

I went to my room, took a hot shower, put on my housecoat, and lay down on the bed. I got to thinking, "I'm going to be in Vegas for three long days." Then the question arose, "Why did I just say, 'long days'? Before, I've always wanted to stay in Vegas as long as the money lasted. What's wrong with me? I've never felt like this before. I've got a full agenda, an agenda that I should be looking forward to, but for some reason I have no interest in my upcoming meetings. I used to love being around the L.A. boys and the stars, seeing their new movies, and enjoying all the cocktail parties and liquor. Now I can't even get excited about gambling, and I know gambling isn't a sin. Pastor Short told me to have a good time and bring home lots of winnings. No, it's just that I'm depressed, and I know exactly what I'm depressed over—Marvin's death.

"I have rethought that luncheon at Burdines until there is absolutely nothing left to rethink. I need to leave it alone. There is no point in my trying to figure out why Marvin is dead, and why he died the way and the time he did. Pastor Short was right: some things are not for me to know. It's just that I feel so miserable on the inside. Part of me wants to go back to my old ways, while in my heart I know those old ways are temporal, artificial, and superficial." I thought at that moment, "I wish I knew someone in this hotel who was strong in the faith, who could go out to dinner with me and talk with me about spiritual things."

———

I returned to Miami early Friday evening. Doneata picked me up at the airport, and the two of us went out to dinner with Jack and Ann Mitchell. We went to an Italian restaurant in Miami Springs called Joe Peppi's. Joe Peppi's was Jack's favorite restaurant. It was one of those little Italian restaurants that you had to have heard about before you would go there to eat. It was located in the middle of a group of old, small

Dolly Parton, Jack Mitchell, and Burt Reynolds

buildings in a run-down area of Miami. It was a favorite hangout for Dan Marino, Don Strock, and several other Miami Dolphins football players. Joe was a big Dolphins fan and had pictures of the Dolphins players and Dolphins memorabilia scattered throughout the restaurant. Joe also had a picture that Jack had given him of Jack with Burt Reynolds and Dolly Parton. That particular picture was framed and hanging on the wall right beside the front door.

Joe Peppi, the owner, was a big, and I mean big, Italian man. In addition to being the owner, Joe was also the head chef and a strolling musician. Quite often while you were eating your meal, Joe, accompanied by a guitarist, would stroll from table to table singing love songs in Italian. I remember once when Jack and I went to dinner together at Joe Peppi's, I was enjoying my chicken Parmesan and potatoes when Joe Peppi strolled by our table singing. Jack stood up and made his way beside Joe Peppi and started singing love songs with him. I could hardly believe Jack was singing in front of everyone with Joe. Jack did have a good voice and enjoyed singing at Joe Peppi's. So this particular evening when he stood up to sing, I was not shocked or embarrassed because I was used to such. I thought, "It's amazing what a person can get used to, but at least Jack sounds good. It would be embarrassing if he could not carry a tune. I wonder what Doneata would do if I stood up and started singing with them? She would probably slip under the table because I could not carry much of a tune, neither do I know Italian. I guess I'll spare her the humiliation."

After spending the last three days in Las Vegas, I would have preferred to have gone home, put on some shorts and a T-shirt, and had some pinto beans with chopped onions and corn bread with Doneata and the children. But, I knew how important it was for Doneata to have an evening out, especially after having such a busy week in the home.

Jack, Doneata, and Ann were enjoying their meal and talking softly. I thought of the conversation we had had on the way to the restaurant. We talked about Sadie. Jack had said that she was taking Marvin's death very hard. I thought, "Poor Sadie. It was only the two of them for all those years. I wish they'd had some children. It would be much better if Sadie weren't left alone." We had all agreed that we needed to be extra sensitive to Sadie in the weeks ahead. I made a mental note to check up on her.

Jack was talking to me. I interrupted him: "What did you say, Jack?" He was asking me to bring him up to date with my Las Vegas trip. He then proceeded to tell me about his week at the office. "Larry, I hired an old friend of mine by the name of Bill Copley as the new Director of Advertising and Marketing. Bill is a good man. He's been in the business a long time. Bill and his wife currently live in Washington, D.C. His children are all grown and living away. The Copleys will be in Miami in three weeks."

"That's good, Jack. You're going to need a good man to take some of the workload off your desk."

"Larry, have you been keeping up with the stock this week?"

"I looked at it Thursday. Wasn't it up a quarter?"

"Larry, it closed today at twenty-eight." Jack took out his pen and started figuring on his napkin. "Larry, do you realize if this happens and that happens, that means, I'm going to have this much money." Jack then held up his napkin with about twenty numbers all lined up in a row.

"Jack, you spend too much time playing with your Wometco stock. Everyone knows that when the Colonel passes on, the company will eventually sell, and your stock will be worth trillions." I thought about how much of my own Wometco stock I had sold through the years to pay my family's medical bills. If it weren't for my stock options, I would be head-over-heels in debt.

As we were about to leave the restaurant, Ann said, "Larry, you and Doneata remember to pray for Jack next week. He goes back to see the doctor on Tuesday. The old boy hasn't felt that well this week."

I looked at Jack. "Are you okay?"

"Oh, it's nothing," he replied. "I've just had a lot of indigestion here lately, and I have been tiring easily."

"Well, you'd best stay healthy, old buddy, because I'm not about to let Stanley send me over to your office and have me play General Manager for you."

Jack laughed, "No, I don't think that would sit too well with Eddie."

As it turned out, someone did go to the hospital that next week, but it wasn't Jack. Tuesday night I started vomiting and passing blood. Doneata rushed me to our doctor's hospital in Coral Gables where I was found to be in critical condition with a bleeding ulcer. I stayed in the hospital, heavily sedated for over a week.

My physician and I had several conversations while I was hospitalized. Dr. Friedman blamed my poor health condition on the stress of being a film buyer in the highly competitive theatre business. In addition to being my personal physician, Dr. Friedman was also my friend. And true to his Jewish roots, he often dispensed advice with his prescriptions. This time was no exception. "Larry," he said, looking at me more like a father than a peer, "I don't care how much money you are making. Look at you; it's not worth it! You should get out from under that pressure, even if you have to sell your house and drop your standard of living. You're killing yourself, and I'm not going to be responsible."

I knew that he was right about the stress related to my work. But I never shared with Dr. Friedman that he had misdiagnosed my reason for being sick. It wasn't my work—that is, as far as the responsibilities associated with the Film Department. I could buy film in my sleep. No, my problem was coming from the spiritual struggle within. I was continually at odds with myself. Every day I was going to work doing everything within my power to get those unwholesome films into my company's theatres and then going home every night and trying to have a Bible study with my family. I was going in two separate directions at the same time, and it was literally tearing me apart on the inside.

When I got home from the hospital, I called our pastor and made an appointment to have breakfast together. We met on a Thursday morning at Denny's. The hostess seated us in a booth toward the back of the restaurant. After taking a sip of hot coffee, Pastor Short asked me, "Larry, when is the doctor going to let you return to work?"

I laughed. "The doctor is not the problem. Dr. Friedman told me I could return to the office yesterday. The problem is Eddie: he won't let me back in the office until Monday."

"Larry, your boss is one in a million."

"You can say that again. Eddie has always been more like a father to me than an employer."

Over our breakfast, my pastor insisted that I tell him all about my recent trip to Las Vegas. He really enjoyed hearing me tell him about my meetings with movie stars and their latest films. Then we talked about our families, and we both agreed that we must get our families together in the very near future.

Between bites of breakfast, Pastor Short made small talk about our families. "Larry, Joan, the children, and I really enjoy fellowship with you and your family. Joan and I can unwind around you and Doneata; you are one of the few couples that we feel like we can relax and just be ourselves with."

The waitress refilled our empty coffee cups. Then Pastor Short looked straight at me and said, "Okay, Larry, you didn't invite me to Denny's to eat bacon and eggs—we could have done that at your house. What do you want to talk with me about?"

I replied, "Pastor Short, I have a very serious problem that has been troubling me for some time now. I have tried to resolve it on my own but can't. I need to talk with someone about the problem. Both Doneata and I thought you, being our pastor, would be the perfect counselor for me to discuss it with."

Pastor Short sat listening to every word I had to say. And despite the burden on my heart, I couldn't help but notice how distinguished he looked in his navy suit and polka dot tie with his red beard, mustache, and neatly combed hair. He looked more like a Shakespearean actor than a minister. His appearance, in my mind, gave credibility to his opinions.

"Pastor," I continued, "before I came to know the Lord, I would have told anyone that I have the greatest job in the world. Wometco has been an absolutely wonderful company to work for. You yourself commented earlier about how good Eddie Stern has been to my family and me. I feel very confident that Wometco is going to offer me the Film Department, if and when Eddie makes the final decision to go ahead and retire."

Pastor Short interrupted, "That's great, Larry. What a promotion!"

I gave him a "please-hold-your-comments-until-I've-finished" look, then continued. "Being the Head Film Buyer for Wometco is the dream job that I thought I always wanted. But now, well, I'm just not so sure anymore." I had Pastor Short's undivided attention. I could tell he was listening to every word I had to say.

"Pastor, the problem is not with my work but the nature of my work. Before I became a Christian, I loved all types of movies, anything and everything. As long as it came on a reel, I enjoyed watching it. But since my salvation experience, certain movies are really starting to trouble me. It is very hard for me to watch a woman undress on the screen, and then attempt to have a Bible study that evening. And it's not just the nudity; it's a lot of things: the language, the music, and the violence. The violence in these new movies is extremely graphic.

"As a Christian, my concern is the overall direction I see the motion picture industry heading. Pastor, don't you understand what I am trying to say?" He nodded in agreement but remained silent. "Now maybe you have a better understanding about some of the struggles I have been going through since I came to know Christ. I think my ongoing struggle within is why I ended up in the hospital with bleeding ulcers last week. I'm not sure what I should do. Maybe I should leave the industry and get into another line of work. Well, Pastor Short, you tell me. What do you think I should do? I have got to do something, or I'm going to self-destruct!"

He just sat there for what seemed like forever before he did anything. Then he stretched his arms, rubbing the back of his neck with his fingers as if it were aching. He turned his head from side to side, then frowned as he closed his eyes. As his eyes slowly opened, he shrugged his shoulders up and down. Then he took in a deep breath and exhaled it as if he were doing a physical workout. Sitting there watching him go through this series of expressions, I thought to myself, "Is this a stall or some sort of routine he goes through?" He finally gave me a warm smile and said in his Scottish brogue, "Larry, I think I could stretch a mile if I wouldn't have to walk back." We both chuckled. His facial expression then became very serious as he started to speak.

"Larry, I have tried to listen very carefully to every word that you have said. First let me ask you a question. Do you feel the Lord is leading you into any type of ministry?"

"Ministry? Me, no, no I don't. However, if the Lord called me into full-time Christian work, that would be fine by me as long as I knew that was His will for my life."

"Larry, we have many men today in full-time Christian work that shouldn't be in it. Do you know why they are there?"

"No."

"They are there because it is a job. It meets their financial needs. They are not there because of a calling, just financial security."

"Well, what does all this have to do with what I have just told you?"

"Only this: you're looking at the motion picture industry as something that is evil. Yes, it has evil in it, but name a business that doesn't? If you worked for the *Miami Herald,* you would have to deal with sensuous advertising material. If you worked for a radio station, television station, or your neighborhood Seven-Eleven store, they all would have their compromising situations that the Christian man would have to struggle with daily in his soul. Larry, what if you worked in a supermarket?" Robert raised his eyebrows, tucked his chin to his neck, and stuck out his bottom lip as he leaned his head over the table and said in a very curious voice, "Have you seen some of those magazine covers lately? Wow, Larry, pornography is not just in your movie theatres—it's everywhere. At least at Wometco you don't have to work on Sunday or sell beer and wine: even they are a problem to those Christians who are into legalism."

His words caught my attention, particularly the word "legalism." I wondered where I had heard that word. Then I remembered Marvin told me I was beginning to act legalistic. I made a note to find out what the word meant. Pastor Short had continued to speak without my hearing him. "I'm sorry, Pastor, will you repeat what you just said?"

"Larry, I said that if you worked at the supermarket you would have to work on Sundays, sell pornographic magazines, and beer and wine." He paused a moment, took out his handkerchief, and blew his nose. In the process, he made an absolutely ridiculous sound. It was all I could do to keep from laughing. I looked around the room and noticed some other folks were giggling at him. It provided a bit of comic relief in the middle of what, for me, was a very tense situation.

Pastor Short continued, "Excuse me, now where were we? Oh yeah, Larry, have you ever thought about the content in some of those lewd books and magazines that are available for you and your family to read right from the shelves at the public library?" He paused again, took a deep breath, and smiled as he exhaled. "Larry, I could go on and on, but I think you see where I am heading. No, I don't think you should consider quitting your job. I think you, my good friend, have a unique ministry right where you are, and the problem is that you haven't realized it yet."

Pastor Short then took out his New Testament as he was talking, "Larry, let me read you a passage of Scripture from the fifth chapter of Matthew, starting at verse 13: 'Ye are the salt of the earth: but if the salt have lost his savour, wherewith shall it be salted? . . . Ye are the light of the world. A city that is set on an hill cannot be hid.' And, Larry, verse

16 concludes with, 'Let your light so shine before men, that they may see your good works, and glorify your Father which is in heaven.' "

Pastor Short laid his Bible on the table; then he placed both his hands on his sides and leaned over the table stopping short of my face. Then he spoke to me in a tone of voice that you would expect a father to use when making an important point to his child: "Larry Vaughn, I think you have a marvelous opportunity, right here, at Wometco, to be salt in the film industry. Not all Christians are called to be only in Christian service. You can be a powerful influence for the gospel in the motion picture industry if you will let your light shine before men so that they may see your good works, and glorify your Father in heaven. Larry, I think it would be a grave error for you not to use this opportunity to witness for Christ in the film business."

Pastor Short leaned back in his seat, crossed his arms, and rested his chin in the palm of his right hand. With his fingers, he created small circles, back and forth, around his lips. He then took his long right index finger and slowly moved it back and forth from himself to me and said, "Larry, laying all that aside I think you should look at your family. I personally would be scared to death if I were unemployed today. Larry, good jobs are hard to come by. You have a large family with great medical concerns. You're not going to be able just to walk into another job like you now have. How long did you say it took you to get to where you are at Wometco? I believe you said a lifetime. Scripture says that you do have a responsibility to your loved ones to meet their financial needs."

After a long minute of silence, Pastor Short looked down at his watch. Then, using his thickest and deepest Scottish brogue, he said, "Larry, do you know what time it is? It's 10:45. You have got to be exhausted." He slapped the table and said, "We must be on our way before I have Doneata and Eddie upset with me for keeping you out too long." Pastor Short grabbed the check and held his finger up in the air as if to say, "I know I should let you pay for my most remarkable services rendered, but I would rather you owe me one." He then gave me a large wink that wrinkled the entire right side of his cheek and said, "Maybe our next outing will be taking the wives over to The Rusty Pelican."

I smiled and replied, "Yes, and that treat will most certainly be on me."

Licking his lips, Pastor Short said, "Larry, such a thoughtful and kind gentleman you are."

I thanked him for being available. "My family and I appreciate you and your family very much. You have most certainly given me a lot to think about. Let me go home and discuss our conversation with

Doneata. Then the two of us will pray about it, and I'll act accordingly."
We shook hands and went our separate ways.

That afternoon I took Doneata out by the pool. She sat upright in the chair for the better part of an hour with her hands in her lap, listening to every word that I had to say. I tried to tell her, word for word, everything that was said during my meeting with Pastor Short. Then the two of us talked for a long while. Doneata got tears in her eyes and started crying. I went and got her a tissue.

She wiped her eyes and said, "Honey, all we want to do is what is right and pleasing in the sight of our Lord. The Lord knows our hearts. If your being at Wometco is God's perfect will for our lives, then so be it —Wometco is where we want to be. I just don't want you making yourself physically ill while worrying about being out of the Lord's will."

As always, I started mentally thinking through the events of the day. "This is really great news," I thought. "Now I can be a Christian and stay in the film business. I even have the blessing and encouragement from my pastor. As a Christian businessman, what more could I possibly want?"

After that day Doneata and I felt that it was God's purpose for my life for me to witness to my friends and coworkers in the film industry.

———

During the next few months we spent a lot of time in fellowship with the Short family. I had never known a couple quite like Robert and Joan. Every time we got together it would be a time of food, fun, and relaxation. Robert loved to play Pac-Man on the Atari. And we always got a kick out of watching him play the game, because he played with so much enthusiasm. Quite often the little boy came out in Robert, especially on those occasions when he was having too much wine to drink. He would start wanting to play a game, then as the evening grew on and the wine consumption increased, Robert would start acting rather silly—especially in light of his being a minister. Joan would have to be the one to get him home and to bed before he got himself in trouble.

As a Christian, well, sometimes I just didn't understand Robert's lifestyle. In his office at church, he was a very serious man. The distinguished Pastor Short was a master when it came to putting words on a piece of paper or explaining a section from his basis of theology. The Scottish gentleman in him gave him the aura of being very well educated, polished, and (he would add) totally Reformed in his theology. But when he was away from the church, Robert turned into a good ole' boy who was out to have a good ole' time. I often found myself wondering on those evenings, "Robert is really a fun-loving guy, but I wonder if he really has a genuine calling to be a minister of the gospel?"

One Friday evening after entertaining the Shorts in our home, Doneata and I went to bed for the night. I turned the light off. Then I reached over and turned the light back on. I started the conversation.

"Honey, the Shorts are such a wonderful family, and Robert has been such a dear friend to me." I sat up in bed and looked over at Doneata, "But do you want to know what I think?" Doneata ran her fingers through her hair; then she turned to fluff up her pillow as if to say, "I have a feeling we're going to be talking for a while."

Doneata replied sleepily, "What's that, honey?"

"Well, I think since Pastor Yaegar left Parker Road, we, personally, have had a lot of fun with the Shorts. However, spiritually, Doneata, I think we have become stagnant." Doneata sat there in bed resting her chin on her knees. She thought a minute; then she nodded her head up and down in agreement.

"Larry, you've got a point. You think the world of Robert, and I dearly love Joan and their children. What has been really bothering me is the way Robert is so free in his alcohol consumption."

"Well, we certainly haven't done anything to discourage him from drinking so much," I said, as much admitting my behavior as criticizing Pastor Short's. "I personally have drunk more wine in the short while that I have known the Shorts than I have in the past year."

"Larry, I'm glad to hear you say what you just said. I think we need to be careful with our relationship with the Shorts."

"Honey, let's start looking around for another family in the church that we can spend some time with. A family that puts a greater emphasis on spiritual matters."

———

Doneata phoned me one day at the office. "Larry, do you have a minute?" She was just bubbling with excitement.

I smiled at her infectious enthusiasm. "Honey, all I have been doing today is sitting here waiting on my private line to ring and hoping to hear your sweet voice on the other end."

"Larry, be serious, I've got some wonderful news to tell you."

I'd heard those words before, so I asked her, "Honey, you're not pregnant again, are you?"

"I had better not be, Larry Vaughn. Now listen. This is important. I've just heard the most interesting message on the radio from a preacher out in California. Oh, I wish I had taped it."

I could tell she was upset with herself. "Honey, what was the text?"

"It was taken from the book of Isaiah. The preacher was talking about America and how God is going to hold the people in America accountable because this country has turned away from those truths that are found in His Word. Larry, it was so convicting. I hope I can remember to tell you everything that the preacher said."

"Did you get the preacher's name?"

"Yes, I did. It's 'James T. Clarkston.' He has a very large ministry in California. I called the radio station to find out if he has a program daily. They told me that he is on Monday through Friday from 10:00 to 10:30 a.m.. Tomorrow I'll be sure to tape him so you can listen to him."

"That's great, honey. It sounds like an answer to prayer. We have been spiritually dry for sometime now. Doneata, before you hang up, I've got some great news for you."

"You do?"

"I most certainly do."

"Well, what is it?" she asked, with impatience in her voice.

"If you will call the radio station back and ask them for the tape number and an address, you can get a copy of today's message."

"Oh, why didn't I think of that?"

"Because I wouldn't have been able to think of it for you and be the hero for the day."

"Well, keep up your heroic deeds, Clark Kent. I'll see you tonight."

As it turned out, Pastor James T. Clarkston was a godsend. Doneata taped his radio message every morning, and I listened to it every evening. Little did we know that first day that Pastor Clarkston was about to become the most instrumental Christian man in our life for the next several years. I have listened to literally thousands of his messages on tape, read all of his books, and made several trips to various conferences to hear him speak in person. It was wonderful to be able to hear good expository preaching of the Word of God from a strong man of God, even if we did have to hear it on radio and not from our local church.

One evening, after I had finished a five-mile jog, I cooled off in the pool. I lay there with my arms stretched along the side of the drainpipe and my neck propped up against the side of the pool, watching the sun set over Miami. When I got out of the pool, Doneata came outside and sat down beside me.

"What were you in such deep thought about?" she queried. Sensing my surprise, she answered my unasked question, "Yes, I was watching you from the bedroom window. I could tell those wheels were turning."

"Honey, I was thinking about the series on 1 John that Pastor Clarkston has been preaching through. God's Word is really convicting. I think I have finally memorized verses fifteen through seventeen of chapter two. Let me see if I can quote them to you: 'Love not the world, neither the things that are in the world. If any man love the world, the love of the Father is not in him. For all that is in the world, the lust of the flesh, and the lust of the eyes, and the pride of life, is not of the Father, but is of the world. And the world passeth away, and the lust thereof: but he that doeth the will of God abideth for ever.'

"Honey, I think what the apostle John meant when he wrote those verses is that we are not to actually love the things of this world. I'm not talking about all things—that would be absurd—but those things that leave God out, those things that are a rival to Him. This afternoon while I was screening two movies, that particular passage of Scripture came to my mind. For the most part, those verses describe exactly what Hollywood does. Hollywood glorifies the lust of the flesh, and the lust of the eyes, and the pride of life. It's like this world that we live in is a part of an organized system that is headed by Satan, and God is left completely out of the picture. Unfortunately, I think Satan is using Hollywood to exalt himself and to try to make people forget there is a God."

Doneata got up out of her chair and came and sat down on the chaise longue beside me. She put my hand in hers. In her eyes I saw a look of genuine concern. She squeezed my hand as she said, "Honey, why don't you just go ahead and quit your job? You have struggled with movies on and off, mostly on, since you got saved. You know I'll support you in whatever decision you make." Doneata gestured by extending her arm and hand as if she were pushing back away from us in one clean sweep our house and pool. "Larry, I don't need any of this stuff. All I want is for you to have peace and for us to be in God's will."

"Doneata, you know what I just don't understand? The one thing that I am always struggling with, movies, is the exact thing that everybody—honey, when I say everybody, I'm talking about *all* our Christian friends—enjoys watching. It makes no sense. Why can't we enjoy movies the way everyone at Parker Road does—including Robert and Joan?" I paused to look at her to sense her reaction. She just gazed at me without answering.

"Doneata, I don't even think I told you what happened last Sunday after Sunday school. Do you remember meeting 'Freddie and Rhoda Barrett'?"

"Is she the one who's expecting?" Doneata asked.

"Yeah, and her husband is tall and dark haired. Freddie is one of the partners at the law firm 'Peterson, Flank, Johnson, and Barrett.' Robert told me he's one of the most respected attorneys in Miami. Anyway, after Sunday school I walked over to the coffee pot during the fellowship time; that's when the two of them walked over to me. I guess it was only natural for Freddie to do the talking since he's a lawyer." I began recounting for Doneata the details of the conversation.

"Good morning, Larry." Freddie and his wife both gave me a big smile. "Are your ears burning? Rhoda and I were talking about you on the way to church this morning."

"Well, you folks don't have a whole lot to talk about if I'm the topic of conversation."

Rhoda giggled as Freddie straightened my tie, which I doubted was crooked. He continued, "Larry, 'John and Gloria Strickland' were over at our house for dinner last week. Your name came up during our conversation on movies. John told us that you are the film buyer for Wometco and that you have your own private screening room."

"Well, that statement is partially correct." Freddie looked confused, so I figured I'd better explain my title. "I'm the Assistant Film Buyer for Wometco. I do have a V.P. that I answer to."

Freddie look relieved. "But, you do have a room where you watch movies before they are released to the public, right?"

"That's correct," I answered, wondering where the conversation was going.

"Larry, Rhoda and I love going to the movies. We would like to have you and Mrs. Vaughn over for dinner one night and hear about some of your experiences with movie stars."

I thought to myself, "No time soon, Brother," but wanting to be polite, I gave a noncommittal answer. "Well, maybe the four of us can get together one evening."

Freddie started fidgeting, pulling his cuffs down beyond his coat sleeve. Then he started wiping dust off his coat, and I could tell he was trying to work himself up to what he had to say. Sure enough, he cleared his throat and put one hand in his pocket and the other hand on my shoulder and said, "Larry, Rhoda and I would like to ask a favor of you. Would you think it rude or too bold of me to ask you if we might come down to your screening room and watch a movie with you sometime?"

I always hated when people put me on the spot. I tried to think of a quick reply. I then remembered what Pastor Short did that day at

Denny's while I was waiting on his answer. I thought, "I'll act like Robert did while I'm thinking of a nice way to tell this guy, 'No way, Jose.'"

I'm sure I didn't do the stretching, neck rubbing, shoulder shrugging, and breathing routine like Robert did, but what I did do gave me enough time to come up with an answer. I'm not a very good actor, but I tried to put on a very sympathetic, disappointed appearance as I said, "Freddie, Rhoda, I would love to be able to say yes to your request, but, unfortunately, I must say no. I am so sorry, but if that privilege were extended to you and your family, then I would also have to make it available to all of the other families at Parker Road. I'm sure you can see where that would become a very large problem." They looked so disappointed; I knew that I had just ruined their upcoming worship service.

Freddie mustered up an artificial smile and said, "We understand. It's just that we love going to the movies so much." He gave me a great big smile as he said, "Especially movies at Wometco."

As I turned to leave, Freddie said, "Larry, one other thing then I'll let you go."

I thought, "Now what? Of course, some passes!" I reached for my wallet as he started to talk.

"You wouldn't by any chance have a couple of passes, would you?"

"Sure, Freddie, you and Rhoda enjoy a movie this weekend on me."

Doneata, who to this point has patiently listened, interrupted, "Larry, you never said anything to me about that."

"On the way home from church I thought about mentioning it; but we had the kids in the car, and I didn't want them to hear the conversation. Then later I just forgot about it. Honey, I have folks from Parker Road call me at the office, at least," I paused to think, "two or three times a week asking for passes. You know what I am going to start doing?"

Doneata looked at me as if she were getting sick to her stomach. "No, what?"

"I'm going to discontinue giving passes to anyone. Why should I make it free for people to sin? At least they should have to pay to watch that stuff."

"Larry, promise me that you'll do that starting right away." Doneata's voice had an unusual earnestness to it, and I replied in kind.

"I promise. Starting right now, freebies are history."

———

The phone was ringing. Doneata answered, "Hello, Vaughn residence."

"Hello, Doneata. This is Ann."

"Hi, Ann. I was just about to call you to get an update on Jack. He's in room 454 at South Miami Hospital, right?"

"Doneata, they have found more tumors."

"Ann, no! Where?"

"They found three."

"Three?"

"Yes, three. There's one on his lung, one on his spine, and another one on his liver."

"Ann, I'm so sorry."

"We're taking them one at a time. Jack is in good spirits considering the gloomy news."

"I'll call Larry. I'm sure he will want to stop by to see Jack on his way home from the office. Ann, do you need anything?"

"Just prayer."

"Our prayers you and Jack have."

I stopped by the hospital on the way home. On the elevator to the forth floor, I was trying to get my thoughts together. "I must be very upbeat. Now is when I need to be an encouragement to Jack. He must not see my concern and my fear." I continued praying quietly to myself as I walked into the room.

As I walked into the room, Jack was lying in bed reading the newspaper. "Hey, partner, what are you doing back here? These beds are supposed to be for sick people."

As he dropped the paper down, Jack peeped over the top of it at me and smiled. "Larry, come over here and sit down, right here beside me on the bed. Ann said she told Doneata about my tumors. Larry, you know what the good news is?"

"No, but I'd love to hear some right about now."

Jack laughed. "There are only three tumors and not four."

I smiled at the dear old man and shook my head. "Jack, you don't need to be in a hospital—you need to be in an insane asylum."

Jack straightened the blanket on his bed while I fluffed his pillow. Then he got very serious. "Larry, I might end up in a wheelchair or bed-ridden, but I'm not going to give in to it. I'll fight it with my last breath."

"Jack, I know you will. Let's take it one day at a time. Now, tell me everything the doctor had to say."

It seemed to do Jack good to talk about it. He tried to remember everything word for word. When he finished giving me all the details, I asked him if I could have prayer with him. He nodded his head in agreement. I prayed for Jack's health needs and for strength for Ann. After I prayed, Jack and I talked a little while, then I left the hospital.

Driving home from the hospital I was thinking to myself, "Jack's favorite pastime is watching the Wometco stock go up and down, up and down. I doubt if he lives long enough to see any real financial fruit from all those years of labor. That man is dying; I'm sure he would give all his stock, right now, without a second's hesitation, for a clean bill of health. I must pray that God will do a mighty work in Jack's life and save him before he dies."

Twenty-One

The Compromise

"Good morning, Eddie."

"Top of the morning to you, Larry." Eddie was trying to organize several stacks of papers on his desk. "Larry, have you made the film rental settlements with Tri-Star on the Stallone film?"

"Not yet. It's on my agenda for today."

He stopped looking through the stacks of papers and said, "Well, at least I know why I can't find the settlements. Larry, let me know how you come out on the settlement. I'd like to see our film rental percentages take a drop this period."

"Eddie, I'll do the best I can." I paused a moment, then continued. "Eddie, will you be in the office all day today?"

"I'll be here until around 3:45. I have an appointment with the barber at 4:15. Look." He started pulling strands of silver hair out from the side of his head. Smiling, he continued, "Don't you think it's starting to get sort of long?"

"Yes, I guess you do need your ears lowered." I paused a moment, "Eddie, I would like to talk with you around 3:00 this afternoon on a personal matter."

Eddie motioned for me to close the door, "Let's talk right now."

"I don't have the time, Eddie. It's Monday, and I've got too much work to do in the next hour to get into it."

Eddie shrugged his shoulders, "Okay, Larry, we'll chat later."

That afternoon, my intercom started buzzing. "Larry."

"Yes, sir."

"I thought you said you wanted to see me at 3:00."

I looked at my watch; it was 3:10. I thought, "Where has this day gone?" "Sorry, Eddie, I'll be there in one minute." I cleared off my desk and told Betty to hold my calls while I was in Eddie's office.

Eddie was sitting behind his big desk in his high-back leather chair with his shirt sleeves turned up a third of the way. His tie was loosened, and the top button on his shirt was unbuttoned. His silver gray hair had lost its part and was tossed, more or less, completely out of place. Both of his elbows were propped up on the desk with his chin resting in the palms of his hands. He looked as if he were tired and in deep thought.

I asked, "Eddie, are you okay? You look like you've had a rough day."

"To be honest with you, Larry, I've been sitting here for the last ten minutes trying to figure out what it is that you want to talk with me about."

"I'm sorry, Eddie. I didn't mean to be late. Time just got by me. Anyway, what I have to say won't take but a few minutes."

I sat down in the black leather chair that was closest to where he was sitting. "Eddie, what I am about to do is one of the hardest things that I have ever had to do in my entire life." When I said that, Eddie didn't move a muscle; he just sat there looking at me as if he were expecting some bad news. "Eddie, I am here to officially give you notice that I will be leaving the company."

He looked at me without any emotion and said, "And where may I ask might you be going?"

I thought, "That's exactly what John Huff said to me when I gave him my notice at ABC."

"Eddie, I'm not leaving you to go with another theatre circuit. You know I would never do that." I looked away from Eddie and dropped my eyes toward the floor and said, "I'm leaving Wometco for personal reasons."

Eddie had a look of relief on his face.

I went on to say, "Eddie, there must be no misunderstanding between us. My decision to leave Wometco has absolutely nothing to do with you or any of the Wometco people. As a matter of fact, my feelings for you and this company are what's making it so hard for me to give this notice. But, I have no other option. I have thought this matter through completely, and I must leave, as I said earlier, for personal reasons—reasons which I care not to discuss." Eddie sat back in his chair and looked at me as if he were totally bewildered. I went on to say, "Eddie, I am prepared to give you up to a ninety-day notice."

Eddie stood up and walked over to the refrigerator and took out a can of tomato juice. While opening the can, he acted as if he were upset with himself. "I must be blind as a bat! I should have seen the stress that you've been under."

I thought, "You're right, Eddie. I'm under a lot of stress, but you don't know anything about the spiritual stress that I have been dealing with."

"Larry, what's wrong with me, not realizing what you've been under?"

I interrupted, "Eddie, you're misreading my reason for leaving. I told you it has nothing to do with you or the company. Again, Eddie, I must leave for personal reasons."

He took a large swallow of the tomato juice; then he sat back down in his chair. He gave me the "Eddie Stern" look that everyone had always warned me about—a look that I had seldom seen during the seven years that I had worked for him.

He hit the desk with his knuckles, "Larry, listen to me. I want you to leave the office this afternoon, and I don't want to see or hear from you for two full weeks. I want you to go home and spend some time with your family."

I interrupted, "But, Eddie—"

He stood up and extended his arm at me with his hand open as if to say, "Stop." "Larry, not another word. Freida will mail your check to your home the next two weeks. We will talk two weeks from today, at 8:30 a.m. There will be no further discussion on this matter until then." He then left the office for his barber appointment.

I just sat there in his office a few minutes. I thought to myself, "Well, I knew he was going to get upset, but I wasn't planning on dragging this notice out two more weeks. No use in calling Eddie or trying to talk with him—his mind is made up on this two-week delay."

Stanley walked into the office, "Hi, Larry, where's 'The Don'?"

"Stanley, you just missed him. He's gone to get his hair cut."

Stanley smiled and said, "Well, I guess Eddie figures if it grows on company time, why not get it cut on company time."

We laughed as he waved good-bye and left.

I spent those two weeks off mostly in personal Bible study. I never bothered to inform Pastor Short of giving Eddie my notice because I knew, from past discussions, the pastor's opinion on the matter.

Our family seemed always to be having doctors' appointments. This time it was for Larry Jr. We had noticed that he was starting to have abnormal behavior where he would start drooling from his mouth uncontrollably at times, his eyes seemed to have a strange look as if he were in some sort of a haze, personality changes, and when he was sleeping, we noticed the left side of his body would jerk uncontrollably. During those two weeks off, Doneata and I spent two days over at Miami

Children's Hospital where Larry Jr. underwent twenty-four-hour-a-day monitoring of activity in the cells in his brain.

After the test results came back, Doneata, Larry Jr., and I met with our pediatrician, Dr. Flicker, and a neurologist, Dr. Duschanney. Dr. Duschanney did most of the talking. "Mr. and Mrs. Vaughn, your son is having multiple seizures going off in his brain all throughout the day. We don't know what is causing this. There could be several factors involved; however, we have some very good medications that have given us some good results when treating seizures of this nature. We would like to start treating Larry immediately with a combination of medicines for a period of several months. We will have to have Larry come back for an overnight visit periodically, so we can monitor his seizure activity on a twenty-four-hour schedule."

Driving home from the hospital, I commented to Doneata, "Well, two out of three is not that good."

"What do you mean, two out of three?"

"I mean David having had leukemia, and now Larry Jr. having seizures. That's two out of three. Praise the Lord Mentora is healthy."

"Honey, we can also praise the Lord that David is doing so well. Don't forget, the doctors were ready to give up on him and look at how well he is doing."

"You're right, Doneata. We really have a lot to be thankful for. Even Mentora is now a wonderful child. It's just that she stretched the 'terrible two's' from the time of birth until she was three years old!"

Doneata asked me, "Larry, still no regrets on leaving the company?"

"None at all. I have a perfect peace about leaving the theatre business. I know the Lord is going to meet our needs because I know what we are doing is pleasing to Him. It doesn't matter if Robert Short or every single member at Parker Road thinks that I've gone nuts. I know in my heart this is the right thing to do. Monday, I'll wrap things up with Eddie, and we'll move forward from there."

———

Monday morning I walked into Eddie's office at 8:30 sharp. "Good morning, Eddie."

"Hello, Larry, please shut the door and sit down." Eddie commented, "Larry, you look rested. How do you feel?"

"Eddie, physically I am doing very well."

"Good, now tell me what you did while you were away from the office, and I want to know all about the family."

I spent the next ten minutes relating everything that had happened during my two weeks away. He was especially inquisitive about my appointment with Dr. Duschanney, and Larry Jr.'s test results.

Eddie finally brought the question up, "Larry, are you still determined to leave the company?"

"Yes, sir, I am."

Eddie's countenance was starting to change as if he were getting annoyed with me.

"Larry, how long have you worked for me?"

"Seven years."

"How many raises have you had to ask for?"

"Not one." I didn't like where this meeting was headed, but I guess I should have expected it.

"Larry, I brought you into this department and treated you, not like an employee, but like a son. I don't understand how you can even consider doing something like this to me—not as good as I have been to you." Eddie paused a minute, "You know, Larry, during your past seven years with Wometco, the company has also been very good to you." Eddie raised his eyebrows, "A million dollar insurance policy on David, some very lucrative stock options, and a very good salary increase every single year that you have been with Wometco, not to mention your generous expense account."

I just sat there. What could I say? Every word out of his mouth was the truth. I thought, "Sure, I could remind him about the millions of dollars I had made for the company by utilizing my film buying and negotiation skills. And because of those abilities, he and Jerry were free to travel all over the world without Eddie having to be concerned with what's happening at the office. But that was what I was being paid to do. No, I had to hear the man out, without my making any negative comments."

Eddie looked at me with somewhat of a smirk on his face, "Okay, your mind's made up. You're leaving, so be it. But don't you think you at least owe me an explanation as to why you are leaving? Don't I deserve that much?"

I thought about what he said: "I do owe him that much. He is not going to understand, but I do owe this fine friend and boss of so many years an explanation."

"Okay, Eddie, I'll tell you why I am leaving. When I came with the company seven years ago, I loved the motion picture business with all my heart, soul, mind, and body. Movies were my whole life. But, Eddie, do you remember the day I came in this office and told you that I had become a Christian, that I had made a profession of faith in Jesus Christ as my Lord and Savior?"

Eddie had a strange look on his face. I could tell his mind was searching back, trying to pull out of his memory bank exactly what I was talking about.

I went on, "Eddie, ever since I became a Christian I have had a continuous struggle with movies. The screening room is driving me crazy. I go down to the screening room and watch a movie filled with sex, violence, and bad language; then I go home and try to have a Bible study with my family. I can't do it, Eddie. I'm going in two different directions at one time, and it is destroying me on the inside."

Eddie just sat there with his shoulders dropped, his arms were resting at his side, and his mouth was open. "Eddie, what I am trying to tell you is something has got to give: either my work or my relationship with Jesus Christ. Unfortunately, for you and Wometco, I have chosen Christ."

For the first time in seven years, I had Eddie Stern speechless. He just sat there and said nothing. He finally closed his mouth and looked at me as if he were stunned. He took off his glasses and proceeded with his fingers to wipe off his face.

"Larry, this is one call I missed. I have been racking my brain trying to figure out what could possibly be wrong with you. I thought of everything from marital problems to your having a nervous breakdown, but this never entered my mind. I would have never guessed you, Larry Vaughn, to be a man of the cloth."

"What? Eddie, I'm not going to be a preacher. I just can't continue to put all those movies we screen week in and week out into my mind. Eddie, I know you don't understand, but those movies are affecting my relationship with my Lord."

Eddie got very quiet. He didn't say anything for maybe five minutes, but I could tell he was thinking through everything that I had just said.

Finally Eddie broke the silence, "Larry, I have an idea. Hear me out. What if I made it possible for you to continue on with your present job responsibilities except you would not be required or expected to screen any films—no films at all?"

"Eddie, I don't understand how I can be a film buyer without watching films."

"Simple. I'll watch the movies when I'm in Miami, and when I'm not in town we'll bring in a couple of men from out in the field to watch the films. After screening the movies, they, in turn, will report to you. Meanwhile, you'll continue to be responsible for payment of film rental, maintaining your important relationships with the film distributors, negotiating with the film companies for products, traveling, etc." Eddie snapped his fingers and pointed at me as if to say, "Well, what do you think of that?"

I looked across the desk at Eddie as I thought, "He's looking at me as if we are playing a game of chess, and he just put my king in check. This unusual proposal I was not expecting. A film buyer that doesn't watch movies would be like a race car driver that doesn't drive race cars!"

"Eddie, I don't know. I'll have to think about this."

Eddie got a very impatient look on his face and said very emphatically, "Larry, I'll tell you what you better think about: your wife, your medical bills, your children, and how you're going to provide for their needs. By taking my offer, you can have your cake and eat it too. Don't make a foolish decision that you'll live to regret for a long time."

I listened to what Eddie had just said. Who is going to insure my children with my medical needs? My present salary coupled with my group insurance was more than enough to meet all my present and future medical and financial needs. I thought about my younger son. "I'm not sure what's going on with Larry Jr. and his seizures right now. I'm sure no insurance company would touch him."

"Eddie, you've got yourself a deal. I'll be pleased to stay on with the company under those conditions as discussed."

Instantly, I saw the old Eddie return, "That's great, Larry. I told Jerry this morning I was going to find a way to work this problem out to where you would stay on with us. Now let's get to work. Go get your books— you've got some catching up to do."

Before going back into Eddie's office, I phoned Doneata to tell her the news. "Honey, I'll give you the long version of the meeting tonight, but the short version is that I am staying on with the company. As of today, I am going from screening 200 to 250 movies a year to none!" Doneata did not understand. I promised her I would fill in all the blanks when I got home.

―――――

On the bus ride to Dadeland that day, I got to thinking, "I'm so glad everything worked out with Eddie and me the way it did. This has been the most wonderful seven years as far as employment. I've certainly had my share of good times being employed at Wometco."

Larry and Goldie Hawn at the NATO convention at the Fountainbleau

About that time I passed a billboard advertising the Fountainbleau Hotel on Miami Beach. Now there was a good memory. How long ago was it? Four, maybe five years ago when the National Association of Theater Owners had a convention at the Fountainbleau. The Fountainbleau was one of the largest and most famous hotels on Miami Beach. In earlier years it was one of the most famous hotels in all of the world. The company put Doneata and me up in an oceanfront room for the whole week. All we did was eat, sleep, and spend time with the Hollywood elite. That week was like a paid vacation with all the trimmings.

I thought back to a breakfast Doneata and I had in the restaurant of the Fountainbleau. We were sitting there in a booth and Doneata said, "Larry, there's Steven Speilberg in that booth across the way. Do you know him?"

"No, I've never had the pleasure of meeting him."

"Larry, his food hasn't come yet; let's go over and introduce ourselves to him."

"Honey, if it were anywhere but in a restaurant. I don't want to disturb Mr. Speilberg in a restaurant."

"Do you mind if I go over and talk with him?"

"Not one bit, Doneata. You do what you want to, but I'll meet him somewhere besides his breakfast table."

Doneata got up and walked over to Mr. Speilberg's booth. There was another gentleman whom I did not know sitting across from him. Mr. Speilberg was propped up in the corner of the booth with his leg resting on the seat. All I could see of Doneata was her back, but I noticed Mr. Speilberg straightened himself up in his seat and made room for Doneata to sit down. She sat down beside him, and they seemed to be in a heavy conversation. I thought to myself, "Maybe I should go over and introduce myself; he certainly doesn't seem to mind Doneata interrupting their conversation. I wonder what she is talking to him about?"

They talked several minutes before the waiter brought their breakfast to the table. As soon as the food arrived, Doneata got up from the booth, shook both their hands, and politely left.

She returned to our booth with the cutest smile as if she were saying, "I know something that you don't know."

"Okay, Miss Jet Setter, do you mind telling me what all that was about?"

"Oh, Steven was just inquiring if I would be available to star in his next film."

"And what did you say?"

"I told him I would have to think about it, that I would phone him later, after I check my calendar."

Doneata was so cute. She was just a giggling.

"All right, tell me what you two were really talking about."

"Larry, you could guess all day, and you would never guess what he asked me."

"What?" Doneata had my curiosity up.

"Well, when I introduced myself to him and told him that you were my husband, he asked me, 'Why is Wometco Theatres out of business with Columbia Pictures?' "

"You're kidding!" I could hardly believe my ears.

"No. He wanted to hear the whole story. That's what we have been talking about all this time."

"Well, I'll be. Doneata, you would think a man of Steven Speilberg's stature—you know, the most successful director in the history of motion pictures—wouldn't be aware or even concerned about Wometco's problems with Columbia Pictures."

"No, honey, you're wrong. He said he would like to see Wometco back in business with Columbia because he likes the way our Miami theatres can gross."

I thought, "Well, how do you like that!"

"Larry, I didn't think you would mind my telling Mr. Speilberg the story. So I told him about how one of the Columbia bigwigs insulted Eddie Stern's wife at a dinner one night in Los Angeles. And how since that night the Wometco and Columbia Pictures relationship has gone downhill."

"Well, Doneata, there's actually more to that story than what you told Mr. Speilberg, but you were correct in the part that you told him. That was the spark that was used to dissolve our business relationship with Columbia Pictures. By the way, did you get his autograph?"

Doneata looked at me as if I had just asked the stupidest question. She then took out of her dress pocket a small sheet of paper and waved it back and forth as she said, "Of course I got it."

The bus pulled in to Dadeland as I thought, "Yes, not only I, but Doneata too has had some good times because of our association with Wometco."

I walked over to my car feeling good about how the events of the day had turned out.

————

In the past I had been used to screening movies, weekly—anywhere from ten to fifteen hours a week. I now found myself with that many hours each week available for use in other areas of work. Now I was free for lunch every day instead of only one or two days a week. Many days I thought of my old lunch partner, Marvin Reed. I sure did miss Marvin. Not a day went by that I didn't think about how Marvin and I used to go out to lunch together.

Since I had the time, I decided I would start going over to the park on Biscayne Boulevard a couple of days a week. The park would be an excellent place to share the gospel with some of the many street people who were always hanging out at the park. I would usually look around and pick out an individual that I thought would be willing to listen to me present to him the plan of salvation. During that year, I shared the good news of Jesus Christ to many of the homeless who came to the park to spend their days.

I had a system that seemed to work. Now that I look back on it, what I most likely was doing was paying the derelicts to listen to me give them the plan of salvation. After I finished the study, I would give them a couple of bucks and encourage them to buy something to eat with the money. I knew in my heart that most of the time the money I gave them probably was used to support their alcoholism or drug addiction.

I got to know many of the street people by name as we would see each other several times a month. We would sit and talk about all sorts of things. It amazed me that some of them seemed to have been, at one time or another, just ordinary people. By ordinary, I mean they seemed to have average intelligence, personality, looks, etc. But, eventually something happened in their lives that put them over the edge with society. They lost all contact with family, friends, and even their former identities. They were complacent about being "derelicts" of society.

One of the most embarrassing moments in my life came from my association with one of these derelicts. His name was Bernie, and Bernie and I had several conversations about God and His Son, Jesus Christ. Bernie looked exactly like what he was—a bum. He wore pants cut off above the knees with holes in them; they probably hadn't been washed that year. His shirt was just as bad, an old slipover, faded, gray tank top. Bernie's hair and beard had at least a year's, maybe two-years', growth since being cut. He was always bare footed, and his feet were totally black from being unwashed.

One afternoon I went to lunch with Stanley Stern. On the way back from lunch, Stanley and I heard a voice calling, almost yelling, "Larry, Larry." We both turned to see who that was hollering so loudly, and there across the street about fifty yards away was Bernie. He continued to holler, "Larry, Larry! Jesus loves you, Larry, and so do I."

Stanley looked at me and had the funniest look on his face; he looked as if he had just taken a swig of castor oil. He asked, "Do you know that guy?" Bernie was walking faster toward us, starting to holler again.

I said, "Stanley, excuse me; I'll be right back." I double timed it across the street to Bernie, feeling in my pockets along the way for some "hush money." I reached Bernie before he started yelling again. I slipped five bucks into his hand and said, "Not now, Bernie. I'm with my boss. I'll see you later in the week."

Bernie gave me the goofiest smile and said, "Okay, Larry." As I hurriedly walked back to Stanley, Bernie yelled to me, "God bless you, Larry."

Stanley was standing there with a look of disbelief on his face. He said, "Larry, do you really know that guy?"

I dropped my head and said without looking at Stanley, "Oh sort of, I gave him a few bucks one day, and now he thinks we're buddies."

I could tell at that moment that Stanley Stern, the Executive Vice President of the Entertainment Division of Wometco Enterprises, wasn't impressed with me or my derelict friend.

———

The last six months of Jack's life were spent for the most part in South Miami Hospital. I dropped by three to four evenings a week to see him. Many times he never even knew that I was there. I felt bad for Jack but even worse for Ann. She was the one that was always there by his side, daily watching her husband's life slowly slip away. Ann knew it would only be a matter of days or weeks at the longest before Jack—her love, her husband, and her very best friend—would be no longer breathing and living on this earth.

One afternoon after leaving Jack's room, I met Stanley on the way out of the hospital. We were standing outside the main lobby.

"Larry, how is Jack today?"

"No change, Stanley. He's about the same. I didn't stay but a few minutes; Jack's having trouble staying awake."

"Probably all the painkillers they have him on."

As I started to leave, Stanley said, "Larry, wait a minute. I just wanted to tell you that Eddie shared with me everything that you have been going through the past few months. Larry , without a doubt, you did the right thing by staying with the company."

"Well, Stanley, I was prepared to leave, but Eddie and I got everything worked out."

"Larry, did you know you are just like me?"

I smiled and asked, "In what way, Stanley?"

"In providing for the needs of your loved ones. Larry, it would break your heart if you couldn't give your family those material possessions they needed to get along in this life. Larry, it costs a fortune just to live today—let alone raise a family with special health needs. I know you, if you had left the business, you would have lived to regret it every day for the rest of your life. Why, the first time Doneata or one of your children had a need that you couldn't meet, it would have driven you crazy." Stanley put his arm around my shoulder and gave me a gentle tug. "Larry, I just wanted to tell you that I'm glad for you and especially for your family that you came to your senses and made the right decision."

It was during this same time period that the legendary Colonel Mitchell Wolfson passed away. The dear old gentleman who had started an empire with only one small theatre had finally passed on. Some fifty plus years ago Mitchell Wolfson and his partner Mr. Meyer started the Wolfson Meyer Theater Company—the giant conglomerate that is known today as Wometco.

Twenty-Two

Broad Horizons

It didn't take very long after the Colonel's passing for Wometco Enterprises to be put on the market for sale. Several companies expressed much interest in purchasing Wometco; however, the stockholders' best offer came from a group of investors out of New York by the name of KKR & Associates. KKR & Associates had a reputation for making large corporate-leveraged buy outs. Their billion dollar offer was all the Wometco shareholders needed to hear to sell the company.

Two of the main players responsible for putting the deal together on the Wometco side were Arthur Hertz and Michael Brown. Arthur was for many years Wometco's Chief Financial Officer, and Michael was the Executive Vice President of Wometco Enterprises.

I had never had much conversation with Mr. Hertz or Mr. Brown because Eddie always kept a tight lid on the Film Department. I cannot remember seeing either one of those gentlemen in the Film Department. In my first eight years with the company, I don't remember Mr. Hertz or Mr. Brown asking me one single question about film buying. They spent all their time working in the corporate headquarters next door with Colonel Wolfson and the other department heads within the company. Even though I never had any direct business dealings with the two gentlemen, I knew very well the reputation of each man.

Arthur Hertz was a very stout, heavy-set man in his late forties or early fifties. He combed his slick, black hair straight back without a part. He carried himself exceptionally well for his size. He was an immaculate dresser: always wore a suit, never a sports coat. Mr. Hertz looked his part: a senior executive with a reputation for being an extremely tough businessman.

Every time I saw Arthur Hertz walking to his Cadillac, he would have twelve to fifteen manila folders packed full of papers tucked under one arm. In his other hand, he would have his large leather briefcase which was always bulging at the seams from being overstuffed with more documents and papers. Mr. Hertz had the reputation of being a workaholic. He also had the reputation of being a very intelligent man. I understand he worked nights at a supermarket while putting himself through the University of Miami where he graduated at the top of his class with honors. His entire business career had been at Wometco.

Eddie once told me that Art Hertz was very political minded. Art knew everybody from national political leaders, to state governors, senators, and those politicians in between. Art was divorced. His two sons lived in Miami with him.

Michael Brown looked to be a younger man than Art Hertz. Maybe in his early to mid forties. Michael had basically the same work characteristics as Art Hertz, but he didn't look anything like Art. Michael was a short black-headed man maybe a little like Dustin Hoffman in appearance. Michael was a "facts and figures man." He was noted more for his extra-keen business skills than for his political skills. Michael dressed immaculately. He wore very expensive suits, shirts, ties, and shoes. Michael was married to a lovely lady, and they had two teenage children.

I always thought Hertz and Brown seemed to complement each other with Hertz being the mouthpiece, the front man, the politician, possibly the risk taker of the two; and Brown being the quiet one, the man behind the scenes, the thinker. Together they made a great one-two punch for the Wometco team.

Eddie called me into his office to give me the news. "Larry, I just got off the phone with Stanley; he was over at the hospital. The doctor says it's only a matter of days with Jack."

"Eddie, that's so sad. The company sells, Jack finally gets his payment for his stock, and it means zero to him."

"Well, at least Ann won't have to be strapped financially."

"That's true."

"Larry, Jack is not what I called you in here to talk about. Have you heard through the grapevine who's trying to buy back pieces of Wometco from KKR & Associates?"

"No, why don't you bring me up to date?"

"Art and Mike are trying to put together their own leveraged buy out and buy back certain parts of the company from KKR & Associates."

"Which parts?"

Eddie raised his eyebrows as if to say, "I'm impressed."

"They're going after all the Wometco vending, the Miami Seaquarium, plus the Puerto Rico and Florida theatres."

Eddie scratched his head as he smiled and said, "Larry, my man, things sure do keep changing around here.

"Larry, it doesn't matter to me personally who ends up with Wometco because I've decided to go ahead and retire. I told you eight years ago that when the Colonel is no longer here, then I'm leaving. Well, the grand old gentleman is gone, so I'm going to announce my retirement Friday. I have a feeling Mr. Hertz and Mr. Brown will be very interested in talking with you about a film buying position with the new Wometco in the not-too-distant future."

"Well, Eddie, I would like very much to talk with Mr. Hertz and Mr. Brown at the opportune time."

That evening on the way home from work, I stopped by the hospital. Jack never knew that I was there. I spent a few minutes talking with Ann. I had prayer with her; then I left. I had been home from the hospital maybe an hour when we received the call that Jack Mitchell had passed away. As I hung up the phone, I thought. "In a way it's a blessing: both Jack and Ann have suffered a lot these past six months."

Jack was buried a few days later. The thousands of people at Wometco, as well as the hundreds of people in the motion picture industry that knew and loved Jack, all mourned his passing. Jack had been a dear friend, and I knew in the days ahead I was going to miss him terribly.

After the funeral Ann came over to me, and we gave each other a big hug. She looked me straight in the eye as if to say, "What I am about to tell you is very important."

"Larry, Jack told me to have you come over to the house and go through his closet and take whatever suits of clothing you want before I give anything away. He wanted you to be sure to get whatever you want first before anything was touched."

"Ann, I'll stop by this weekend. I will consider it a privilege and an honor to be able to wear Jack's suits."

Jack was a dresser. Since we wore the same size suit, I went to his home that Saturday and picked out several tailored suits and sports coats, which I indeed felt privileged to be able to wear in the years ahead.

The next few weeks, I found myself having to fight off anxiety. Nothing seemed concrete, stable, or secure anymore. Jack was dead. Eddie had announced his retirement next month. Art and Mike were working twenty-four hours a day trying to put their deal together to buy

Wometco. Larry Jr. wasn't doing well at all on his medications. The doctors wanted him to go back into the Children's Hospital for more testing. I guess the best thing I had going for me was the messages I was listening to daily from Pastor Clarkston. He really helped me to keep everything in its proper perspective. My security returned when I remembered that God knows even how many hairs are on my head. Nothing can happen in my life without God allowing it. "Yes," I thought, "right now, especially right now, I ought to be concentrating on those heavenly things of God. By faith, I must give to God these temporal concerns of this world—concerns that I now seem to be putting undue emphasis on. I know He wants what's best for my life and the life of my loved ones. He wants me to put my trust in Him and not be concerned with my immediate circumstances."

———

It was a Monday afternoon just before 5:00 when I received a call from Art Hertz's secretary. "Hello, Mr. Vaughn, Gail here. Mr. Hertz asked me to give you a call and see if it would be possible for you to meet with him and Mr. Brown in the morning at 8:00 a.m."

I thought to myself, "That's too early." But I said, "Yes Gail, tell Mr. Hertz that 8:00 a.m. will be just fine."

On the way home that afternoon I thought about the upcoming meeting with Mr. Hertz and Mr. Brown. Even though I'd seen these guys weekly for the past eight years, I really didn't know them. We had never even sat together at any of the company dinners. Outside of small talk about movies, I hadn't even talked to them. "I had better get my thoughts together before the morning. Yes, I need to have a plan. What am I after from these guys? What are my expectations? They will never allow me to have the autonomy in the Film Department that I'm used to having. There's just too much money and risk involved for them not to expect to be kept informed.

"I think I'll demand two things: a raise and a contract. Then I'll see what their expectations are. Now what kind of a raise should I ask for? I think I'll shoot for $25,000 a year. Later on I can ask for stock in the new company. I'd better be careful with the contract. Sure, I'm locking them in, but I'm also locking myself in. What if I don't like working for them, or they don't like me working for them? I'm going to ask for a year contract, and that's all. After a year we'll know each other much better. Should I ask for V.P. stripes? No, I don't think so. Right now I would rather have the cash and the contract. If one of the other two don't work out, then I'll ask to be made an officer in the company. I'd better bathe this meeting in prayer tonight. I've heard about how tough these guys are at negotiating."

I walked into Art Hertz's outer office at 8:00 a.m. sharp. For some reason I was nervous, very nervous! But, I put on my "poker face" and said to myself, "Okay, Larry, go in there with both guns blazing. Act as if you're John Wayne, and you'll end up getting exactly what you want."

I tapped on his door and heard, "Come on in." I opened the door; Art was sitting behind his desk smoking a cigar. His tie was loosened and the top button on his pinstriped shirt was unbuttoned. His shirt sleeves were turned up to his elbows. He was working through several stacks of papers, one sheet at a time. His desk was covered with documents and files. Looking at him you would have thought it was 8:00 in the evening instead of the morning. He was really going at it.

Michael was sitting at the end of the sofa with a legal pad in one hand and the telephone cradled between his chin, shoulder, and ear. He was writing as fast as he could while listening to the party on the other end of the phone. I felt out of place standing there all fresh from a good night's rest.

Art motioned toward an empty chair and said, "Sit down, Larry. Mike will be off the phone in a minute." I sat down and started rehearsing in my mind those things which I was about to say.

Mike hung up the phone, made a comment to Art, then looked over at me and said, "Good morning, Larry. Welcome to the new Wometco."

I smiled as Mike walked over and sat down beside me. He flipped over the page on his legal pad to a fresh page and then prepared himself for note taking. Art did most of the talking.

"Larry, it's almost a done deal. Mike and I, along with our lenders, are about to consummate the purchase of several properties of the former company which will include the Wometco Florida and Puerto Rico theatres. Mike and I would like for you to stay on as our film buyer for the Florida theatres. How does that sound to you?"

"That sounds just fine to me. I was anticipating that I would have the opportunity to work for you gentlemen in the Film Department."

Art replied, "That's great. We're looking forward to working with you." Art looked at me and said, "Now, Larry, what else do we need to talk about?"

I thought to myself, "Here goes nothing!"

"We need to discuss salary and a contract."

Mike and Art glanced at each other, and then they both looked at me. Art asked as he puffed on his cigar, "What do you have on your mind?"

I thought to myself, "Remember, Larry, you're doing an imitation of John Wayne. Ask for the contract and salary exactly like John Wayne would say it."

"I think a salary increase of $25,000 the first year would be in line with the additional responsibility I will have once Eddie is gone. As far as contract, I would like a one-year contract. That will give you gentlemen enough time to know if you're pleased with the work that I do, and it will give me enough time to see how I like working for the two of you."

Art asked, "Is that it?"

"That's it."

He looked at Mike. "Have a contract drawn up for Larry, you, and me to sign. Larry, your increase will start effective March 1, 1985."

As I stood to leave, Art motioned for me to sit back down. "Larry, your demands have been met; now here are mine." He coughed, then took another puff on his cigar. "Two of the largest and most aggressive theatre circuits in the country: American Multi-Cinemas and General Cinema Corporation have both targeted the Miami market as an area of expansion. They are going to be building their new state-of-the-art eight-plex and ten-plex theatres right in our own back yard. I'm paying you very good money to make absolutely sure we keep the big pictures playing at Wometco Theaters. Eddie tells me you have an excellent reputation with the film community. You're going to need all the help you can get once AMC and GCC get their new theatres off and running. I'm not buying Wometco to lose money, but to make money."

I looked at Art as if I were John Wayne himself. "Art, I will not be able to guarantee you and Mike that Wometco will play every big picture every time and shut the other guys out completely, not when the other guys are AMC and GCC. That's impossible. It can't be done. No circuit has enough muscle to shut down AMC or GCC Theaters. But this much I can promise you and Mike; as long as I am your head film buyer, Wometco will get, at the very least, its fair share of the big pictures in all of the Florida theatres."

Art looked at Mike as if to say, "He's awful sure of himself, isn't he?" Then he stood up, extended his hand, and said, "It's going to be a lot of hard work growing together, but if we make money, then Larry Vaughn makes money."

I shook both their hands and left the room. As I closed the door, I sighed; I was relieved the meeting was over. I thought to myself, "I went in there with both guns blazing just like John Wayne would have done. But now that it's all over, my knees are knocking, and I feel more like Woody Allen than John Wayne."

———

What does someone do with a $25,000-a-year raise in 1985? I sold my home in Cutler Ridge and bought a much nicer, new home in Kendall Lakes, which was one of the up-and-coming areas of Miami to live in. This particular home was one the builder had been using as a model. It was an absolutely lovely home. It had off-white Italian tile from the entrance hall into the family room and throughout the kitchen and breakfast area. The whole house was open and very spacious. The breakfast room, kitchen, and family room all overlooked a huge brick patio area which was enclosed with dark domed screening. There were three large bedrooms and two full baths, plus a vanity area in the master bedroom. There was a large dining room which joined a step-down sunken living room. The dining room back wall was all beveled glass. There was a state-of-the-art security system installed throughout the house. The back yard was about a quarter of an acre in size. It was completely enclosed with a six-foot privacy fence. This home had everything but a pool, and a pool was the one thing that years ago I had lost interest in maintaining and cleaning.

The film community threw a surprise going-away party for Eddie Stern. My job was to find a way to get Eddie to Jacksonville. Then they ("they" being a group of Eddie's closest friends) would take over from there. I leaned on Eddie to take one last trip to Jacksonville with me to help solve a problem I was having with one of the film distributors. I told him we could fly up in the afternoon, have dinner, do our business, and return to Miami the following afternoon. He took the bait and agreed to make the trip.

When we got to the restaurant for the so-called meeting, there must have been 75 to 100 film people there to "roast" Eddie Stern. They sent him into retirement in grand fashion. It was a wonderful luncheon, a luncheon that I'm sure Eddie Stern has never forgotten.

The first Monday in the office after Eddie retired was a somewhat strange experience for me. I thought back to the very first time I had seen that office. It was that Sunday morning some eight years ago when I flew down to Miami from Charlotte to interview for the job of assistant film buyer with Wometco. Oh, how I was so impressed that day with everything: Eddie's conversation with Joseph E. Levine, his larger-than-life office, the king-size desk, and, yes, Eddie Stern himself. Now, some eight years later the office, desk, and responsibility that went along with it were all mine. It felt good to sit behind my king-size desk in my very large office.

Betty buzzed me. "Larry, Mr. Hertz is on line two."

"Good morning, Art."

"Good morning, Larry. Are you free for lunch today?"

"Yes, sir, I am."

"Good, Mike and I want to take you to The Standard Club at 12:30."

"Fine. Shall we meet in the parking lot?"

"That will be fine."

I wondered, "Is this one of those get-to-know-you meetings?"

The Standard Club is a private club located downtown on Biscayne Bay right in the heart of the banking district where Miami's elite in the business community gather for lunch and special occasions. I had eaten there probably two hundred times in the past eight years, but my lunches had always been with film executives in town from Dallas, New York, or L.A. This was my very first luncheon with Art and Mike.

While the waiter was bringing our iced tea, Art started the conversation. "Larry, Mike and I would like for you to enlighten us further about the process involved in purchasing film for our theatres. This is one area of the theatre business that we have a general knowledge of, but not a thorough knowledge of."

"Gentlemen, I'll be pleased to tell you whatever it is that you want to know about film buying. Let me start out by saying that I buy film several ways—it depends on which film company I am talking to. Let me give you an example. Tri-Star Pictures is my vendor everywhere in Miami, except in North Miami. In North Miami Tri-Star plays all their pictures in AMC's theatres. Now, what this means is that every picture Tri-Star releases, I play. That's great when we're opening Sylvester Stallone's new film, *Rambo*, in May. *Rambo* is a grand slam that is going to make Wometco lots and lots of money because we're their main customer in South Florida. That's the good news. The bad news is that I also have to play their losers. Sometimes holding an auditorium for a loser keeps us from going after a more important and much bigger picture with another company.

"More and more of the film companies are getting away from offering their product out on competitive bid. The reason is that the film companies are making a lot more movies today than they used to make.

For example, Disney used to release four to six movies a year. Now they are talking about cranking out twenty to thirty movies a year. When a company is bidding their product, then we—we being the theatre circuits—can pick and choose what pictures we want to go after. We will bid for the good movies and express no interest in the bad pictures. The film companies are now finding it in their best interest to stop the bidding process and allocate their pictures to play in the theatres of their choice. By doing this, they are assured that they will get all of their pictures played."

Art commented, "I heard that's what is starting to happen. Larry, my concern is this: say the big national theatre circuits like AMC and GCC make a deal with the film companies to play their pictures in their theatres everywhere. What does that do to circuits like Wometco?"

"That's a good question, Art; but it should not be a legitimate concern for you or Mike."

"Why not?"

"Because of our relationships, Art; that's why. I've been doing business with these companies for the past sixteen years. The way the film companies do business with theatre circuits changes every so often, but regardless of how they change, we always get our share of the pie. Sometimes we even get a bigger piece than we deserve.

"Take Orion Pictures, for example. We play Orion 100 percent wherever we have a theatre. You know, Orion is as hot as a firecracker. Yet, we play all of their movies."

Art asked, "Is that relationship on solid footing?"

"Is cement good enough for you?"

Art nodded as if he understood, but I could tell he really didn't understand all the information I was giving him.

Mike spoke up. "Larry, do you think all the companies will eventually discontinue offering their pictures out on competitive bid?"

"Yes, I do. As long as the marketplace is flooded with pictures the film companies would rather be ensured of a home for all of their pictures than to bid the big ones and have to worry about getting their little pictures played off."

Art asked, "Do you feel comfortable that you will be able to continue to get product from all the companies?"

"Art, there is only one fence that needs mending that I am aware of, and that is with Columbia Pictures. As long as Eddie Stern was the head buyer, my hands were tied. Now that Eddie is gone, I am going to try to get Wometco back in business with Columbia Pictures. But you two must be patient. You must remember all those years that we have been out of business with Columbia Pictures, someone else has been playing their pictures. You can't expect Columbia to walk away from their good, loyal customer that has been taking care of them all this time and start playing Wometco just because Eddie Stern is gone, can you?" Art stuck out his bottom lip as he shrugged his shoulders.

I continued, "Give me some time with Columbia, but remember, sometimes you have to crawl before you can walk. And this is going to be one of those times. As far as bids, I think once I have made my bids up, I should go over them with one of you for final approval. I do need some freedom. I don't want to waste your time or my time on the small stuff. Say on bids of $15,000 and up we should talk."

Art looked at Mike and said, "That's fine."

On the way back to the office I felt like the lunch had been a good one. These two men have stuck their necks way out in buying these theatres. I think I told them what they wanted to hear. Now I just had to be sure to deliver the goods, or within three months they'd be using me as fish bait over at the Miami Seaquarium.

––––––––

Standing at the foot of the hospital bed watching the nurses go through the tedious process of hooking all the small, fine wires from the monitor to Larry Jr.'s head made me wonder if our medical problems were ever going to end. Dr. Duschanney was very concerned about the way the medications were having very little, if any, effect on Larry's continuous seizure activity. In a few short months we had seen our three-and-a-half-year-old son's body digress back into infancy. Larry was back in diapers, constantly drooling at the mouth, and staying continuously doped up from the combination of medications his body was being given on a daily basis. We were hoping this hospital visit would give us some much-needed answers to those questions about Larry's uncontrollable seizure-related problems.

After two long days of watching Larry Jr.'s brain cell activity being monitored on a moment-by-moment basis, Doneata and I finally met with Dr. Duschanney. From the beginning I could tell he wasn't pleased with the test results. He made no attempt to hide his genuine concern.

"Mr. and Mrs. Vaughn, the results of our tests confirm why Larry's behavior has been the way it is. Every medication or combination of medications that we have tried on Larry has been totally ineffective. His brain is continuing to have uncontrollable, multiple-seizure activity which is being manifested in the obvious, abnormal reactions that are being manifested throughout his body." Dr. Duschanney gave us a very sympathetic look; then widening his eyes he said, "I mean there are a lot of fireworks going off all the time in that child's head." Dr. Duschanney stopped talking, looked down at his papers, and started bobbling his head from side to side as if to say, "What next?"

After a moment Dr. Duschanney sat up erect in his chair, took off his reading glasses, and tossed them on his desk as he cleared his throat to make a statement. "Mr. and Mrs. Vaughn, I think we should now consider the possibility of your son having a surgical procedure that will, hopefully, alleviate the seizure activity in his brain." Doneata went straight to her purse for a Kleenex. I knew she was about to start crying. "However," Dr. Duschanney continued, "I must warn you, having this operation does not in any way guarantee that Larry's seizure problem will be rectified. It is an alternative consideration, only to be used when medication has proven to be completely ineffective. Let me explain the surgery to the two of you so that you may weigh your options."

I thought to myself, "I wish Doneata were at home, and I could spare her from having to hear this firsthand. It would be easier on her if I could sugar-coat the bad news to her rather than have this guy give it to her point-blank."

"Mr. and Mrs. Vaughn, the first thing you need to be aware of is that this particular surgical procedure has been performed only sixty-six times in the United States. The majority of the operations have been performed in two hospitals up North, but one operation was performed here in South Miami within the last two months."

Doneata interrupted, "How is that child doing?"

"I'm sorry to report, not well. The child is still in a coma." Dr. Duschanney coughed and cleared his throat. "If we perform this surgery on your son, our intent will be to go into the front right side of the brain and remove a portion of the temple lobe area. This is the area where all of Larry's abnormal cell activity is coming from. By removing this area of the child's brain, it should enable us to anticipate one of the following results. One, the child could be totally free from abnormal cell activity— in other words, normal. That's the best case scenario." Dr. Duschanney held up two fingers and continued to talk. "Two, by having this surgery Larry would not be free from experiencing seizure activity; however, we would then be able to control Larry's seizure activity with medications. That's still a good result." Dr. Duschanney now painfully held up a third finger. "Three, the surgery would have no effect, at all, on Larry's condition. His abnormal seizure activity would not be affected by the surgery."

"Of the sixty-six surgeries performed so far, those are the results we have received. Larry's odds would be evenly split. At best we have a 33 percent chance for a complete recovery, a 33 percent chance to be able to control his seizures with medications, and a 33 percent chance that the operation will mean absolutely nothing as far as controlling the seizures."

"Now, let me give you the possible side effects: blindness, paralysis, and death. All three are possibilities with this type of brain surgery." Dr. Duschanney paused, dropped his head, and said, "I'm really sorry that I don't have better news for you folks, but all I can do is give you the facts as they are."

I smiled and nodded as if to say, "We understand. None of this is your doing. We will be okay."

Dr. Duschanney relaxed in his chair as if he had just finished a very unpleasant chore. Doneata's eyes were full of tears, and she was starting to shake. I knew it was all she could do to try to hold her composure. I reached over and squeezed her hand.

I looked at the little white-headed Dr. Duschanney. He looked his part: a surgeon, a thinker, one of the intellect of our society. He was in his late fifties, a short man, very thin, pale, almost frail looking but so intelligent that he constantly was trying to drop down to our level of understanding to explain the problem in words that Doneata and I could comprehend. I thought to myself, "If this were a poker hand, I would fold and ask for a re-deal. I don't like having to play this hand that I have been dealt."

"Dr. Duschanney, you have given Doneata and me a lot to think about. Let the two of us sort through all of this information and get back with you. If we decide to have you operate, when would you want to schedule the operation to be done?"

"Within the next three months. Actually, a surgeon from the Northeast will fly down to do this particular surgery. The surgeon specializes in this surgical procedure. For the child's sake, the sooner we operate the better off he will be."

I thought to myself, "So much for weighing our options." Then I continued, "Okay, thank you for your time. You'll hear from us by the first of next week."

Driving home from the hospital, Doneata started to cry. I tried to ignore her hurt and pain. I knew we had to get away from our feelings. Yes, somehow, we must get beyond our emotions.

"Doneata, listen to me. I was feeling in that doctor's office just like you do right now, but I don't feel that way anymore. No, I most certainly don't. I'm not discouraged at all."

Looking over at me with tear-filled eyes, Doneata said, "Go on. I want to know exactly how you feel."

"Okay, let me tell you. I think God is going to heal Larry's brain completely, and He is going to use the surgery as the means by which He chooses to heal Larry. Honey, I believe it with all my heart that God will protect Larry in and through the surgery; and the surgery will not be done in vain. God is going to use Dr. Duschanney to perform a miracle in our son's life. All we have to do is bathe the operation in prayer. The Lord will take care of the rest."

Doneata squeezed my arm and said, "Oh, Larry, what would we do in times like this without the Lord?"

"Honey, I would be on my way to get drunk as a skunk. Isn't that the way a lot of people react to hardships in this life? Doneata, I wish Pastor Clarkston were here with us right now. I know exactly what he would say. 'Brother and sister Vaughn, let's take this situation to God's people and have them pray for a miracle in your son's life. Psalm 130:5 tells us, "I wait for the Lord, my soul doth wait, and in his word do I hope." You folks must put your hope in Him and Him alone. Forget the circumstances. Circumstances are what those without faith have, but we are in the hands of the One Who controls those circumstances. Oh, how blessed are we to be called children of the living God.' "

"Larry, it sounds to me like you're starting to preach."

"No, I heard it on a message from Pastor Clarkston recently which just happens to be for Larry and Doneata today."

Doneata actually got a smile on her face as she said, "Honey, I'm glad we had this talk. I feel like God is in control, and we are going to have a victory."

"Good. Now, let's work on getting some prayer support before the day of the surgery."

———

That afternoon Doneata called her friend Arlene Milburn to ask Arlene and her family to remember Larry Jr. during their prayer time. We had met the Milburn family when they visited our Sunday school class a few weeks earlier. In no time at all we had become very close friends. Bob and Arlene, along with their two children, Steve and Lori, had recently moved to Miami from Goose Creek, South Carolina. Bob was a tall Georgia boy who had worked his entire business career with the K-Mart Company. He and I hit it off very well right from the start. He was just a laid-back kind of guy with no pretenses. Bob reminded me of Red Skelton in both his looks and actions. I thought Bob was funny without intending to be funny. He was full of warmth and had a wonderful personality. Bob knew no stranger. He could be a good buddy to almost anyone. He said the reason he and I got along so well is that we had absolutely nothing in common, that is, of course, outside of our relationship with our Lord.

Arlene ended up being Doneata's very best friend. They did absolutely everything together. I nicknamed them Lucy and Ethel. Doneata was Lucy and Arlene was Ethel. The nicknames fit perfectly, because those two girls were always getting themselves into the most comical situations. The Milburns were young in their faith but hungry to grow in God's Word. Our families made a good mix. We built a friendship that was going to last for a lifetime.

Prior to Larry Jr.'s scheduled surgery date, Doneata and Arlene started going around to various churches in the Miami area showing ministers a picture of Larry Jr. and asking the minister to share with his congregation Larry Jr.'s upcoming surgery.

I checked Larry Jr. into Miami Children's Hospital four days before his scheduled surgery date. Dr. Duschanney said, "Because of the seriousness of the surgery, we must put Larry Jr. through this test one more time, just to make absolutely sure all the seizure activity is contained in the temple lobe area of his brain." Larry was put in a brand-new room in a new wing of the hospital. The nurses came in, carefully placing each wire and socket into its proper place on Larry's head; and then started the long process of monitoring his brain cell activity.

A few hours later the nurse came in to report that there was a problem with the equipment. The nurse said, "Mr. Vaughn, there must be something wrong with the monitor that we are using. Everything is showing up normal on the screen. I am going to unhook Larry Jr. and put him on another monitor. You know, this is a new room, and it is going to take time for us to get the bugs out of the works."

I responded, "That's fine. You go ahead and do whatever it is you need to do." Thinking no more of it, I went back to my book.

The following morning the nurse and Dr. Duschanney came into the room together. Dr. Duschanney was the first to speak, "Mr. Vaughn, we are going to have to move Larry Jr. into another room. We can't get the equipment on track in this room. We spend all this money for the best equipment money can buy, and what happens? It doesn't work properly."

"I understand. Larry Jr. didn't care for the wallpaper in this room anyway." We all chuckled as we starting packing to move to another room.

Later that afternoon Dr. Duschanney came into Larry's room. He looked worn out. He sat down in the chair located across from Larry Jr.'s bed. He took his reading glasses and propped them up on his forehead. He had a frustrated look on his face. He took in a deep breath as if to say, "What a day!"

"Dr. Duschanney, you look like you've seen better days. This must have been a rough one for you."

Dr. Duschanney held his arms out with his hands open as if he were trying to feel for raindrops and said very emphatically, "Mr. Vaughn, your son is making me out to look like a fool." I sat up, because I was really curious about what he was talking about. "Mr. Vaughn, I know what I am about to say is going to make absolutely no sense, but your son for the past day and a half has had no abnormal activity in his brain." I just stared at the man, trying to figure out if I had heard him correctly. "Mr. Vaughn, I'm telling you there is absolutely nothing wrong with Larry. He has gone from continuous long-term multiple-seizure activity to zero seizure activity." As if embarrassed Dr. Duschanney continued, "We can't operate where there is no problem. 'Dr. Ramphus' is waiting to perform the surgery and now has arrived with no surgery to perform!"

I thought to myself, "What's wrong with me? Have I been asleep or just plain blind to what's been going on here these past two days?" Gathering my thoughts, I replied, "Dr. Duschanney, I can explain exactly what has happened."

Rubbing his eyes and acting as if he wasn't really interested in my uneducated theory, Dr. Duschanney said emphatically, "Tell me; I'm looking for an answer."

"It was God. God has healed Larry Jr." Dr. Duschanney looked at me as if I were talking about the Easter bunny. I thought, "I must get that smirk of disbelief off his pale face."

"Dr. Duschanney, let me explain. My wife and I are Christians."

He raised his eyebrows as if to say, "Here we go."

"We have been calling Christian people all over the country asking them to pray that the Lord would use this surgery to heal our son. Dr. Duschanney, we have over two hundred churches alone praying for Larry Jr. Your equipment is not broken, and Larry Jr. is not sick. I never put the equipment and the rooms together with Larry's seizures because I was so sure God was going to heal him through the surgery. Don't you see what has happened here? God has performed a miracle right before our very eyes."

I could tell the good doctor was not buying what I was selling. "Now, Mr. Vaughn, let's not get carried away with God performing some supernatural miracle just yet. There is a very good possibility that your son's seizure activity will return in the very near future."

"Dr. Duschanney, with all due respect to your medical expertise, you're wrong." That statement produced a frown on the doctor's face. "When God does a healing of this nature, it is permanent. I can't believe that I didn't suspect something yesterday when the equipment gave a clear reading. It's just that I was 100 percent sure Larry Jr. would be healed in the operating room. But isn't God good? He spared us that."

Dr. Duschanney was just sitting there with a frown on his face, halfway listening to what I was trying to tell him. I could see his wheels spinning; his mind was searching, searching for an answer. He was desperately trying to find something tangible that he could grasp on to.

After a while Dr. Duschanney came up with his own theory. "Mr. Vaughn, what could have very well happened is that your son, at the eleventh hour, realized the seriousness of the surgery. His body could have reacted by healing itself, rather than going through the trauma of the surgery. That is a very good possibility of what could have actually happened." He seemed pleased with his theoretical evaluation of the situation. "Anyway, Mr. Vaughn, don't be surprised if the seizures return. I expect the seizure activity to return in the near future; and when it does, then we'll reevaluate our position and act accordingly."

I was getting irritated with his disbelief. "Dr. Duschanney, you think what you like. You won't see Larry Jr. again in this hospital for seizure problems. No, as of today, seizures are no longer a concern in the Vaughn household."

That day was the end of Larry's seizures. Larry never again had another seizure that we are aware of. It took Doneata and me several months to wean Larry off his medications, but within a few months he was a totally normal child. That was the wonderful part of this miraculous event. The sad part of the story was the wise Dr. Duschanney's total blindness to the miraculous healing power of God in our son's life.

———

I spent the better part of the following week in Atlanta meeting with various executives from the film companies. I had the opportunity to tell several film distributors about how God had miraculously inter-vened and healed my son without his having to go through surgery. All of the men seemed to listen with great interest as I told the story. It gave me an excellent opportunity to share the gospel with several men.

One division manager in particular, Jim Dixon, shared with me during a business dinner, "Larry, you know, several years ago I heard that you had become one of those born-again Christians, and you know what? I have been watching you for years to see if your conversion was for real."

I felt an urgent concern. "Jim, that scares me to hear you say that. I hope I haven't disappointed you too much since you started watch-ing me."

"Larry, you haven't disappointed me at all. No, not once." Jim raised his eyebrows and blew out a puff of hot air. He smiled as he said, "I still remember the old Larry Vaughn very well. If things didn't go exactly like you thought they should go, you would start cursing and threaten to go over my head to the home office." Shaking his head with a big frown, Jim said, "Larry, sometimes you could be a miserable soul."

I knew that man he was talking about. I wanted to crawl under the table. He continued, "Larry, I would have to listen to you rant and rave until you had absolutely nothing left to say. But since you became a Christian, not once have I seen you display that type of attitude, and I'm always watching. I noticed how the industry as a whole has recognized you as being a Christian man. You're always the individual who is asked to give the invocation at convention dinners. When you first started being called on to pray before meals, I just thought to myself, 'Looks like Vaughn has found his new spot on the dais; he has been pigeonholed to be the Christian to ask the blessing.' "

Jim gave me a funny look as if to say, "You ain't gonna believe this." Then he continued. "Larry, there have been times when I have actually tested you to try to force you to lose your temper, but you wouldn't retaliate. You told me you thought my position on the issue was wrong, and you would like to suggest that we do such and such; but I couldn't get you to lose your temper."

I thought to myself, "Praise the Lord that He has blinded this man to my sinfulness."

"Larry, you are the man that God used to bring salvation into my life. Today I am a born-again Christian because of how I have seen God work in your life."

"Jim, why didn't you tell me?"

Jim smiled. "I just did."

"No, I mean sooner. When did you become a Christian?"

"Three months ago. I even have my whole family in church. They all know about you."

"Well, I just don't know what to say. Our God, isn't He wonderful!"

"Yes, Larry, He is. I can't wait to get home and tell my family about God's healing Larry Jr."

"Jim, next trip to Atlanta I expect to meet your family."

"Larry, come in on a Wednesday, and we'll take you to a prayer meeting."

"Jim, that's a date."

Flying home on the L1011, I sat staring out the window, watching as the afternoon sun started to make its descent into the west. Below me, all I could see were lazy blue and white pillows of clouds as the evening was preparing to make way for nightfall. The words to a song I heard Mentora singing last week came to mind. I think she learned the little song in Sunday school. "From the rising of the sun, to the going down of the same. The name of the Lord is to be praised."

Twenty-Three

The Unexpected Bouquet

The next few months I was kept very busy at the office. I really enjoyed working for Art and Mike; the three of us seemed to get along just fine. Stanley was in and out of the office, but for the most part Stanley was being used by Art and Mike as a consultant with the new Wometco. Stanley, like the other senior executives of the former company, was now financially independent and could do whatever he chose to do with his time and money.

Art and Mike divided the responsibility of overseeing the various departments within Wometco between themselves. As far as titles, Art was Chairman of the Board, and Mike was President of Wometco. Of the two men, Art was the one I was the most involved with daily. When film executives were in town, I would quite often invite Art to have dinner with us. Of course, Mike was always more than welcome to come along, but Mike's involvement seemed to be more with Peter Moreno, our man in charge of the Puerto Rico Theatres, than with the domestic operation.

Every Tuesday morning we had an executive meeting in the board room at 8:00 a.m., which I always thought was sixty minutes too early. However, I never shared that point of disagreement with the bosses. Art, Mike, Bill Copley—who replaced the late Jack Mitchell as General Manager—and I attended the meetings. After a brief time of small talk and coffee we would dig right into the business at hand. I was always first on the agenda. I would submit a report showing what each theatre in the company grossed at the box office the past Friday, Saturday, and Sunday. On that same report I would show what the other theatre circuits grossed that same weekend. By doing this, we could look at each individual market and see exactly how our theatres were doing against the opposition theatres.

I always felt somewhat like a sports analyst on Tuesday morning trying to explain why the theatre in Ocala did so well over the weekend. Orlando was soft, but next weekend was going to be great in Orlando. We were in trouble in Gainesville. Miami and Ft. Lauderdale did this, but this coming weekend in Boca Raton, well, you'd best prepare yourself for this. During some of those meetings I would think to myself, "I'm like a football coach: I'm only as good as last weekend's results."

Art and Mike seemed to be sensitive to their being overweight, especially since it was near the time for them to have their company physicals. One day during lunch, Mike made a proposal to Art and me. As Mike rubbed his stomach and looked across the table first at my stomach and then at Art's stomach, he said, "Gentlemen, the three of us need to go on a diet."

I noticed Art immediately got a frown on his face as if to say, "Now, why did you go and bring up that subject?"

Mike continued, "I've got a suggestion about how we might encourage one another to lose some weight, that is if anyone is interested."

I looked over at Art, who was still frowning, and then back to Mike, who was sitting, waiting with a curious look on his face. I said, "Sure, I'm interested." Even though I was a jogger, I still had allowed my weight to climb up to 210 pounds. I could stand to lose 20 to 25 pounds.

Mike and I both looked at Art. Art grit his teeth, stuck out his bottom lip, and shook his head from side to side as if to say, "It's useless. I can't lose any weight." I almost laughed, but then I thought, "I'd better not!" Art exhaled a large gust of air in frustration at the thought and looked at his watch as if to say, "Time might be becoming an issue." Then reluctantly he replied, "Go ahead, Mike. Tell us what's on your mind."

Mike smiled, pulled his chair up closer to the table, and put both elbows on the table as he prepared to share with Art and me his well-thought-out proposal.

"First thing, gentlemen, is we need a new set of scales to weigh with. I am prepared to fund the cost of the scales with my own personal resources."

I glanced at Art. He didn't seem impressed with Mike's generosity.

"The scales will be placed in the closet in my office. They are to be used once a week, every Tuesday morning prior to our 8:00 a.m. meeting. Our first weigh in will be next Tuesday morning. Each person's weight on that day will be his starting number. Now, here's how the rules will work."

I glanced over at Art again. This time the expression on his big, round face was already one of defeat. I almost laughed. Mike leaned over toward Art to explain the rules very carefully.

"During the week, if you gain a pound or more it will cost you $10 for each pound you gain to each of the other two players. For each pound you lose during the week, you will receive $10 from the other two players. That's it. We will weigh in every Tuesday, add, subtract, and pay off. What do you guys think?"

I said, "Count me in. I need to lose some weight. I'll feast between now and Monday, then on Tuesday I'll start on my crash diet."

Art started popping his big knuckles on his fat fingers. I thought, "I wonder if Art's popping of his knuckles in any way represents what he would like to be doing to Mike's neck at this moment."

Art said, as if under duress, "Okay, count me in as of Tuesday."

With a big smile on his face, Mike said, "Great! This will be good for Wometco. You know, a healthy Wometco management is a happy Wometco management."

Art looked at me as if in disgust and said, "Let's go."

Financially, Mike's weight-loss program turned out to be a windfall for me. The show and tell every Tuesday morning amounted to anywhere from $30 to $80 cash for me. The $10 swing gave me all the incentive I needed to cut back on food and jog longer. For Art, it wasn't incentive enough for him even to skip dessert. I lost twenty pounds; Mike lost about fifteen. And Art—well, he gained a few pounds during the program. Unfortunately for me, after a few weeks Art humbly asked Mike and me to dissolve the program.

After six months with the new Wometco, Art and Mike awarded me with my V.P. stripes. My official title was Vice President in charge of Film Buying and Booking. I was glad that I had waited and not had to ask to be made a Vice President. It felt good to know that in six months I had won them over, that Art and Mike had complete confidence in my film-buying abilities in the highly competitive Florida theatre market.

––––––––––

The limousine driver put the last piece of luggage into the trunk, slammed the lid down, and then we were on our way to the hotel. Art and Mike were sitting directly across from me; Doneata was sitting beside me. Janet Brown was sitting on the other side of Doneata. The ladies were having a good time just talking with each other about everything they wanted to do while "the boys" were busy working at the upcoming NATO convention.

THE REEL STORY

NATO is short for the National Association of Theater Owners. NATO holds an annual meeting in major cities throughout the United States. This particular meeting was being held in Los Angeles. The convention started on Monday evening and concluded on Thursday evening. There must have been four to five thousand theatre people in attendance, which included both exhibitors and distributors.

I don't remember the name of the hotel the convention was being held in, but it was an old hotel that had been restored to a magnificent piece of architecture. I enjoyed our stay there as much as any hotel I have ever stayed in. And because of my position in the film industry, that list included some of the best hotels in the country: the Beverly Wilshire in Beverly Hills, the Waldorf Astoria in New York City, and the Ritz Carlton in Atlanta. The money and power associated with my position in the film industry brought along with them a good many perks: and they all suited me just fine.

Because of this particular hotel's uniqueness, it made for a most delightful stay. Doneata especially enjoyed our room; it was furnished with a beautiful cherry bed, dresser, table and armoire, a quilted bedspread with thick linens, plush carpeting, and two high back chairs for sitting, reclining, and relaxation. We had a beautiful view of Los Angeles from our window.

That evening Mike and Janet went to the dinner at the convention while Art, Doneata, and I had dinner away from the hotel in a quaint

Michael and Janet Brown with Danny DeVito (center)

little Italian restaurant with Bruce Snyder. Bruce was the President of Twentieth Century Fox Film Distribution. Down through the years, Bruce had been a good friend to me and the old Wometco Theaters. I was excited about introducing Bruce to Art and the new Wometco. The four of us had a wonderful dinner in a table located off to the corner of the restaurant. After dinner, Bruce suggested we go back to the hotel and have after dinner-drinks before turning in for the evening.

While the four us were sitting in the lounge at the hotel, Joel Resnick walked up and said hello to me. Joel was the newly appointed chairman of Orion Pictures Distribution. I introduced Joel to Doneata and Art. Of course, Joel already knew Bruce Snyder. Joel chatted with us for a couple of minutes; then as he started to walk away, he made a statement loud enough for all to hear.

Smiling at me as if he knew something that I didn't, Joel said, "Larry, I hope you've enjoyed your past relationship with Orion Pictures, because it's about to come to an end." Joel then abruptly left the room as a feeling of uneasiness and concern came over me.

There I am sitting with the president of Twentieth Century Fox, the chairman of Wometco, and my wife, and this guy torpedoes me in the presence of them all. Art wasn't sure how to act. With Bruce sitting there, it was a rather awkward time to be discussing a potential problem with one of our best customers in front of another of our best customers.

I looked over at Bruce. He smirked and said, "Larry, do you know what that was all about?"

I said, "No, tell me."

"Joel is trying to make himself look important in front of me; that's all it was, Larry. Joel's trying to throw his weight around in front of me."

I said, "Well, let's not let his actions ruin a wonderful evening. Bruce, I wish it hadn't come up during our time together."

Bruce shrugged his shoulders as if to say, "No big deal."

Later Bruce said his farewell and left for the evening. Art couldn't suppress his concern with Joel Resnick's statement one second longer. Immediately, Art said very emphatically, "Larry, what's this all about with Resnick?"

"Art, I don't know why he would say something like that except for the obvious reason. You know Resnick was a senior officer at American Multi-Cinemas before moving to Orion Pictures. In markets where Wometco operates theatres, AMC has never had the opportunity to play Orion product. You know, in the past Wometco's relationship with Orion has most likely been a real point of contention with Resnick while he was working for AMC." I thought to myself, "Maybe he doesn't realize that his allegiance is to Orion now."

I could see the steam starting to come out from under Art's collar. "Larry, isn't Orion Pictures the company you told me we played 100 percent, and this is one of those relationships you said was sealed. I believe you said, 'Sealed in cement.'"

"Art," I replied, "my relationship at Orion is not with Joel Resnick; it's with Bob Cheran, the President of Orion Distribution, and Charlie Jones, the Southern Division Manager." (I thought to myself, "As it just so happens, providentially—") "You, Mike, and I are scheduled to have lunch tomorrow with the Orion people—Bob Cheran, Charlie Jones, and the Executive V.P., Buddy Golden. Tomorrow at lunch we'll see just how good our cement really is with Orion Pictures."

When we got into the room, Doneata said, "Oh, Larry, I felt so bad for you. That was just awful."

I tried to laugh off my frustration. "Doneata, don't feel bad for me. That's called business. That's what I get paid the big bucks for, putting out fires like this one."

Doneata looked really worried. "Larry, do you think everything will be okay?"

"Honey, I think Cheran will back me on this one. I've done too much for Orion down through the years for them to take a walk now. However, we need to seriously bathe this luncheon tomorrow in prayer. If I lose Orion Pictures, it will create a great void in my major film supply, especially in the Miami area where Orion has really helped to fill auditoriums with big pictures."

I don't remember who was at breakfast Tuesday morning because of the importance of the Orion luncheon that day. At 12:30 we met in one of the hotel's restaurants. I remember we were seated at a round table located in the center of the restaurant: Bob Cheran, Buddy Golden, Charlie Jones, Art, Mike, and me. My best friend at the table was Charlie Jones. He was my original connection with Orion, and we went back to the Michael Heffner days in Charlotte. For years Charlie had worked for Twentieth Century Fox. I had been the one to help him out in the summer of 1977 by giving him a few playdates on his "little space picture," *Star Wars*. Now Charlie was responsible for sales for Orion Pictures from Texas to the Carolinas. When I had taken a chance on *Star Wars* years earlier, I made both Charlie and me a great deal of money. Now I needed that relationship to hold strong.

This was not one of those luncheons where you have some small talk, ask about everyone's family and dog, then eat a hearty lunch before you get down to the business at hand. No, it was just the opposite. I started out telling them exactly what Joel had said the night before. Bob Cheran hit the table so hard I was expecting to see twelve waiters respond to his command.

Bob said, "Over my dead body will we sell product away from Wometco. Who does Joel think he is to come into this company and start messing with my customers?"

I thought to myself, "Praise the Lord for answered prayer."

Buddy spoke up. "He thinks he still works for AMC."

Bob said, "Well, he doesn't. Larry, I want to apologize to you, Art, and Mike for last night. I'm truly embarrassed that happened, and I do wish Bruce hadn't been there." Then Bob looked me straight in the eye and said, "Larry, as long as I'm President of Distribution at Orion Pictures, you don't have a thing to be concerned about. We're there as long as you need us."

After the luncheon I asked Art, "Well, is the cement going to hold?"

Art gave me a reassuring smile as he winked and said, "Yes, Larry, I believe it will."

That evening we were supposed to go meet Sylvester Stallone at a private party. I was in the shower trying to get refreshed from the stress of the day when Doneata stuck her head in the bathroom door and said, "Larry, you have a telephone call."

From the shower I shot back, "Honey, see if I may call them back in ten minutes." I got out of the shower, dried off, put my house coat on, and went into the bedroom. Doneata handed me the note: "Call Mr. Resnick at room 2307."

"Well," I said to no one in particular, "this is going to be an interesting conversation." I dialed the phone and heard a familiar voice on the other end.

"Hello?"

"Hi, Joel, Larry Vaughn returning your call."

In a very cordial tone of voice Joel said, "Larry, what are you trying to do to me?"

"I beg your pardon."

"Larry, you've got the boys all upset with me. Bob called wanting to know what I was doing making threats to his customers. Larry, don't you know I was just joking with you last night?"

"Joel, neither I nor anyone in my party found any humor in what you had to say."

"Well, I meant nothing in what I said. Of course you're our customer. I can't believe you took me seriously."

"Okay, Joel, let's drop it at that," I responded.

"No hard feelings?"

"No hard feelings, Joel."

I hung up the receiver thinking, "I sure hope Bob Cheran has a long-term contract with Orion."

That evening at the Stallone party, I ran into Bruce Snyder and told him of the events of the day.

Bruce laughed as he said, "I'm glad it's back to business as usual with you and your friends at Orion." And that's just the way the balance of the week was—business as usual. That is, up until the Thursday evening grand finale.

On Thursday evening there was a private party prior to the closing ceremony in a room adjacent to the Grand Ballroom of the hotel. The party was by invitation only to a select group of maybe 150 VIP's. Immediately following the party would be the dinner and closing ceremonies in the Grand Ballroom at 8:00. The dinner was for all 4,000 to 5,000 attendees.

Larry Vaughn and Sylvester Stallone

Ron Howard and Larry Vaughn at the private party

I had tickets for Art, Mike, Janet, Doneata, and me to attend the party. I told them to be sure to make it to the party, because there were going to be several heads of film studios there along with some big-name stars: Ron Howard, Danny DeVito, Michael J. Fox, and Clint Eastwood were all supposed to be there along with several other big names in the business.

We arrived at the party right at 6:30, and as we went into the room, the first thing I noticed was the scrumptious buffet of lobster, roast beef, shrimp, baked ham, turkey, and a variety of baked breads. Doneata looked at the food and said, "Honey, if I start eating this, I won't be able to enjoy my dinner."

I responded, "Doneata, don't forget that at the dinner you're eating one of 5,000 pieces of chicken. Let's enjoy ourselves right here."

The room started filling up with people, and somehow Doneata and I got separated. I found Ron Howard standing over in a corner by himself and walked over to introduce myself to him. I talked with him several minutes, telling him how much I appreciated his last film, *Cocoon*, and how I had been a fan of his from his Opie days on the *Andy Griffith Show*. Ron Howard is a genuinely nice man. For someone who has grown up in front of the camera as a star and is now behind the camera as a respected director, he seems to have a lot of humility—that's not something you see a lot of among the Hollywood elite.

I started looking for Doneata, and I couldn't find her anywhere. I ran into Danny DeVito and started to talk with him. While talking movies with Mr. DeVito, I looked across the room and saw Doneata standing beside Clint Eastwood. He whis-

Danny DeVito and Larry Vaughn

pered something in her ear, and she immediately pointed over toward me. He looked at me and nodded his head, as though he were agreeing with her on some point.

I thought to myself, "I wonder what they are talking about? I'd best mosey on over to them." It took me a minute to get there, but I finally made my way over to them.

Clint Eastwood extended his hand and said, "Hello, Larry Vaughn. Your wife and I have been talking about you. She tells me that you have been faithful in playing all my films."

"Mr. Eastwood, I believe that to be correct. I have done a lot of business with Warner Brothers down through the years, and I don't think I've missed playing many of your motion pictures."

We talked about the industry a few minutes; then Doneata and I stepped aside to let some other folks have a chance to speak with him.

I said, "Let's get some more food before we leave."

"Larry, if I do, I won't be able to eat any dinner."

"It doesn't matter. Let's get another plate of this good stuff." We reloaded and found a resting place.

At this point I had to find out what Doneata and Clint Eastwood had been talking about. I began, "Doneata, did you have the opportunity to meet all of the celebrities?"

"Yes, I did. I especially enjoyed meeting Michael J. Fox. Larry, I had no idea he was so young. He was very kind to me. We talked several minutes, but I could tell he was very tired."

"Honey, everyone is tired. These conventions will wipe you out by the time you leave to go home. I'm glad you had the opportunity to meet everyone. Now, let me ask you a question."

"What's that?"

"What did Clint Eastwood whisper in your ear earlier?"

Doneata put her hands on her sides and gave me a very serious look. "Larry Vaughn, do you know what he asked me?"

"No what?"

"He wanted to know what I was doing later this evening!"

My mouth dropped, and I stammered, "You're kidding?"

"No, I'm not!"

"And what did you say when he asked you what you were doing later this evening?"

"I pointed toward you and said, 'I'll be with my husband—that tall man right over there.' That's when I had the opportunity to tell him that you were the buyer for Wometco."

"Then what did he say?"

"He said, 'Have I met him?' I said, 'I don't know. I'll call Larry over.'"

Clint Eastwood and Doneata Vaughn

At this point, I was thinking to myself: "Humph! Clint Eastwood's trying to come on to my wife." We finished our hors d'oeuvres and moved on into the ballroom for the banquet.

The grand ballroom was decorated mostly with Clint Eastwood memorabilia because he was being honored by NATO as the "Star of the Decade." We ended up with fairly good seating—our table was located about two-thirds of the way back, but it was situated directly beside one of the two main aisles which led in and out of the ballroom. We really didn't have to be seated near the dais because we had talked with nearly everyone on the dais at the party earlier in the evening.

The most interesting event of the evening, as far as I was concerned, happened at the closing of the ceremony. All the awards had been given out; all the speeches had been made, and all the stars were preparing to leave the dais to exit the ballroom. Clint Eastwood was the first to leave the stage along with Barry Reardon and other Warner Brothers executives. Eastwood, being first, set the tempo for everyone behind him. He happened to exit the aisle that our table was closest to. A spotlight was following him as he walked the aisle toward the back exit.

While walking toward the exit, Mr. Eastwood spotted Doneata. He stopped on the spot, which meant that the twenty celebrities behind him also had to stop. He stepped over the crowd-control ropes and

Larry Vaughn and Clint Eastwood

walked past the security guards, who were separating the tables from the aisle, and walked the fifteen feet or more over to our table. Mr. Eastwood then proceeded to pick up the bouquet of flowers that were being used as the centerpiece on our table. He then graciously handed the bouquet to Doneata. He gave her a warm smile, then turned and walked back to the security guards and crossed back over the rope, where all the other celebrities and executives were just standing there waiting for him to return so that they could leave the ballroom.

Doneata had nowhere to hide. She just stood there totally embarrassed with five thousand people looking at her and her bouquet of flowers.

––––––––

It felt great to be back in Miami after having spent most of the previous week in Los Angeles.

I spent most of the day at our church, Parker Road, on Sunday. In the morning at 9:30, we had Sunday school, followed by fellowship time at 10:30. Then, the morning worship service at 11:00. I then had to be back at church at 5:00 p.m. for an hour and a half long leadership class on training to become an officer. I and several of the other men in the church were studying with Pastor Short. The day concluded with the evening worship service at 7:00.

By the time we got home from church, fed the children a snack, and got them into bed, it was pushing 10:00.

I told Doneata, "Come on, let's go out on the patio and talk a few minutes before we go to bed."

She made two cups of hot tea and brought them to the outside table. Then she looked at me and asked, "Honey, is there anything special you want to talk about?"

"Doneata, I was just thinking on the way home tonight about the worship services today. You know, everybody at Parker Road is so friendly, but have you noticed how no one at church seems to ever talk about things of the Lord? I don't know, maybe it's just me, but I got absolutely nothing out of either one of Robert's messages today."

"Larry, you keep listening to Pastor Clarkston speak on radio. Then you go to church and have to listen to Robert preach. Well, you seemed to get let down."

I thought a minute and then responded, "Doneata, that's not it. I don't expect Robert to preach like Pastor Clarkston, but I do wish I could go to church and get fed every once in a while.

"As far as conversation in general, there is very little difference between what the members of Parker Road talk about during the fellowship time on Sunday morning and what the film people talked about during those cocktail parties last week in Los Angeles. I think Parker Road has more of a country-club atmosphere about it than a place of worship. If I didn't have the preaching and sound Bible teaching of Pastor Clarkston, then I would have no one teaching me sound biblical truths and principles."

"Larry, how is the officer training class going?" Doneata asked.

"Fine. Robert is a much better teacher than a preacher. Doneata, I guess I shouldn't be complaining so much. As long as we're at Parker Road, we can do just about anything we want to and be accepted just the way we are. Everyone at church thinks it's wonderful that I have been made a Vice President at Wometco. I have yet to hear one negative comment from anyone about my being in the entertainment industry. But, let me tell you something, Doneata. If we up and moved to Pastor Clarkston's church, I think we would have to make a lot of changes in our life before those folks would even let us join their membership. Those people out there are striving for holiness. They are God-centered. You can tell that by the way the man preaches. Parker Road is man-centered, and you can tell that is true by the way Robert preaches."

I looked at my watch; it was 10:45 and time for bed.

"Doneata, I don't know why I can't just leave well enough alone. It just seems to me that the Christian people at Parker Road have the same interests as the unsaved film people. Pastor Clarkston keeps talking about our being strangers and aliens, peculiar people: in the world, but not of the world. I don't know anyone at Parker Road who fits that description. It bothers me sometimes the way we have the freedom in Christ to do anything and everything. It seems like that freedom is what's wrong with you and me and the folks at Parker Road."

I paused a minute to judge Doneata's response. She was listening intently, so I continued. "I know it's not a sin to drink and gamble, but for some reason it doesn't seem right for us to live our new life in Christ the way we did before we came to know Him as Lord and Savior. At least, that's what I keep getting out of Pastor Clarkston's messages."

At this point, Doneata interrupted me. "Larry, I told you a long time ago that I thought gambling was wrong for a Christian, but I wanted the Lord to convict you that gambling was wrong without my having to nag you about it. As for drinking wine, Larry, if you feel we should not drink wine that is fine with me. I just want it to be your decision."

"Oh, I don't know what I want. When I get out of town, I want to drink fine wine and gamble. When I get around Pastor Short, I want to do the same; but when I study the Bible and listen to Pastor Clarkston's messages on radio, I feel like my gambling is a poor witness, and I'm just not so sure about where I stand on drinking wine right now."

I stretched and smiled at Doneata, "If anyone knows, you know how much I enjoy a bottle of fine wine."

Doneata was starting to yawn from the long day. "Honey, we'd best turn in and finish this conversation tomorrow. You have got to get up early in the morning."

"Doneata, there is really nothing left to say. These things just keep churning around in my head." I held my hands up and shook my head as if I were trying to dry my hair with an imaginary towel. "I can tell you one thing. I sure do go from one extreme to the other."

"What do you mean?"

"Talking about movies with Sylvester Stallone one day and trying to understand what Pastor Clarkston means when he talks about being strangers and aliens the next day. Doneata, in the last week we have experienced the very best of both worlds. One world is totally controlled by darkness, and the other is controlled by light."

––––––––

As the small commuter jet was making its descent from Philadelphia into Atlantic City, I went back over my well-thought-out plan. No gambling on this trip, period. I am a new creature in Jesus Christ. I am not going back to my old ways of throwing around large amounts of cash in the casino. My money could be used for a much better purpose, like in the Lord's work. Besides, what if some other men are watching me like Jim did for all those years. What a poor testimony and stumbling block my gambling could be in their life.

I'm staying at Merv Griffin's Resort Hotel, and the Show East Convention is being held next door in the adjacent hotel, Donald Trump's Taj Mahal. Now, how can I get to the many convention activities without going the obvious and shortest way, which is through both hotels' casinos? Let me think. It will be out of the way, but I could go to the first floor elevators at the Merv Griffin Hotel, then walk immediately out the side exit doors, which lead to the Boardwalk. I could then walk up the Boardwalk to the Taj Mahal and enter the Taj Mahal through their Boardwalk entrance. I would then have to take the escalator upstairs and cross back over to the convention activities. It would take a lot longer to do it that way, but I would bypass having to walk through the casinos to get to the convention meetings. It would be worth the extra time and effort in order to bypass, not one, but two casinos and have to deal with being tempted to gamble.

I had to prepare myself mentally: this is going to be a long week. It's now Tuesday morning, and I'll be here until Friday morning. I thought to myself, "If anyone would have ever even suggested that I, Larry Vaughn, would be flying into Atlantic City for three days and all the cash I would have on me was a hundred bucks for taxis and newspapers, I would have laughed in his face and told him he was crazy. But, this is a confirmation to me that my salvation is of God—that it is real. He is most certainly the only One who could have changed my heart in this once most-loved area of my life."

I was right. It ended up being a very long week. I spent all my free time in my room doing Bible studies, listening to tapes from Pastor Clarkston, and jogging up and down the Boardwalk. I think one of the saddest sights I've ever seen in all my life was all the old people that were being bused into Atlantic City from the New York area on those junkets to gamble for the day.

Those old folks would come in once a month and put the better part of their monthly social security check into the casino's slot machines. Then, once their cash was gone, they would go outside and sit on the Boardwalk, waiting for the scheduled departure time so that the bus could take them back to their homes. How empty their lives looked. How I appreciated the gift of eternal life that I had been given, especially when I looked into their sad eyes as they just sat there waiting for the lonely ride home.

That particular week I spent many hours on the Boardwalk examining the different types of people that live in a city that is known around the world for its gambling casinos. Pimps, prostitutes, drugs, crime, and poverty: they all go hand in hand with legalized gambling.

I had some very good business meetings while in Atlantic City. I spent all my time during the day attending convention activities, in addition to several luncheons and dinners with various film executives. On the plane home Friday morning, I prayed a prayer of thanksgiving to the Lord: I thanked Him for His protection during the week. I also thanked Him for helping me not to yield to the temptation of my flesh.

There were times during that week that I felt like a magnet was actually trying to draw me to my old friend, the blackjack table. When the temptation was at its greatest, I would leave the building and recite some recently learned memory verses that dealt with being tempted.

Yes, the Lord was good. I got on the plane with cash in my pocket. Outside of meals and the hotel bill, I never used my VISA card once. Those individuals who really knew me, if they were there, could have said they had seen a true miracle happen in my life during that week. I didn't gamble so much as a dollar. No, not once did I place a bet in a casino.

———

The following Monday afternoon Charlie Jones flew in from Dallas to settle the film rental payments on the film *Platoon*. It was always good to see Charlie Jones. Down through the years, Charlie had become one of my very best friends in the film industry. As a matter of fact, I was best man at Charlie's wedding when he and his wife, Thelma, were married several years earlier. Charlie was a tall, rugged man. He was in his mid-to-late fifties. Charlie had built up quite a reputation for himself in his many years in the film industry. He was known as a tough, no-nonsense Southern Division Manager who did a very good job for Orion Pictures in spite of his personal lifestyle.

Charlie was an excellent golfer. He always either won or came in second or third at the many film industry golf tournaments that were held throughout the year. Charlie was a high roller when it came to placing a wager on a game of golf, a blackjack table, or a high-stakes poker game. Charlie's reputation as a two-fisted drinker preceded all of the above. More often than not, Charlie would start drinking liquor early in the afternoon and end up getting himself in trouble later in the day because of something he did or said to someone as the day and his alcohol wore on. Yes, Charlie seemed to enjoy living his life to the fullest, always walking on the edge, continuously toying with disaster.

Charlie and I were best buddies before I came to know Christ as my Savior. Charlie and I have spent literally hundreds of hours at the dog track, horse track, playing gin rummy, or in a high-stakes poker game. After I became a Christian, Charlie never really understood my conversion experience. I tried talking with him on several different occasions about how Christ came into my life, but Charlie seemed totally blinded to anything of spiritual interest.

Once in Miami, not long after I came to know Christ, Charlie and Thelma came to spend a weekend with my family and me. During their stay with us, I let Charlie drive one of my cars. He never commented, but I often wondered if it bothered Charlie driving around town with a car that had a big red heart on the bumper that said, "Jesus died for you."

I picked up Charlie at the airport around 4:30 and drove him over to his hotel, The Grand Bay in Coconut Grove. Some people would say The Grand Bay is the best place to stay in all of Miami. It was most certainly the hotel of choice for the various film distributors who always seemed to be in town for one reason or another.

I spent the remainder of the afternoon with Charlie in the hotel's lounge. That evening Charlie and I were going to have dinner with Art in one of the private clubs in the Grove at 7:00 p.m. Art picked us up in front of the Grand Bay at 6:45. We made small talk while taking the five-minute drive to the restaurant. I was a bit concerned about Charlie's overindulgence in alcohol that afternoon. I didn't know whether he had been drinking on the plane ride to Miami, but I knew Charlie was totally relaxed by the time we left the lounge at the Grand Bay. The first thing Art did was order Charlie a drink. I could see this was going to be one of those long, Charlie Jones evenings.

Art spent the next half hour asking Charlie industry-related information. Art loved data, data, and more data. After Charlie brought Art and me up to date with everything that was going on in production at Orion Pictures: with the industry as a whole and the latest news about what other theatre circuits were doing as far as expanding their theatre operations.

Finally, Charlie held his hands up as if he were being robbed and said, "Art, that's enough shoptalk. I came to Miami to see my good friends at Wometco. I'm here to spend money. To wine and dine you and Larry." Laughing, Charlie said, "I'm here especially to wine you."

I said, "Charlie, you can wine and dine us when we're in Dallas. As long as you're in our town, we do the wining and dining."

Art spoke up, "Yeah. Whom do you think you're having dinner with? We're not one of those other cheap theatre circuits. In Miami, your money is no good, Charlie Jones."

Charlie smiled at Art, and then in a business tone of voice he said, "I wish you guys were as friendly at settling the film rental payments on pictures as you are in picking up dinner checks."

Charlie then looked at me and stuck out his tongue at me. When he did that, Art looked totally dumbfounded at Charlie's most unusual behavior. Then Charlie said with a smirk on his face, "Larry, you're a miserable guy to settle film rental payments with. I think I'll make Joel happy and start playing my pictures with AMC."

I looked at Art and said, "You see the type of character I have to do business with."

Charlie motioned to the waiter for a refill on his drink and said, "Larry, are you saying I don't have no class, or just low class?"

"Charlie, I didn't say anything about your class; I was talking about your character. I'll discuss your class tomorrow after we have finalized the film rental payments on *Platoon*."

Charlie nudged Art and said, "Art, how would you like to settle the film rental payments on *Platoon* with me right here and now and leave Larry out?" Holding up three fingers as if to say, "Scout's honor," Charlie said, "Art, I promise I'll give you a better settlement than I will him." Charlie pointed toward me as he puffed his cheeks out and stuck his finger up in the air.

I thought to myself, "Charlie is getting stone drunk. Art is used to dealing with bankers, not people like Charlie Jones. It's going to be interesting to see how Art handles this proposal. We have only about twenty theatres playing *Platoon,* which has grossed several hundred thousand to over a million dollars."

Art said, "Charlie, if I settle with you, then I will have Larry upset with me for not allowing him to do his job. I'd best let the two of you work out the settlement of the payment of film rental on *Platoon* between yourselves."

I thought, "Very good, Art."

Charlie started waving at Art, "Tell your money bye-bye. I'm offering a one-time *Platoon* sale."

Art gave a very cordial smile and said, "No, you and Larry work out the settlement."

I don't think Art really knew how to take Charlie. I knew Charlie was just giving Art a hard time.

Then Charlie said, "Okay, Larry, let's settle the picture right now across the board. One percentage number and it's done. Larry and I will write down what we think a fair film rental payment to be on a napkin. Then, we'll place the two napkins in this cup and Art will pick one of the two napkins. The napkin Art picks is the final settlement on *Platoon* for all the Wometco playdates." Then Charlie held up his fist and looked at me as if to say, "But, you'd better be fair." Charlie then paused to explain the rules, "The figures have to be in line with what I can get New York to approve and with what Larry can get—" Charlie pointed toward Art, " 'moneybags' over here to be pleased with."

I leaned over the table and eyeballed Charlie. "Let's do it." The concern in Art's face was obvious. By his expression alone, I knew Art felt Charlie's method of conducting business was entirely inappropriate.

No, Art didn't appreciate or understand this haphazard way of settling the film rental on a mega-film like *Platoon*. Art's pick of a napkin from the cup could mean literally thousands of dollars in Wometco's plus or minus column.

Charlie thought a few seconds and then jotted down his number on his napkin. I did the same. We then placed the two napkins in a cup, and Charlie held the cup up over his head and mixed up the numbers. He then held the cup in front of Art and asked Art to pick one of the napkins. Art, with a look on his face as if to say, "I can't believe I'm having to do this," reached for a napkin. Immediately, Charlie pulled the cup away before Art could take a napkin, and then Charlie looked in disbelief at me. Charlie said, "You were going to go through with it, weren't you?"

"Absolutely. Why not."

Charlie looked at Art and, shaking his head from side to side, he pointed his finger at me as he said, "Art, you've got a dangerous man working for you."

While Charlie was talking, Art's big hand dove for the napkins in the cup. He wanted to see the numbers that Charlie and I had written down. Charlie's number was fifty-seven-and-a-half percent. My number was fifty-two-and-a-half percent. Charlie said, "Art, Larry, is a very dangerous man. If I were you, I'd get me another film buyer. One who's not so hard on distributors." Then, leaning back in his chair and placing both his hands over his heart, Charlie said, "And their hearts. Now if you gentlemen will excuse me, I'm going to try and find the men's room."

Art did not try to hide from me his disapproval of Charlie Jones's shenanigan ways. When Charlie got out of sight, Art became very straightforward in what he had to say to me: "Larry, I haven't figured out exactly what all is involved between you and your vendors in the way you obtain films and settle film rental payments for films played in our theatres. However, one day soon I expect to understand exactly what it is you do. Between now and then, I wish you would be more careful with the company's money."

I knew before Charlie ever left the table that Art was upset. I figured I'd best try to explain: "Art, I told you when I first came to work for you that I purchase film and settle film differently with each distributor. When you get back to your office tomorrow, look at your film rental settlement sheets with Orion Pictures. You will see right there in black and white that no one, I mean no one, gives us better film rental settlements than Charlie Jones." I knew I was now talking in language that was crystal clear to Mr. Arthur Hertz: figures in black and white.

Art shook his head in disbelief and said, "Larry, what do you think you'll end up settling *Platoon* for?"

"It will average out somewhere between fifty-four to fifty-five percent. I'll come over to the hotel and have breakfast with Charlie in the morning; then we'll go to the office and get the work done."

"Well, if Charlie hadn't backed down, we could have ended up paying a bump of two-and-a-half percent on every one of our playdates on *Platoon*." Frowning as he shook his head from side to side, Art said, "Larry, that's a lot of money on a million dollars or better."

I shrugged my shoulders. "That's true. Or, we could have ended up saving two-and-a-half percent on a million dollars. Art, this is all part of film buying. Don't let it get next to you. Here comes Charlie."

The dinner came and the three of us started enjoying our delicious gourmet meal. After a few minutes Charlie put his fork down and looked over at Art and shook his head from side to side as he pointed at me and started laughing. "Art, did Larry ever tell you about the time in Las Vegas where he had Red Skelton come over to our table and wish me a happy birthday?"

Art asked, "*The* Red Skelton?"

"That's right. Larry, tell Art what happened that night."

"Well, first of all, it happened in Atlanta and not Las Vegas."

Charlie stuck out his bottom lip and bobbled his head from side to side as if to say, "The city doesn't matter."

I continued, "It happened, oh, I don't know, maybe four or five years ago. There was a large group of us having a surprise birthday dinner for Charlie at the Terrace Garden Inn. There were mostly film distributors at the table. We were all sitting there roasting Charlie, when one of the guys noticed Red Skelton standing over by the elevator. Charlie said that he couldn't believe we were staying at the same hotel with Red Skelton. He said he had always been a fan of his. Charlie seemed so serious in his statement. I thought to myself, 'Charlie, working in the business, has seen so many movie stars. I'm surprised that he hasn't already met Red Skelton before now. I think I'll go introduce myself to Mr. Skelton and see if I can persuade him to come over and wish Charlie a happy birthday.' So, I got up and walked over to Mr. Skelton.

" 'Pardon me, Mr. Skelton. My name is Larry Vaughn.' He looked at me with that famous face that had warmed the hearts of literally millions of people for close to half a century and said, 'Hello, Mr. Vaughn.'

Pausing to think a moment, I continued, " 'Mr. Skelton, like yourself, I'm in the entertainment business. I'm the assistant film buyer for

Wometco Enterprises in Miami, Florida. I'm here tonight with a group of men celebrating the birthday of one of those gentlemen sitting over at that table.' I pointed toward our table. 'His name is Charlie Jones. Mr. Jones is a Branch Manager with Twentieth Century Fox Film Corporation. As a matter of fact, all of those men at that table are involved in the film industry. They are each employed by one of the major film studios. Mr. Skelton, would it be too great an imposition for me to ask you to step over and just wish Mr. Jones a happy birthday? When he saw you standing here, he commented about how much he would like to meet you.'

"Mr. Skelton looked at me and responded, 'Why no, not at all. I would love to meet Mr. Jones, as well as the rest of your party.'

"I introduced Mr. Skelton to Charlie first. They talked for several minutes about the film industry. Then Mr. Skelton wished Charlie a very happy birthday. I then introduced Mr. Skelton to each of the other gentlemen at the dinner table. Mr. Skelton was extremely cordial and polite, talking and asking questions to each man that he met. After he made the rounds, met, and talked with everyone, I then ushered him back over to the elevator. I most sincerely thanked him again for making Charlie Jones's birthday such a memorable event. He entered the elevator and wished me a good night."

Charlie said, "Art, Larry worked for Eddie Stern so long that he even acts and thinks like Eddie. That is exactly what you would expect Eddie to have done under the same circumstances."

Art said, "I wish I had been there that evening. I would like to have met Red Skelton."

Charlie responded, "Art, I'm disappointed in you. I thought you meant you wished you had been there because it was my birthday." We all laughed as we made our way out of the restaurant and back to the hotel.

Twenty-Four

Decisions

Thanksgiving and Christmas seemed to come and go all too quickly. It was now mid-February, and I found myself once again on an airplane, this time going to the Show West Convention in Las Vegas. I had prepared myself for the long flight out to Las Vegas. I had my headphones, tape recorder, and Pastor Clarkston's series on 1 John, which I had already heard once, but I had been wanting to hear the complete series through for a second time.

I sat there in my seat looking out the window thinking to myself, "I must do in Las Vegas just as I did while I was in Atlantic City. Stay away from the casino and spend all my free time in my hotel room in Bible study and prayer." I knew this time the temptation to gamble would be greater in Las Vegas than it was in Atlantic City. The reason is that, in Las Vegas, there's no Boardwalk to escape to, to get away from the never-resting, never-sleeping gambling casino. Plus, the main floor of the Bally Hotel is all casino. You can't go anywhere at the Bally without having to walk through the casino. I thought to myself, "This trip I'll have to be extra careful not to yield to any of the many temptations to gamble."

I paused from listening to my tapes to look out the little window into the vast open sky. I could see little specks on the ground representing mankind. "How insignificant man must appear to Almighty God," I thought. I sat back and tried to rest. I decided to flip through the magazine I had picked up earlier. I was turning the pages rather quickly when something caught my eye. I turned back two pages and saw an article on Chuck Colson. "Wow," I thought, "doesn't that bring back memories. Let's see, how did it all begin? I believe it was a phone call, yes, a phone call."

I received a call from Dr. Jim Hurley. Doneata and I had come to know Dr. and Mrs. Hurley and their three children through Parker Road.

Dr. Hurley was a young man in his mid to late thirties. Jim was known by everyone at Parker Road as a thinker, or the individual to ask when clarification was needed about the exact meaning of a portion of Scripture, particularly those deep things of God. Jim taught a Bible class in one of the local theological seminaries. He also kept himself busy lecturing and writing for magazines on theological issues. Jim had studied theology firsthand under Dr. Francis Schaffer.

After a few minutes of small talk, Jim came to his point. "Larry, the purpose of this call is to ask you if you would be free in two weeks to spend the weekend with me in prison?"

I thought he was joking. "Jim, would you mind repeating what you just said?"

Jim was laughing on the other end. "Larry, let me explain myself. I have been asked by Chuck Colson's organization, Prison Fellowship, to put on a Friday night and all-day Saturday Bible conference in the South Dade Correctional Institute. Larry, I got to thinking about whom the Lord would have me invite to go along and help me on this conference. Your name came to my mind."

"Jim, I don't know if I'm the right person for this sort of thing or not. I might not be much good working in an environment that, well, fortunately I'm not used to being in." We both laughed at my rather awkward statement.

"Larry, all I ask you to do is pray about it and give me a call—say by tomorrow evening, with a yes or no. I believe you could be a great help in this ministry, Larry, if you'll only step out in faith and be willing to make the sacrifice of a weekend."

I always hated it when someone put things that way. It would be hard enough to say no to Jim; but, if this is from the Lord, then it's almost impossible to say no, that is, without making myself and my family very miserable in two weekends when I'll be sitting at home disobedient and out of God's will instead of ministering with Jim in prison.

I told Jim, "You will hear from me no later than tomorrow evening."

I called Jim the next day. "Okay, Jim, I'll go with you in two weeks to the prison."

"Larry, your participation is an answer to prayer. I'm sure you're going to receive a very special blessing for making this small sacrifice for the Lord."

"Jim, I just hope the Lord will be able to use me in this type of ministry."

Jim replied, "Don't you worry about that. You will be used greatly."

"I don't know. I must admit I still have some reservations, but I have made the commitment to go with you. I will be in prayer between now and then that all will go well the weekend of the conference."

As it turned out, that weekend was the beginning of a three-and-a-half-year ministry I had working with Prison Fellowship. After that first weekend's experience, it was obvious to me that the Lord had given me a special ability in working with the incarcerated. Years later, I now am able to look back and see how the Lord, at that time in my life, used Dr. Jim Hurley to open the door of opportunity for me to have a unique ministry at the South Dade Correctional Institute.

I started out going down to the prison every Thursday evening as a citizen-volunteer to participate in an hour-long worship service with the prisoners and a few other citizen-volunteers from other area churches. After the prison chaplain, Chaplain Hunt, got to know me better, he asked me if I would consider getting involved more in the ministry at the prison. To my knowledge I was the only citizen-volunteer that Chaplain Hunt made this type of a request to. He asked me if I would consider taking on an inmate with some very special emotional and guilt problems.

The man's name was "Wayland Blackburn." He was a man in his mid-thirties who was serving a twenty-year sentence for a sex-related offense. The first time I met Wayland, he kept his eyes glued to the floor during the entire conversation. As a matter of fact, I did all the talking. Occasionally, Wayland would utter a grunt or mumble a "yeah" or "nah," but that was the extent of what he had to say. Chaplain Hunt asked me if I would be willing to work with Wayland, one-on-one, on Saturday mornings for a period of time. Chaplain Hunt went on to tell me that he had exhausted his own personal energies and time in working with Wayland and thought that maybe some one-on-one counseling and Bible study with an individual like me would help to bring Wayland out of his emotional shell.

I saw a lot of changes for the good in Wayland during the two years I discipled and counseled him at the South Dade Correctional Institute. Later he was transferred to the Florida State Hospital for the Criminally Insane in West Fort Lauderdale. There I continued working with Wayland until he was released from prison.

We made it a point to keep up with each other by letter or phone during his first two years out of prison. He called me one day from his home in West Texas to tell me that he had met a girl and asked her to marry him. Shortly thereafter they married and moved away. I haven't heard from Wayland since.

I am not sure if Wayland Blackburn ever made a genuine profession of faith in the Lord Jesus Christ. I do know that for several years he had the opportunity to be exposed to sound, one-on-one Bible teaching. He memorized literally hundreds of Scripture verses, and he experienced, in his darkest hours, a time of genuine Christian love.

During those years, Chaplain Hunt and I became very good friends. I remember once he went to the warden with an unusual request. He asked the warden if he could have special permission to take two of the inmates—one a convicted murderer and the other a bank robber—out of prison long enough to speak during a Sunday evening worship service at Parker Road. I know the Lord touched the warden's heart because he agreed to this most unusual request from Chaplain Hunt. Those two inmates, both of whom became Christians while in prison, gave a wonderful testimony to the saving grace of Jesus Christ in their lives to the congregation of Parker Road during that very special service.

I was staying so involved in Prison Fellowship that I thought at one time that maybe the Lord was leading me into the ministry on a full-time basis. Prison Fellowship came into being through a series of circumstances the Lord brought into the life of Charles "Chuck" Colson. Mr. Colson was Special Counsel to President Richard Nixon during the infamous Watergate investigation. Because of Colson's involvement in Watergate, he went from having super power to jail almost overnight. It was during this transition from fame to shame that God performed a mighty work in this man's life and saved him. After Mr. Colson was released from prison, the Lord laid on his heart the idea of forming a Christian organization to help men who have been incarcerated. Hence, Prison Fellowship came into being.

I had the opportunity to meet Mr. Colson at a private reception when he was in Miami to speak at one of our sister churches. A mutual friend introduced us to each other at the reception. I told Mr. Colson how I had been very active for several years as a citizen-volunteer for Prison Fellowship. I gave him a brief summary of my background along with my résumé. He seemed interested in hearing what I had to say. He told me as soon as he returned to his Virginia office, he would talk with his personnel manager about our conversation and someone from his office would get back in touch with me.

Shortly thereafter I was invited by Mr. Colson to fly to Virginia and spend a day with one of the key men in the organization. When I received the invitation to visit Prison Fellowship's home office, I thought to myself, "This must be the door the Lord is going to use to have me exit the motion picture industry." During the flight from Miami to Virginia, I was so excited about the possibilities of my working for a Christian organization that I didn't think the plane would ever touch ground. Unfortunately, the excitement didn't last long. After spending the day and finding out what the job description involved, I had no interest in going with the organization.

I wanted to go into prisons and get involved with those men who had lost their marriages, their children, and their loved ones because of their incarceration. I wanted to use biblical principles to help comfort those men and to expose them to the Word of God. I wanted to use Christian principles to help rebuild bridges of communication between men and their families so that when those men got out of prison they would have a home and a family to return to. Prison Fellowship's intent was to employ me to go into the business community, not prisons, and get the business community involved in helping to meet the financial needs of the organization. Organizations like Prison Fellowship with accruing expenses most certainly needed men and women to gather funds; I just had no interest in being one of those fund raisers.

The morning after I returned from Virginia, I called Prison Fellowship to inform them that I would not be interested in coming to work for them in the position that was offered. I thanked them for their time and expenses incurred in flying me to Virginia, but I felt at that time that I was to continue on with Prison Fellowship as a citizen-volunteer only.

The stewardess interrupted my thoughts as the evening meal was being served. I graciously had to pass on the dinner, because I had an 8:00 p.m. dinner in Las Vegas that evening with a V.P. of Columbia Pictures. I put the Colson article down and went back to my tapes on 1 John.

The plane arrived in Las Vegas on time at 6:00 p.m. I had two hours to get to the hotel and get checked into my room before my 8:00 p.m. dinner. Riding in the taxi from the airport to the hotel, I asked the taxi driver, "What's the latest news in Vegas?"

The cabby acted hungry for conversation. "Mister, last week the strangest thing happened downtown. This guy walks into one of the casinos. I believe it was the Golden Nugget. Anyway, the guy has two bags, one in each hand. One bag has five hundred thousand dollars in cash, and the other bag is empty. He walks over to the Pit Boss at one of the craps tables and says he wants to put the whole five hundred grand on the next roll of the dice."

"What did the Pit Boss say?"

"He told the man with that much cash riding on the roll of the dice, he would be glad to open up a new table for him to shoot on. The guy says, 'If it's the same with you, I'll just let the money play on this table with these people.'

"Now mister, a woman was rolling the dice at that particular table, so the guy said, 'I'll play the lady's next roll of the dice.'

"The Pit Boss said, 'Okay, if that's the way you want to play it.'

"So, the lady rolls the dice and comes up a winner. The guy had them put his winnings, five hundred thousand dollars cash, into the empty bag. He then left with two bags of cash totaling a million dollars. Now, what do you make of that?"

I thought a moment, and then I said, "I'll tell you friend. I think it was one of two things. One, this could have been a very desperate man that had to have five hundred thousand dollars, and he was willing to lose just that much money to get it. Or, it could have been a great publicity stunt put on by the casino. See, that's all we've talked about the last five minutes."

The cabby said almost angrily, "You know, I didn't think of a publicity stunt idea. I wonder if it was?"

He pulled the cab up to the entrance of the Bally Hotel, and there were people standing around outside everywhere. I knew something was wrong. I got my luggage and walked up to the Bell Captain. "What's going on with all these people just standing here?"

"Sir, the computers are down. We're running two to three hours late on getting people checked into their rooms."

I looked at my watch: it was 6:30. I had an hour and a half until my dinner with Columbia Pictures. I asked the Bell Captain, "Where can I store my luggage until my room is made available to me?"

"Sir, if you don't mind tagging your luggage, I'll be happy to see that it is sent to your room once you have checked in. Just leave it right here."

I thanked him and slipped him five bucks. I then went inside the hotel.

I took the escalator downstairs to the basement of the hotel where the mall is located. I spent the next hour browsing in the shops, trying to kill time until my dinner. At 7:45 I walked over to the registration desk. The situation looked even worse than earlier. There was a very long line of people trying to get room assignments. I decided to go on to dinner and then try to check in later.

At 8:00, I met the Columbia people and had a very nice dinner in one of the hotel's many fine restaurants. Shortly before 10:00 p.m., I went back over to the registration desk. The check-in situation was still impossible. The lady told me it would still be an hour or two before I could expect to get into my room. I turned around and thought, "Now what?" Staring at me was the casino with all its glitz and glamour. I was tired and didn't want to go outside the hotel because of security reasons. I thought to myself, "I've got a couple of hours to kill. It's not going to hurt me to walk through the casino and watch some of the people gamble."

As I slowly walked through the casino, I heard a familiar voice say, "Larry Vaughn, get over here and sit down."

I turned to see Wayne Lewellend sitting at a blackjack table. (Wayne is the President of Paramount Pictures Distribution.) I walked over and started talking with him.

He said, "Come on, man, get out some money and let's get this table smoking."

"Wayne, I don't have that much cash on me."

"Do you want me to let you have some money?"

I thought a moment. "No, hold my seat; I'll be back in a minute."

I don't have any excuse for what I did next. As it turned out, my actions were totally oblivious to the messages from 1 John I had been listening to earlier in the day on the airliner. Leaving Wayne at the table, I walked over to the cashier's window.

I thought to myself, "Las Vegas and Atlantic City are the only two cities in the country where a one hundred dollar bill gets absolutely no respect. I'd better get a lot of cash."

I asked the teller for a cash advance in the amount of $3,000 on my VISA card. I thought, "What the heck. I can't get into my room for a couple of hours. I might as well play a few hands of blackjack."

I went back to the table, and Wayne was waiting on me. Optimistic Wayne said, "Larry, my friend, tonight is our night. I can just feel it."

A few minutes later, Jimmy Spitz walked over. (Jimmy is the President of Columbia Pictures.) Jimmy sat down and talked to us as we played, but he didn't do any gambling.

Well, the old Larry Vaughn came to life. I started gambling like I had in years gone past. At one time I was up more than $20,000. On one hand alone, I won $6,000. Jimmy left the table around midnight. Wayne and

I stayed and gambled together until 6:30 the following morning. After all was said and done, Wayne had won about $4,500, and I walked away more than $15,000 ahead.

Wayne looked at me as we cashed our chips into hundred dollar bills. "Larry, I knew last night we were going to have a hot streak. I'm sure glad you ran into me. Let's go celebrate our winnings over some bacon and eggs."

Wayne and I then went to breakfast and talked about some of the many outstanding hands we had during the all-night blackjack game. Wayne made me promise that we would gamble together again before the convention was over.

After breakfast, I went over to the registration desk to see if my room was finally ready for me to check in. The lady at the desk was very polite as she apologized for the delay. She then informed me my standard room had been upgraded to one of the tower suites by the hotel management. I immediately thought back to around 2:30 that morning. That was about the time that the Casino Boss asked me if I had checked into my room. I told him that the line was too long earlier, and I would check in after I left the blackjack table.

I thought, "They have marked me down as a high roller and up-graded me to a tower suite. This is like going back to the Michael Heffner days." That's exactly what they did. My room was a huge beautiful suite that was reserved for high rollers. The Casino Boss at the Bally wanted to make sure my stay with them was a pleasant one.

I looked at my watch; I was supposed to meet Art and Mike in less than an hour. I thought, "Having no sleep last night is going to make for an extra long day today."

I took a quick shower and changed into a fresh suit of clothes. I took a safety pin and pinned the envelope with over 150 hundred dollar bills to my inside breast coat pocket. The safety pin makes for a good protector against those individuals who have mastered the art of picking pockets. Then hurriedly I left the room to meet with Art and Mike.

I said absolutely nothing to anyone about how I had just spent the last eight hours gambling. I was hoping it would remain a well-kept secret between Wayne, Jimmy, and me. But it didn't. During the day, it seemed like everywhere I went someone had heard of my good fortune at the blackjack table the night before. Finally, I realized the consequences of my actions. My all-night card game with Wayne Lewellend was the talk of the convention. By midafternoon my winnings were being exaggerated by some to be over twice what I had actually won.

I was beginning to get a real sick feeling in my stomach, as I realized how in one short night I had tarnished my Christian witness with the film community. My concern now was that I no longer would be remembered as Larry Vaughn the Christian, but now it would be Larry Vaughn the big winner. Just when I thought things couldn't get any worse, they got worse.

At 6:30, Tuesday evening, I was standing in the lobby waiting to meet Art and Mike for a business dinner when Jim Dixon, my new brother in Christ, walked up and patted me on the back. "Hello, Larry, glad to see you."

"Hi, Jim, it's so good to see you."

Jim had a strange look on his face. "Larry, congratulations, I hear you did very well on the tables last night."

I wished I were a snake so I could just slither away somewhere. I needed to explain: "Jim, I want to talk to you about last night."

Jim interrupted, "Larry, there's my party. I can't talk right now; I'll catch you later."

As Jim hurried off, I thought, "Jim shared with me in Atlanta that he had watched me for five years, and not once did he see me stumble in my Christian testimony. Jim said my testimony played an important part in the Lord's bringing salvation into his life. I wonder what Jim is thinking right now, right this minute. He's probably confused, disappointed, and hurt that I behaved the way I did last night."

I don't remember with whom Art, Mike, and I had dinner that evening. I had totally lost my appetite. I picked at my food just enough so that it wasn't obvious that something was wrong with me. I didn't think the dinner would ever end. All I wanted to do was to be able to go to my room. Yes, go to my fancy suite. My fancy suite reserved for the high roller and the big spender. Maybe there I could at least be left alone.

When I finally got to my suite, I sat down on the sofa. I sat there alone thinking for the better part of an hour. I started to examine my salvation. "How could I have done such a thing? And I did it so soon. I mean, I go out and gamble the night away before I have even checked into my room. Just a few hours earlier on the plane I had studied and listened to Pastor Clarkston's messages about God's being Light. Here I am trying to memorize 1 John 1:5-7. Can hypocritical me still remember the verses?"

> This then is the message which we have heard of him, and declare unto you, that God is light, and in him is no darkness at all. If we say that we have fellowship with him, and walk in darkness, we lie, and

do not the truth: But if we walk in the light, as he is in the light, we have fellowship one with another, and the blood of Jesus Christ his Son cleanseth us from all sin.

There it is in black and white, straight from the Word of God: "God is light, and in him is no darkness at all. If we say that we have fellowship with him, and walk in darkness, we lie, and do not the truth." I thought to myself, "It makes no sense at all. I must not be truly saved. I keep trying to mix and match those things of light and darkness."

I thought, "There's a verse. What is it? There's a warning about people who do things like I have just done. Oh, which verse is it? Where is it found in Scripture? I believe it is in Numbers. Yes, it is Numbers 32:23: 'Be sure your sin will find you out.' Well, unfortunately, because of my actions Monday evening, I can certainly say, firsthand, Amen to that verse."

I thought a few minutes. "Satan knows because of my history of gambling that I am still vulnerable in that area of my flesh. If I keep the money, I'll never have victory over gambling. The temptation to play cards will always be there every time I get near a lousy casino. No, for me to have a spiritual victory over this area of my life, I must get rid of the money. But, what should I do with it? Take it and give it to some needy organization, or maybe the church's building fund? It's a lot of cash. Let me think, who should I give it to? To begin with, I should have never had the opportunity to give the money to anyone. If I go and start giving the money away, I'll end up looking like a Good Samaritan, instead of the schmuck that I really am. No, I think I will give the money back to its rightful owner—the casino. I don't want their money, and I don't think the Lord would bless this money to any good cause that I gave it to."

I got up, put on my coat, and went downstairs to the casino. I thought, "I'd better not do it here in Bally's casino. Too many people know me in here. Someone might see what I am doing and get the wrong idea. I think I'll go across the street to Caesar's Palace. The chances are better that no one will recognize me at Caesar's Palace."

I walked over to Caesar's Palace and went to the very back of the casino. I found a seat open at a blackjack table. A large, black gentleman was dealing the cards. I walked up to the table and took the remaining three hands that were open. I opened the envelope and divided up the $15,000 between the three hands I was playing. I looked at the dealer and said, "The money plays." The big, husky dealer raised his eyebrows when he saw the amount of cash I wanted to play on each individual hand. He then turned his head in the direction of the Casino Boss and said in a loud voice, "The man's money plays." The boss walked over, looked down at the three stacks of hundreds and said, "Okay," to the dealer. The dealer dealt the cards.

There were two other men playing besides me. Neither of them was playing for any serious money. The two men played their hands out, and when the dealer came around to me I held all three of my hands the way they were dealt to me: on one hand, I held on seventeen, another fourteen, and the last sixteen. The dealer hit a four on his sixteen to give him a twenty. The dealer immediately looked up at me with sadness in his eyes.

He said, "Friend, I am so sorry."

I said, "Don't be. That's exactly what I came over here to do."

He had an expression of confusion on his face as I slowly walked away from the table. I then left Caesar's Palace and made my way back across the street to my room at the Bally.

The next day I cornered Jim in the hotel lobby. "Jim, I have felt very bad about my behavior in the casino Monday night."

"Larry, you shouldn't feel bad. The Bible doesn't say it's wrong to gamble."

"Jim, the Bible has a lot to say about man and his sin. What I did Monday evening was sin. I was a poor testimony to you and the rest of the film community. I have felt absolutely miserable because of my actions Monday night in the casino. As you know, in the past, before I became a Christian, I enjoyed gambling very much. Gambling for many years was the only god I knew. But, in the last year, God's Word has convicted me that gambling is a sin."

I smiled as I shook my head from side to side in disbelief. "Jim, I guess Monday night I left my spiritual armor in my suitcase. My actions were those of the old Larry Vaughn—you know, the Larry before Christ. Jim, I am here now to ask your forgiveness for my being a stumbling block to you."

"Larry, I think you're making a bigger deal out of your playing blackjack than it really is. I really don't feel like gambling is a sin. I do think gambling should be done in moderation, as Scripture tells us we are to do all things in moderation."

Listening to him talk, I couldn't help but think, "This poor guy must attend a man-centered church like Parker Road."

"Jim, just to keep the record straight, I want you to know that I gave all the money back that I won."

"You did what?"

"The money is gone. I gave it all back. I knew God wouldn't bless one penny of it. I had to give it back to gain victory over this stronghold in my life."

I could tell Jim was taken back with what I had just told him. We talked a few more minutes. When he left, I felt like I had regained some of the ground that I had lost with him on Tuesday. Even though Jim said he saw nothing wrong with my gambling, I could tell a change for the good in his countenance after I had talked with him Wednesday and asked his forgiveness for my actions on Monday.

———

I spent the next few months staying very busy at the office. Wometco, like other theatre circuits, was in an expansion mode. Art and Mike were trying to protect our position in the Miami area by building several new state-of-the-art multiplex theatres. The company, as a whole, was having a very good year.

Art Hertz and Doneata Vaughn at a theatre opening

Early one Tuesday morning, I received a phone call from David Forbes's secretary. David Forbes was the recently appointed President of Distribution for MGM/UA. She asked me, "Mr. Vaughn, Mr. Forbes is going to be flying in to Miami this Thursday afternoon. He wanted me to call and ask you if he might be able to stop by and meet with you around 3:30?"

"Yes, that will be fine. Or, better yet, why don't you ask Mr. Forbes if it would be okay for me to pick him up at the airport. And if his schedule permits, I would love to take him out to dinner Thursday evening."

"Mr. Vaughn, Mr. Forbes will be flying out of Miami for New York directly after his meeting with you. As for your picking him up at the airport, that won't be necessary. I have already made arrangements to have a limousine pick him up, take him to your office, and return him to the airport. Mr. Forbes didn't want you to have to bother with going back and forth."

"Okay, tell Mr. Forbes that I'm looking forward to meeting him Thursday."

I hung up the phone wondering why David Forbes would fly through Miami for such a brief meeting with me. I had seen his picture in all the trade magazines. He wore his salt-and-pepper hair short. His hairstyle, coupled with his conservative suits and unusual eyeglasses, gave him somewhat of an Ivy League look. The wood frames on his glasses were small and round, which made them stand out in his pictures. He used to be associated with the late Steve McQueen. I can't remember exactly what it is he used to do with McQueen. He was either his press agent, publicist, or something along those lines.

Mr. Forbes now had a big job with one of the oldest and most famous of all the major studios. But, also one of the most troubled studios. In recent years MGM/UA had been bought and sold several times over. The company had been struggling for some time in trying to get big-name directors and producers under contract. They desperately needed some big pictures to help get MGM/UA back on track. The industry thought it was a move in the right direction when MGM/UA brought Forbes aboard to head up their distribution arm.

Betty buzzed me at 3:30 sharp. "Mr. Vaughn, you have a Mr. Forbes here to see you."

"Betty, send him on in."

I got up and walked toward the door to meet him as he entered the office.

"Hello, Larry Vaughn, I have been looking forward to meeting you."

"Likewise, David, please come in."

As I went to close the door, I told Betty to hold all my calls. He looked just like he did in his photographs. I thought to myself, "He looks like an educated, very reserved, and polished businessman. He looks like one of those individuals who make it a point to stay on top of everything. I think he will be good for MGM/UA."

David sat down at the far end of my large desk. Because of its size, sometimes my desk could be a bit intimidating to certain persons. I have been accused, in the past, in jest, of having the legs on my end of the desk a fraction taller than the legs on the back end of the desk, which would give someone the feeling of being looked down on during a conversation. Looking down the long desk at David Forbes made me feel uncomfortable. I got up from behind my desk and sat down in one of my black chairs directly across from him.

We made small talk about Wometco, MGM/UA, and the industry as a whole for a few minutes, and then David got right to the purpose of his visit.

"Larry, let me tell you why I am here today. I wanted to meet you and talk with you about the possibility of your joining the senior management team at MGM/UA. I have two men I intend to interview for the position of General Sales Manager, Eastern region for domestic distribution. Of course, you are one of the candidates. I am going to interview the other gentleman tomorrow afternoon. I shall make my decision by the time I get back to the studio in L.A. on Monday. Now, let's talk."

David spent fifteen to twenty minutes talking about his plans for reorganizing the distribution arm of the company and what my job responsibilities would be if I were the individual chosen to be the General Sales Manager, Eastern region. He said, "Larry, your responsibility would be the placement of our motion pictures in those theatres located throughout the entire Southeastern United States." He concluded his introduction with, "Larry, this would be a golden opportunity for you. The sky would be the limit." Smiling, he said, "Well, have I whet your appetite or not?"

I sat back and pushed my chair away from the desk. I gave him a warm smile of appreciation for his consideration. I then said, "You know, there are a lot of people that would give anything to have an opportunity to be a part of the new management team that David Forbes is putting together at MGM/UA. But, David, in all honesty, I don't believe I'm your man."

He had a very inquisitive look on his face as if to say, "Really?"

I went on to say, "Let me explain. First, I am deeply honored that my name would even be brought up in consideration for such an important position with MGM. However, let me give you a little more information about myself that you aren't aware of."

He loosened his tie just a little as I started to talk.

"David, first and foremost, my responsibility is to God." I had his attention. He was listening to every word that I had to say. "You see, David, I am a Christian man."

He interrupted me, "Like in being 'born again'?"

"Yes, that's correct."

He nodded as if to say, "I understand."

I continued. "After God, my second area of responsibility or loyalty is to my family. I have a wife, who is a wonderful Christian woman, and three lovely children. Then, my third responsibility is to Art Hertz and Michael Brown here at Wometco. Those three areas: God, family, and work pretty much take care of a twenty-four-hour day in my life."

I paused a minute. Then I leaned over and put one elbow on the desk, resting my chin on my hand. "Now, David, what I think you are looking for is a man who is going to be loyal to you and MGM/UA first and foremost. And that's okay. It's just that, well, after what I have just told you, I don't see me being that man."

While nodding his head in agreement, David said, "I think I understand." He thought a moment; then he said, "Larry, I would like to thank you for being so open and honest with me this afternoon. It has indeed been a pleasure meeting you. On your next trip to L.A. I would like to have the privilege of taking you out to one of my favorite restaurants for dinner."

"David, that is a dinner I'm sure I'm going to enjoy, as I would like to get to know you much better."

We shook hands. I thanked David again for his considerations and wished him much success with his new challenge at MGM/UA.

Twenty-Five

The Controversy

In June of 1988, Art and I made a trip to New York City to attend a black-tie dinner in honor of Wayne Lewellend. While in the city we were riding down Fifth Avenue in a limousine on the way to a private dinner party. I had a few free minutes alone with Art. I though to myself, "Now would be the opportune time to bring up some very important business that I have been needing to discuss with him."

"Art, I need to run something by you."

"Shoot."

I looked at Art sitting there all decked out in his tuxedo. He seemed to be enjoying immensely the smoking of his fine Cuban cigar.

"Art, there is a picture coming out this fall that we need to talk about. It's going to be a very controversial film, especially among the Christian community. The name of the film is *The Last Temptation of Christ*. It's being directed by Martin Scorsese. As you know, Scorsese has made some powerful and important films in the past. He is an excellent film-maker. I, personally, am appalled that Scorsese would associate himself with such a deplorable film." I looked directly at Art. "Art, in my opinion this picture should have never been made. It is going to be extremely offensive to those individuals, like myself, who are followers of Jesus Christ." I stopped talking briefly to let what I had just said sink in. I then looked very sternly at Art. I wanted to drive home to this man how important it is that he support my decision that Wometco would not play this picture.

I felt it was also extremely important that I furnish Art with all the facts going in. "Art, I'm also disappointed to inform you that one of our good customers, Universal Film Exchange, is distributing *The Last Temptation*. I haven't had any discussions yet with Universal about Wometco's playing the film, but I'm sure I'll be hearing from Phil

295

Sherman within a few weeks." I frowned as I shrugged my shoulders. "My intention is to tell Phil we will not play the film in any of our Florida theatres. *Temptation* is scheduled to be released to the public sometime around mid-September or October.

"Art, because of the subject matter of *Last Temptation,* this is one picture that I personally want absolutely nothing to do with. I also think it would be in Wometco's best interest not to play this controversial picture."

Art cracked his window a little more to let some additional smoke out of the car. He then looked at me as if to say, "Why are you telling me all of this?" Then he began speaking. "Larry, you're my film buyer. If you don't want to play the picture, then we don't play the picture."

I breathed a deep sigh of relief, "Thanks, Art, for supporting me on this one." Art looked down at the floor, wiped some spilled ashes off his pants, and shrugged his shoulders. He seemed to give the matter no additional thought. If Art had only known that night the agony that lay ahead because of that decision, I'm sure he would have spent further time and much deeper discussion about his position on playing *The Last Temptation of Christ* in his Wometco theatres.

While in New York at a cocktail party, I met a very interesting man. A man that I had heard about for years. His name was A. Foster McKissick. Mr. McKissick and I had one very special thing in common: we were both from Greenville, South Carolina.

The first time I ever heard the name Foster McKissick was some twelve years before when I was working for John Huff at ABC. I was told at that time that Mr. McKissick was one of the wealthiest men, if not *the* wealthiest man, in South Carolina. He was an entrepreneur on a grand scale. Mr. McKissick was very diversified in his business holdings: he had vast real estate properties and was into banking, car dealerships, credit companies, etc. He owned and operated an oceanfront resort, Litchfield by the Sea, a planned community at Litchfield Beach, South Carolina, located a stone's throw away from Pawleys Island, South Carolina, or about seventeen miles south of Myrtle Beach, South Carolina. Litchfield by the Sea had several oceanfront high-rise condominium buildings which were absolutely beautiful. There were several swimming pools, tennis courts, and blocks of homes and townhouses.

At Litchfield Beach Mr. McKissick also owned and operated a hotel, The Waccamaw House; Webster's, a restaurant; three 18-hole golf courses; a pro shop; and the Litchfield Country Club. And last, but by no means least, he owned a twin theatre.

Recently, Mr. McKissick had sold the majority of his theatre circuit to United Artists Theaters. At that time United Artists Theaters was the largest theatre circuit in the United States. I believe Mr. McKissick's circuit had in the neighborhood of 250 screens. Prior to the sale to UA, Mr. McKissick's theatres were scattered from Virginia to Texas and on into Oklahoma. I was told by several people that the theatre business was Foster's true love. But, one day, United Artists Theaters came knocking at Foster's door with a pocketful of cash, and Foster, or maybe it was his board of directors, just couldn't say no.

Upon meeting Foster, I thought, "He's not at all like what I had expected him to be." I had heard so much about Foster McKissick down through the years that I was expecting to meet a man that carried himself like a Mitchell Wolfson, Arthur Hertz, Stanley Stern, or maybe even an Eddie Stern. But, Foster was just the opposite. Everybody at the dinner except Foster was in a tuxedo. Foster was wearing a dark blue sports coat, with an oxford blue shirt, and a dark blue inexpensive company tie with the Litchfield insignia which had sea oats on it. His pants were a pair of tan khakis, almost like work pants. His shoes were a pair of inexpensive loafers. He had a pipe tucked between his belt and his slacks.

I remember commenting to someone about Foster's not being in a tuxedo. The individual looked at me as if I had just made a stupid statement. "Larry, that's A. Foster McKissick you're talking about. You will never see Foster in anything different from what you see him in right now. That's his uniform, or at least that's the only outfit I have ever seen him wear. No, you won't find a yellow, white, or striped shirt in Foster's closet. He always wears the same outfit, day in and day out. And you know what, Vaughn? If you're A. Foster McKissick, that outfit is accepted as the dress of the day by whomever you're with, or wherever you are. Years ago Foster burned the rule book when it comes to what's acceptable and what's not.

I thought to myself, "I'd like to get to know Foster McKissick better. He's most certainly got a style all his own." I studied Mr. McKissick a moment. He looked to be in his mid-to-late fifties. He had a nice round face and seemed to enjoy talking about the theatre industry while smoking his rustic cherry pipe. He had a full head of brownish-gray hair that went well with his silver-framed glasses. Yes, looks and actions can be deceiving. Mr. McKissick, at best, looked like just one of the guys. Not the A. Foster McKissick he really was: a man of great wealth, vast power, and much fame.

———

Toward the end of that summer is when the nightmare began. I'm not exactly sure who or what was used to ignite the spark. It could very well have been a theatre customer asking one of our managers for general information. The manager, being unable to answer the question, referred the lady to my office. Anyway, I received a phone call from this lady asking when might she expect the film *The Last Temptation of Christ* to open in the Miami area. I informed the lady the film would most likely open sometime during the month of October. She then asked me if I knew which Wometco theatres in the Miami area would be playing the film. I informed her that Wometco would not be playing *Last Temptation* in any of our Miami theatres.

She asked very emphatically, "Well, why not?"

I said, "There are several motion pictures that play in Miami that never play in a Wometco theatre. This is just another one of those pictures."

She proceeded to tell me how disappointed she was that Wometco wouldn't be playing the film because she was looking so forward to seeing *Last Temptation* in her theatre of choice, which happened to be one of the Wometco theatres. We talked another minute or two, and that was the end of the call.

About an hour later, I received another call from a woman in reference to Wometco playing *Last Temptation*. I told her basically what I had told the first lady about why Wometco wouldn't be playing the film. This lady was more inquisitive about my company's reasons for not playing the film. She was very vocal in expressing her displeasure over our decision not to play the film.

"Mr. Vaughn, Wometco plays all the important films in the Miami area. I can't believe you have already made a decision, and a bad decision I might add, not to play such an important film as *The Last Temptation of Christ*."

"Lady, I'm sorry to disappoint you, but that's the way it is. We book our theatres months ahead. We can't possibly play all the pictures that are released by the film companies in our theatres alone. This is one motion picture that you will have to see in one of our competitor's theatres."

"Then, they will play *Last Temptation*. Is that correct?"

"Lady, I can't speak for another circuit about whether they will play *Last Temptation* or any other film."

"Mr. Vaughn, may I ask your title?"

"I am Vice President in charge of Film Buying and Booking."

"Thank you." She then hung up the phone.

I thought to myself, "I know her type. A letter documenting her displeasure in me for not playing the film is going to follow with copies to everyone in the company."

Within half an hour I had another phone call with someone else inquiring about when *Last Temptation* was going to open in Miami, and if Wometco would be playing the film. I was beginning to wish I had a taped message that I could play and not have to keep going through my spiel every few minutes. They say the third time is a charm, but that wasn't true with this call. This particular lady got so upset with me for not booking the film in Miami that she promised me she would never again patronize a Wometco theatre. Then she said some very harsh words to me before she slammed the phone receiver in my ear.

I buzzed my secretary. "Betty."

"Yes, sir."

"Is there supposed to be a full moon tonight?"

"Well, I don't know sir. May I ask why you have asked?"

"Betty, this afternoon I have received not one, nor two, but three strange calls from women all inquiring about the film *The Last Temptation of Christ*."

"Well, Larry, I hate to be the bearer of more bad news, but I have two more messages on my desk for you to call in reference to that particular film."

"You're kidding!"

"No, sir. I was just waiting for you to get off the phone before I brought them in to you."

"Well, just hang on to them for right now. There will probably be more as the day goes on."

"Yes, sir."

I started doodling on a piece of paper. Doodling has always been a great help to me in trying to figure things out and in making important decisions. I was now trying to figure out why all of a sudden there was such an interest in *The Last Temptation of Christ*. It has to be either something had recently broke in the media about the film, or these calls were all related to each other. I don't think all these calls today are just a coincidence. I thought to myself, "I'm sure glad I had that talk with Art in the early part of the summer. At least I have the company backing me up on this one."

That night I shared with the family the five phone calls I had had that day in reference to *Last Temptation*. I asked Doneata and the children to make this situation a matter of top priority during their personal devotional time. We then prayed that the Lord would give me wisdom in handling the public in the days ahead, as we knew the calls of the afternoon were only the beginning. I didn't sleep very well that night. I kept tossing and turning and thinking about the potential problems that might come up because of that movie.

The next day I received another call on *Last Temptation*, but this call was from one of the local talk-radio stations. The city of Miami has many radio stations, but unfortunately for me this call came from the secretary of "Mark Powell." Mark Powell was one of the most popular and outspoken radio personalities in the Miami market. His show was always right up at the top of the ratings surveys. He was known for his controversial subject matters and his abrasive behavior.

"Mr. Vaughn, my name is 'Jane Weatherby.' I am secretary, assistant, and well, you might say, head gopher for Mr. Mark Powell. How are you doing today?"

I thought to myself, "Fine before I had to talk with you." Screwing up my courage, I responded, "Just fine, Ms. Weatherby. And what may I do for you on this beautiful Wednesday morning?"

"Mr. Vaughn, I'm calling you in reference to the much-anticipated opening of the Martin Scorsese film, *The Last Temptation of Christ*. When might we expect the film to open in the Miami area?"

"Ms. Weatherby, I believe Universal is planning on opening *Last Temptation* in New York and L.A. in September, and the rest of the country will follow sometime in late September or early October."

"Wonderful, there is so much interest already in this film. I think it's going to be an important film at the box office, don't you?"

"Well, Ms. Weatherby you never really know how a film is going to do at the box office until it opens."

"Mr. Vaughn, you don't sound very excited about the film. Have you had the opportunity to trade screen *Last Temptation* yet?"

"No, I haven't seen the film."

"Mr. Vaughn, may I ask you a question?"

I thought to myself, "She took her time getting to the purpose of her call." I replied, "Certainly you may."

"How many theatres in Miami will Wometco be playing *Last Temptation* in?"

"Ms. Weatherby, Wometco will not be playing the film in Miami."

"Oh no, don't say that." She sounded so artificial that I had to count to ten to keep from losing it with her. "Mr. Vaughn, I was hoping to see *Last Temptation* in a Wometco theatre."

"Well, I'm sorry to disappoint you, Ms. Weatherby; but we won't be dating the film."

She paused a moment. "Mr. Vaughn, has your company taken a position on not playing *Last Temptation* because of its controversial subject matter?"

"Ms. Weatherby, why is this the first time I have ever heard from you in reference to films that we choose to play or not to play in our theatres? Several films play every week in Miami, but not in a Wometco theatre."

"Mr. Vaughn, *Last Temptation* is different from just any other film."

I thought to myself, "You can say that again."

"In my opinion, *Last Temptation* is a must-see film. Mr. Powell and our station management want to make absolutely sure that those persons who live in the Miami area have the opportunity to see the film, if they so desire. We would be greatly disappointed in Wometco Theaters if Wometco would not play the film because of the subject matter. If you did that you, in essence Wometco, would be telling us, the public, what we should see or should not see. Why, you would be taking away our First Amendment rights. Mr. Powell feels very strongly that every American should have the opportunity to see *The Last Temptation of Christ,* if he or she so desires to. It's only right to let those individuals who choose to see *Last Temptation* see it, and those who would find it offensive—then they don't have to see it. Mr. Vaughn, don't you think Wometco owes the community the right to decide for themselves what they can or can't see?"

This lady was giving me a headache.

"Ms. Weatherby, my company's decision not to play *Last Temptation* is in no way an attempt to say what you or anyone else can or cannot see. We are operating our theatres as a business, not a public service—just like your station operates as a business. I doubt Mr. Powell would appreciate very much if I called him and demanded he speak on a certain subject because I felt the community should be able to hear about the subject in question. I doubt that anyone tells Mark Powell what he should or should not speak on." There was silence on the other end of the phone. I could tell her ears were closed to what I was saying.

"Mr. Vaughn, Wometco also operates theatres in other cities within the state. Is that correct?"

"We operate theatres in Fort Lauderdale, Boca Raton, Orlando, Gainesville, and Ocala."

"Are you the individual responsible for the purchasing of film in those areas as well as Miami?"

"Yes, I am."

"Is your position on not playing *The Last Temptation of Christ* the same in those markets as it is in Miami?"

"That is correct."

"Oh, I see. Mr. Vaughn, one more question, then I will let you run. You have been so kind to give up so much of your valuable time to me this morning."

I thought to myself, "Oh, shut up."

She was very direct in her next statement: "Mr. Vaughn, are you a Christian?"

"Ms. Weatherby, I find that question to be totally out of line considering the content of this discussion. But I guess I should expect no less from someone associated with Mark Powell."

She made no reply.

"Ms. Weatherby, my personal religious convictions should have no bearing on a business decision that is made by the senior management of Wometco Theaters. However, I shall answer your question. Yes, I am a Christian."

That wasn't all she wanted to hear. She probed a little further.

"Mr. Vaughn, are you a Christian, like in being born again."

"Ms. Weatherby, your question is superfluous. Being born again is the only way a person can truly be a Christian."

She didn't try to hide her animosity toward me. "Thank you, Mr. Vaughn, for answering my questions."

As I hung up the phone, I thought to myself, "I hate to do it, but I'd better listen to the Mark Powell Show today."

I don't know how bad I was expecting the godless Mark Powell to be that afternoon, but he was worse than I could have possibly imagined. He was irate that Wometco would take such a position on not playing *The Last Temptation of Christ.* He went on to say, "Just who does Larry Vaughn and Wometco Theatres think they are to tell us what we can and cannot see. Wometco has taken away our First Amendment rights, and I'm not going to stand for it. And neither should you!"

I forgot how long his show was on the air—two or three hours. It seemed like forever. Mr. Powell asked his listeners to get on the phone and call Wometco and tell Wometco exactly how they feel about our inexcusable, communistic actions.

Powell went on to say: "Good people of Miami, let's jam Wometco's switchboard with complaints of our displeasure because of their actions. If they won't let us decide what we can and can't see, then we'll boycott not only Wometco Theatres, but the Miami Seaquarium, their Baskin Robbins Ice Cream Parlor, and whatever else Wometco owns and operates. Who needs Wometco? I'll tell you who, good citizens of Miami—you don't!"

Driving home having to listen to Mark Powell spew off at the mouth almost made me sick. Wometco Enterprises was a household name in south Florida. I didn't hurt for myself; I knew in the bottom of my heart I should have left the industry years ago. I knew all this was just spiritual warfare, and I should expect no less. No, my concern was for Art and Mike. This negative publicity was going to really get their attention. They were good men. I felt really bad that they were going to have to go through all of this controversy.

I thought, "Tomorrow is going to be a very tough day at the office."

When I got home, I went over all the events of the day with Doneata. I told her, "Well, one thing good about all of this is it's a no-brainer on my part."

"Honey, what do you mean by 'no-brainer'?"

"By that I mean that I cannot be associated with the film. If Art and Mike cave in to the pressure, then I'm out of the business, and that's God's will for my life. If they support me, then I'll hang in there because I know God will give me the physical and emotional strength to endure the storm."

Doneata replied, "I'm going to call the Shorts and some other people and ask them to start praying."

"Honey, that's an excellent idea."

We went to bed around 11:00 that night. I might as well have stayed up and done a Bible study or done some work around the house. I found it impossible to get my mind off the events of the day. I lay tossing and turning in bed for the better part of the night. I finally got up at 3:00. I went to the kitchen table, read a chapter from the Psalms, and had a time of prayer. I could tell from my nausea and sour stomach that my ulcer was trying to act up. I figured I'd better double up on my Tagamet the next few days.

I sat there alone by myself thinking, "Satan is really manifesting his hatred of God by having this film made for his demonic purposes. When I think back to how the motion picture industry has changed in the past thirty years, it becomes crystal clear to me how Satan has used Hollywood as one of his primary tools for getting into a person's mind and filling it full of all sorts of evil and perverted thoughts."

I took in a deep breath and blew out in a moment of frustration as I thought, "Sooner or later I am going to have to find a way to make a permanent break from any association with this godless business."

I walked into the den, got out a pencil, some paper, and my calculator. I went back to the kitchen table and started figuring the bills. Let me see now, exactly how much is my monthly overhead? Well, the house mortgage is $1,400 each month. Doneata's Cadillac is costing me another $500. My car payment is $250. Then, there's the children's private education, plus medical expenses, clothing, utilities, groceries, etc."

I put the pencil down, leaned back in the chair to where only two of its four legs were resting on the floor, stretched my arms at length, and yawned. I thought, "My materialistic ways are what's keeping me between the rock and the hard place. Tomorrow, at this time I may very well be out of work with not a penny coming into the home. Maybe that's the Lord's perfect will for my life. However, if the Lord sees fit to bring me through this crisis, then I am going to start making some serious changes in my lifestyle. I think it would be wonderful if the Lord made a way for me to get out of Miami, exit the film business, and maybe, even move back to the Carolinas."

I looked at the clock: it was 4:25. I thought, "I should go back to bed and try to get some sleep."

Somehow, a few hours later, I mustered up the energy needed to get out of bed, shower and shave, and be at the office by 8:30. Art buzzed me at 8:35.

"Hello," I answered.

"Larry, can you come over here right away?"

"Yes, sir. I'm on my way."

I walked into Art's office. Mike was also there along with "Albert Stringer." Albert was the recently appointed Executive Vice President of Wometco. The three of them looked at me. No one, as expected, was in a very good mood.

Art bit his bottom lip and pointed his big finger at the telephone. "Larry, look at the telephone."

I noticed all the lines were lit up.

"All of our phones are ringing off the hook with moviegoers irate at us over our decision not to play *Last Temptation*. Mark Powell is making us out to be some sort of communistic dictators. Have you heard what he's asking people to do?"

I frowned as I nodded my head. "Yes, Art, I have heard every word."

Albert spoke up. "The decision about playing *Last Temptation* should have been discussed, in detail, among the four of us before now."

I looked at Albert. "Albert, I talked to Art about this film months ago. He and I discussed it in detail."

Albert looked at Art.

Art said, "Larry, that's true, but I had no idea about how negatively the community would react to our position of not playing the film."

Art lit up a cigar, made a ring of smoke in the air, and then looked directly at me.

"Larry, the calls started nonstop late yesterday afternoon. Our girls are getting told off and cursed at because that radio station keeps encouraging people to call. Mr. Powell has done a very good job at getting the citizens of Miami up in arms over our decision not to play the film."

Art turned his back to us and looked out the window.

Albert said, "I think we need to re-evaluate our position on playing the film."

I jumped in. "Albert, the decision of whether we are going to play *Last Temptation* has already been made." I said with complete confidence, "We are not playing the film."

I held my breath and started praying, "Lord, I need Art and Mike's support now more than ever. Please touch their minds and give them the wisdom and strength to do the right thing."

Albert was ready to roll up his sleeves and slug it out with me when Art interrupted, "I don't like Mark Powell or anyone else telling me what I can or can't do with my theatres. Let's leave it alone for now and see if maybe it won't just blow over in time."

I thought, "Thank you, Lord, for answering prayer."

I looked at Albert—his anger was showing in his eyes. I knew there was much more that he was wanting to say about our decision not to play the film.

That afternoon, *The Miami Herald*, one of the leading newspapers in the country, called and asked me basically the same questions that Ms. Weatherby had asked the day before. The next morning, I found an article on the front page stating something to the effect that Larry

Vaughn, the Christian film buyer for Wometco Theatres, announces that Wometco will not be playing *The Last Temptation of Christ.*

I wondered, "When I get to work this morning, should I go to my office or go ahead and do the inevitable, which is to go on over to Art's office?"

Sure enough I was back in a meeting at 8:30 with the three of them. Art held up the front page of the paper. Oh, he was fit to be tied.

"Larry, I'm sure you've seen this article."

"Yes, sir. Art, while we're on the subject of newspaper articles, I might as well tell you, yesterday I also talked with one of the New York newspapers."

Art shook his head in disbelief of all the happenings around him and said, "Is this nightmare ever going to end?"

I spoke up. "Art, if you had agreed to play the film, you would have the same repercussions—only the negative calls and mail would be from the Christian community."

In an act of total frustration, Art threw the newspaper article across his desk. I felt really bad for Art and Mike having to go through all of this trauma because of not playing a picture that they knew absolutely nothing about. They really didn't understand what all the controversy was over.

Waving a handful of letters in the air, Art said, "Larry, look at the mail we have received in protest of our position on not playing this film."

"Art, I have a desk full of hate mail myself."

"Well, I need to see those letters."

"Fine, I will have them brought over to your office within the hour."

Albert wanted to pick up with where he left off yesterday. He appealed to Art. "Art, I believe you and Larry were too quick in your decision not to play the film. For the record, I think it would be in the best interest of the company for us to reconsider and play the film."

I looked at Albert. "Well, you're not the film buyer—I am. And the decision has already been made; we're not playing the film." If looks could kill, I would be a dead man.

Art interrupted my thoughts as he said, "You two stop it." He turned to me and asked, "Larry, what does Universal have to say about all of this?"

"I haven't heard a word from them on the subject."

Art raised his eyebrows and gave me that look as if to say, "You will."

During these rather testy meetings, all Mike seemed to do was look at whoever was talking and take all the information into his memory bank. That's the way Mike was. He was the quiet thinker. I knew when he finally did make a statement, it would carry a lot of weight in how Art would look at things. After a few minutes, Art suggested we all get back to work and table the immediate problem at hand. I felt blessed that I was able to leave the meeting still in one piece. I knew Albert was after my head.

That afternoon, I received the expected phone call from Phil Sherman. Phil, at that time, was the General Sales Manager Eastern Division of Universal Film.

"Larry, what's going on in Miami?"

"Phil, I don't know exactly how all this got started. I think it started with an inquiring customer who talked to me and, after not liking what I had to say, went to one of the top talk-radio stations. Then they got hold of it, and everything started snowballing in the wrong direction. I can tell you one thing: I wish that picture, *Last Temptation*, had never been made."

"Larry, I haven't even asked you to play the picture, and Miami's already national news."

"Yeah, I know."

"Larry, do you want to hear the good news?"

"Phil, I'd love to hear some good news right about now."

"Controversy sells tickets, lots of tickets. Because of all the adverse publicity already received on *Last Temptation* in Miami, I think Miami has the chance to be one of our better engagements on the film."

Phil paused a moment. "Larry, I want you to play the picture on an exclusive-run basis in Miami. The company wants to go one run only in the Miracle Theatre."

"Phil, forget it. I'm not playing the film."

"Larry, I have seen the picture. It's a very good film. People are making a mountain out of a molehill on this film. There is absolutely nothing offensive in the picture. Scorsese has made a fine film that deserves to play in the Miracle Theatre. I'll tell you what I'll do. I'll put a print on a plane today; you look at it tomorrow morning and call me after you have seen the film."

"No, Phil, I will not look at the film."

I could tell Phil was starting to get very upset with me.

"Larry, does this hold true for all the other Wometco markets in Florida?"

"Yes, it does."

"You know, Larry, Florida is a very competitive theatre market. Universal has a lot of important films coming up in the months ahead. Wometco needs Universal far, far more than Universal needs Wometco."

"Phil, I don't see how I could keep my theatres booked with good playable pictures without the support of Universal Film. Wometco Theaters needs Universal Film like Larry Vaughn's lungs need air for my body to stay alive. Phil, if you walk away from me over *Last Temptation,* the results will be devastating to me as well as my company. However, I am not going to play *The Last Temptation of Christ* in any Wometco theatre as long as I am in charge of the film department."

He paused a moment. "Okay, Larry, if that's your final decision, then I guess we have no more to talk about on that subject."

Phil hung up, and I felt sick at my stomach.

Driving home that night, I went over in my mind my conversation with Phil. I have always had such a good relationship with the management team at Universal. I thought, "I sure hope it's not over. Without their product, I will be at a great disadvantage in trying to keep film in my theatres. I'm going to have to pray that God won't let Universal go out of business with me over this deplorable picture."

It was another sleepless night. I think I tossed and turned until sometime around 5:00 a.m. Then, it was all I could do to get out of bed at 6:30 to meet the new day.

All this happened in the span of four weeks. The radio station kept digging at us, people kept writing hate letters, and individuals kept calling our office to let us know that they would no longer support any Wometco theatre. Finally, Art called what was to be the final meeting on *The Last Temptation of Christ,* except this time I was called into the meeting last. The meeting had started earlier with Art, Mike, and Albert. They chose to call me in after they had talked for some time among themselves.

Art started out doing the talking. "Larry, we, as individuals and as a company, have gone through several weeks of sheer agony over our decision not to play this film, *Last Temptation.* I personally can't go anywhere without the subject coming up. My phone at home rings off the hook with friends wanting to give me their opinion on the matter. The same thing is happening with Mike, Albert, and I'm sure with yourself. I was hoping the whole controversy about us not playing the film would blow over within a few days, but it hasn't. Now, my question to you gentlemen is where do we go from here?"

Albert spoke first. "I'm embarrassed and disappointed that we're not playing the film. All along I thought the decision not to play *The Last Temptation* was the wrong thing to do. It has definitely hurt our image in the community. It could affect our long-term relationship with Universal, and I personally think the picture is going to do very well at the box office."

Albert then turned from Art to me. With a smirk on his face, he eyeballed me and spoke in a very sarcastic tone. "I think we all know what I have just said is the truth. The question is: What is Larry going to do if we have a change of heart and play the film? Well, they won't ask you, Larry, so I will. What will you do if we decide to have a change of heart and play the film?"

Before I could reply, Art looked at Albert and said, "Mister, you're out of line. That question is not yours for the asking." Then in a moment of built-up anger and frustration, Art slammed his fist down on the conference table. "Enough is enough!" he shouted. I glanced down at the table to see if it had cracked.

Looking straight into Albert's eyes, Art said, "I don't want to hear another word on this subject again. We are not going to play the film, and that is final, over, done with, period! Does everyone understand?"

I went back to my office thinking, "I have just experienced a true miracle. God touched Art Hertz's heart and mind to have him support his Christian film buyer, when the circumstances would rule for him to do completely different."

I breathed a deep sigh of relief. I knew in my heart that now I was up for anything. I had just experienced the power of God working through Art Hertz's life in protecting me from those powers of darkness.

It's hard to believe, but many good things came out of that bad experience with *The Last Temptation of Christ*. Because of all the publicity, churches all over the country got wind of the situation in Miami. Christian people by the thousands were praying for me and the company. Letters of appreciation started pouring in to Wometco from everywhere. People were thanking Art, Mike, and me for not playing the film. I remember walking into Art's office one morning.

Art, puffing on his cigar, motioned toward a stack of mail on the floor as he said, "Look, Larry, more mail from your friends." The Christian thank-you letters were actually outnumbering the earlier hate mail.

The next time I talked with Phil Sherman, it was like we had never had that last conversation about my playing *Last Temptation* in the Miracle Theatre. It was business as usual. He never mentioned my not playing *Last Temptation,* and I could tell there were absolutely no ill feelings between Phil and me. My relationship with Universal was as solid as it ever was.

Because of all the adverse national publicity Miami received on the film, the other major theatre circuits shied away from playing *Last Temptation* in Miami. AMC played it in other cities, but not in Miami. United Artists Theatres wouldn't touch it, nor would General Cinema Corporation. I was pleased later to hear that GCC's mostly Catholic board of directors made a company decision not to play the film anywhere.

There for a while it looked like *Last Temptation* would actually end up not playing in Miami, but a small, independent theatre owner—eager to make a fast buck from the publicity—negotiated with Phil to play the film. After all the controversy and advance fanfare on the film, I was pleased to see that his engagement did only fair business at best.

Twenty-Six

The Dark Cloud

I had a spiritual victory in February of 1986 when I returned to the Bally Hotel in Las Vegas for the annual Show West Convention. After twenty-five years, I, Larry Vaughn, had finally lost all interest in the one thing that had controlled my life for so many of those twenty-five years: gambling. I spent the entire week at the Bally, either attending convention activities, having meals with film executives, or in my room studying and meditating on Scripture and praying.

The plane ride home from Las Vegas was a much more pleasant plane ride than the plane ride a year ago. I remember sitting in my seat and bowing my head and giving thanks to our great God for protecting me from even having a desire to participate in those evil temptations of the flesh. The emotional, guilt-ridden experience of winning all that money and then giving it all back was not for naught. God used that experience in my life to cure me and release a major stronghold that had been embedded in my life for so many years.

————

There was always a mountain of activity going on at Wometco. I was about to start my fifth year of service with Art and Mike. For the most part, it had been an exciting adventure being part of the management team at the new Wometco. During the past four years, the company had renovated several older Wometco theatres and brought them up to more modern standards, purchased two theatres in Miami from Loew's Theatres, and built several new multiplex theatres. As far as the stability of the company, things just couldn't have been better. Art and Mike believed in sharing the company's prosperity. Salarywise, I was probably one of the best-paid film buyers in the country.

I received a call one Tuesday afternoon from Frank Jones. Frank had been the assistant film buyer under the old Litchfield organization before Foster McKissick sold his theatres to United Artists. Frank was a funny-looking guy. He had a big mouth full of pointed teeth that he showed quite often because he was always smiling and laughing. He had a huge balding head with big sagging brown eyes that always had dark circles under them. Frank had a very deep voice. When he talked, it sounded as if he were talking from the very bottom of his belly. He had a very outgoing personality. He was always the one called on at a film function to tell a wild story to get the audience laughing.

Yes, Frank Jones was most certainly an interesting individual. He had worked for Foster ever since Foster had been in the theatre business. He was a divorced man with two grown children: a son and a daughter. Neither of Frank's children lived in the area. Everyone in the industry who knew Frank liked him. Frank had the reputation of being the individual that always closed the bar. Yes, Frank was always the first to arrive at a party and the last one to leave. He was always out to have a good time. I had never had any business dealings with Frank Jones, but I think when it came to film buying, Frank depended more on his friendships and Litchfield's relationships with individuals than his negotiating skills to get the better product in his theatres. Frank Jones and I were total opposites.

Frank asked me, "Partner, are you going to be home this evening?"

"Yes, Frank, I will be."

"Great, Larry, would you mind if I give you a ring tonight on a personal matter?"

"No, Frank, that will be fine. I have a tennis game from 6:30 until 8:00 p.m. I will be home after about 8:10."

"Good. You may expect a call from me then."

I hung up the phone thinking, "Frank must be looking for work."

Frank called me around 8:30. After a few minutes of small talk, Frank asked me, "Larry, the purpose of this call is to see if you are still happy working for Wometco."

I was surprised to hear him say that was why he called. My answer was instant. "Very much so, Frank." I paused. "But, why do you ask?"

"Well, Larry, do you remember meeting Foster McKissick last summer in New York?"

"Sure, how can anyone forget meeting A. Foster McKissick? He's one-of-a-kind."

Frank gave his famous big laugh. "You got that right, brother." Frank started talking very quietly as if he didn't want anyone else to hear what he was about to say. "Larry, Foster has decided to go back into the theatre business. I might add in a very large way. He is talking about building a new circuit of theatres all across the United States. His intent is to build a circuit with 750 screens. His expansion plan calls for an opening of one to two theatres a week."

"What?"

"That's right. He anticipates opening one to two theatres a week."

I thought to myself, "At Wometco during a good year, we will open only one or at the very most two theatres."

"Frank, Foster better have a lot—I mean a lot—of cash to build theatres that fast."

Frank laughed. "He does."

Frank had my curiosity up. "Well, tell me, Frank, if I had any interest, how would I fit into Foster's plans with this new theatre circuit?"

"Larry, you heard about Foster's former head film buyer, Allen Locke, having a stroke?"

"Yeah, I was sorry to hear about Allen's health problems. He is such a nice guy. How is Allen doing?"

"Larry, Allen's having a tough time. He's having therapy, I believe, twice a week. Foster offered Allen the job of managing the Pro Shop at the Litchfield Country Club, if and when he's able to go back to work. But I don't think Allen has any interest in the Pro Shop at this time. Anyway, because of Allen's poor health, he will not be able to go back into film buying. When Foster, Ulmer, and I started looking at the various film buyers out there, your name ended up being first on our list of men to talk to."

I thought a moment about what Doneata and I had been recently praying about: that the Lord would provide an opportunity for our family to get out of Miami, leave the film business, and maybe, one day, even end up moving back to the Carolinas. Well, this isn't leaving the film business, but it could most certainly be a move in the right direction.

I thought a moment. "Okay, Frank, tell Foster that I would like very much to talk with him."

Frank sounded shocked. "Well, Larry, you just never know. That's exactly what Foster was hoping you would say." Frank paused a moment. "I don't want to sound like I'm rushing you, but could you and your wife possibly make a trip to Litchfield Beach this weekend? Would that be too soon for you to meet with Foster?"

I thought a moment. "Frank, pending no problem with our friends keeping the children, this weekend will be fine."

"Okay, if you get your baby sitters, here's what Foster would like to do: He would like for you and your wife to fly up to Litchfield by the Sea Friday afternoon and return to Miami Sunday afternoon."

"Fine, Frank, I'll take care of the tickets on my end and phone you tomorrow with my flight information."

"That's great, Larry." He chuckled. "This call is going to make Foster McKissick's day."

Doneata and I arrived at the Myrtle Beach Airport around 5:30 p.m. Friday afternoon. Frank was at the gate waiting for us. He drove us the seventeen miles south to Litchfield Beach. The company had made arrangements for Doneata and me to stay in one of the furnished townhouses located on one of the golf course fairways near the Litchfield Country Club.

The home was professionally decorated inside. Everything was immaculate. The refrigerator and pantry were fully stocked. Our bedroom and den gave us a beautiful view of the River Club Golf Course.

After bringing in the luggage, Frank handed me a set of car keys. "Larry, the car parked in your driveway is for Doneata and you to use while you're staying with us. Here's a map of the area. If you have any questions, I'll be happy to answer them for you, or I'll most certainly find someone who can answer them for you."

Frank looked at his watch. "We are to meet Foster and his wife, Sophie; Ulmer and Bill Eaddy; Jack Jordan and his fiancée, Carol, for dinner at the Country Club at 7:00 p.m."

Frank gave Doneata and me that big, genuine, caring smile of his and said, "You be ready for me to pick you up at 6:50."

———

Frank, Doneata, and I walked into the beautiful Litchfield Country Club, which looked like a stately Southern mansion from a bygone era. I almost expected to see Rhett Butler and Scarlett O'Hara walk by on their way to dinner. The Litchfield Country Club reminded me of the mansion Tara in Margaret Mitchell's *Gone with the Wind*.

We went to a private room upstairs which had two sofas and several chairs. I could tell the furniture had been rearranged to make an area for conversation. Everyone was already seated waiting for our arrival. Foster was the first one out of his chair. He walked over to me and shook my hand. I then introduced him to Doneata. Foster formally welcomed Doneata and me to Litchfield. He introduced his lovely wife, Sophie; his Executive Vice President and General Manager of Litchfield Theaters,

Ulmer Eaddy and his wife, Bill; and Jack Jordan, his director of advertising and marketing, along with Jack's fiancée, Carol.

Bill wanted to get her explanation in first: "My father had his heart set on a boy, and when I came along, he gave me the name he had picked out for his son." Then giving us a real cute smile, Bill said, "I've never wanted to change it; so, Bill I am."

We all laughed at the novelty of her story. One waiter came and took drink orders while another waiter brought in two trays of delicious hors d'oeuvres.

We had a wonderful time getting to know one another. Doneata took a special liking to Bill Eaddy right from the start.

After an hour or so, we moved into the elegant dining room of the Litchfield Country Club for our evening meal. Foster insisted Doneata and I have she-crab soup as our appetizer. He said very proudly, "My chef is the best cook in the area. His she-crab soup is the best in all of South Carolina." Doneata and I were both glad that we listened to Foster and took his advice. The soup was delicious. The meal itself was scrumptious.

During the meal, I noticed Foster kept taking his fork and eating off Doneata's plate. I thought to myself, "Foster should have ordered the red snapper because he's eating most of Doneata's." Then a few minutes later, Foster started eating off Bill's plate.

Finally, Sophie explained to Doneata and me Foster's most unusual behavior. "Foster McKissick does what he calls 'grazing' when having a meal. That means he would rather eat off your plate than his own."

Sophie shook her head and threw her hands up in the air as if to say, "I have given up on trying to change him."

"Doneata, maybe you can break him from that bad habit. No one else has ever been able to."

Foster held his fork up in the air as if it were a flag and said, "Well, I don't know why it always happens that everybody's food always looks better than mine. I just like to have a taste to see if your food is as good as it looks." We all laughed at Foster and his most unusual habit.

I couldn't help but notice how kind Foster was to the waiters and the waitresses. He seemed to know everyone's name from the water server to the hostess. After dinner Foster asked the waiter to have the chef come to our table so he could thank him personally for such a fine dinner. After dinner we all caravanned over to the McKissicks' oceanfront townhouse at Litchfield by the Sea.

By the time the evening was over, Doneata and I knew everyone much better. Sophie was a wonderful lady. Exactly what you would expect Mrs. A. Foster McKissick to be: a very cordial, pretty, and intelligent lady. She had polish, class, and lots of it. But she didn't have that air of being better than the rest. No, she complemented her famous husband well. She was quite a lady in her own right. I enjoyed talking with her very much.

Ulmer Eaddy was Foster's right arm when it came to Litchfield Theaters. Ulmer was an older gentleman who had spent his whole life in the theatre business. He knew every facet of the business. He could talk real estate, popcorn, or film buying. Ulmer was one of the key players in the Litchfield organization.

Jack Jordan was no stranger to me at all. Jack was in his late sixties. He and I had worked together for John Huff many years earlier in Charlotte, North Carolina, at ABC. Jack held the same position, director of advertising and marketing, at Litchfield that he did at ABC many years ago. Jack had a wonderful personality. He was a hard-working company man. In his free time he liked to play golf, party, and have fun. Jack and Frank Jones were a lot alike when it came to, after hours, letting the good times roll.

At about 11:30 p.m., we decided to call it a night. Foster asked me, "Larry, can you find your way back to the Country Club from where you're staying?"

"Yes, sir."

"Good then. The Bishop [that was Foster's nickname for Eaddy] and I want to meet with you in the morning at 10:00 a.m. in my office. It's located on the ground floor of the Country Club. When you go in the main door, it's the first door on your right."

"Fine." Doneata and I thanked everyone for a wonderful evening; then we left for our home away from home.

Saturday morning Doneata slept in while I prepared myself for my 10:00 a.m. appointment. When I got to Foster's office, Eaddy and he were busy going over some real estate information. They cleared off the desk, and the three of us started to talk.

Foster said, "Larry, I'm going to move the home office from Easley, South Carolina, to right here at Litchfield Beach. These days, all you need to get work done is a telephone, a fax machine, and an airplane. I just so happen to have all three right here at Litchfield." He paused, "Well, actually, we keep the company jet at the airport in Georgetown, which is only twenty minutes from here."

Foster went over the expansion plan of the new company with me from A to Z. I was surprised that he shared as much information with me as he did, without my having made a commitment to come to work for him. After he walked me through the new company, he said, "Larry, in the very near future I am going to need a film buyer."

I looked at Foster and Eaddy and said, "I'm interested very much in talking with you gentlemen about buying film for your theatre circuit." I continued, "There are only two nonnegotiables in my coming to work for Litchfield."

Both Foster and Ulmer looked at me to hear what it was I was about to say.

"I need to have a good private Christian school to educate two of my children. My daughter, Mentora, is going into the eighth grade; and my younger son, Larry Jr., is going into the second grade. My older son, David, because of his past health problems, is going to need some one-on-one tutoring before he can be expected to get his much-needed high school diploma. I also must be able to find a good church for my family and me to worship in."

Foster nodded as if he understood. "Larry, there are several good churches right here in the Pawleys Island area. There are even more churches toward the Myrtle Beach area. I'm not sure about a private Christian school."

I interrupted, "Foster, my wife made some phone calls Thursday when we found out that we would be coming up for the weekend. This afternoon, if you don't have anything on the agenda for us, Doneata and I are going to meet with Mr. Weeks, the principal of Calvary Christian School; and while we're at it, we would like to check out some of the churches in the area."

Foster sat back in his chair and put the palms of his hands on the back of his neck. "Larry, I guess the only thing left to talk about is money." He looked at me with a curious look on his face. "What kind of money are you making at Wometco?"

I wrote down a number on a sheet of paper and slipped it across the table. Foster looked at the paper then at Ulmer. "Larry, we don't pay any of our people that kind of money."

I thought I might as well be honest. "Foster, that's just my base salary without any of the perks."

He pulled on his ear lobe as he said, "Larry, I want you, but the question is," he held his hands open in the air, "Can I afford you?"

"Foster, let me ask you a question. How many screens do you have up and running right now?" The movement of his eyes passed the question over to Ulmer who responded, "Not many, maybe thirty."

I thought for a moment and then said, "Well, gentlemen, let's not let money kill the deal."

Foster had an inquiring look on his face as he said, "Larry, what do you have in mind?"

"Maybe we'll have to come up with some sort of a compromise on my salary where it can grow as the company and my areas of responsibility grow. Foster, you and Eaddy put your heads together and get back with me."

I thought a moment, and then I decided I would go ahead and share with Foster and Ulmer what I was thinking. "Foster, one thing in your favor is that I am a Christian man. My wife and I have been praying that the Lord would open a door of opportunity for my family to get out of Miami and move back to the Carolinas. It looks like there's a possibility God is going to use you in making that happen. If so, then we'll work out the financial end to where neither one of us will get hurt."

Foster looked at Eaddy and said, "You know, Bishop, I like the way Larry says things." Foster thought a moment. "Larry, Bishop will call you sometime in the next few days and the two of you will talk further about the deal."

"Foster, that's all I wanted to hear."

Doneata and I spent the better part of that Saturday afternoon driving around looking at Pawleys Island, Deerfield Beach, Surfside, and the South Myrtle Beach area. We went over to Calvary Christian School and talked with Mr. Weeks about the school. We were pleased with what we saw and heard. Our first impression was that Calvary Christian would be a good place for Mentora and Larry Jr. to get an education.

We called and talked with one of the ministers from one of the Reformed churches in the North Myrtle Beach area. The pastor sounded like a fine man, but his church was too far away for us to visit with any long-term expectations of joining. He recommended we visit "Plantation Church," a sister church of his at Surfside Beach. He told us the pastor was known for his strong gift of the preaching of the Word of God.

That evening, the McKissicks, the Eaddys, Frank, Jack, and Carol, plus Doneata and I all went out to one of Foster's favorite restaurants for dinner. Then it was back to his home.

Our weekend at Litchfield Beach was a wonderful experience. I tried to imagine leaving the hustle and bustle of a major city like Miami,

Florida, and living and working in this little corner of paradise nestled between Myrtle Beach and Georgetown, South Carolina. Foster commented, "I never lock my house at Litchfield because there's no reason to. We don't have any crime here. I also never take my keys out of the ignition in my truck or cars. There are no car thieves around here."

I said, "Foster, you make Litchfield Beach sound like 'Camelot.' Does it also only rain at Litchfield Beach after sundown?"

"Well, I can't go that far, but Litchfield Beach is a great place to live and raise a family." I could tell Foster really wanted to work it out for me to be a part of his team.

Doneata and I talked on the plane ride home. "Larry, I do think Litchfield could be a springboard to your exiting the film business."

"So do I, honey. It's just that I have such a big job now it's going to be hard for Foster to come up with a plan to make it work financially. But, if he gives me a figure that's anywhere in the ballpark or near the ballpark, I'm going to take it."

"Good. This is what we have been praying would happen."

"I'll tell you something else Doneata. If the Lord makes it possible for me to go with Litchfield, this will be my last move in the theatre business."

"What do you mean?"

"I mean, if I go with Litchfield, I'm going to promise the Lord that after Litchfield I will not go to work for another theatre circuit or film company."

"Larry, how long do you think the Litchfield job will last?"

"Doneata, I think Foster is building a circuit to sell. If so, it will most likely take him five to seven years to grow the circuit to the size he wants it to be before he sells it. Of course, that's just a guess, but probably a pretty good one."

Doneata put my hand in hers and squeezed it. "Larry, I wish we didn't have to wait so long to know what is going to happen."

"Me too, sweetheart."

It was about three weeks later when the call came in from Ulmer Eaddy. "Larry, I apologize for not getting back to you sooner, but things have been crazy here at the office."

"That's fine, Ulmer. I'm just glad to hear from you now."

"Larry, Foster and I want to fly down to Miami and meet with you this weekend. Would it be possible for the three of us to have dinner Friday evening?"

"Only if you let it be my treat. I've got to do something to reciprocate for that wonderful weekend you folks showed Doneata and me at Litchfield Beach."

"Well, we'll see. Could you meet us in Fort Lauderdale Friday afternoon at 5:30 at our hotel? We're staying at the Jockey Club."

"Sure, I know where it is. I will see you then."

When I arrived at the Jockey Club, Foster and Eaddy were relaxing in two chairs at an outside table. After a few minutes of small talk, Foster looked at Ulmer and said, "Bishop, let's get the business out of the way before we go to dinner."

Foster sat up erect in his chair and said, "Larry, Bishop and I have come up with a plan that we think will work for both of us. There's got to be a little give-and-take on both sides, but how does this sound to you?"

Foster then looked at Ulmer. "Go ahead, Bishop, give Larry the proposal." Ulmer took out his pad and pencil. "Larry, the bad news first. We'll have to start out by shaving your base annual salary by $10,000, but we'll give you a new Ford Crown Victoria to be used for your personal use as well as business use. While you're trying to sell your home in Miami, we'll furnish you with a completely furnished three-bedroom home located on the golf course at River Club to live in for six months rent free with all utilities paid, including the phone. Of course, you'll have to pay for any long-distance charges."

Then Foster chimed in, "Larry, I'll grandfather you a full membership to the Litchfield Country Club, which is worth $7,500. You'll have at your and your family's disposal all golf, tennis, swimming, and Country Club privileges."

Then Ulmer said, "Larry, we'll pay all your moving expenses 100 percent."

Foster then looked into my eyes. "As Litchfield grows, Larry Vaughn will grow." Foster leaned back in his chair and said, "Bishop, is that it?"

Ulmer, checking off each point on his list, said, "I believe it is."

Foster said, "Oh, if you take the job, your immediate superior will be the Bishop, then me."

I noticed that statement seemed to embarrass Ulmer.

"Foster, you have yourself a deal. When do you gentlemen want me to report to work?"

Foster said, "We thought we would leave that decision up to you."

I thought a moment. "Gentlemen, today is Friday. When Arthur Hertz comes into his office on Monday morning, my letter of resignation will be on his desk. I will give him a two-week notice—that's all he'll need because the theatres are booked with very good product for the next three months. The timing couldn't be better, leaving in the end of May with his theatres set for the summer. I would like to take another two weeks off and report to Litchfield on, say, the first of June."

Foster looked at Ulmer. "Bishop, have one of the attorneys draw up a contract for Larry and me to sign."

I looked at Foster. "Foster, as far as my end, I don't need a contract. Your handshake is all I need to seal the deal."

Foster elbowed Ulmer in the side. "I tell you, Bishop, I like the way Larry thinks." That handshake consummated the deal.

We left the Jockey Club and went out to a delicious dinner at one of Fort Lauderdale's better restaurants, The Down Under. That night was the start of many memorable evenings I was to have with Foster McKissick and Ulmer Eaddy.

On Monday mornings Art usually calls me by 8:45 a.m. to get a quick update on the weekend receipts at the box office. This particular Monday I did not hear from him until nearly 11:00 a.m. Then the call came in.

"Hello?"

"Good morning, Larry."

"Good morning, Art. How are you today?"

"Larry, I was fine until I opened my mail. Would you mind coming over here for a few minutes?"

"No, sir. I'll be right there."

I walked into his office. Art was sitting behind his desk, and Mike was sitting in the guest chair directly across the desk from Art. I sat down in the chair beside Mike.

Art spoke first. "Larry, Mike and I received your letter of resignation this morning."

"Yes, sir. Well, I can't say I haven't had mixed emotions, but I think thirteen years is long enough for me to spend in one place."

Art stared at me and gave me that look as if to say, "Okay, Larry, quit beating around the bush. What is it that you're after?"

Art took out a fresh cigar and started twirling it with his fingers. "Larry, why don't you tell Mike and me what it is that you want."

"They think I'm here to negotiate," I thought to myself. "Art, I don't want anything. I'm leaving."

Art said very emphatically, "Larry, you know you're not seriously considering leaving Wometco. Now, what is it that you want?"

"Art, I have already made a commitment with another company." Both Art and Mike had a surprised look on their faces. "I'm not trying to get anything out of you and Mike." I looked at Art. "You gentlemen know that's not the way I operate." I paused a moment. "It's just that I have taken another film-buying position with another theatre circuit."

Art was shocked. "Larry, you mean you have already made a commitment to go to work for someone else?"

"Yes, sir. That is correct."

"Where are you going?"

"I'm going to work for Foster McKissick."

Art thought a moment. "Foster McKissick—I thought he was out of the theatre business."

"He was, but in the very near future Mr. McKissick is going to build another circuit. I have made a deal with him to be his film buyer."

I looked at the genuine concern on Art and Mike's faces. I figured I best say something positive. "Art, Mike, I have your theatres already booked with top product through the month of August. Whomever you bring in will have plenty of time to get acclimated to the Florida market without having to worry about having good, playable product in the Wometco theatres for the summer."

Art's wheels were churning. He stood up and started walking around the room. "What about the lawsuit that is pending with 'Haskins Theatres.' If it ever goes to trial, and it looks like it very well might, then we'll need you to testify."

"If and when that happens, I'll just have to fly back down to Miami to testify. If your New York lawyers need me to give any additional depositions, then have them call me, and I'll make myself available. Foster is very much aware of the lawsuit and the pending jury trial in Miami."

Art shook his head as if he were angry with himself. "Larry, I wish you had talked with Mike and me before giving Mr. McKissick a final commitment. Maybe we could have made it worth your while to stay on with Wometco."

"It's not the money, Art. You have always taken very good care of me financially. It's just, well, I want to go back to the Carolinas. It's a personal thing with me. I have enjoyed working for the two of you very much."

I smiled as I pointed my finger at them. "You two are demanding as all get out, but I always liked a challenge. You men have been extremely generous to my family and me. By the way, I had a talk with Foster about

Wometco. Since Wometco is not presently in opposition to Litchfield in any markets, Foster doesn't mind your calling me periodically for information. If you so desire, I shall be a consultant for your new film buyer for say four to six weeks. That will give him the time needed to get acclimated to the Florida theatre market."

I looked at the disappointment on Art's and Mike's faces. "There will be no charge to you gentlemen for this service."

That was a tough meeting for not only Art and Mike but also for me. It's hard to leave a company that you have given thirteen years of your life to. However, when you pray specifically for God to open doors to make an escape, and then those doors are miraculously opened, you have no choice but to enter them and find out what's on the other side.

Art and Mike gave me a wonderful going-away luncheon at Christy's, which is one of the finest Angus prime beef steakhouses in Coral Gables. It was at that time I was given a plaque of appreciation for my thirteen years of service with Wometco. The home office employees also gave me a very nice going-away party and a very special gift: an executive briefcase. I was pleased to be able to leave Wometco without any animosity between Art and Mike and me.

Most of the major film companies in California never really understood why or how I could leave a top film market like Miami, with all its visibility and power, to work at Litchfield Beach, South Carolina. Even though all the distributors had the utmost respect for A. Foster McKissick, they just couldn't understand my walking away from one of the top film-buying jobs for a position with much less recognition, power, and challenge. If I had one V.P. tell me, I must have had five V.P.'s tell me, "Larry, you're going to work for a wonderful man; but, careerwise, you've just taken a step backwards." Many times I thought to myself that my friends would really think I had lost all my marbles if they knew that I had turned down a top position with MGM/UA.

What the film community didn't know was the constant struggle that was going on within me. Ever since I had become a Christian, there always seemed to be a dark cloud hanging over my head. Sometimes the cloud would blow away for a while, and I would have a period of spiritual happiness, contentment, and joy. But, those times of happiness, contentment, and joy were becoming shorter and shorter as the cloud seemed to return more frequently, interrupting the joy of my relationship with Christ.

One day I figured out what controlled that dark cloud. No, it wasn't here today and gone tomorrow just by chance. What controlled that cloud was my attitude toward sin and my relationship with God. When I gave in to the demands of this world and all those compromises associated with it, the cloud would arrive. And when I strove to walk close to the Lord and depend on Him, by faith, to meet those needs in every area of my life, the cloud disappeared. As I thought about it, I realized that the cloud represented my double-mindedness before the Lord, and my double-mindedness came from my ongoing struggles with my involvement in the motion picture industry.

Twenty-Seven

The Brief Friendship

The family moved with me to Litchfield Beach on the first of June in 1989. We put our house in Miami on the market with a realtor and left it furnished for the realtor to show. We were also able to help meet a need in a Christian family's life during that period of time. We let a teacher and her children from Westwood Christian School in Miami live in our home the five months before it sold. I believe the reason it took five months for our home to sell was that the Lord wanted the teacher and her family to live there during that time.

Living at a country club resort made Doneata and the children feel like they were on an extended vacation. Every morning they would wake up in our beautifully furnished home and look out the window at the golf course. Down the street was the swimming pool and the Litchfield Tennis Club. And, if that wasn't enough excitement for them, then across the street was the beautiful Litchfield Beach and the Atlantic Ocean. Yes, the family really seemed to be enjoying themselves those first few weeks at Litchfield Beach.

I must admit I was enjoying the laid-back change of lifestyle myself. In Miami it had taken me an hour to drive to the office; it now took three to five minutes. On any given day, if I chose to do so, I could go home and have lunch with the family. I was home every afternoon by 5:15 instead of 6:30 or 7:00.

The pace of living at Litchfield Beach was about as far from Miami living as one could get and still be in the United States. I kept finding myself having to put on my mental brakes every time I turned around, both at work and at home. I had spent the last thirteen years at work in a suit and always had to be mentally prepared at a moment's notice to have to deal with bankers or investors. At Wometco, daily there were questions to be answered and explanations to be given. At Litchfield, I didn't even have to wear a suit to work. Our dress of the day was a golf shirt, casual slacks, and loafers.

Foster liked to have a meeting once a week with Frank, Jack, and me. We would usually meet late Tuesday afternoon in the sitting room of the Litchfield Country Club. Foster, Jack, and Frank would drink beer while I nursed a glass of Chablis wine. During the meeting, we would go through four to six baskets of fresh, hot popcorn as we talked about the past weekend's business. Those Litchfield meetings were somewhat different from Wometco's Tuesday morning meeting where Art, Mike, Albert, Bill, and I went over, individually, each theatre's gross, both Wometco's and the opposition's, with a magnifying glass to see who came out on top for the weekend. At the beginning, life was indeed laid back at Litchfield Theaters.

One Tuesday afternoon Foster commented about how much weight he had recently gained and how he was thinking about going on an exercise program. He said, "I think this excess weight is hurting my tennis game." Foster loved to play tennis on the weekends.

I said, "Foster, with all the beautiful places to run around here, you should take up running."

"Larry, I have been a jogger on and off for years. It's just that here lately I've been mostly off more than on with my running."

"Foster, running is something that I have been doing on a regular basis for twelve years. Why don't you and I start running together? It's much easier to run on a regular schedule when you have a partner to run with you. If you're like me Foster, the accountability of having someone to run with makes all the difference in the world."

"Larry, that sounds like exactly what I need. When do you want to start?"

I thought a moment. "I'll be in Dallas all of next week. The following week I plan on being in Atlanta. How about in three weeks?"

"Sounds fine by me."

Foster ordered another beer and some more popcorn. I could tell he was getting excited about the possibility of our running together. He said, "Larry, when I'm at the beach I can run any day of the week but Monday. Mondays, I leave out early and fly back to Greenville for what usually ends up being all-day business meetings."

"Well, Foster, I don't normally run on Sunday. So, why don't we plan on running, say four mornings a week—when we're both in town. Our regular scheduled running days could be on Tuesday through Friday.

Then maybe occasionally we could do an extra run on a Saturday morning."

Smiling as he toasted me with his mug, Foster said, "Larry, you've got yourself a running partner."

"Great! Tell you what I'll do, Foster. I'll come over to your home every morning at say 7:00, and we'll run, say, a two-mile course through Litchfield by the Sea."

Immediately Foster held up his hand and said, "No, Larry, that wouldn't be fair. You can come over to my house one week, and I'll come over to your house the next week. That is the only fair way to do it. You shouldn't have to be the one to drive everyday."

"Okay, Foster, if that's the way you want to do it."

A man of Foster McKissick's stature could have driven anything he wanted to drive, but Foster chose to drive a pickup truck. On the back of his pickup truck was, believe it or not, a trash can! Foster's truck was often seen parked in the grass along Highway 17 South at Litchfield Beach while he was out picking up trash and empty beer cans that had been tossed beside the highway by careless litterbugs. That was just one of Foster's quirks. He couldn't stand to see any litter at Litchfield Beach.

The first morning we jogged together, I couldn't help but notice Foster's outfit. He had on an old pair of faded gray shorts and a red striped jogging shirt that looked like it should have been thrown away years ago. I noticed the sock covering his big toe was sticking out of the canvas on his left jogging shoe.

I said, "Foster, those jogging shoes have had it!" Pointing toward the shoe I said, "Your toe is coming out of the shoe."

Foster gave me a look as if to say, "It doesn't bother me; why should it bother you?" Then he answered me. "Larry, maybe you're right. Looks like I've just about got all the mileage out of these shoes that I'm going to get."

"Well, Foster, maybe Jack, Frank, and I could take up a collection and get you a new pair of running shoes. I know how tight your finances are right now building all these new theatres."

Foster looked at me and nodded his head in agreement. "Larry, that might not be a bad idea."

I didn't know Foster's displeasure with litter played into his thoughts even while he was running, but it did. We would be out jogging at Litchfield by the Sea or over at the River Club, and, if Foster saw a piece of paper, he would have to stop jogging long enough to pick it up. Well, it's kind of hard to jog with the Chairman of the Board and not become self-conscience to those things that irritate him. So when I saw a piece of litter, I would stop, pick it up, and then go back to jogging. I don't know why I wore a stopwatch. This type of jogging was terrible on your time. On a two-mile run, we were running out of storage places to put our collection of litter. Foster came up with a solution.

One morning Foster walked out of his house with two empty plastic grocery bags. Immediately, I knew they were for us to put our trash in. He gave me a look as if to say, "Well, you can't hold all the trash in your hands."

"Larry, this bag is for your trash." Smiling as he waved the other empty plastic bag in the air, he said, "And here's mine. At least now we have somewhere to put the trash."

For several months, Foster and I ran together as our schedules permitted. Both of us started trimming down and looking better physically as our bodies were starting to get into shape. It wasn't always easy though—especially for Foster. Sophie once told Doneata about how Foster acted one morning when it was my turn to come over to his house to jog.

This particular morning it was extremely cold outside. At the beach when that cold wind starts blowing in off the ocean, it can really send chill bumps up your spine. Sophie said that Foster got out of bed and walked over to the window. The rolling clouds were so dark it made it almost look like it was still nighttime outside. The chilling wind was howling and blowing the trees to and fro. It was a miserable morning. Foster turned from the dreary view and looked at Sophie lying there in the warmth of their bed. Sophie said that Foster said almost angrily, "Sophie, I don't want to run today!"

Sophie said she could tell by the way Foster was acting that he was working on a plan to get out of running that particular morning. After a moment, Foster looked at Sophie, snapped his fingers, and said, "I have an idea. Sophie, when Larry drives up, why don't you go downstairs and tell him that I am sick, and I can't run today."

Sophie said, "Oh no, Foster McKissick, I'm not going to do your dirty work for you. If Larry Vaughn can get up in this cold weather and come over here to run, then you'd better be out there to meet him."

Sophie went on to tell Doneata that Foster had the saddest expression on his face as he put his running shorts on. Sophie said, "Doneata, I actually was starting to feel sorry for the old boy."

Then Foster started up again. "Sophie, I sure don't want to run today." Sophie said that Foster then walked back over to the window and said, "The weather is terrible. Oh, I do hope Larry doesn't come out in it today." Sophie said that it was about that time that they heard a tap on the door. Foster looked at Sophie with an expression of sadness in his brown eyes and shrugged his shoulders in despair as he said, "I guess we know who that is." Sophie went on to tell Doneata how much fun she had watching Foster force himself out of the comfort of his warm bed and home that dreary morning at the beach.

After I heard that story, I thought back to that cold, cloudy, and windy morning. As I recall, Foster gave me a very solemn "Good morning" that day. I was wondering during our run if he felt okay. He sure was quiet that day. I don't think he even picked up much litter.

Foster finally broke down and bought himself a new pair of running shoes. That was the same year Frank, Jack, and I went in together and bought Foster a very nice running suit for Christmas. Foster now had the equipment needed to get serious with his running. The only other thing he needed was me, his partner, to get him out and going.

———

Four months after our family moved to Litchfield, I flew down to Miami to testify for Wometco in their lawsuit. In Gainesville, Florida, Wometco operated a three-screen theatre, the Plaza, that played exclusive run, or what you might call one-run-only in the town. This meant that when Wometco played a picture at its Plaza Theatre no other theatre in Gainesville was allowed to play that picture simultaneously with the Plaza. Now, Wometco's Plaza was the only theatre that took that position when playing a film. The three other circuits in Gainesville had agreed with the film companies that they would play films on an exclusive or nonexclusive, maximum two runs in Gainesville.

One regional circuit by the name of Haskins Theatres took objection to Wometco's playing exclusive run on every film it played in the Plaza. The owner of the circuit, "Mr. Rasper," phoned Art Hertz about the situation in Gainesville and asked Art if he would reconsider his position on playing only exclusive run in Gainesville. Mr. Rasper said, "Mr. Hertz, every theatre owner in Gainesville has agreed to play nonexclusive but you. Because your theatre plays exclusive on every picture, we don't have enough movies to keep our theatre screens booked in Gainesville. If you would do as the other circuits do and play nonexclusive at your Plaza Theatre, then there would be three more pictures to go around for all of us."

Art informed Mr. Rasper he would check into the Gainesville situation and get back with him in the near future.

Art in turn buzzed me and asked me to brief him about why I wanted to play only one run in Gainesville.

I said, "Art, I don't mind playing two runs in Gainesville if the other run is playing in the Haskins theatre. The Haskins theatre is in worse physical shape than our theatre is. Given the option, I think the public would rather see a movie in our theatre over the Haskins theatre. We have a better location and a slightly better building. The problem is that if we go to two runs in Gainesville, then that means we will also have to let AMC Theatres have the opportunity to play day and date with our theatre. AMC has two new nice theatres. If we play a picture with AMC, I think they will get the lion's share of the business."

I paused a moment. "Art, I wouldn't be surprised if AMC got as much as 75 percent of the gross, and we end up with 25 percent."

Art frowned as he said, "Playing with AMC would kill our theatre."

"Art, it would happen overnight. When one is given the option to ride in a Cadillac or a Chevy for the same price, he will take the Cadillac every time."

Art phoned Mr. Rasper back and informed him that Wometco would continue to play only on an exclusive-run basis in our Plaza Theatre in Gainesville. Mr. Rasper then advised Mr. Hertz that he could expect to hear from his attorney within a week. Mr. Rasper went on record to notify Art Hertz that unless Wometco changed its position immediately in Gainesville, then Haskins Theatres would have no other alternative than to take legal action against Wometco Theatres.

To make a long story short, Haskins Theatres filed a very serious lawsuit against Wometco Theatres and Twentieth Century Fox Film Corporation. The lawsuit brought forth many serious accusations against both companies. Along with several other very serious charges, Wometco was being sued for restraint of trade and for being in collusion with Twentieth Century Fox.

The gist of the lawsuit was that, while I was employed at Wometco as the Vice President of Film Buying, I was using the clout of Wometco's Miami theatres to force Twentieth Century Fox to adhere to my demands in Gainesville, which was absolutely false. I never did understand why Mr. Rasper picked Twentieth Century Fox to sue along with Wometco in Gainesville. In that particular town, I had other distributors that I did more business with on a picture-by-picture basis.

There were megabucks at stake in this lawsuit—millions of dollars. It all boiled down to the way Larry Vaughn was conducting his business practices in Gainesville, Florida, as the Head Film Buyer for Wometco Theatres.

"Blake Frazier," the attorney for Haskins Theatres, had asked the judge for a jury trial, and that the trial be held in the Dade County Courthouse, which is located in downtown Miami. Mr. Frazier wanted the jury trial to be held right in the back yard of the big powerful Wometco Theatres.

I will never forget one of the questions that was asked me by "Eric Rosenfield." Eric was one of Wometco's New York attorneys.

"Mr. Vaughn, two years ago this October on a Monday afternoon you had a conversation with Mr. Rusty Gautier at Orion Pictures. I would like for you to tell me about that conversation."

I just looked at Eric. I really didn't know how to respond. I responded, "Eric, that was just a run-of-the-mill conversation that I had with Mr. Gautier that day. Why, I talked with Rusty Gautier three to four days a week. How can you expect me to remember one ordinary phone conversation?"

That was not what Eric wanted to hear. "Larry, because of the lawsuit, it is extremely important that you remember verbatim every word that you said that day."

I looked at Eric and said, "I'll try my best to remember it as it happened."

Eric smiled back at me, and then he went to work. It took a while, but the more Eric and I talked, the clearer everything started becoming to me. After a couple of hours, I had told Eric everything that he needed to know. I could have even told him what I had for lunch that day if he wanted to know.

The Wometco/Twentieth Century Fox lawsuit with Haskins Theatres finally came to trial. This was my first, and I hope only, experience on the witness stand. The judge called me to take the stand at about 1:30 in the afternoon. From where I was positioned, I noticed there seemed to be a lot of people in the courtroom. That surprised me; I mean after all this wasn't exactly a murder trial. After being sworn to tell the truth, the whole truth, and nothing but the truth, so help me God, I was instructed to sit down. I looked at the judge, the jury, and then I looked over at Mr. Rasper and his two attorneys.

Across the wooden rail separating the judge, jury, and witness stand from the public sat Art Hertz and Michael Brown—right there on the front row. I could tell Art and Mike were emotionally consumed with every single word that was being said. Sitting beside Art were

Wometco's two New York attorneys: Eric Rosenfield and "Jerome Hindermann." Eric and Jerome were partners from one of the top law firms in New York. It was characteristic of Art and Mike to always get the very best when money was at stake. And these two guys were supposed to be tops in their field. Directly behind Eric and Jerome were several more attorneys from Los Angeles who represented Twentieth Century Fox.

Blake Frazier was the attorney that questioned me the most during my time on the stand. He questioned me for the better part of seven hours. When asking some of his questions, he didn't have his facts exactly correct. I even had some fun with one of his questions: "Mr. Vaughn, isn't it true that you were the best man at Walter Powell's wedding?"

I replied, "No, sir."

Mr. Frazier looked at me, then at the judge, and then over toward the jury as he said again, very emphatically, "Now, Mr. Vaughn, are you telling me that you were not the best man at Walter Powell's wedding?"

I thought to myself, "This guy has Walter Powell mixed up with Charlie Jones, but I'm not gonna tell him." I responded to his question, "That's correct."

Mr. Frazier looked irritated and somewhat confused as he shuffled through some of his documents and papers. He then had a brief conference with one of his associates and Mr. Rasper. After a few moments he said, "Now think, Mr. Vaughn, are you absolutely sure that you weren't the best man at Walter Powell's wedding?"

Once more I replied, "That's correct." I looked at the judge, and then the jury. I shrugged my shoulders lifting my palms face up as if to say, "Your Honor, why does he keep asking the same question over and over?"

The judge, looking over his reading glasses spoke directly to Mr. Frazier. "Mr. Frazier, if my memory serves me correctly, that's the third time you have asked Mr. Vaughn that question. I also believe Mr. Vaughn has answered your question with the same response three times. Now, let's move on." I got tickled inside at Mr. Frazier's mix-up of names. That was one of the very few moments with comic relief.

During his seven hours of interrogation, Mr. Frazier tripped himself up on one other occasion. He said, "Now, Mr. Vaughn, isn't it true that when you were employed by Wometco you used the strength of your buying power in Wometco's Miami theatres to get product for your Plaza Theatre in Gainesville, Florida?"

I replied, "Mr. Frazier, what strength are you referring to?"

"You know, your big-grossing theatres in Miami. Isn't it true that you held those theatres over Twentieth Century Fox as a wedge to get Fox to comply with your request to play exclusive run on their product in Gainesville?"

"Mr. Frazier, I didn't have any real clout in the Miami market."

He looked surprised and almost stunned as he said, "You didn't?"

"No, sir. The better grossing theatres in Miami are the newer theatres that have been built by General Cinema Corporation and America Multi-Cinemas. They had the clout, not Wometco. While I was working for Wometco, I was doing everything I could to try to keep good top pictures in the Wometco theatres and away from those two big national circuits and their new state-of-the-art theatres."

Mr. Frazier looked somewhat confused at that statement. I'm not sure, but I believe I heard his pencil snap in two while I was talking.

The last time Mr. Frazier stuck his foot in his mouth was when he tried to argue that I had a controlling influence over a conglomerate like Twentieth Century Fox. Somehow, I finally got a chance to speak without having to directly answer one of his questions.

I said, "Mr. Frazier, don't we all want to get to the truth of the issue in question? That is the purpose of this trial. All I want to do is tell the truth and you keep cutting me off. Mr. Frazier, don't you really want to hear the truth?" He did not reply to my question. He sat down and had another conference with his fellow attorneys and Mr. Rasper. Later, I was told by our attorneys that that statement was worth a million bucks; at least, when the jurors heard it.

There were also some very hard questions that I had to answer during those seven long hours. What I would do before and after every question that I was asked was pray. Not once did I not pray before and after each question was asked. When I couldn't think of anything specific to pray about, I started reciting the Lord's Prayer.

Art and Mike, without realizing it, made me very nervous. They were sitting on the very edge of the bench, digesting every word. The two of them kept wringing their hands as if they were wet and hurting. It made me very nervous realizing that a loss in this trial would cost them millions.

Finally, my two days of being on the witness stand came to a conclusion. I was free to leave and fly back to Litchfield Beach. As I left the courtroom, Mike and Eric came rushing out to me to thank me for my services. Eric said, "Larry, if we were ever going to make a training tape on how to act on the witness stand, you're the man we would want to use as our example. Your answers were frank, honest, and from your heart. I watched the jury very carefully while you were on the stand. They know you were telling the truth." Mike gave me a firm handshake and eye contact that said it all. I hurried away to catch my plane.

Later that week, I received a conference call from Art, Mike, Eric, and Jerome. They were ecstatic with joy. The verdict was in: Wometco and Twentieth Century Fox had been found not guilty on every single count. And, as for Mr. Rasper and his theatres, he just thought he had problems. He ended up having to pay a fortune in court costs; plus, Twentieth Century Fox went off service with him in every state that he operated theatres in, and that included a lot of states.

––––––––

The one thing Doneata and I really missed while living at Litchfield Beach was being able to hear Pastor Clarkston's daily radio message. Pastor Clarkston was far and away the most instrumental Christian man in my life. I have spent years listening to thousands of his radio messages. I believe I have read all the books he has written. I have done a thorough, three-year study through the Gospel of Matthew using his commentaries. Plus, I have made several trips just to hear him speak at various churches or conferences. Is Pastor Clarkston a perfect man? Absolutely not. I'm sure he's far from it. But, Pastor Clarkston is the man God chose to use in my life to help me mature in my Christian faith. Through his ministry, I was daily fed the Word of God.

At Parker Road, I got theology. Yes, everyone knew their theology, but, for the most part, Pastor Short's messages were just a bunch of "tell the good folks what they want to hear." Then he could go home and enjoy his roast and potatoes without any unpleasant interruptions.

Sometimes the problem is not in what the minister says, but, maybe, in what he does not say. Shying away from unpopular issues—issues that deal with how a Christian is biblically supposed to look at his life, his work, his family, his priorities, his decision-making process, his walk, his entertainment time, and, yes, his sin—can be more damaging to a person's spiritual being than anything. Those years at Parker Road I seldom if ever heard a message that dealt with striving to "be holy as He is holy."

My family and I visited Plantation Church. The first Sunday there, we had to sit on the front row. The church was meeting in a small warehouse while waiting on the completion of the final stages of construction of the new church building. The warehouse was full. There must have been just over two hundred people in attendance. We found out later that they were going to move into their new church building within a year. The preacher was a young man, who had a very commanding presence when preaching from the pulpit. After hearing his Sunday morning message, I knew we would be back that evening to hear more of what that man had to say.

On the way out of church, I introduced my family and myself to the preacher. His name was "Curt Goldfield." He was a tall, slim, redheaded man. I would guess him to be in his mid-to-late thirties. He dressed conservatively. The first thing I noticed about his appearance was how thick his glasses were. I thought, "The poor fellow must be blind when he doesn't have his glasses on." He and I talked for several minutes. I told him how we had recently moved to Litchfield Beach from Miami, Florida, and how we were now looking for the Lord's direction in finding a church home.

As people were leaving the building, he introduced my family and me to several families in the church. The people were all very friendly to us. Pastor Goldfield then asked if he might pay me a visit in the days ahead. I suggested he and I have lunch one day the next week. He said he would check his schedule and call me Monday morning to set up a lunch appointment.

The family and I went back to Plantation for their Sunday evening service. There was no problem finding a seat since there were only about thirty to forty people at the service. We enjoyed the fellowship and having the opportunity of being able to hear the preaching of the Word.

On the way out of church, Pastor Goldfield came over to me and said, "Would Tuesday be a good day for us to have lunch?"

"Yes, sir. Tuesday will be fine."

Pastor Goldfield thought a moment. "Now, where should we go for lunch?"

"Well, I have a suggestion. If you don't mind taking the fifteen-minute drive down to my office at Litchfield."

"No, not at all."

"Good, I would like to take you to the Litchfield Country Club for lunch. The club has wonderful sandwiches, burgers, and fries."

That Tuesday, we met for lunch as planned. Pastor Goldfield and I walked through the Litchfield Country Club's restaurant to the outside porch where I had reserved a table in the corner. The porch was always the seating of choice at the restaurant, mainly because of the picturesque view of the outside flowers, the huge great oak trees, and the manicured greens of the golf course. The porch was completely enclosed with all glass—the roof as well as walls. It was like eating outside, without having to put up with the flies, mosquitoes, and temperature. Our table in the corner gave us a wonderful view of the golf course with its winding cart paths and the summer flowers which seemed to be in bloom everywhere.

We both ordered iced tea to drink. After a time of small talk, Pastor Goldfield told me about his wife and four children. Then he talked about Plantation Church. He said, "The church came into being about ten years ago. A small group of folks were meeting every Sunday at the Holiday Inn when they decided it was time to move into a building and pray about the Lord's bringing them a full-time preacher. The people came from several different," he smiled as he repeated very emphatically, "very different denominational backgrounds." He shook his head and gave me a sympathetic smile. "Larry, we started with a real mix of people at Plantation. Some of the folks had a Methodist background, others were Baptists, and a few were Presbyterian." He took a sip of his tea. "As it turned out, they bought an old carpenter's shop to worship in and hired me right out of seminary to be their pastor. Plantation is the first and only church that I have ever pastored." Smiling, he said, "You might say we, my congregation and I, have grown together the past ten years."

I asked him, "With the various backgrounds of the people, how did you folks end up in a Reformed denomination?"

"Someone from the denomination came and talked with the people, and they liked what they heard. They decided that this denomination was the direction the Lord was leading them to become a part of."

"So, after they decided on their denomination, the Lord brought you into the picture."

"That is correct. I am the senior pastor. I have two elders that have been on the board forever, and we also have four deacons."

We talked for another thirty minutes or so. I asked him the standard questions about their youth group, Bible studies, etc. Since I had spent many years in that particular denomination, I knew his position on doctrinal issues—that was one subject we didn't have to spend any time on. After coffee and dessert we began to wrap things up. I thought to myself, "For a first meeting, my lunch with Pastor Goldfield has been a good one." Driving back to the office, I thought to myself, "Plantation is probably going to become the church that the family and I end up serving, growing, and worshipping in."

———

My first seven months with Litchfield gave me a lot of memories. Some of those memories are wonderful memories: like when Foster would get the gang together, and we would go out on the river for an evening cruise on *The Litchfield Lady*.

The Litchfield Lady was a yacht that Foster kept docked a few miles north of Litchfield Beach. This was by no means a run-of-the-mill yacht that you would go out and buy at a place that sells boats. No, *The Litchfield Lady* was a beautiful piece of craftsmanship designed for those few individuals who could afford and appreciate the very best in yachts. When I first saw *The Litchfield Lady*, I thought to myself, "This must be a yacht like the Kennedys would own."

Foster loved cruising down the river on *The Litchfield Lady*. There would always be a captain and one first mate aboard. The captain, of course, took care of steering us through safe waters, and the first mate was responsible for serving the delicious hors d'oeuvres of rare roast beef, fresh baked ham, shrimp, and fresh baked rolls. He also doubled as the bartender.

As the sun started to descend into the west, that's when the singing would begin. Foster loved for us to sing those old gospel hymns. "Amazing Grace" was his favorite. We usually had to sing "Amazing Grace" at least twice. I would look over at Foster and think, "He has got to be the most unusual man that I have ever known."

———

Those first seven months, I spent an enormous amount of time traveling for the company. Ulmer wanted me to see all the Litchfield theatres; plus, he wanted me to see our new theatre sites that we had already made commitments to build on, as well as new theatre sites that we had on our list for possible consideration. In my spare time, I was flying around the country meeting with all the film companies, bringing them up to date with the new Litchfield Theatres.

It was also during this time that South Carolina had an unwanted visit from a hurricane by the name of Hugo. Hugo gave Litchfield Beach a solid one-two punch, followed by a knockout blow. Our beautiful oceanfront sand dunes were gone. The golf courses had trees down everywhere. Many of the homes had terrible wind, roof, and water damage. The entire Grand Strand area from North Myrtle Beach to Georgetown, South Carolina, was a mess. It took several months and several million dollars to get everything put back together like it was before Hugo blew through South Carolina.

After Hugo slammed into the Carolinas, I got a call from my old friend and former employer Art Hertz. "Larry, didn't I try to tell you not to go? Now look at what happened to you. You leave Miami after how many? Thirteen years. You go to of all places, South Carolina, and there you get nailed by a hurricane." Art was having a good time. Of course, he was just ribbing me.

The real purpose of his call was to make sure the family and I were okay. We talked a few minutes about things in general. He then had another call come in. Before he hung up, we promised each other that we would keep in touch. I hung up the phone thinking, "Art, was a good friend. I hope his new film buyer does a good job for him." I then laughed to myself as I thought of Art and Mike's Tuesday meetings. Why did I just think "hope." They will make sure their new buyer does a very good job for them, or in three months he'll be fish bait over at the Miami Seaquarium.

After five months, our house in Miami sold, right after the lady and her children who were living there no longer needed it. We left our River Club home and rented a home in Wachesaw Plantation, which was about eight miles north of Litchfield. Our intent was to live in Wachesaw Plantation for one year. During that year, we would purchase some property and build a home.

Shortly before Christmas, my family and I joined Plantation Church. Once again we had to go through the mandatory eight-week new members' class, but we were glad to now be officially a part of a local body of believers.

In December, Foster, Eaddy, Jack, Frank, and I flew in the company jet to Atlanta for a retirement party for Mac MacAfee, a fine gentlemen who had spent the majority of his life at Paramount Pictures. The dinner was being held in one of the large banquet rooms at the Ritz Carlton Hotel in Buckhead. I had almost decided to stay at the beach and not make the trip, as I was trying to fight off a terrible cough and cold. But, I had been asked by Paramount to give the invocation at the dinner, and I held Mac MacAfee in such high regard that I let my emotions overrule my poor health.

By the time we got to the hotel, I was in bad shape physically. I thought I was coming down with the flu. My body started aching all over. I struggled through the dinner and ceremony; then I spent the rest of the evening in my room. Well, the really bad news is the next day Foster woke up feeling just like I did. On the plane ride home he was coughing, sneezing, and starting to look like he was getting very sick. In between coughing and sneezing, Foster with red, watery eyes looked over at me and said, "Well, Larry, one thing good came out of your going on this trip with us."

Sneezing and coughing, I said, "What's that, Foster?"

"For the past seven months I have been trying to find a nickname for you. Well, I've finally found it."

I hesitated to ask, but I did. "Okay, Foster, what is my nickname?"

As if he were King Arthur himself, Foster stood up and said, "From this day forth, you shall no longer be known as Larry Vaughn, but," he paused momentarily to give every ear the necessary time to listen up, "you shall be known as 'Germ.'" Foster then sat down as everybody in the plane broke out in laughter. Foster elbowed Jack as he pointed toward me and said, "Germ has given me the flu." That nickname, Germ, stuck. From that moment on, that's the only name Foster ever called me by except when we were with businessmen that wouldn't understand why anyone would be named "Germ."

That Christmas Mentora prayed for snow, mainly because living in Miami all her life she had never seen snow. Doubting Larry told Mentora not to get her hopes up because I didn't want her to get too disappointed if it didn't snow. Well, it snowed all right. As a matter of fact, it snowed a record fifteen inches at the beach. The snow stayed frozen on the ground for three days. That snowfall taught me another important lesson: be careful what you pray for because God most certainly answers prayers, especially Mentora's!

———

During the Christmas holidays, I had a heart-to-heart talk with Doneata one evening. We got the children all tucked in their beds for the night; then we went into our bedroom. I felt so good about a decision that I had been struggling with that I wanted to share it with Doneata.

Doneata slipped under the covers while I sat up on the bedspread with my legs crossed as if I were an Indian about to smoke a peace pipe. "Honey, God has been working in my life, and there's something I need to talk with you about."

Doneata could tell by the expression on my face that what I was about to say was important. She sat up in bed, reached over and got my pillow, and fluffed it in place directly behind her pillow. Then smiling at me as she ran her fingers through her hair, she said, "Honey, let's talk."

"Doneata, God has been so very good to us that I just can't believe it."

"Larry, that's a fact."

"Look at where God has placed us. We're living back in South Carolina. Doneata, do you remember when in Miami we prayed specifically that God would bring us back to the Carolinas?"

"Of course I do."

"Honey, things are better right now than I could have ever imagined them to be. Look how God has blessed our children: Mentora and Larry love going to Calvary Christian School. David enjoys working for Litchfield Landscaping. He's always telling me about how Foster will drive up to where he's working, park his truck, and get out and talk to him a few minutes. Foster really likes David. Why, Foster commented to me the other day, 'Larry, David's a fine young man. I like that boy. There's nothing artificial about him.' Now those words came from Foster McKissick.

"As for me personally, things couldn't be better at the company. I absolutely love working for Foster and Ulmer." I paused a moment. "I must admit I do pretend a lot when it comes to the excitement of all these theatres being built."

Doneata said, "Why is that?"

"Well, I'm happy for the company that it's expanding and growing; but, well, it just bothers me that we're building buildings where people are going to go and put a lot of things into their minds, evil things that God never intended them to see or hear."

Doneata closed her eyes as she nodded in agreement. "Larry, I understand how you feel."

"But, Doneata, as far as the workload, all I do is keep putting on my mental brakes."

"Honey, you haven't mentioned the greatest blessing."

"Well, I was coming around to the church, but I was saving that for last. Doneata, we are most certainly getting fed the Word of God at Plantation. The people as a whole don't seem that serious about their relationship with their Lord, but it's not because they aren't getting fed. I can tell Pastor Goldfield is striving to live a holy life. His messages are good. He puts a lot of time, prayer, and preparation into his sermons; and look at his family. His wife seems to be a very godly lady. I can tell, can't you?"

"Absolutely, Larry. I want to spend more time around godly women like Janie. She's an encouragement to me."

I stretched out across the bed and said, "Doneata, here's where I'm heading with this conversation. I have been spending a lot of time in Bible study and prayer, both at home and away during my recent business trips. I feel like there is more service in the future that the Lord is wanting to do with my life than He has done in the past. I have no idea what it is, but I believe there is something else the Lord wants me to do. However, because of one particular area in my life, I think I'm limiting myself in how much the Lord can use me."

Doneata just sat there trying to figure out exactly what I was trying to say. "Honey, what I'm telling you is that I am prepared to make a covenant with God that I will not ever drink any more wine or any other form of alcohol, ever again, as long as I live. I know Scripture doesn't say it is wrong to drink alcohol, but this is something that I believe God is convicting me of that is wrong for my life. If I give up my love of wine for Him, I think He will replace it with something better." I looked at Doneata. "This is not something I am asking you to do, but it is something that I feel the Lord would have me to do."

Doneata put her arms around me and gave me a big hug. "Larry, for years I've waited to hear you say that. I knew in time, the Lord would remove the desire for wine from your life." She hesitated a moment, and then she asked me, "Larry, may I ask why you are making a covenant with God about this? To my knowledge, you have never made a covenant before."

"Honey, I'm afraid if I don't make a covenant with God about this particular area of my life, then it won't stick. I'm afraid that someday, somewhere, I'll change my mind and start back drinking wine again. You know, Doneata, the temptation can be great to go back to doing something that you really enjoy doing very much when everyone else does it. I'm talking about friends outside the church as well as brothers and sisters in the church. A covenant with God doesn't give me that option of going back to my old ways. Scripture tells us that you had better not make a covenant with God unless you intend to keep it."

Doneata replied, "Well, I want to join you in making that covenant." Squeezing my hand and giving me the cutest look she said, "After all, we are one." At that moment Doneata and I got down on our knees beside the bed and prayed a prayer of thanksgiving and confession to our Lord. We then made a covenant with God that no form of alcohol would ever again touch our lips. That was a wonderful evening as I continued to take another step in my ongoing desire to empty this unworthy vessel of those things that are displeasing to God in my life.

I know the Bible does not say it is wrong for an individual to drink wine. But, for some unknown reason, at the time I felt like God was using His Word to bring about changes in the way I had been seeing things. I felt that His will for my life was for me to be a different kind of man. I didn't understand it at the time, but I felt like God had set me apart for a special purpose.

————

That February was an especially busy month for me. Foster felt like we needed to spend some time on the West Coast visiting some of the distribution heads and sharing our upcoming expansion plans with each of them. I called the studios and set up breakfast, lunch, and dinner with all the presidents and general sales managers of the various film companies.

Frank and I arrived in L.A. midafternoon on Monday. Because of a previous commitment, Foster wouldn't be able to join us until late Tuesday afternoon. Frank and I had dinner Monday evening with Wayne Lewellend. Wayne insisted on taking Frank and me to one of his favorite restaurants. The meal was absolutely wonderful. Wayne was not only a good customer of my former company, Wometco; but he also thought the world of Foster McKissick and Litchfield Theatres. After sharing with Wayne our future expansion plans, he seemed excited about the new Litchfield organization.

Tuesday morning Frank and I had breakfast with Jimmy Spitz, the president of Columbia Distribution. Then it was lunch with Mitch Goldman, president of New Line Cinema.

Foster's flight arrived in time for him to join us for dinner Tuesday evening with Bruce Snyder, president of Twentieth Century Fox Distribution. Wednesday, Thursday, and Friday the agenda was the same: more breakfasts, lunches, and dinners. At 10:30 Friday evening our business was done. We had met with every distribution head in town. We left L.A. Saturday morning feeling like all the film companies were excited about what the new Litchfield was trying to accomplish.

We flew to Georgetown on Saturday evening. When I got off the plane at 7:30, I was exhausted.

Foster said, "Germ, why don't you go home and take a quick shower, and then you and Doneata join Sophie and me for dinner at the Country Club."

I thought to myself, "If I have to eat another rich meal, I'll throw up." I didn't like to say no to Foster, but I really needed my rest. "Thank you, Foster, for the offer, but I'm worn out. I think I'll go home and crash."

————

Doneata and I put down a deposit on a beautiful piece of prime real estate—an acre of land in a new development known as Wilderness

Plantation. Right at the front of the property was a huge great oak tree that Doneata just fell in love with. She wanted to have our house built where she could sit out on our front porch and look at that beautiful great oak tree. Doneata has always loved trees. This particular acre of land didn't come cheap. However, the community itself was absolutely gorgeous. I thought we would enjoy living at Wilderness Plantation; and financially, I felt to build there would be a good investment for us in the long run.

God's timing is always perfect. The following Sunday after putting the verbal contract on the property, Pastor Goldfield preached a very strong sermon on how materialism is taking over Christian people in this day and age, especially Christians who have lived and been brought up in the United States. Well, the whole time he was preaching I felt like he was preaching to me and me alone. I got to thinking about the piece of property I had just purchased and how much it was going to cost me to build the house I was planning to build on that property.

When we got home from church, I asked Doneata if she would check on the roast and then meet me in the bedroom for a few minutes before lunch because I had something important I wanted to discuss with her.

When she came into the bedroom, I said, "Honey, what did you think of Pastor Goldfield's message today?"

Doneata said, "Larry, I knew that's what you wanted to talk to me about. I felt like he was talking about us all during his message."

"Me too, Doneata. I want to call Mr. Taylor and ask him if he will let me out of the deal on the property at Wilderness Plantation. I'll tell him he can keep the deposit on the land, but I would like to be let out of the deal. I'll leave it up to him. Even though we haven't signed a contract yet, he does have my word. If he holds me to it, then we'll just have to buy the property and resell it."

"Larry, I feel exactly like you do, that we should drop our sights and buy a less-expensive home."

"Okay, let's stop right now and pray about this call to Mr. Taylor— that the Lord will touch this man's heart so that he will let me out of the contract."

My conversation with Mr. Taylor couldn't have been better. I told him the truth: that I had re-evaluated the cost of the property, and what it would cost me to build a home at Wilderness Plantation was more money than I actually wanted to spend. He was pleased to let me out of the deal and even thanked me for the call. I felt like losing the deposit on the property was, by far, the lesser of the two evils.

That afternoon, I thought, "Now, there's nothing biblically wrong with a Christian building a nice home with funds that you have left over after the tithe. But, for some reason God doesn't want me building that estate home at Wilderness Plantation. God not only spoke to me, He gave Doneata a confirmation that it was the wrong thing for us to do. For some unknown reason, God wants us living below our means. At the time, I really didn't understand what was going on, but I knew God was preparing me for something. I just didn't know what it was.

Doneata and I ended up buying a modest home in Deerfield Plantation. The home was two years old but had never been lived in. The builder went bankrupt while the house was under construction, and the house ended up being the property of the bank. We bought the house in as-is condition. What we liked best about it was its location. It was convenient to everything, especially Plantation Church. It was less than five minutes away.

———

The next six months I stayed very busy with new theatre openings. True to his word, Foster McKissick was opening theatres every week or so. We were doing just fine when all of a sudden a financial crisis hit Litchfield Theatres. Foster McKissick had a $50 million lawsuit filed against him by United Artists Theaters. United Artists was suing Foster because of a new theatre that the company had recently built in the Atlanta area which UA said was competing with one of their existing theatres. When Foster sold his former circuit to United Artists, there was a noncompete clause in the contract of sale. The United Artists suit stated that Foster had violated the noncompete clause by building the theatre in question.

Because of the lawsuit and some other factors, Litchfield Theatres all of a sudden found itself strapped for cash. We were having some very difficult days at the office just trying to keep our theatres open and the bill collectors from actually shutting the company down. All of this happened during a period of several months. We had tractor trailers loaded with theatre equipment sitting parked with no place to put the equipment. We were caught in the middle of a financial disaster.

I remember standing outside the office one afternoon talking with Foster about the situation. Foster and I had just finished a conference call with Wayne Lewellend over a large film payment that was overdue at Paramount. Foster looked at me and put his hand on my shoulder. He said, "Germ, for the first time in months I can see light at the end of the tunnel. I think we are going to be able to work things out. I really feel optimistic that everything is going to be okay. I have to go to Greenville in the morning for a very important meeting tomorrow. I will be back at the beach late tomorrow afternoon or early evening. We will go over everything once I get back." Foster gave me that warm assuring smile of his as he said, "Hang in there, Germ; things are starting to look up."

It was around four in the morning when we received the phone call. Doneata woke up to answer the phone. I immediately came out of my deep sleep as I heard the concern in Doneata's voice.

She said, "What? Oh no. When? It can't be. What can we do?" She then started crying as she said, "Okay, thank you for calling. Please call us if you hear any news."

Doneata jumped up out of the bed and went toward the bathroom. I said, "Doneata, what's wrong? Who was that on the phone?"

"Just a minute, Larry; I'll be right back." Doneata came out of the bathroom with a box of tissues. Her eyes were already red and full of tears. She sat down on the bed beside me and tried to regain her composure. "Larry, I've got some bad news to tell you." She paused a moment, then took a deep breath and said, "Foster's plane went down in the ocean last night."

I jumped out of bed. "What? What did you say?"

"Foster's plane crashed in the ocean last night. He was flying back to the beach from Greenville with a friend of his in his friend's plane when they crashed in the ocean somewhere off the coast of Georgetown. Right before the crash, Foster radioed in, 'Mayday! Mayday! This is Foster McKissick. My pilot has gone to sleep.' Larry, the Coast Guard is out right now looking for them; that's all we know."

My body felt limp. I thought I was about to get physically sick, but I only cried.

A few moments later I said, "Doneata, let's take this situation to the Lord. If Foster and the pilot are still alive, let's ask the Lord to protect them until they can be rescued." We got on our knees beside our bed and took our concerns and fears to our Lord.

That morning driving in to the office, I had plenty of time to think and pray. I thought to myself, "Why is it that I have had to experience so much death in my life? Farrell, my mother, Roger Hill, Marvin Reed, Jack Mitchell, and Stanley Stern." My thoughts went back to the day Stanley walked into my office and sat down on my sofa to share with me that he had a malignant brain tumor. He said, "Larry, I'm going to die, and there's absolutely nothing I can do about it." Stanley was so despondent and tired. The year before, Stanley had watched his wife, Madeline, die with cancer of the brain. Now, he was facing the same turmoil and pain that he had to watch her go through.

I thought of how Stanley got up from the sofa and walked over to my desk to sit down in one of the chairs. He took his checkbook out of his jacket pocket and looked at me. "Larry, why don't you let me write you a check. I have all this money and have absolutely nothing to do with it. My mother's needs at the nursing home have been provided for until the time of her death. Larry, let me do something for you and your family."

I felt so bad for Stanley. I got up from behind my desk and walked over and put my arms around this dear friend of many years. "Stanley, I have no financial needs. You know, financially, Art and Mike take good care of me. If you want to make a donation to someone, then you make a donation to someone who has a need."

That day I wanted to talk to Stanley about the Lord, but it was not meant to be. Stanley was a man of the Jewish faith. He was a man who had no interest in Christianity.

As I pulled into the Litchfield parking lot, the sky was littered with helicopters. They were everywhere. Propelling their way out over the Atlantic Ocean in search of a downed airplane and hopefully two men, alive and in need of rescue.

Eventually the plane was found resting on the floor of the ocean. Neither of the bodies were ever recovered. Foster McKissick, the man who was known and loved by all who knew him, was never to be seen again. As for me, I had lost a man that I had come to know and love in a very personal way. I had lost a very good friend and my jogging partner.

There was a memorial service for A. Foster McKissick held that weekend at Litchfield Beach. The funeral service was held two days later in Greenville. Friends and relatives gathered by the hundreds to pay their last respect to the man who had played such an important part in so many lives down through the years.

Twenty-Eight

Responsibilities

The following weeks were very trying times at Litchfield Theatres. The Board of Directors was trying to find direction about what to do next. There weren't that many options available for them to take. The company was faced with $30 million of defaulted debt, two foreclosures, numerous lawsuits, and a negative net worth.

The Board of Directors appointed Douglas D. Richardson as Chairman of the Board for both the Litchfield Theatre Division and the Litchfield Real Estate Division. Doug had come aboard the company as a consultant several months before Foster was killed. Doug's expertise was finance. He knew all the players when it came to banking and finance. He was the man ultimately responsible for Litchfield's remarkable financial turnaround. Ulmer Eaddy remained on as the Executive Vice President of the Theatre Division.

The very first thing Doug did was sell off some of the theatres and take the much-needed cash and pay down some of the outstanding debt. It hurt to sell away some of our better theatres to the opposition, but by doing so, it gave us the immediate cash needed to help keep the company going until we could decide what to do next.

Doug's next consideration was the filing of Chapter 11 bankruptcy. That option would give Litchfield protection by the court to restructure the outstanding debt and reorganize the company's current holdings. The bankruptcy idea was put on hold for the time being.

Our concern with filing Chapter 11 bankruptcy was that it had never been done before by a major theatre circuit. The primary concern was how the film companies would react to our being in bankruptcy. Would they continue to furnish a theatre circuit in bankruptcy top pictures in a highly competitive theatre industry? Or, would they choose to sell their movies to the opposition theatre company who was on solid footing, financially speaking?

I started receiving calls from my friends in distribution. Their question was, "Well, Larry, what are you going to do? Are you going to stay and go down with the ship, or are you going to let us help you find another job?"

My pat answer was, "No, I'm here for the duration. As long as Litchfield Theatres needs me, that is how long I intend to be here."

My friends in the business thought that was a loyal, but rather foolish, statement for me to make. What they weren't aware of was the promise that I had made to the Lord when I came with Litchfield—that after Litchfield I would exit the theatre industry. Bearing that in mind, I had no other option but to sit and see how God was going to work in and through all of this financial turmoil at Litchfield Theatres.

Doug called what ended up being one of the most important meetings of the year late one Sunday afternoon. There were five men in the meeting: Doug; Ulmer; Ken Martin, the Chief Financial Officer; Tom Henson, our attorney; and me. The purpose of the meeting was to decide whether Litchfield Theatres should pursue going into Chapter 11 bankruptcy protection.

Doug and Tom did most of the talking. After two hours of going over facts and figures, Doug said, "Gentlemen, if we can get the film distributors to cooperate with us, then I suggest we file for Chapter 11 bankruptcy."

Doug then looked at me. "Larry, can you make a call to someone in distribution and feel him out as to how his company would react to our filing Chapter 11? Talk to him and get back to me, if possible, later tonight." In frustration, Doug threw his pencil across his desk. "If the film companies won't continue to serve us top product, then we're dead in our tracks."

I left the meeting to go home and call one of my very best friends in the business. Bert Livingston is the Vice President and Southern Division Manager for Twentieth Century Fox Film Corporation. I had met Bert several years before when he was the Jacksonville Branch Manager for Fox. Down through the years, Bert and I have become very good friends. Not only friends on a business level, but also very good personal friends. Bert also worked for another very good friend of mine, Bruce Snyder.

I dialed Bert's home number.

"Hello?"

"Hi, Jaynie, Larry here."

"Well, hi, stranger, how are you doing?"

"Jaynie, I'm doing okay, all things considered."

She paused a moment. "Larry, Bert told me all about Mr. McKissick. I sure was sorry to hear about his untimely death."

"Jaynie, one never knows what fortune or misfortune tomorrow might bring; only the Lord knows."

"That's true. Well, I guess you want to talk to Bert."

"If he has a minute."

"Hold on, Larry, I'll go get him. He's in the den playing a game with the kids."

"Hi, Larry."

"Bert, I apologize for calling you on a Sunday evening and taking you away from your family."

"Stop it. You call me anytime you want to. What's doing? Is everyone okay at home?"

"Yes, Doneata and the family are all doing well. Bert, I have an important question to ask you. I have been in a meeting the past two-and-a-half hours with Doug Richardson, along with our attorney and some other men. We are trying to make a very important decision that could ultimately decide the future of Litchfield Theatres. Doug asked me if I would contact someone in distribution and feel him out as to his thoughts about what Litchfield is considering doing. He wants to know how your company would respond to our—" I paused a moment, "well, our filing Chapter 11."

Bert thought a moment. "Larry, where are you calling from?"

"I'm at home."

In his usual chipper voice Bert said, "Okay, I'll call you back in a few minutes."

About twenty minutes later the phone rang.

"Hello?"

"Larry, guess who I just got off the phone with."

"Silas Marner."

"Very funny. I was lucky enough to catch Bruce at home. I told him about our phone call of a few minutes ago."

"And?"

"Bruce said to tell you Twentieth Century Fox's relationship is not with Litchfield Theatres but with Larry Vaughn. As long as you tell me that your film rental will be paid as it has always been paid, then we don't care whether Litchfield Theatres is in bankruptcy or not."

"Oh, Bert, that is wonderful news! All it takes is one distributor to go along, then I think everyone else will follow."

"Larry, Bruce and I want to see you guys pull it off. Whatever we can do to help, we're willing to do."

I thanked Bert for his support; then I hung up the phone and called Doug.

I told Doug verbatim what Bruce had told Bert.

Doug said, "Larry, what is Bruce's position with Fox?"

"Why, Bruce is President of Distribution."

"Larry, that is exactly what I wanted to hear. Now, first thing in the morning call the rest of the companies and get back to me as soon as you have talked with everyone."

Monday morning I called Frank Jones into my office first thing. I gave Frank some companies to call while I called the rest. By 4:30 that Monday afternoon, Frank and I had all the major film distributors notified of our intent to file Chapter 11 bankruptcy. Along with that notification, we had the support of all the companies that it would be business as usual as long as Litchfield continued to make its film rental payments in a timely manner.

Late Monday afternoon Doug, Ulmer, Ken, Tom, and I met. With the good news of support received from the film companies, we were now ready to proceed forward with our plan of filing Chapter 11 bankruptcy protection. Now that the immediate heat was off, we could roll up our sleeves and get down to some serious work. It looked like, for the time being, God was leaving a door of opportunity open for me in the film industry.

––––––––

A good friend of mine, "George Phillips," called me one Sunday afternoon and asked me if I would mind his nominating me to be on the elder board at Plantation Church. During the past year, George and I had grown to become good buddies at Plantation. George was an elder himself and had a wonderful wife, "Shelly," and three lovely children. George was one of those guys who are friendly with everyone they meet. He was always going out of his way when it came to showing good Christian hospitality to a friend or a stranger.

George informed me that during a recent elders' meeting, Pastor Goldfield commented to him and "Bill Hart," the other elder, that he felt the timing was right to add three additional elders on the board. Pastor Goldfield told the men he was anticipating an increase in membership with the church moving into the new building. I told George I would pray about my name being submitted to the congregation for a vote, and I would speak with him later in the week on the subject.

A few days later George and I had another discussion about my becoming an elder. He started out the conversation by saying, "Larry, we desperately need you on the Session." Acting as if he were mentally and physically exhausted from the responsibility required by being on the Session, George said, "Larry, the pastor, Bill, and I can't continue on the way that we have been going. I mean the three of us being responsible for a congregation the size of Plantation Church is at times," he paused, "well, it's just overwhelming." As if George were Uncle Sam himself, he pointed his finger straight at me as he said, "I want you to come on the Session so I can—" he let out a sigh of frustration, "take a long-overdue break." Dropping his big burly shoulders and putting his arm around my comparatively small shoulders, George said, "Well, what do you say? Are you with us?" He then made a fist out of his large, oversize hand and took dead aim at my nose and said, "Or are you against us?"

I smiled at George's way of expressing himself. I couldn't help but like this big, fun-loving guy. "George, Doneata and I have prayed about it; and if you still feel led to submit my name to the congregation, it will be fine by me for you to do so."

George slapped me on the back as he said, "Larry, it's going to be great working on the Session with you."

I looked at his big, warm smile and said, "You'd better not count your chickens before they hatch. Being nominated and being elected are two different things." George smiled as he gave me a big hug.

The Sunday that the congregation voted on the nominees, I was surprised to find out that I was the only man nominated that every single member at Plantation voted to go on the elder board. I felt that was a sign from the Lord that it was in His will for me to be on the elder board.

I went through an intense twelve-week study course that was taught by Pastor Goldfield on the doctrines of Plantation's faith before I was installed as a Ruling Elder on a Sunday morning along with two other men: "Clarence Finley" and "Brendell Knight." We now had six elders at Plantation: five Ruling Elders and one Teaching Elder. The Teaching Elder was, of course, Pastor Goldfield.

At Plantation we didn't have a Wednesday night worship service as some other churches have. What we had was Wednesday night home church. We had three homes that held Bible studies. My home, being so close to the church, was one of the homes used each Wednesday for study. I taught a study every Wednesday evening on the Gospel of

Matthew. This study went on for the better part of three years. You might say it went at a snail's pace. During those three years we never did complete the study of the Gospel of Matthew.

As I look back, it became crystal clear to me why the Lord laid it on Doneata's and my heart not to build that estate home at Wilderness Plantation. If we had built at Wilderness Plantation, we wouldn't have this home at Deerfield available for ministry on Wednesday evenings. Plus, with the present financial uncertainty of Litchfield Theatres, I personally didn't need to be carrying a lot of personal debt.

———

During a Sunday evening worship service, Pastor Goldfield announced to the congregation that he would be leaving Plantation Church. This was only a few weeks after I had been ordained as an elder. Pastor Goldfield said the Lord had called him to another church in Mississippi. Wanting to stay in God's will, he accepted the call and notified the Session at the church in Mississippi that he and his family would be with them within three months.

Our elder board met the following week to make a decision about how we were going to continue to function during the interim period that Plantation Church would be without a pastor. In this particular denomination, there were two options for a church to choose from when it didn't have a pastor. While the church was without a pastor, the elders could invite an interim pastor in to preach and handle the day-to-day operations of the church. During this interim period a Pulpit Committee would be formed, and they in turn would invite men in to candidate for the position of pastor. The interim pastor would preach when there was nobody invited in to candidate. Or, the elder board could elect one of their own members to act as Moderator of Plantation Church during the interim period.

Our elder board voted unanimously to elect one of our own elders to act as Moderator, rather than bring in an interim pastor. I was the man chosen by the other elders to be the Moderator of the Session. I felt somewhat uncomfortable taking on that kind of responsibility, but the other elders felt that I was the one most qualified for the position. Little did I know that interim period without a pastor would last for exactly one year.

During that year, I stayed extremely busy at Litchfield trying to do everything I could to help Litchfield Theatres erupt out of bankruptcy, as well as be responsible for a 220-member congregation at Plantation. Every Sunday I would have a guest preacher in my home for Sunday lunch. On Wednesday evening I would have anywhere from five to twenty-five members of Plantation in my home for a weekly Bible study. I was also president of Plantation's Men of the Church, which meant a monthly men's breakfast meeting and program for up to 100 men. There were weeks that I saw very little of my family as Litchfield Theatres and Plantation Church occupied nearly all of my time.

Even though God blessed that year at Plantation, both physically and emotionally, it was a hard year for me. The former pastor, Pastor Goldfield, had such a strong presence about himself that very few people would challenge him on controversial issues. But, once Pastor Goldfield and his family had packed their bags and left Myrtle Beach, that's when certain individuals started stepping out rather boldly to see exactly how far they could go in having the Session change some of the policies at Plantation Church.

When it came to our five elders, we had a real mix of men. My friend, George Phillips, the man who had nominated me to become an elder, had a very kind, warm personality. Everyone in Myrtle Beach knew George. George reminded me of a politician; he always wanted to go the way the crowd went. George was one of those individuals who wanted no one to be upset with them.

Bill Hart was our senior elder. Bill was always looking to find ways to give a helping hand when help was needed. At our men's monthly breakfast meeting, Bill was always one of the first men there to help make the coffee or pour the orange juice.

Bill and his lovely wife, "Gloria" lived only a few houses down the street from us. The Hart family brought a lot of warmth to Plantation Church. Every week Bill would stand at the outside entrance to the church and welcome people as they entered for worship. Immediately after the worship service, Bill would be at the exit door to thank everyone for coming to Plantation. Yes, Bill and Gloria Hart brought warmth to the ministry at Plantation.

One area Bill always needed prayer in was his ongoing struggle with smoking cigarettes. I guess we all have our weaknesses, the Lord knows I have mine, and tobacco was Bill's. He just couldn't kick the habit of smoking cigarettes no matter how hard he seemed to try. I remember when Larry Jr. rode his bicycle by Elder Hart's home one day and saw Elder Hart sitting there on his lawn mower enjoying a cigarette. Larry was so surprised and disappointed that Elder Hart would smoke cigarettes right there in his own front yard.

Brendell Knight, like myself, was one of the new men on the Session. Brendell was probably in his mid-thirties. He was married with three children. Brendell had an interesting background. He was brought up in a very conservative Christian home. Brendell was even educated at a very conservative, fundamentalist university. He was married to a lovely lady, "Jennifer."

After college Brendell spent several years at a liberal law school. I often wondered if that's what changed Brendell's views concerning how a Christian ought to think and act. It always seemed as though Brendell's choices and actions were liberal.

I remember one Sunday evening when Brendell threw a Super Bowl party and invited several families from Plantation Church to watch the Super Bowl rather than meet with God's people during the Sunday evening worship service. I found it discouraging to have one of our elders encourage people to put football ahead of meeting with God and His people.

The Lord didn't lead me to vote for Brendell to become an elder. I thought he was an intelligent man, but in spiritual matters I found him to be young and immature in the faith. But, when he was elected to the elder board, I prayed the Lord would use this position in Brendell's life to help mature him for the work He had called him to do at Plantation Church.

The last elder was Clarence Finley. Clarence came on the Session the same time that Brendell and I did. Clarence was an older man. He tended to keep to himself. When Clarence had something to say, he would say it, but only after he had completely thought through what it was he was going to say. Clarence and his wife had retired in West Virginia and moved to Myrtle Beach. He was a good friend to me during the years that I knew him. Of all the elders, Clarence was the one most Reformed in his theology.

As for me, I was the elder that was considered to be the most conservative of the group. I remember once during a rather testy meeting Brendell commented, "Well, I guess it's good we have Larry on the Session. We need one conservative man on the Session to help give it a balance."

One of the many responsibilities of being the Moderator of the Session was to make sure the pulpit was filled each and every Sunday with a fine man of God, bringing the people at Plantation His Word week in and week out. That year without a pastor, I invited preachers in from all over the country to speak during our Sunday morning and Sunday evening worship service. I never formally notified the other elders about whom I would have coming in to speak on any given Sunday. I would bring the elders up-to-date with the men I had set to speak during the upcoming month at our monthly Session meeting.

I'll never forget the time I invited Richard Owen Roberts to come speak to our congregation for a three-day series of messages. I called Mr. Roberts and asked him if he would speak to our people on Friday evening, then speak at our men's breakfast on Saturday morning, and conclude his messages on Sunday during the morning and evening worship services. Mr. Roberts is noted for being one of the foremost authorities on revival in the world. I had heard him speak numerous times before. He had spoken at our sister church in Myrtle Beach as well as at Plantation when Pastor Goldfield was still there.

Pastor Goldfield had often commented to Tommy Swaim, a good personal friend of mine who also happened to be the chairman of the Building Committee, that if Richard Owen Roberts walked into Plantation on any given Sunday unannounced, he would gladly step aside and let Mr. Roberts have his pulpit. One can't really appreciate that statement unless he knew how much Pastor Goldfield guarded his pulpit.

Well, when I told the elders that I had invited Mr. Roberts in to speak at Plantation, they each, one by one, shared with me their displeasure in my inviting Mr. Roberts to come and speak.

One of them said, "Larry, Mr. Roberts speaks way too long. His messages are too hard on people. We need someone who makes us feel good." Then another elder chimed in, "You're right! Mr. Roberts is no fun." And another said, "That man's too serious for me." Clarence just shrugged his shoulders as if to say, "Well, whatever the majority wants."

I thought to myself, "I've already invited Mr. Roberts to come and speak. What's wrong with these men? Mr. Roberts is one of the godliest men I know. Mr. Roberts is without a doubt a man who walks with God, and it shows in his preaching. Mr. Roberts's preaching is head and shoulders above most of the sermons that we're accustomed to hearing. I must try to reason with these men and appeal to their conscience to reexamine exactly what it is they are saying."

I just sat there for a moment thinking to myself, "What am I, Larry Vaughn, doing here in this position? I didn't ask to become an elder. I didn't seek the position of elder, and I most certainly did not want to take on the responsibilities associated with being the Moderator of the Session. But, it was these exact men who asked me to be their leader. Now, as unworthy as I am, I must try to lead them in the way I would think the Lord would have them lead the congregation of Plantation Church."

I got up from behind the desk in the pastor's study and walked around and sat on the corner of the desk. "Men, let's think for a moment about what it is that we are saying here." Two of the men gave me that look as if to say, "Here he goes again."

"Gentlemen, we are the Ruling Elders of Plantation Church. The decisions we make in this room tonight will affect the entire congregation: either for good or bad. I'm sure we all want to put our personal feelings aside and do what we think God would have us to do." I shrugged my shoulders. "You four men may very well be right, and I may be wrong in wanting to bring Mr. Roberts in to speak at Plantation. Who knows? Maybe the timing is not right." I paused a moment and nodded my head as I said, "I do believe God works through His elders." I shrugged my shoulders again, as I said, "The reason I thought it would be good to have Mr. Roberts come in at this time is because of the present condition of Plantation Church."

I thought a moment. "Gentlemen, we need someone, not just anyone, but a man who is strong in his faith, like Richard Owen Roberts to come in here and talk to the congregation of Plantation Church about our S-I-N. We've already had several conversations about how nobody comes to church on Sunday night anymore. Our deacons aren't here half the time on Sunday morning, and I seldom see them here on Sunday evening. The people's giving is way down. Financially, we're okay. But that's only because, right now, we don't have to pay a pastor's salary."

I looked around the room. "At the men's prayer meeting on Wednesday morning, we have the same three to four men. We can't even get the five of us to show up for prayer on a regular basis." The next thing on my agenda to bring up seemed inappropriate for me to address. I thought my jumping on them for their movie-going would sound hypocritical because of my being in the film business. But be it as it may, I took a deep breath and continued, "And while we're on the subject of sin, I know I'm in the movie business; but it makes a terrible example for an elder to be seen at R-rated movies. Scripture tells us that we are to be holy as He is holy, because without holiness no one will see God. When members of the church see elders and their wives at R-rated movies, then what kind of a signal does that send to the people?"

One of the men wanted to change the subject. "Larry, Richard Owen Roberts is a fine man. I just think the timing is wrong for him to come to Plantation. I say we vote on it and let the vote decide whether he comes or not." The other men nodded in agreement.

I thought to myself, "This vote is for the record only because I already know the outcome."

I said, "Okay, men, let's vote." The vote was four to one against Mr. Roberts's coming. I replied, "I'll call Mr. Roberts and tell him that we must cancel his engagement and that maybe he can come and speak at another time." The men all nodded in agreement.

An elder isn't supposed to go home and talk with his wife about a Session meeting, but I did anyway. I felt like I just had to say something to someone before I made the much-dreaded phone call to Mr. Roberts. Maybe talking things over with Doneata was the way I was using to muster up the courage needed to make the call.

"Doneata, I believe God works through His elders; it must be me that's wrong. For some reason God doesn't want Mr. Roberts speaking at Plantation. The vote stands. I must call Mr. Roberts and try to find some way to gracefully bow out of having him come."

Doneata listened to what I had to say. She had very few comments as she agreed with what I said. We then had prayer, and Doneata went to sleep.

I didn't sleep much that night. My soul was in a turmoil trying to figure all this out. I could find no peace or understanding about why things happen the way they do. It was hard for me to believe these men on the Session were the same men I used to go out to lunch with and have in my home. At the start, I thought we were all like-minded when it came to those serious things of God. I ran my fingers through my already messed-up hair as I thought to myself, "I don't know what to think anymore. I know one thing; it's getting late. I guess, at times, maybe, I'm just too serious minded." I looked at the clock. It was 4:30. I knew I must try to get some rest before the night turned into the morning.

The next morning at 7:30, I received a phone call from Clarence Finley. "Larry, I have been thinking about that vote last night. I would like for us to get the guys together and have another vote. I went home last night, and I was miserable. I don't think my head touched the pillow all night. I think what we did last night was wrong, and it needs to be discussed further."

I was so thrilled to hear Clarence say what he said. I told him, "Okay, Clarence, I'll call the men and set up another meeting before I call Mr. Roberts. Who knows? Maybe they are having second thoughts also."

I told Doneata, "God has been working in Clarence Finley's heart. He wants me to get the Session together again on the issue of Mr. Roberts's speaking at Plantation." Right there on the spot Doneata and I gave thanks to our Lord for touching Clarence's heart and mind. We then prayed about the future meeting with the other three elders.

I got the five of us together Sunday morning after the worship service. Clarence did most of the talking. He told the other elders basically what he had told me on the phone earlier. Clarence said, "Men, I don't think God was in that vote the other night. I think we should take another vote."

In past years, I have played in too many poker games not to be able to read expressions on certain men's faces. I knew those three wouldn't budge on the Roberts issue. This time the vote was three to two. That afternoon I called Mr. Roberts, and all he said was, "Larry, it's okay; I completely understand."

To me that decision by the Session not to allow Mr. Roberts to come and preach was a turning point in the ministry at Plantation Church. Spiritually speaking, things were already going downhill, but from that day forward it seemed like God removed His Spirit completely from the ministry at Plantation Church. And that was a shame because there were some serious Christian people worshipping at that church who had a desire to grow in the grace and knowledge of our Lord and Savior, Jesus Christ. But, because of an impotent Session, those sincere folks had to suffer spiritually along with everyone else.

We have all heard that old saying, "You must be careful what you ask for." Well, it wasn't four weeks later that Plantation Church had a man come and candidate. This man, "Terry Pink," was to become the new pastor at Plantation Church. As we found out later, everything about Terry Pink—from his preaching, to his actions, to his personal lifestyle—was about as far from Richard Owen Roberts's preaching, actions, and personal lifestyle as the east is from the west.

That Sunday Pastor Pink came in to candidate. I had him and his family over for lunch after church. He had a lovely wife and four absolutely adorable children. After lunch he and I went out on the back patio and talked. We both sat down on the patio lounge chairs. He crossed one of his legs over the other and rested the palms of his hands behind his head. He smiled as he talked. He was so laid-back in his manner that he almost made me nervous. Anyway, he told me everything I wanted to hear. We talked for about thirty minutes. He knew all the right answers when it came to conservative issues. Later that afternoon, he met with the Pulpit Committee and had a good meeting with them. It wasn't long at all before the moving van had the Pink family moved into their new home located not more than six houses away from mine.

During the months ahead, Pastor Pink started doing some strange things that concerned me greatly. He taught the new-members' class every Sunday morning during the Sunday school hour. He had inserted into the bulletin: "The new-members' class is where we have fun." I thought, "Have fun! It should be where people learn what the Christian walk is all about." After watching his actions for a few weeks, it became clear to me that we had hired a man whose qualifications fit that of a youth minister more than a senior pastor. Terry Pink just wanted to have a good time. He always looked fresh and ready to go in his starched shirt, Dockers pants, and penny loafers. He was always ready for a good laugh or some extracurricular activity at a moment's notice.

I thought, "If he would only take some of that energy and zeal for fun and put it into its proper channel in the ministry at Plantation." After a few weeks, I went to him one Sunday morning after church and told him I would like to meet with him privately one morning. We made an appointment to meet on Tuesday morning at the church office at 6:00.

I went into the meeting speaking from my heart, but I was very direct in what I had to say. I felt uneasy having to address my pastor about the issues at hand. I wanted to help him. I wanted the ministry at Plantation Church to flourish under its new pastor. Anyway, I found myself that morning face-to-face with him. The long-prayed-over meeting was finally at hand. I looked searchingly into his happy blue eyes.

"Pastor, because I am a Ruling Elder at Plantation, I feel it my duty as a servant of our Lord to share with you some of the concerns I have about your ministry. I believe now would be a good time for you and me to talk about those concerns individually."

Pastor Pink had his pad and pencil out. His eyes were dancing eagerly. He reminded me of a boy at his first day of school writing down his supply list of needed materials for the year ahead. Anyway, he made a list of each concern.

"Pastor, my first concern is that you aren't putting enough time into your sermon preparation." He frowned and bobbled his head back and forth as he looked down at his pad. "May I ask how much time do you put into your sermon preparation each week?"

He was quick to reply. "Larry, not enough. It's just that I have been so busy doing other things that I have let my sermon preparations go."

His eyes met mine. They were pleading for sympathy and understanding.

I thought, "A minister's central focus ought to be the preaching of the Word above all else; but remember, Larry, be understanding." So, I nodded as if to say, "I understand what you are saying."

"Pastor, quite often you don't even show up for Wednesday morning prayer. I understand your schedule may not permit your being at every Wednesday prayer meeting, but it's just that you are seldom at any prayer meeting. Your absence discourages me and the two or three other men that do show up."

He looked at the ceiling as if he were trying to think up a good answer to that concern. Then he looked at me. I looked straight into his eyes and said, "Pastor, I hope you are spending time alone with the Lord each day."

Pastor Pink thought a moment, and then he said, "Larry, my prayer life is nowhere near what it should be." Dropping his head, he said, "No, I haven't been spending much time in prayer lately."

I said, "Pastor, I hope you don't mind my being perfectly frank with you."

He looked surprised at that statement. I guess he thought I was already being frank with him. "No, Larry, go right ahead."

"Pastor, I told you when you came to Plantation that the elder board as well as the congregation were divided about the future direction of the church. Part of the church is looking to hold to those more traditional, conservative values and the other part is looking to go in the direction of the liberal view. You told me on my patio the Sunday that you came in to candidate that you didn't have a liberal bone in your body. Well, my concern after watching you these past few weeks is that you are allowing Plantation to go liberal, and liberal very quickly I might add."

He acted shocked. "Larry, I don't want to be responsible for Plantation's going liberal."

"Then, Pastor, you'd better get back on track. Your elders and deacons are looking to you for direction. If you will just stop and look at them and see how worldly they have become in their thinking, then maybe you'll have a better understanding of my concerns."

We talked a few more minutes, but that was the gist of the conversation. His once-happy blue eyes sobered somewhat during that meeting. I hoped his inner man was sobered as well. I often wondered if Pastor Pink understood the importance of leading the flock of Christ. We closed our time together with each of us lifting up in prayer the ministry at Plantation Church. He thanked me for my concern and promised to try to do better. We were supposed to meet again the next Tuesday morning for more prayer. I had agreed to hold him accountable. I knew only time would tell.

It didn't take much time to tell. In the weeks ahead it was as if Pastor Pink and I had never had that Tuesday morning meeting. There wasn't the smallest change in any of the areas that he and I had talked about that morning. We never met another Tuesday morning as planned. Pastor Pink always had something come up or whatever have you. I started thinking about resigning from the Session, because I felt like I was just a cog on the wheel. I don't know why the Lord had called me to see things differently from the other elders, but it's perfectly clear to me that I was seeing things very differently from the way they saw them.

Our good friends the Milburns invited my family and me to come and spend New Year's Day with them and their daughter. We thought the timing couldn't be better. I thought it would be great to get away from the frustrations of the problems associated with Pastor Pink and the Session for a few days.

When I returned home, my phone was ringing off the hook. One of the members at Plantation asked me if I had heard about the New Year's Eve service that was held at the church.

I said, "No, I have been out of town."

This individual went on to give me a little information about the events of that evening. "Well, they did open and close the service in prayer, but in between all kinds of strange things were taking place."

I asked, "For example?"

"Well, Brother Vaughn, the preacher and his wife were dancing in the aisle while one of the ladies in the church played the boogie-woogie on the church piano."

I thought to myself, "No! Must I hear more?"

"One of the elders played that song—oh, Brother Vaughn, I can't think of the title. You know, it's the one about the night the squirrel got loose at some church and they thought revival was breaking loose as the squirrel kept finding itself in some very unusual places."

"Yes, I've heard portions of the song. I must make note to check into that."

"Brother Vaughn, I wish you had been there."

I thought a moment. "Let me ask you a question. Were any other elders at this service?"

"Why, yes, they were all there."

"And this took place in the sanctuary?"

"Why, yes."

I thanked the person for the call. As I hung up the phone, I got a sick feeling in the pit of my stomach. I felt very hot all of a sudden. I sat down and put my hands through my hair. I thought to myself, "Ichabod. God's Spirit has left that place. It's no different from any one of the fifty or more entertainment centers located at Myrtle Beach."

That next day Doneata and I went for a walk. As we walked past Pastor Pink's house, he was in the yard doing some work. When he saw us, he waved and said hello and turned to walk away rather hurriedly.

Doneata said, "Larry, what's wrong with Pastor Pink's mouth? It looks swollen." I motioned for her just to keep walking. "But, honey, did he have a dentist's appointment today?"

I replied, "Honey, there's nothing wrong with his mouth outside of its being full of tobacco. You didn't know that he chews, did you?"

Doneata looked shocked. "Well, I knew Larry Jr. saw beer in his refrigerator, but I didn't know he chewed tobacco too."

I smiled at Doneata's innocence. "Well, now you know."

Sunday after the worship service I questioned the elders about what I had heard that went on at the New Year's Eve service. Pastor Pink's only reply was, "That's hearsay, and you shouldn't pay any attention to it." It took about half an hour to drag it out of him, but everything happened as I was told earlier. I had hoped he and the elders would have had some remorse for the New Year's Eve service, but they didn't. What does one do when every person on the Session opposes him?

A few days later I submitted my resignation from the Session at Plantation Church. It was just a few weeks later that I realized that it was absolutely wrong for my family and me to sit under Pastor Pink's ministry. I wrote a letter to the elder board asking them to take the Larry Vaughn family off the role at Plantation Church.

Twenty-Nine

The Prelude

Whereas at Plantation Church everything seemed to have unraveled, it was just the opposite at Litchfield Theatres. Doug brought a new man on board, Stephen Colson, as president of Litchfield Theatres. Steve, a former General Cinema executive, had excellent operation and management skills. The theatres were grossing beyond our wildest expectations. All the necessary pieces of the corporate puzzle were coming together to make it possible for Litchfield Theatres to be thrust out of bankruptcy. Litchfield Theatres was out of Chapter 11 within a year. Things just couldn't have been going better for the company.

There were lots of big movies being released, and we certainly had our share of the business. We were pounding our annual projections into the ground. Where a year earlier it looked as if all was lost, we now saw not only a chance to maintain our current presence in the marketplace but also an opportunity in the not-too-distant future to start back building theatres again. Yes, it wouldn't be long at all before Litchfield Theatres, Ltd. would be back as a major player in the film industry.

Whereas all of my time used to be divided between my responsibilities at Litchfield Theatres and Plantation Church, I now found myself being kept very busy traveling for Litchfield. After all those years at Plantation, it seemed very odd not being associated with Plantation Church. I drove by the church every day going to and from work. I would think quite often of how different the ministry at Plantation was before the arrival of fun-loving Terry Pink. I was glad the theatres were now occupying most of my time and thoughts.

The following months were exciting times at Litchfield Theatres. Doug would have four or five of us over to his home on a midweek day for eight hours of brainstorming. Doug would lock the door, take the phone off the hook, and we would go at it for hours at a time. Then the next week I would be out looking at new theatre sites or traveling to Atlanta, Dallas, or Los Angeles for film-buying meetings. Yes, it was an exciting time at Litchfield. I was happy for the Board of Directors and for the shareholders that Litchfield Theatres had more than met anyone's financial expectations.

The company was doing so well that we were considering moving the home office to Charlotte, North Carolina. Doug wanted to be closer to our lenders, and I wanted to be closer to a major airport. One big drawback about living at Myrtle Beach was the flight connections, or should I say the lack of flight connections. It would be nice to live in a city that had direct flights to Dallas, New York, and Los Angeles.

On a personal note, I thought a move to Charlotte would be great. Living in a larger city, I knew there would be several good choices of churches where our family could get week in and week out the strong preaching of the Word of God. Also, I thought it would be nice to get into a church with people who strove to live by Scripture.

Doneata and Mentora went to Charlotte to look around at churches, Christian schools, and housing. They spent two days there with Doug Richardson's wife, Wilma, looking the town over. Charlotte had certainly changed since the eighteen years ago that Doneata, David, and I had lived there. Doug and Wilma had a home in Charlotte as well as a home on one of the fairways at the Litchfield Country Club. Wilma was the perfect hostess and guide for Doneata and Mentora's two days of church, school, and house hunting.

While the girls were busy looking for churches, Christian schools, and homes, Doug and Ulmer were being kept busy with the real estate people looking for the proper site selection for our new office building in Charlotte. The announcement hadn't been made official to the home office employees yet, but it looked like in the not-too-distant future the move was going to become a reality.

————

While I was in Spartanburg, South Carolina, looking at a possible site to build a new eight-plex theatre, I dropped by one of our other theatres in the city. It was a Friday evening, and I noticed several teenagers and families standing out in front of the theatre looking at the large display frames advertising all the films that were currently playing in the theatre. Most of the films were R-rated. I did have one good family film playing at the time that was suitable for all ages.

What really grieved me was when I noticed some of the R-rated display posters that were inserted into the "now playing" frames located outside the theatre. One of the display posters had a lewd picture of a very seductive woman advertising one of the R-rated features. It disturbed me personally that those families there to see the G-rated film had to be exposed to such sensuality. I felt responsible for those families having seen the lewd picture; after all, I was the film buyer.

When I walked into the lobby, I noticed there were several families standing around watching the television monitors advertising all the films playing in the theatre, as well as coming attractions. That was the way people passed time until their particular film started. I thought to myself, "I wish there were some way those families would not have to be exposed to those previews. The film companies always put the most exciting parts of the movie in the preview to whet the audience's appetite. Sometimes, the most exciting part is actually the very part we should not be exposed to. I do hope there are no Christian people in here." And then I noticed the variety of display posters that were scattered throughout the lobby. And there for a second time was the same poster I had seen outside.

I walked over to the concession stand. I overheard a teenage girl talking to her date about the movie they were about to see. It was the same one I saw advertised on the poster outside. I looked around and noticed several other young couples waiting on the same film to start. I thought to myself, "Why are these couples paying to see the seductive woman undress on the screen?" I asked myself the question, "What's wrong with women today? Have they really changed to the point that they don't object to their date, mate, or steady looking at other women? Surely, deep down inside, it must bother wives and girlfriends for the man they are with to look at all the nudity on those posters, on the television monitors, and in the movie itself. It's no wonder that America is the nation that leads the world in divorce."

I had recently read a newspaper article that said nearly 1.2 million marriages were dissolved by the courts in 1994. That figure was triple the figure of 1960. I thought a moment, "I can understand one reason why there is so much divorce today. People today, more than ever before, spend their entertainment time watching other people undress and do unspeakable things on screen. And what about our children? We may think children don't notice certain things, but we fool ourselves. They notice much more than we think they do, especially young boys who are brought into an environment that has sensuality, horror, violence, and bad language. What adults watch in moderation, children, when given the opportunity, will watch in excess."

That same newspaper article predicted one out of every two marriages in 1995 would end in divorce. I wondered how much of a role the entertainment industry as a whole played in those staggering divorce figures. I wondered how much of a role I had played in those figures.

A familiar verse from Job came to my mind: "I made a covenant with mine eyes; why then should I think upon a maid?" Scripture tells us that outside of a man's personal and intimate relationship with his wife, God never meant for him to look upon a woman. Most certainly, this is not the way Hollywood displays women in posters and on the movie screen.

I realized how sensual material affected me. I stood there thinking, "I'm made of flesh and blood, and I have the same struggles that every other man living on planet earth has to deal with." I looked at all the men leaving the theatre. There were young fathers with their wives and children, some fathers and sons, more couples than anything—either dating or young married men and women. I wondered if there were any Christian husbands, fathers, or single Christian men in the crowd. I thought to myself, "If some of those men are Brothers in Christ, then they, like myself, should know right from wrong." Right there I prayed silently that God would convict any Christian man who might be there that night, that God would touch his mind and have him reevaluate how he spends his entertainment time, and that God would grant him wisdom in what he allows to be brought into the mind of his wife and children.

I left the theatre that night feeling bad about how all those things that were once considered to be evil are accepted without question by the masses today. A family comes to the theatre to see a good film, and they have to wade through all the R-rated promotional material just to get to their G-rated movie; that bothered me.

I got in my car and thought about all the films that had entered my mind during the many years I had been in the film industry. And I realized that the mind is like a computer. What goes in through either the eyes or the ears is locked in there forever. And I was helping young men and young women to fill their minds with impure thoughts.

Driving across town to my hotel, I thought about the Wometco lawsuit and specifically about the questioning from the New York attorneys. I was amazed at the way Eric Rosenfield brought back to my mind everyday events that had happened two years earlier. If Eric Rosenfield wanted to know some information about a film that I saw, say some fifteen years ago—even though in my lifetime I have seen thousands of movies—I could tell Eric whatever it was he wanted to know about the particular movie in question if he worked with me long and hard enough.

Those images and thoughts are all stored away deep in the back of my mind. That's why we must be so careful to protect our mind from those things we allow it to see and hear. The worst thoughts can be brought back with much less work than Mr. Rosenfield used.

———

I heard the phone ringing, but I was in such a deep sleep that I really didn't want to wake up to answer it. After about the fifth ring, Doneata came dashing from the bathroom, talking to me as she hurried toward the phone.

"You'd better wake up and get at it. I've already had my shower."

I heard Doneata answer the phone and say, "Hello. Good morning. . . . yes . . . he's right here."

Doneata handed me the phone as she motioned to me that a cup of coffee was on the way.

As I reached for the receiver, I looked at the clock; it was 7:05. "Hello. Good morning, Ulmer; you're up mighty early. Is everything okay?"

Ulmer's voice was trembling, and he spat out words that, at first I couldn't comprehend: "Larry, we had a robbery in one of our theatres last night. Two of our employees, the assistant manager and an usher, were killed."

The fog of sleep left me as the reality of Ulmer's words rocked me. "What! Two men killed. Oh no, Ulmer, I can't believe it." I jumped out of bed, put on my housecoat, and started walking toward the den.

"Ulmer, this is like waking up in a nightmare! Tell me exactly what happened."

"Larry, after the last feature started, two men came into the theatre. The lobby was empty except for one usher who was walking around waiting on each of the individual auditoriums to empty out as each movie ended. The assistant manager was sitting in the office counting up the day's receipts."

Ulmer was quiet a moment; then he continued. "One of the men knocked on the office door. Since he was a former employee, the assistant manager let him in the office."

I interrupted him. "Ulmer, you mean one of the killers used to work for Litchfield?"

"Larry, I'm afraid so."

I felt sick at my stomach as I asked Ulmer, "Then what happened?"

There was a long pause on the other end of the line. I could tell Ulmer was having a really hard time trying to tell me the story. "Well, Larry, you won't believe it, but," he hesitated a moment, "they took the usher out back of the theatre and executed him. One bullet in the head."

Chills went up my spine. "Ulmer, why in the world would they kill the usher? He had to be just a kid."

Ulmer sounded heartbroken. "Larry, who knows why evil men do those evil things that they do? My guess is the men knew that the usher could identify them, and they would rather kill him than have to worry about his being able to identify them."

I agreed.

Ulmer cleared his throat. "Then, the two men took all the cash in the safe and made the assistant manager leave with them. The three of them left the theatre in the assistant manager's van."

I interrupted again. "How do you know all of this?"

"Larry, it just so happened that, as they were pulling away from the theatre, the theatre manager's son drove up and noticed the former employee riding with the assistant manager in his van. The manager's son knew something was wrong because the theatre was left unattended while it was still open. He went inside and could find no employees. He started looking everywhere for the usher. He eventually found the young man's body outside at the back. He went back inside and phoned the police. The police arrived at the theatre within a matter of minutes. They had a full description of the van. The assailants drove about thirty miles and stopped the van out in the country on a deserted highway." Ulmer paused again. "Larry, it was there that they executed the assistant manager by putting a bullet in his head."

From his tone of voice, I could tell Ulmer was mentally, as well as physically, exhausted from telling me about these terrible double murders. "Larry, that's all I know right now. It's a terrible story, but that's how it was told to me."

As impossible as it may sound, I wanted to find some words of encouragement to give to Ulmer. "Ulmer, this is going to be a long, hard day for you and the families and loved ones of those young men who were killed last night. Doneata and I will be sure to bathe this terrible tragedy in prayer." I thanked Ulmer for the call and told him I would see him later in the day.

I told Doneata the unbelievable story just as Ulmer had relayed it to me. Together we prayed for Ulmer and the families and loved ones of the two young men who were murdered that night. We prayed that God would manifest Himself to the families, friends, and loved ones of the deceased men in a very real and special way that day, that somehow through this terrible tragedy God would use it to bring someone to Christ.

Driving to work, I thought about what Ulmer said: "One of the men used to work for us." In that particular town, we operated two theatres. One theatre was known for playing the Disney films, comedies, and the more sophisticated adult-type entertainment. The other theatre, where the robbery and killing took place, was known for playing the action, ethnic, and horror-type films. That particular theatre was what we call in the theatre business an "action house."

I wondered as I drove down Highway 17 South toward Litchfield Beach that dark, dreary morning how many of those evil, violent films those two killers had watched before they decided it was time to act out what they had been watching for entertainment. It disturbed my soul that these senseless murders had happened. My heart cried out for those two dead men. They were so young; they had their whole lives ahead of them.

My mind drifted to the verses in Matthew that deal with the eye and how important it is that we guard our eyes from evil: "The light of the body is the eye; if, therefore, thine eye be single, thy whole body shall be full of light. But if thine eye be evil, thy whole body shall be full of darkness."

Those two men had committed two heinous acts of murder and robbed a theatre because their eyes had allowed their whole bodies to become full of darkness. There is absolutely no way to tell, but I couldn't help wondering if those two men had never been exposed to all the violence in those R-rated movies, would they have dared even to think about doing such an unspeakable thing. I thought to myself, "These violent action movies that are being made today are making men's eyes to become evil and their bodies full of darkness. And that darkness leads to all sorts of evil things." I felt sad that I was the person who was responsible for putting those R-rated films in that theatre. I had helped those murdering young men to fill their eyes with evil and to commit such sin.

I needed some way to resolve, once and for all, the struggle that kept resurfacing time and time again—the terribly unsettled conscience about my work. I had lived with an uneasiness about the effect of my involvement in the film industry on my own spiritual life, the life of my family, and now the lives of countless others. What could I do? Doneata's words came to my mind: "Honey, why don't you just go ahead and quit your job? You have struggled with movies on and off, mostly on, since you got saved. You know I'll support you in whatever decision you make. All I want is for you to have peace and for us to be in God's will."

———

When planning a business trip to Atlanta, I decided to drive rather than fly, as I wanted to make a stop in Columbia and look at a potential theatre site the company was considering building a ten-plex theatre on. On the drive to Atlanta, I put a tape in the cassette player that was given to me by a man I met while I was the Moderator at Plantation Church. The man that gave me the tape was the Reverend Mark Kittrell. I met Mark when he came to Myrtle Beach to speak to the staff and students at Calvary Christian School. Mentora was so impressed with his messages that she heard at Calvary that I sent Doneata to hear the Reverend Kittrell preach the next day. Doneata came home just as excited as Mentora. I asked Doneata to invite Mark and his wife, Tammisue, and their son, Caleb, over to dinner as I would like to invite him to speak at Plantation.

We had a wonderful evening together with the Kittrell family. Mark and his family travel all over the country, where Mark speaks at Christian schools and churches about how God has worked in his life. God blessed Mark with exceptional athletic abilities, especially in the area of basketball. If he so desired, Mark could have played basketball in the National Basketball Association. He was that good—good enough to be in the pros; but, Mark chose to put aside those temporal pleasures of this world to go into full-time Christian service.

At the close of the evening, Mark gave me a sermon on tape from the pastor of his home church in Greenville. He said, "Larry, the Lord really blessed my soul when I heard this message. I think if you listen to it, it will do the same for you."

I asked Mark and Tammisue, "Do you folks have a good home church?"

They looked at each other and smiled. Then Mark said, "Brother Vaughn, we have a wonderful home church. Our pastor, Pastor Minnick, is a fine man of God. He is the man of God that I am striving to be like."

That statement meant something coming from a godly man like Mark Kittrell. I said, "Well, Mark, you have whet my appetite. I am looking forward to hearing the message and visiting your church, if for some reason I am ever in Greenville on a Sunday or a Wednesday night."

Mark was right. As I listened to Pastor Minnick's message on tape, it did my soul good; this man's message was from our Lord. Pastor Minnick's doctrinally sound expository preaching of the Word reminded me very much of Pastor Clarkston. I saw much similarity in

Pastor Minnick's message and in messages that I had heard from Pastor Clarkston. Yes, I most certainly wanted to hear more from the gifted Pastor Minnick.

Thirty

Carrots, Carrots, Carrots!

It was a Friday morning in January when Steve called me into his office for what ended up being one of the most important meetings of my life. I walked into his office at 8:30. Steve got up from behind his desk and closed the door. He went back to his desk, sat down, and started doodling on a piece of scrap paper. Looking very serious, Steve said, "Larry, we have got to talk." I recognized the urgency in the tone of his voice. "What's up, Steve?"

Steve got up from behind his desk and walked to the empty chair beside me. He sat down and put his hand on my arm. "Larry, I received a phone call a couple of weeks ago from Mike Campbell."

I thought to myself, "Mike Campbell, he's the president of Regal Cinemas." Steve took his right hand and started rubbing the back of his neck. I wondered, "Is his neck stiff or is he just trying to buy a couple of extra seconds before proceeding?"

"Larry, I didn't take the call seriously at first; however, after several conversations with Mr. Campbell and later with our Board of Directors, it looks like Litchfield Theatres is going to merge with Regal Cinemas."

I thought to myself, "That would be a great move for Regal Cinemas. They are already the up-and-coming theatre circuit in the country, and now to have the Litchfield circuit would be a big feather in Mike Campbell's hat."

Steve loosened his tie, crossed his legs, and cracked his knuckles as if to say, "The hard part's behind me." Then he continued speaking. "Of course, Larry, you do understand there are several steps that have to be taken before a merger of this magnitude can happen. The proposed merger has to go before the courts; the Regal shareholders have to vote on it. There's a number of hurdles that we have to overcome before it can actually happen."

As Steve talked, I was thinking to myself, "Well, it looks like this is the door the Lord is going to use to get me out of the theatre business."

"Steve, let me ask you a question. If all goes as expected and there is no glitch in the works, when do you think the merger will take place?"

Steve puckered his lips and started mentally walking through the time frame of the merger. He leaned back and rolled his eyes to the back of his head; then he looked down and started counting on his fingers. Bobbling his head from side to side, searching through his mind for an accurate answer, he replied, "Oh, I don't know, Larry. I'd guess the merger could be over and done with by early to mid summer."

Steve then got up and walked around the room. He started straightening a picture on the wall; then, he turned and looked directly at me. "Larry, none of the Litchfield senior management is going to be invited to go with Regal." Steve shrugged his shoulders. "They have their own management team in place. Unfortunately, they don't need another president, executive V.P., or head film buyer." He looked at me as if to say, "That's the bad news." Steve cleared his throat as he said, "Regal does want to talk to our district managers and equipment people. They are the only home office personnel Regal has expressed any interest in." Steve looked disappointed that Regal didn't invite me to go with them. I thought now would be a good time to cheer Steve up.

"Steve, don't be disappointed for me. I've heard nothing but wonderful things about Mike Campbell and Regal Cinemas, but I wouldn't go with Regal if they offered me a job."

Steve looked shocked. "You wouldn't?"

"No, sir. I have no interest in staying in the film business. Litchfield Theatres is my swan song in the film industry."

Steve looked relieved, but surprised at that statement. "But, Larry, what will you do?"

"I have no idea; but whatever I do, it won't be in the film business."

He just sat there and stared at me a few moments. I felt uneasy. I was trying to hide the fear that had all of a sudden overwhelmed me. I thought to myself, "What will I do? I'm a forty-seven-year-old man who is about to walk away from the only business I know."

Steve was talking, and I was so deep in my thoughts that I missed what he was saying. "I'm sorry, Steve, would you mind repeating what you just said?"

He exhaled then proceeded to repeat the sentence. "Larry, Mr. Campbell wants the Litchfield management team to stay in place until the takeover is completed."

"Steve, that's fine by me." I shrugged my shoulders. Smiling, I said, "It's not like I have any place to go. I'll be here as long as Litchfield Theatres needs me."

Steve and I talked a while longer, but that was the gist of the meeting.

That private meeting soon became public information, as there's a saying in the film business which seems to have merit: "There are no secrets on film row." My phone started ringing off the hook as the distributors heard the news.

One of the first calls I received was from Bruce Snyder, the president of Distribution at Twentieth Century Fox. "Larry, I just heard the news this morning about Litchfield merging with Regal Cinemas. I just wanted to call and let you know that I just got off the phone with Mike Campbell, and I told Mike he'd better take you with him. Larry, my man, don't be surprised if you don't hear from Phil Borak in the very near future."

Phil Borak owned and operated his own film buying agency. He did all the film buying for Regal Cinemas out of his Cincinnati, Ohio, film buying office. "Bruce, your taking the time to call Mike Campbell on my behalf was very kind and thoughtful. You're a good friend, and I do appreciate your concern for my well being."

"Larry, if Regal doesn't work out, you let me know; and we'll work on another angle."

As I hung up the phone, I thought to myself, "No, I'm not going to miss leaving Hollywood and the years of struggle that I have had trying to justify staying in this godless industry, but I'm sure going to miss the many dear friends that I have come to know and love down through the years."

Bruce Snyder's phone call got results. Sure enough, Steve buzzed me later that afternoon and informed me that he had talked with Mike Campbell. Mike called to tell Steve that he felt he had been too quick in not expressing interest in Larry Vaughn, not having had the opportunity to talk with his film buyer about a possible position with their film department. Steve informed me that Mr. Campbell was going to have Phil Borak give me a call later in the week.

Friday morning, I got my call from Phil Borak. "Hello, Larry Vaughn, I understand Mike is planning to add some more screens to his ever-growing circuit."

"Phil, that's what I hear. It looks like you're soon going to have a lot more screens to be responsible for."

"Larry, that's the purpose of this call. I talked with Mike. I want you to take a couple of days off and fly up to Cincinnati and spend some time with me. I think I've got an operation up here that might interest you. From what I've heard about you, I think you and I could make a real good team."

I thought to myself, "There's no point in keeping the man hanging."

"Phil, I do thank you for your consideration; but there's no point in my wasting your time or money. I have no interest in moving to Cincinnati or staying in the film business." I paused a moment. "So, there's really no reason for me to fly to Cincinnati."

Phil thought a moment before he made a reply. "Larry, I think you're a bit hasty in your decision making. Why, you haven't even heard my offer yet. Larry, I hope you don't mind my saying so, but it's not good business to turn down a job without hearing all the facts. Larry, at least fly up to Cincinnati and let's have dinner together. Let me tell you what I was planning on doing with you; and, of course, you owe it to yourself to at least talk about what the job will pay."

Laughing, I said, "Phil, if I did that then I would probably end up going to work for you."

"Well, that's what Mike and I want you to do."

I paused a moment. "Phil, I do appreciate your interest, but you're wasting your time."

Phil got very serious in his tone of voice. "Larry, you mean thanks but no thanks?"

"Nothing personal, Phil; but I just have zero interest."

"Okay, if you change your mind before I hire someone," he paused, "then let me know."

It seemed like Phil just had to add one more statement. "Larry, I do wish you would give more thought to this proposal. You would be the perfect man for the buying of product for the South and Southwest. Why, that area of the country you know as well as your own back yard. You not only know the lay of the land, but you also know all of the players."

I thought it best to go ahead and change the subject. "Phil, I do hope I can meet you sometime, and we can have dinner together; but, it will have to be somewhere in the South."

He caught the drift and gave me what sounded like an artificial laugh as he hung up the phone.

I thought to myself, "Phil Borak sounds like a man that I would really like to get to know."

As I placed the phone receiver back in its cradle, I was pleased with myself for not waffling with Phil on my decision to leave the industry. However, on the inside I remained overwhelmed with fear—the fear of leaving the business that I had spent all my adult life in and stepping out into the unknown.

I thought about my good friends at Litchfield Theatres: both those in senior management as well as those individuals on the board of directors. I knew they would be disappointed when they found out that I wouldn't even meet with Phil Borak.

I could imagine what they would think: "Surely, Larry will at least meet with Mr. Borak. What kind of businessman is Larry anyway? It's nonsense to say no without hearing the offer!" Then I thought about my good friends of many years in the film industry; how they won't understand that I wouldn't even take the time to fly to Cincinnati and have dinner with Phil Borak and hear what he had to say. I sighed as I mumbled softly, "I know my own limitations. It's best that I leave the industry without any further negotiations with anyone to stay in the business."

Wall Street received the news of the Litchfield Theatres' proposed merger with Regal Cinemas very favorably. The day the news broke is the day Regal's stock started climbing and continued to climb on the Nasdaq Stock Exchange.

At the office and on the home front, I was not waffling on my decision to leave the theatre business. Nonetheless, on the inside I was scared to death about what I was going to do once the merger was consummated. My whole life has been the motion picture industry. Outside of those childhood jobs—a morning paper route, stocking some grocery store shelves, and my tour of duty in the National Guard—the only money I have ever worked and earned was money associated with the film industry.

I thought to myself, "Why does the industry have to be putting out such bad product? Why can't it be different?"

I thought back to when I was a child living in Athens, Georgia. Oh, how I loved the movies. That's where I would spend every Friday night and all day Saturday and Saturday night. That's what I lived for, the weekend, so I could go to the movies. Unfortunately, Tarzan, Roy Rogers, and Gene Autrey are long gone.

I thought about how it was when Walt Disney was alive and how, even though Mr. Disney was far from being perfect, he did attempt to make some movies with wholesome family values. Yes, I can remember the day when I could recommend a Disney film to a family to watch as wholesome family entertainment. Today, I couldn't recommend Disney movies to Christian families. For the most part, the Disney company is no different from any other film company. So now, instead of being able to say to a Christian family, "Hey, have you and the family seen the latest Disney film?" I have to do just the opposite and warn Christian families to be very careful with the so-called family entertainment that the Disney company is producing.

The fact that the advertisement states Walt Disney doesn't mean the film is suitable for the Christian family. For the most part, Disney films are made by men and women who don't know Christ; and as a result, in some of those films there are all sorts of hidden evils that the Christian family must be aware of: the new age, the sexual innuendoes, the undermining of family values, and the music. Unfortunately, the Disney company of today has very little in common with the original Walt Disney Company.

These thoughts reassured me that I had made the right decision. "No, I see no ray of hope that the motion picture industry is going to change directions for the good. I must stand firm in my commitment to leave this industry that I once loved with all my heart. And, by faith, I am going to believe that my God, the God of the Bible, will continue to meet all of my needs in the days, months, and years ahead.

———

Doneata and I were trying to decide where we were going to live after the Litchfield/Regal merger was finalized. With my being out of work, we could move just about anywhere since I was going to be looking for work anyway. For several reasons we decided to consider moving back to Greenville, South Carolina, although Greenville today has very little in common with the Greenville that Doneata and I had left some twenty years before. After much thought and prayer, we decided to move the family to Greenville after the merger.

Doneata and I drove to Greenville to spend a weekend and look the town over. I remembered the tape that Mark Kittrell had given me from his pastor, Pastor Minnick. I told Doneata, "Sunday morning, before we head back to the beach, let's go visit Mount Calvary Church; I would like to hear Mark's pastor, Pastor Minnick, preach."

I remember well what Pastor Minnick's text was on that particular Sunday morning. He was preaching through the Ten Commandments. His sermon text was part one of a two-part message on the Fourth Commandment: "Remember the sabbath day to keep it holy." As a matter of fact, Pastor Minnick's message was so good that I told Doneata that we should make plans to come back to Greenville the next weekend to hear the conclusion of Pastor Minnick's message on the Fourth Commandment; which we did. After visiting Mount Calvary Church, Doneata and I were encouraged to find out that there are some good churches, but it seems they are just hard to find.

The next weekend in Greenville, I went to visit a pastor and good friend of mine from my denomination, "Dr. Ray DePraeter." While I was the Moderator at Plantation, I had several conversations with Dr. De-Praeter. As a matter of fact, it was Dr. DePraeter who recommended Terry Pink to Plantation Church's pulpit committee. Doneata and I went to Pastor DePraeter's new members' Sunday school class; and as the Lord would have it, Doneata and I were the only ones there.

Dr. DePraeter pulled up three chairs, and the three of us sat there and talked for the better part of forty-five minutes. He said, "Larry, I received a call the other day from Terry Pink. Terry told me that I would probably have you and your family come visit 'Bird Road.'" Dr. DePraeter was aware of the reasons that I resigned from the elder board and later removed my family from the membership at Plantation Church. In that same conversation, Dr. DePraeter apologized to Doneata and me for recommending Terry Pink to the pulpit committee at Plantation Church. We talked quite some time; then Dr. DePraeter made a statement that really struck a nerve with me.

He said, "Terry has asked me to come and preach at Plantation in January." Now, Dr. DePraeter didn't actually say he was going to accept Terry's offer to preach at Plantation, but by the way he made the statement, he insinuated he was considering going.

I thought to myself, "How could this fine man of God consider supporting the ministry at Plantation knowing the type person Terry Pink is? Well, I guess nobody's perfect."

Driving to lunch after church that day, I told Doneata, "That's it. I knew it before I ever got to Bird Road today, but the Lord gave me a confirmation during our talk with Dr. DePraeter this morning. I am leaving the denomination that we have worshipped in and served in all these years, and we are going to seek fellowship with those folks at Mount Calvary Church."

I looked over at Doneata; she was very quiet. I could tell she was giving serious thought to every word that I was saying. I took in a deep breath of air and exhaled the air along with my frustration, as I said, "Doneata, I'm wiping the slate clean. There is going to be no more struggle with those evil forces of the motion picture industry, and I'm leaving this denomination that we have spent so many years in. I know the Lord wants us to worship with people that are like-minded in spiritual matters. In order for us to do that, I believe we have to make a major change in where we worship."

———

Doneata and I arrived back at the beach about 10:30 that Sunday evening. Mentora greeted us at the door. She said, "Dad, a gentleman from Dallas has been trying to reach you all day. He has called several times. He says he must talk with you as soon as you come home."

"What's his name, and where is his number?"

"His name is Mr. Fainn; here's his home phone number."

I looked at the note. "I wonder what's up with Curtis. I'd better call and find out what's so important that it wouldn't keep until Monday." Curtis Fainn was a branch manager for Universal Film.

"Hello?"

"Hi, Curtis, I hear you need to talk with me."

Curtis sounded desperate. "Larry, man, where have you been all day?"

"Curtis, didn't my daughter tell you that Doneata and I were in Greenville looking for a place to live?"

"Larry, I have got to talk to you about something very important."

"Okay, Curtis, my time is your time."

"Larry, are you sitting down?"

"Out with it, Curtis!"

"Mr. Rasper wants to hire you to be his Head Film Buyer."

I thought Curtis was joking. I started laughing, and finally Curtis interrupted my laughter by saying, "Larry, I'm serious. Mr. Rasper wants you to come to work for him. He knows you have been in Greenville looking at houses. He said for me to tell you if you have already bought a home, he will buy the house from you and resell it."

I thought a moment and then responded, "Curtis, you're serious, aren't you?"

"Larry, Mr. Rasper's head film buyer is retiring this summer, and Mr. Rasper wants you to take his place. Larry, I don't think he really cares what kind of money you want. Mr. Rasper said, 'Larry Vaughn is first man on my list.'"

"Curtis," I said, "let me ask you a question. Why would a man that I cost millions of dollars in a Miami courtroom want to hire me?"

Curtis chuckled. "Larry, I asked Mr. Rasper the same question."

"Well, what did he say?"

"He said, 'If Larry Vaughn can cost me millions when working for Wometco, then he can make me millions while working for me.' "

I thought to myself, "Well, it's obvious Mr. Rasper puts his money above his personal feelings."

"Curtis, I assume Mr. Rasper had you be the go-between with anticipation that I had no interest in talking with him personally."

"Larry, I like Mr. Rasper. He's always been very fair with me. He called and asked me if I would call you and ask you if you would be willing to come to his Charlotte office and sit down and talk with him."

I thought to myself, "I wish Art Hertz could hear this conversation. He wouldn't believe it—not in a thousand years!"

"Curtis, will you do something for me?"

"Name it."

"Call Mr. Rasper and tell him that I am honored that he would consider me for the position of Head Film Buyer for his circuit; but tell him I have already made a commitment to leave the film business and am going ahead with my plans to move to Greenville."

Curtis said nothing for a moment. Then he said very emphatically, "Larry, I think you're nuts! You should at least talk to the man. I think he would pay you whatever you asked for to get you to come with him."

I did not reply to Curtis's statement. That message of silence led Curtis to agree to make the call for me.

As I hung up the phone, I felt weak, as I knew I had just passed up a very big carrot: a chance to live in Charlotte and make top dollar doing what I do best. No, I didn't particularly care to work for Mr. Rasper; but, if I tied him up with a five-year contract making a certain amount of dollars a year with bonuses and other perks, then I could very well expect to be financially independent by the ripe old age of fifty-two.

I thought to myself, "*Somebody* sure wants to keep me in the film business."

My final job offer came from a circuit located in Dallas, Texas. The Head Film Buyer of the company called me to inform me the owner of the company would like to send me an airline ticket and have me come out and spend a couple of days with him and his people. This particular circuit was very aggressive in the West and Southwest. They were now looking to expand their operations into foreign markets. With their foreign expansion plans almost in place, they needed a film buyer to head up their Southwest operations. Again, I very gracefully thanked the man for the call but declined to make the trip out to Dallas to talk with them. I knew as long as I didn't talk with any of these people, then it would be easier for me to be firm in my stand on leaving the industry.

I received many calls from the film companies concerning my future plans during those last few weeks at Litchfield. Everyone was calling wanting to know what I was going to do once the merger was final. There are no secrets on film row; what was one person's speculation turned into a rumor as all kinds of questions were being asked. Most people thought I was going to open up my own film buying and booking office and work out of my home. Everyone knew that I could easily work two to three days a week at home as an independent agent and make a very lucrative income. Others thought I had stumbled onto something big in the Greenville area. Several individuals asked me if I were in need of investors. Nobody believed the simple truth, which was: "After Litchfield Theatres, I am completely through with the motion picture industry."

The last three days in the Litchfield office were for the most part a time of last-minute communication with the Regal people. All of the important work had already been done. On Monday, the thirteenth of June, I spent the better part of the day going over all the playdates in the theatres with Phil Borak for Regal's upcoming Wednesday takeover. Phil seemed pleased with the product I had selected to play in the theatres.

Tuesday, I spent most of the day on the phone talking with many of the film companies: thanking them for the support they had given Larry Vaughn during the past twenty years and Litchfield Theatres during the past five years.

Late Tuesday afternoon, rather than wait until the last minute, I decided I would go ahead and take my personal items off the wall and clean out my desk. Before I began to put everything away, I took a long look around my office. There were many years of memories with photographs of dear friends, actors and actresses, and, of course, several photographs of the family. I sat there behind my desk thinking, "This moment sure has been a long time in coming. Is it possible that after all these years, I am only one day away from actually leaving the motion picture industry?"

I looked out the window of my office. I could see the sea oats gently blowing in the soft summer breeze. Behind the sea oats rested a pond— the epitome of tranquillity. At that moment, I saw a swan in all its glory glide smoothly across the pond. On the other side of the pond, not too far away, were the sand dunes and the oceanfront homes at Litchfield by the Sea. I looked up at the sky. The clouds were like ripples in the sea, as they were peacefully passing without so much as a small threat of rain. I breathed deeply, trying to fill the moment into my very being. I anticipated that soon my soul would experience a similar tranquillity.

I thought to myself, "God has been so very good to me the past forty-seven years. Even before I knew Him, He was watching out for me. Tomorrow I am starting a new life, but I will take with me some wonderful memories and friendships that took a lifetime to build."

I leaned back in my chair and started to think back to the many dear friends and loved ones God has allowed to be brought into my life in the past forty-seven years. I thought of my foster mother, Mary Vaughn. She loved me so very much. I thought of how it was such a shame that because of her secret she had chosen to live such a sad and insecure life. Even today, I think of my dear mother quite often, always wishing I could have had the opportunity to tell her just once more how much I loved her. If she only knew how much I appreciated the Vaughns' adopting me. It would have made life so much more enjoyable for her.

Then, there was Victor Young, who was in actuality closer to me than my natural brother. I am glad that Victor made a good life for himself. After he finished his tour of duty in the Marine Corps, Victor went on to graduate from the University of South Carolina. Today, Victor is a successful businessman, is married to a lovely lady, Yvonne, and has three children.

Although I haven't talked with Michael Heffner in several years, I will always owe a debt of gratitude to Mr. Heffner for taking a personal interest in me. He gave me an education that you cannot obtain by going to a college or university. He was a man that poured an enormous amount of his time, energy, money, and life into me, while trying to teach me to be able to communicate effectively in the highly competitive motion picture industry. Mr. Heffner is retired and still lives in the Greenville area.

My brother, Buddy and I got together two or three times after our initial meeting. During the past few years, outside of an occasional Christmas card, I seldom hear from Buddy or his family.

I had lunch with Eddie Stern in Atlanta recently. For a man in his eighties, Eddie carries himself exceptionally well. He still has that Cary Grant way about him. I learned a lot from Eddie Stern in the many years I worked for him: a better boss I have never had. Eddie and his lovely wife, Jerry, are both doing well. They spend their summers in their home in Vermont and their winters in Miami.

Art Hertz and I had lunch recently at the Litchfield Country Club. Art came to Myrtle Beach on business and drove down to Litchfield Beach to spend some time with me. Art is doing just fine doing what he does best: making money.

I thought of how my own family has been blessed down through the years. David is now twenty-three years old. Just last year, David graduated from high school. Graduating from high school was a major accomplishment in David's life. His five years of radiation and chemotherapy took quite a toll on his body. Today, David still has to cope with his learning disabilities, but God has been so good in sparing his life. I know David's future is going to be a bright one.

Larry D. Vaughn Jr. has never had one single seizure since God miraculously healed him hours before his scheduled brain surgery in Miami. Today, Larry is in perfect health. God was so gracious in sparing Larry and the family the trauma of his having to go through major brain surgery. This fall, Larry will be going into the seventh grade.

Both my girls, Doneata and Mentora, are excited about leaving the Myrtle Beach area. Doneata is looking forward to the new challenge that awaits us in Greenville. Mentora can hardly wait for the fall semester at the university to begin.

I sighed as I opened my desk drawer for the last time. I grabbed a handful of papers and noticed a pen that had been hiding for some time. I picked up the pen and noticed the Paramount Pictures name and logo on it. I thought of my dear friend, John Hersker, a Branch Manager at Paramount, who gave me this pen several years ago. I thought about how our friendship has grown since that time. At that moment, I made a mental note, "I must keep up with John in the future; good friendships are hard to find."

Then, at the back of my desk, I saw what appeared to be a business card. I picked it up and realized it was A. Foster McKissick's business card. I immediately knew why I had this card in my possession. I laughed as I turned the card over. Sure enough, it was a worthless IOU for five dollars signed by Foster McKissick, given to me on one of those many days he found himself without lunch money. Foster was never one to carry cash on himself. I had traveled several times with Foster only to find out at lunch time that he didn't have a dime to his name. I couldn't help but smile when I saw Foster's IOU.

As I started taking the pictures off the wall, I thought about my many friends and loved ones who are no longer living: my stepbrother, Farrell— his death and the tragic way he died. Farrell's death seemed to have been

Eddie Stern, Jack Mitchell, and Larry Vaughn

such a waste. I thought of the legendary Colonel Wolfson, who left behind an empire known as Wometco Enterprises, and my good friend, Jack Mitchell, with whom I had so many good years at Wometco. Then, my friend Stanley Stern came to mind: the man who came to my rescue with a million-dollar insurance policy when David was diagnosed with leukemia. With remorse, I thought of Roger Hill, the Warner Brothers Branch Manager, who asked me to share my faith with him days before he died in the tragic hotel fire in Boston. Tears came to my eyes when I thought of my best friend at Wometco, Marvin Reed. These men are all gone. Some lived a long, full life; and others died at an early age.

It took only a few more minutes to finish putting my personal items into my briefcase. The last item to go in was my small brown New Testament. I looked around my office: apart from the furniture, the office looked dull and empty. All those things that bring warmth and personality to an office were gone. There were nails on the walls, but no pictures. A desk, but nothing on it.

I put my boxes of memories and my briefcase into the trunk of my car. As I was driving up Highway 17 North toward Surfside Beach, I felt a real peace about how God had been working and answering prayer in my life. Yes, I felt a release that I had never felt before. Reality set in that Tuesday evening: I was no longer going to have to try to mentally balance the scales, those scales in my mind that had created within me such a struggle all of my Christian life. Why had it been so hard for me to let go of those tangible things of this world? Why did it take me so long to place my security completely in God, instead of God plus my work?

I stopped for gas and a Coke at a service station. As I pulled back out onto the highway, I immediately went back to my thoughts of a few moments earlier. I thought about how patient and loving the God of the Bible really is. And I thought about how wonderful He has been to my family and me.

Today, God, through His Grace, has given me the strength to put my trust completely in Him and in Him alone. The glitz and the glamour of Hollywood, the big salary, expense account, power, and stock options—they are all gone. Along with them goes a career that took a lifetime to build. However, what I have now is oh, so sweet! The psalmist said in Psalm 4:8: "I will both lay me down in peace, and sleep: for thou, Lord, only makest me dwell in safety." The struggle within was finally gone. Now, by faith, my family and I are able to rest in God.

On the fifteenth of June 1994, the merger between Litchfield Theatres Ltd. and Regal Cinemas was approved. The merger provided the Litchfield shareholders with over $83 million of consideration, a significant return on their investment.

It was that same week that the Larry Vaughn family relocated to their new residence in Greenville, South Carolina, to start their new life outside of the film industry. In the fall of that year, our family became members of Mount Calvary Church. It was absolutely wonderful to be worshipping with a body of like-minded believers, who strove to live a separated and holy life.

Several months later, someone from Plantation Church phoned me to tell me that Pastor Pink had become involved in an unscriptural situation with one of the ladies at Plantation Church. The denomination took away Pastor Pink's preaching privileges for five short years. He and his family had to sell their home and move away to another state.

When I hung up the phone, I thought of a statement that I had recently read from one of Pastor Clarkston's commentaries, a statement that I had found to be so true in my own life: "Sin has clouded men's minds to the straightforward simplicity of what God's Word says."

THE END

The Vaughn family in 1997